Healing God's Earth

Healing God's Earth

Rural Community in the Context of Urban Civilization

S. Roy Kaufman

Foreword by L. Shannon Jung

WIPF & STOCK · Eugene, Oregon

HEALING GOD'S EARTH
Rural Community in the Context of Urban Civilization

Copyright © 2013 S. Roy Kaufman. All rights reserved. Except for brief quotations in critical publications or reviews, no part of this book may be reproduced in any manner without prior written permission from the publisher. Write: Permissions, Wipf and Stock Publishers, 199 W. 8th Ave., Suite 3, Eugene, OR 97401.

Wipf and Stock Publishers
199 W. 8th Ave., Suite 3
Eugene, OR 97401
www.wipfandstock.com

ISBN 13: 978-1-62032-848-4
Manufactured in the U.S.A.

Scripture quotations contained herein are from the New Revised Standard Version Bible (NRSV), copyright © 1989 by the Division of Christian Education of the National Council of Churches of Christ in the U. S. A., and are used by permission. All rights reserved.

Contents

Foreword vii
Preface ix

Introduction and Thesis:
    Purpose of the Book, Definitions, and Thesis 1

Part A: The Defining Realities

Chapter 1 God's Original Mandate: To Till and Keep the Earth (Gen 2:15) 9

Chapter 2 Our Original Sin: The Desire to Be Like God (Gen 3:5) 21

Chapter 3 The Powers Unleashed:
    Cain Built a City and Named It Enoch (Gen 4:17) 33

Part B: God's Covenants: Paradigms and Strategic Models of Human Experience

Chapter 4 The Call of Faith to Live as a Sojourner:
    Go to the Land I Will Show You (Gen 12:1) 49

Chapter 5 The Character of Empire:
    And the Land Became Pharaoh's (Gen 47:20) 62

Chapter 6 On Wilderness and Promised Land:
    The Israelites Ate Manna Forty Years (Exod 16:35) 75

Chapter 7 The Call to Rural Community:
    So Now I Bring the First of the Fruit of the Ground (Deut 26:10) 89

Chapter 8 Rural Community and Urban Civilization in Conflict:
    A King Like Other Nations (1 Sam 8:5) 105

Chapter 9 The Triumph of Empire and the Persistence of the Rural Vision:
    The LORD Forbid That I Should Give You My Ancestral Inheritance (1 Kgs 21:3) 119

Chapter 10 Exiles and Aliens: Seek the Welfare of the City (Jer 29:7) 134

Part C: The Divine Intervention

Chapter 11 God Made Flesh in God's Own Self:
The Word Became Flesh and Lived Among Us (John 1:14) 153

Chapter 12 The Restoration of Rural Community in the Person of Jesus Christ:
The Time Is Fulfilled, and the Kingdom of God Has Come Near; Repent, and Believe In the Good News (Mark 1:15) 171

Part D: The Christian Experience

Chapter 13 The New Community:
From Every Tribe and People and Language and Nation (Rev 5:9) 195

Chapter 14 The Christian Vision: To Gather Up All Things in Christ (Eph 1:10) 216

Chapter 15 An Urban Future or the Garden Renewed?
I Saw the Holy City (Rev 21:2) 237

Conclusion and Prospect:
Summary, Conclusions, and Prospect 257

Bibliography 263
Subject Index 269

Foreword

It is a pleasure to learn from Pastor Roy Kaufman's perspective on what it means to be a Mennonite believer in a culture that is, if not hostile to, largely ignorant of and uninterested in, the alternative witness of that tradition. Of course, being a pastor of any church in a culture of "none's" (the fastest growing religion in the United States is those who claim no religious affiliation) is difficult. This book also challenges those of us in mainline Protestantism who have made an easy accommodation with the dominant culture.

Kaufman has seen up close that the "forces of urban civilization" have dismantled "rural communities and traditional cultures." Soon one realizes that he is working with typological understandings of dominant values, which he identifies with urban civilization (injustice, greed, and lack of care for one's neighbors), and with the more egalitarian, ecological, and justice-oriented values that he identifies with "rural or local communities."

These essays follow a biblical sequence in which the perceptive author exegetes the context of the original writing and then moves to draw out the implications of those texts for contemporary circumstances. Clearly his emphasis is on the construction of a missional theology that is communal and environmental in nature.

As Kaufman describes the nature of the society God intended, he sees it as exhibiting "a close relationship with the earth," face-to-face egalitarian human relationships, and an active concern for the "weakest and most vulnerable members" of the earth community.

It is also characterized by "a respect . . . for the uniqueness of [this local] place," "a willingness to live within the rhythms of the natural cycle of life," both natural and ecclesiastical, and "a deliberate effort to bring together within the life of the community the economic functions of production and consumption." These values remind me of those I learned in the small town where I grew up sixty years ago and which I see as Gemeinschaft, or folk society. There is a nostalgic attraction to these values, but most of us no longer live there, even if we inhabit rural communities.

And yet, there is a strong Christian engagement with Kaufman's values. So, I find myself pulled between being challenged by Kaufman's biblical, Mennonite, and rural understandings of the Christian life and a perplexity about how relevant those values are in a globalized and justice-starved Gesellschaft, or (post-)industrial society.

Foreword

The location of being challenged by a Radical Reformation pastor is a healthy one. I suspect that, Mennonite or not, Kaufman will make you wrestle with what you believe and how Christ relates to our culture.

Pastor Kaufman ends each chapter with a kind of case study essay exploring the implications of his themes for the mission of the church, particularly in a Mennonite context. His historical review of his native Freeman, South Dakota community is indicative of the virtues of the Mennonite way of life, which in many ways supported the mission of the church. During my visit there in February, 2010, there was clearly a continued sense of being bound together in the community of Christ. However, it is also true as this book makes clear that the task of continuing to engender the vitality of the rural congregation has become far more challenging.

Nevertheless, the nature of sharing and of being interdependent is a force that many in our super-urban communities and congregations look for. Hence, for example, the continuing popularity of small groups within the church. This book identifies the pressures on the rural congregation to remain the body of Christ in a way that is ever widening. The church in Freeman stands as a witness to what has been, and what could be. That is not without its challenges, but then it reminds the mainline church that discipleship is not easy or cheap. It reminds us as well that we are made whole (=saved) by the grace of God and that grace penetrates all.

L. Shannon Jung, Professor
Franklin and Louise Cole Town and Country Ministries
Saint Paul School of Theology
Kansas City, Missouri

Preface

THIS BOOK HAS TAKEN shape over the past ten years or so. It began germinating in my life shortly after I moved back to serve my home congregation at Freeman, South Dakota, in 1999. I began sketching focal statements and an outline in the early years of the new century. However, the book really began to take shape in earnest during a four-month sabbatical in the winter of 2008. During the first six weeks of the sabbatical, my wife and I were on the campus of what is now Anabaptist Mennonite Biblical Seminary, Elkhart, Indiana, during which I boned up on recent scholarship, tested my thesis with the seminary community, and completed the outline, focal statements, and introduction. I remember writing the first pages of chapter 1 later at the Orthodox Academy of Crete, where we spent the last weeks of my sabbatical. After returning from the sabbatical I began writing in earnest and completed about the first half of the book while in full-time ministry before my retirement in August 2010. The remainder of the book was completed by July 2012.

Many people contributed to my writing of this book. First and foremost are the four rural congregations I served as pastor for thirty-eight years—Pulaski Mennonite Church, Pulaski, Iowa; Science Ridge Mennonite Church, Sterling, Illinois; Tiefengrund Rosenort Mennonite Church, Laird, Saskatchewan; and Salem Mennonite Church, Freeman, South Dakota. The good people of these four congregations taught me what I know about rural ministry and rural communities. Their perseverance as alternative communities of faith in the midst of great adversity has inspired me.

The Greek Orthodox Church of Crete, with its strong rural heritage, where my wife and I spent the first three years of our marriage, was influential in my decision to become a rural pastor. There I was also introduced to the rich heritage of Orthodox theology.

In addition, I have a keen sense of the heritage of faith that is mine in my home community here in Freeman, South Dakota. My great-grandfather, Christian Kaufman, was a pioneer minister in the immigrant community that came here from the Ukraine in 1874. I credit my parents, Harry and Adeline Boese Kaufman, with instilling within me this sense of my roots and the agrarian culture that has shaped my life so profoundly, as I hope will be evident in the final essays of each chapter. Though I was the youngest of six siblings by seven years, my siblings have each contributed to my life significantly. My oldest brother, Maynard, by virtue of both his personal mentoring and his academic disciplines, has contributed so much to who I am.

Preface

Finally, I dedicate this book to the memory of my dear wife of forty-three years, Loretta (Epp) Kaufman, and to our beloved three daughters, Joanne, Dora and Susanna, who together have shaped me to be the person I am today. It was they, after all, who put up with the sermonizing that is distilled in the pages of this book, and who by their affirmation and critique encouraged me. Though Loretta rarely gave me direct feedback and probably read but little of the book as it was being written, she didn't have to. She had listened to me long enough from the pulpit to know and approve of what I was doing. She would be profoundly pleased and proud to see this book in publication. During all the writing of this book, she suffered courageously with end-stage renal disease, and she succumbed to complications of pancreatitis on October 13, 2012, just weeks before I received notice that my book had been accepted for publication.

A native of the Mountain Lake, Minnesota, community, Loretta personified the values of rural culture I have sought to describe in this book. She was instinctively sensitive to justice issues common to rural people who struggle with forces of the dominant culture. She lived her life in the immediacy of the face-to-face relationships of daily life in each of the rural communities where we lived. She devoted her life to the making of the home in the context of these communities. Together we learned to garden and can, raising and preserving much of our food. And she honed a marvelous whole wheat bread recipe made with local wheat I grind with a small mill. Loretta loved her flower gardens and houseplants. With profound gratitude for our life together, I gratefully dedicate this book to her memory.

S. Roy Kaufman
Freeman, South Dakota
January 18, 2013

Introduction and Thesis

Purpose of the Book

THE ESSAYS OF THIS book represent my grappling with the Scriptures, and my thirty-eight years of experience as a pastor of Mennonite congregations in rural settings in North America. Growing up in a rural Mennonite community, and throughout my years of pastoral ministry, I have experienced firsthand the stress under which rural people have been living. I have observed directly the forces of urban civilization at work in the dismantling of rural communities and traditional cultures. These essays are an attempt to bring both a prophetic and a pastoral word to the church in its attempts to live as an alternative community within the dominant culture.

Reflecting my experience, the essays of this book will have a certain sermonic character. Each chapter will have as its beginning point biblical texts relevant to the theme. These texts will be explored in their original sociopolitical and historical contexts. Next, there will be an exploration of the historical and contemporary implications of these texts for our own socioeconomic, technical, and political context. Finally, each chapter will explore how the texts are relevant both to Mennonite history and to the experience and mission of the church generally as an alternative community of faith.

My approach reflects the seriousness with which I take the *Confession of Faith in a Mennonite Perspective*, both in its emphasis on the authority of the Scriptures, and in its insistence that "the church is called to live as an alternative culture within the surrounding society."[1]

Along with having a sermonic character, I intend these essays for the people in the pew. While my style here is a bit more scholarly, and the exploration of the biblical texts is more extended than is possible in a Sunday morning sermon, the intended readers are in the first place the constituents of the Mennonite Church in North America. These are my people, and it is they I have sought to serve as a pastor. However, what I write here should be relevant for rural congregations and pastors of all Christian traditions, even though the specific references and examples will be to the Mennonite context in which I have lived.

More specifically, I have a threefold intention with this book. First, I see it as a contribution to the current discussion in Mennonite Church USA and Canada about what it means to be a missional church. While I strongly affirm the movement toward

---

1. *Confession*, 44.

being a missional church, I question whether the current discussions about being missional are adequate. I would insist that mission must be understood holistically, and that it must involve more than the model of individual salvation current in our religious culture. I will argue that the church's mission must be fundamentally about the formation of alternative communities of faith.

Second, as the outline of chapters suggests, this book is intended as a retelling of the biblical story as a unified whole. It has always been important to me as a pastor that people grasp the message of the Bible as a whole. This particular retelling of the biblical narrative takes into account ecological concerns that have not until recently been included in the theological framework of the Christian faith, and it will be this ecological dimension that will make this telling of the biblical story most distinctive.

Third, this book may be seen as attempt to cast Anabaptist Mennonite theology in a framework that highlights not only our distinctive sense of being an alternative community of faith within the dominant culture, but which also takes into account both ecological concerns and the rural history of the Mennonite Church. In current Mennonite thought, the rural past of the Mennonite Church is viewed with suspicion if not hostility. *Die Stille im Lande* ("the quiet in the land") has become a derogatory description of our rural Mennonite past. In the process, the missional implications of being a rural people who have quietly managed to make the earth sustainably fruitful in the most unlikely ecological contexts have been lost. I am convinced that it is precisely our rural history which gives the Mennonite Church a unique opportunity to help shape the mission of the church as a whole for the twenty-first century.

Definitions

In this book, *rural* or *local community* is defined as the context in which humans may best fulfill the mandate of caring for God's creation while living in just, equitable, participatory, interdependent, and sustainable communities. *Rural community* involves relationships of trust and humility and obedience before God, justice and peace and love with one another, and care and harmony and respect for natural communities of life.

Dominant culture or *urban civilization* on the other hand, is understood as the context in which humans have sought to declare their independence from God and their determination to be self-sufficient apart from God. This is a way of living characterized by injustice, inequity, oppression, violence, prejudice, discrimination, domination, control, and exploitation, and governed by the ideologies (idolatries) of racism, individualism, ethnocentrism, materialism, consumerism, nationalism, militarism, and scientism. Inherently unsustainable, urban civilization survives only by the exploitation of natural and rural communities of life, exercised through the political power of nation-states, the economic power of corporate entities, and the technical power of elite specialists.

Introduction and Thesis

It is important to understand at the outset that *rural* or *local communities* can well exist in both rural and urban areas, and *urban civilization* or the *dominant culture* typically informs the values of everyone, rural people as well as urban. We are all complicit in the *dominant culture*, however nonconformed we may consider ourselves to be. This book is intended to bring an understanding of the respective characters of both *rural community* and *dominant culture* or *urban civilization* as spheres of spiritual power operating in the world.

Church and *world* are the more traditional designations for the spiritual realities the title describes. But *church* typically does not denote a politically viable alternative community of faith, much less a community that takes seriously God's mandate to care for the earth. *Local* or *rural community* is intended to designate both that alternative spiritual/social/political/economic reality which is the sphere of Christian living, and the fact that such a community must take into account ecological concerns and ways of life that are sustainable and in harmony with God's creation. And *world* is too nondescript and vague a term to describe the specific socioeconomic, political, technical, and spiritual forces that describe the dominant culture—the domination forces that rule so much of our lives here on earth. *Urban civilization* also points to the historical setting and process whereby these domination forces came into existence.

Thesis

From the beginning of creation, God has intended the human family to participate with God in the unfolding of creation and history. As mortal creatures made in God's image and as God's stewards, humans are called to live in a relation of trust and humility and obedience with God, a relation of justice and peace and love with one another, and a relation of harmony and care and respect for the natural world of God's creation.

Because of our choice not to honor the boundaries and limitations God had established for our stewardship of life, human history has been characterized by rebellion against God, oppression within the human family, and exploitation of the natural world. Human disobedience against God has been institutionalized in the structures of political, economic, and technical power characteristic of urban civilization.

The Bible is the story of God's efforts to enable the human family to regain its intended function within God's plan. These efforts of God involve not only redeeming individual persons from the powers of evil into whose grip humans fell by choosing to disobey God. They also involve the formation of a new community of faith in which God's intention for the human family can be expressed, and in which persons redeemed from the powers of evil may live in the way that God intends humans to live.

This new community will be a *local* or *rural community* characterized by:

- A close relationship with the earth as the source of human life
- Face-to-face egalitarian human relationships

- An active trust in God expressed in daily worshipful dependence upon both the provisions and the limitations God has established
- An active concern for the protection and well-being of the weakest and most vulnerable members of the human and natural members of the community
- Interdependence and a mutually beneficial relationship with other local communities in the region and around the world
- A respect for the natural, ecological boundaries and limitations of its particular place, and an understanding of the uniqueness of its place
- A willingness to live within the rhythms of the natural cycles of life—diurnal, lunar, solar/seasonal, as well as the divinely-instituted weekly, seasonal, and annual sabbatical observances and jubilee provisions
- Conscious attention to the past and the future, considering both the experiences of the past to the seventh generation and the consequences of current decision-making on the future to the seventh generation
- A deliberate effort to bring together within the life of the community the economic functions of production and consumption
- An ability to practice communal self-reliance in terms of providing food, shelter, clothing, and the necessities and energy sources required for the life of the community
- A respect for the ethnic folkways, unique customs, and traditional wisdom inherited from the past and reflected in the membership of the community
- Openness to welcome new discoveries and new techniques made through human creativity that enhance the life of the community in appropriate ways
- A willingness to dispense with techniques that are inappropriate or destructive to communal and natural life
- The creation of distinctive arts and crafts and eagerness to share its unique goods and services with other local communities through mutually beneficial trade
- Solidarity with all other local communities in confronting nonviolently the depredations the dominant culture customarily visits upon local communities
- Openness to welcome sojourners and settlers from other local communities both similar to itself and diverse in cultural heritage
- Openness to welcome refugees from the dominant culture, both its victims and former power brokers looking for a place to fulfill God's intention for humankind
- Openness to be enriched by the uniqueness, diversity, and interdependence of the human family and God's creation

Both God's covenant with Israel embodied in the Ten Commandments and God's new covenant with humanity in Jesus Christ reflect the formation of such local communities of faith, living as alternatives to the dominant cultures of urban civilization current at the time. Both the Israelite settlement in Canaan in the twelfth century BCE and the emergence of the church in the first century CE reveal the formation of agrarian, egalitarian communities with the character outlined above. Quite soon Israelite communities of faith were co-opted to become ethnocentric enclaves, with their own imperialistic ambitions brought to fruition in the reigns of David and Solomon. In their turn, early Christian communities were co-opted by gnostic thought, which led the church to view its mission purely in terms of individual, spiritual salvation, with little if any communal, socioeconomic, political, or ecological implications. Christian communities were also co-opted to the service of imperial ambitions in the Constantinian appropriation of the church, leading to the development of Christendom.

While *rural community* is always vulnerable to the dominant power of *urban civilization*, there are periods of history in which the political, economic, and technical powers of urban civilization coalesce in such a way that they represent a particular threat to the survival of rural communities. We currently are experiencing such an era with the dominance of American imperial political and military power, the development of a global market economy through the agency of multinational corporations, and the vast, immense assault on traditional cultures and local communities around the world, wherever until now people have been able to resist to some extent the allure of urban civilization. Currently, all these traditional cultures and local communities are being exploited by the forces of urban civilization for their natural resources, their human labor, and their consumer potential.

The mission of the church in the twenty-first century must be to reclaim a holistic view of God's intention for the human family and the salvation God offers to us in Jesus Christ. While individual persons do indeed need to be redeemed from the grip of evil in which they are being held by the powers of urban civilization, it is not enough for the church to engage in salvaging individual lives from the wreckage of urban civilization. The church must also be actively engaged in the re-formation of local communities—contexts in which people together can resist the assaults of urban civilization in order to live just, sustainable, and participatory lives together.

The Mennonite Church in North America, by virtue of its rural agricultural heritage and its long history of living as a minority faith community within the dominant culture, is uniquely positioned to advance the mission of revitalizing local communities of nonviolent resistance to urban civilization and standing in solidarity with traditional cultures under siege around the world. Indeed, it may be our opportunity to help the broader church of Jesus Christ find its mission in the world. In order to do this, we need to own our unique history and learn to understand again both God's intention for the human family and the way in which God has been at work recalling and redeeming us for that divine intention.

In the process, we as a Mennonite Church may well need to repent of our own complicity in the values of the dominant culture and our shame of our rural roots.

Our own history, as well as the biblical story of God's intention in forming rural, local communities of faith through Israel and in Christ, can give us the vision to grasp this opportunity we have to shape the mission of the church in our time. In this way, we ourselves can participate actively in the divine purpose of God for history and creation, which is "to gather up all things in him [Christ], things in heaven and things on earth" (Eph 1:10).

Part A

The Defining Realities

Chapter 1

God's Original Mandate

To Till and Keep the Earth (Gen 2:15)

The Human Place within Creation

By God's design, everything in creation is connected, from the atomic particles and atoms and molecules that comprise the stuff of the universe, to the galaxies and stars and planets that are the context for life, to the cells and tissues and organs that constitute the organisms of life, to the chemical reactions and natural cycles and biospheric conditions that govern all life forms, to the cultures and institutions and civilizations that shape human history, to the divine beings and spiritual powers, created and uncreated, that underlie the material universe of time and space.

Within the created order, the human family occupies a unique role. We are made from the earth as mortal creatures, sharing life along with all the myriad forms of life here on earth. Yet we are also made in God's image and have the capacity to share in the eternal life of God. Our lives are bound by the constraints of creaturely existence, and yet we are free to participate in God's creative purpose in shaping creation and history. We have both the ability and the need to relate to one another, to the natural world of God's creation, and to the divine personhood of God. These three relationships form the context for our lives as humans.

We are called by God our Creator to represent the divine presence here on earth, to reflect the divine image clearly in our own lives. In this way we are called to assume responsibility on God's behalf for all forms of life here on earth. This is how we function as stewards, caretakers of a world that belongs to God. We are called to care for the earth as the source upon which the life God has created depends, including our own lives. We are called "to till it and keep it [the earth]" (Gen 2:15).

Healing God's Earth

The Biblical Story

The Human Measure

Having lived for some years in Greece and Canada, I'm familiar with the metric system of measurements. It has always seemed to me an eminently simple and useful system of measurement, using multiples of ten to relate larger or smaller units. I value the meter stick I brought with me from our years in Canada.

The meter is the basic unit of length in the metric system. It seems an appropriate measure for humanity. Humans are typically between one and two meters tall. Our physical world is defined by the metric units of length to the third power. In other words, we can only easily see things larger than a millimeter (thousandths of a meter) or nearer than a kilometer (thousand meters) away. We need the assistance of a microscope or telescope to see things smaller than a millimeter or farther away than a kilometer.

The meter, a little longer than the English yard, has its origin in relation to the size of Earth, being one ten-millionth (10^{-7}) of a quadrant of Earth's circumference of about forty thousand kilometers. If you consider that the meter is one long step for humans, this puts humanity in a measurable relationship with Earth. If you set off in a particular direction and did not diverge for mountains or seas, after forty million steps of a meter each, you would come back very nearly to the place where you began. As a walker with short legs, I struggle to make each step a meter in length. However, it is possible even for me. So by walking five kilometers an hour (five thousand steps of a meter each), for eight hours a day (forty kilometers or twenty-five miles), for five days a week (two hundred kilometers), for fifty weeks a year (ten thousand kilometers), for four years (forty thousand kilometers), one could walk around Earth in four years. Now to be sure, forty million is a lot of steps, but it is conceivable. We live in a comprehensible world, with Earth as our home.

One of my favorite books is *Powers of Ten*. At the center of this book is a picture of a couple having a picnic on the lawn of a park in Chicago. That picture is one meter square. Before and after this picture are pages that progress by the power of ten—decameter, hectometer, kilometer, etc.; decimeter, centimeter, millimeter, etc. In other words, the picture on every page is ten times larger or smaller than the picture on the adjacent page. Using this device, the book moves in forty-two pages from the outer fringes of the universe to the atomic particles that comprise the blood in the man's hand. As humans, we are roughly halfway in size between our solar system (10^{13} meters) and the nucleus of an atom (10^{-13} meters).[1] Of course, the universe is much larger than our solar system, with our sun being only one of some hundred million stars in the Milky Way galaxy, and our Milky Way galaxy only one of some hundred million galaxies in the universe. Still this image gives us a sense of our place in the

---

1. Morrison and Morrison, *Powers of Ten*.

scheme of God's creation. "What are human beings that you are mindful of them, mortals that you care for them?" (Ps 8:4).

It is humbling to realize that life on Earth, including our own life, is the result of cosmic events transpiring over billions of years. Current scientific theory holds that at its birth, the universe expanded at just the right pace—fast enough that it did not collapse upon itself before the stars and galaxies could form but slow enough that stars could form before there would only have been a sterile scattering of matter into space. We are told that the ninety-two naturally occurring elements that are required for life were shaped by the death of a first generation of stars within the universe, leading to a new generation of stars, including our Sun.[2] As we explore our own solar system, it becomes obvious that life could only emerge on a planet strategically distanced from the sun for life-giving water to be present. What coincidences are these that give birth to the profusion of life we see around us?

The Human Origin

As humans we are preoccupied with questions of our origin and our destiny. This seems to be especially true of Christian people. Creation and end times, or eschatology, are subjects Christians ponder, sometimes to the exclusion of more pertinent subjects having to do with our faithfulness to God. Sometimes, these issues become most polarizing and divisive, both within the church and in the world. We are often confronted with a choice between a secular evolutionary model of life origins and a religious creationist model, as though these were the only options available. Both of these models focus on *how* we humans came to be.

In the biblical understanding, the answer to the question of where we come from is focused quite differently and quite simply. We come from God and we return to God! It is that simple! God is the origin and the destiny of both human life and creation as a whole, because God is the Creator, the one through whom all things have come into being, the one in whom we and all things "live and move and have our being" (Acts 17:28). The Bible, in other words, is unrelentingly theocentric in its outlook.

I would venture that our preoccupation with origins has to do with the ambiguous and unique character we have as humans within creation. On the one hand, we were clearly made from the earth and share a creaturely existence along with all the other forms of life God created. After all, we were created on the sixth day along with all the other creatures that live upon the land (Gen 1:24–31). We, like all these other creatures, were brought forth from the earth (Gen 1:24). We, like all these other creatures, were given "every green plant for food" (Gen 1:30). The green plants, which were the crowning achievement of the first three days of creation (Gen 1:12), become

---

2. For a discussion of these phenomena, see Swimme and Berry, *Universe*, 18, 60–61.

the source of sustenance and life for the crowning achievement of the last three days of creation—land animals and human beings (Gen 1:29).

And indeed, it is so! Whether directly or indirectly, human life, like that of all other life forms in the animal kingdom, depends on energy derived from the process of photosynthesis occurring within green plants utilizing the energy of the Sun. We are clearly creatures dependent upon the earth generally, and green plants specifically. We, like all other creatures and life forms God has created, are mortal. We have a natural cycle of life, with birth, growth, maturation, reproduction, and death being the normal state of affairs. Within that normal cycle of life, we, like all other creatures, are subject to natural disasters (storms, floods, droughts, fires, volcanoes, earthquakes), illnesses and diseases and disabilities, accidents, and violent predation by other animals or humans, any one of which can interrupt and end the cycle of life abruptly. Whether cataclysmic or through the normal aging process, we can count on death as the final closing of our earthly life.

As if to emphasize the point, Genesis 2 goes on to affirm that we humans are made "from the dust of the ground" (Gen 2:7). "You are dust, and to dust you shall return" (Gen 3:19). We are humans (*adam*), made from the dust of the ground (*adamah*). In Hebrew, it is the same wordplay found in English, when we say that *humans* are made from *humus*. If that were not enough to confirm our origin and our composition, we come to life and live only by the breath of God (Gen 2:7). This of course is true not only for humans but for all living things. "When you hide your face, they are dismayed; when you take away their breath, they die and return to their dust. When you send forth your spirit [breath], they are created; and you renew the face of the ground" (Ps 104:29–30). We are clearly mortal creatures dependent not only upon the earth but directly upon the Spirit of God for the gift of life. We cannot live apart from either the earth or the breath of God who made us.

Still, this is not all that needs to be said about our origin as humans. We are also the only creatures made in the image of God. "Let us make humankind in our image, according to our likeness" (Gen 1:26). Whatever else it may mean to be made in God's image and likeness, it surely means that we have the capacity to relate to God in a self-conscious manner, and thus to participate with God in the unfolding of creation and history. While not explicitly identified as such, the God speaking in Genesis 1:26 is a triune God—Father, Son and Holy Spirit—who lives as three persons in full mutuality and interdependence in a perfect communion of love. As Catholic theologian Catherine LaCugna says, this God, intimately known to us as Father, Son and Holy Spirit, is revealed as relational in the divine being itself. "God's way of being in relationship *with* us—which is God's personhood—is a perfect expression of God's being as God. . . . God for us is who God is as God."[3]

If we are made in the image of this God, then what sets us apart from other creatures is our ability to relate self-consciously to others, to God, and to God's creation.

---

3. LaCugna, *God*, 304–5 (italics in original).

Self-consciously means, of course, by choice. All other creatures, so far as we know, have little if any choice about how they govern their lives, being limited by the confines of heredity and instinct. While heredity and instinct also play a role in shaping human life, it is the human ability to choose that seems to set us apart from all other forms of life God has created. Other creatures exist to praise and glorify the Creator by their being. Human beings choose whether or not they will praise and glorify their Creator.

If we try to put ourselves into the mind of God, we might imagine the Creator God wishing to have one creature in creation that brings praise and glory to the Creator not as a matter of course but as a matter of choice. *Being a relational God, I desire to be in relationship with one of my creatures that is not determined by creation but which comes as the free and loving response of the creature.* Of course, being such creatures and knowing our history, we might object that such a project was fraught with peril! If a mortal creature was free to praise and glorify God by choice, it would also be free to withhold such praise and glory. Yet, God, being a relational God of love, took such a risk, determined to enter into such a relationship with a mortal creature, no matter what it might cost in the end. Ironically, it is our freedom to choose that marks us as made in God's image. We are made as free moral agents, capable of relating to the divine being, and thus capable of participating in eternal life, mortal creatures though we are.

If it is this ambiguous and unique character that leads to our preoccupation with our origin and our destiny, it is important to understand that our mortality and our uniqueness must both be affirmed and held in tension. Creationists are right in rejecting views of humanity that deny the uniqueness of humankind created in God's image. But they are wrong if and when their high view of human uniqueness leads them to minimize or deny the reality of our creaturely identity and mortality, and thus also to distort the human role within God's creation. Evolutionists are right in affirming the human bond with all other life forms. They are wrong if they use their theories about the development of life on Earth to deny the possibility that humans are uniquely created in the image of God.

The Human Vocation

The unique character of human life on Earth points toward the role humans have within God's plan. Humans have the ability to name and order God's creation, as we see in Genesis 2:19–20, where God brings all the creatures to the human being to see what he would name them. "The man gave names to all cattle, and to the birds of the air, and to every animal of the field" (Gen 2:20). Presumably, the human ability to name the animals extends also to all the other life forms, chemicals, compounds, and elements that make up the world as we know it. We have been busy naming and making order of God's creation ever since! It is a human propensity, and interestingly, a propensity God respects. "Whatever the man called every living creature, that was its name" (Gen 2:19). God gives us the privilege of naming and ordering God's creation, and God respects the names that we give to things.

The human role within creation is closely related to our creation in the image of God. In the Eastern Orthodox liturgical tradition, icons play an important role. Frescoes of biblical events and people adorn Orthodox sanctuaries, including icons of Jesus. While these are important as decorations and even as a means of teaching biblical stories, the icons as stylized portraits represent something more in Orthodox theology. They represent a re-creation or re-presentation of the person or the event portrayed. So the icons in an Orthodox sanctuary re-create salvation history and indeed the universe as a whole to the eyes of the worshipper. Typically, the image of Christ as Παντοκράτορ (pantocrator), ruler of the universe, is the icon painted inside the dome at the center of the sanctuary. This affirms the Orthodox belief that Jesus, as the Lord of the universe, oversees all that happens, both within the liturgy but also in the life of the people and the life of the world.

Icon derives from the Greek εἰκών (eikon) which means image or likeness. It is the term used to translate "image of God" in the New Testament and the Greek Septuagint. Thinking about Orthodox icons in this context is helpful in understanding what it means to be made in the image of God as humans. To be made in the image of God is to re-present God within our bodily life. As creatures made in God's image we are to represent or to reflect God's character in our lives, both to the people with whom we live, and within God's creation among the creatures to which we relate. When other people or other creatures look at us, they are to see God's character reflected, the way a mirror reflects the image of a person standing before it. Here we see foreshadowed in creation God's intention in redemption, that in the incarnation of Christ we see the image of God perfectly reflected.

This is indeed a high calling, fraught with grave responsibility. It raises the question as to God's character. If God is understood to be an autocrat with absolute and arbitrary power over his subjects, then of course it is appropriate for humans to relate to others and to God's creation in a despotic manner. If God is understood to be a divine being whose essence is defined in terms of relational, self-giving love, then our re-presentation of God will look quite different. Much of the content of this book will work at seeking to understand the character of the God we are called to re-present. Presently we will argue that the character of God is most clearly seen in the self-giving love that led Jesus to offer his life on the cross. Jesus, in other words, is the one who reflected most clearly in his life the image of God.

It is in this context that we should understand the divine mandate for humankind to "have dominion over the fish of the sea, and over the birds of the air, and over the cattle, and over all the wild animals of the earth, and over every creeping thing that creeps upon the earth" (Gen 1:26). In the context of God's character of self-giving love, having dominion means not the freedom to use and abuse God's creation for human benefit, without regard for the worth and dignity of this creation. This has often been the caricature of human dominion ascribed to Christianity by its critics, and sadly, it has sometimes also been the way Christians themselves have acted and seen their role. But in fact, having dominion over creation in the context of representing a God of self-giving love means instead being made responsible for the welfare and the well-being of creation. If God takes note of each sparrow that falls and all the hair on our head (Matt 10:29–31), then we, too, are to be mindful of the life of every creature, however insignificant it may appear to us. If God dignifies matter in the creation of a living being, however useless it may seem to us, then that creation is deserving of our care and our attention. We have been made responsible by God for the life and creation God has made.

This human role has often been described as one of stewardship, a concept not much in favor in contemporary thought. Yet stewardship derives from the realm of ecology and economy. A steward is one charged with responsibility for the welfare of the οἶκος (oikos), the home. This Greek word for household or home is the root for ecology (oiko-logos), the study of our human, earthly home, and economy (oiko-nomia), the rule or management of the household. A steward, οἰκονόμος (oikono-mos), has no claim upon the household for which he or she is responsible. A steward is engaged to care for a household that belongs to another. In this case, the steward is responsible for the care of God's household, the earth that belongs to God. The corollary of this is that we are held responsible when things go wrong in this οἶκος. In other words, as mortal creatures made in the image of God, we become participants with God in the unfolding of creation and life, by God's design. We are all economists (οἰκονόμοι) of the home (οἶκος) of God.

To speak of the earth as God's household or God's home is to think of the earth as God's dwelling place. It is not that God's presence is confined to or limited to the earth, in a pantheistic sense. It is instead that God creates with the intention of being at home within the world God creates. God's desire is to walk "in the garden at the time of the evening breeze" (Gen 3:8), in fellowship with the creatures and the myriad forms of life that God has made, including human beings. In some sense, our stewardship of God's creation is what enables God to be at home in God's creation. If we fail in our stewardship, we spoil the intimacy that should characterize the divine presence within creation. That is why, at the end of the Bible and the end of this book, we will come to the vision of God coming to dwell in the new heaven and the new earth, a world newly redeemed through the life, death, and resurrection of Jesus Christ.

In Genesis 2:15, the human vocation is expressed in terms of being put "in the garden of Eden to till it and keep it." The garden of Eden was that place in the east, planted by none other than God in God's own self, as the home for the human that God had formed from the dust of the ground. There was found in that garden every tree "pleasant to the sight and good for food" (Gen 2:9), as well as the tree of life and the tree of the knowledge of good and evil. The garden then becomes the symbol for the earth as the place of human habitation, the sphere where human life is sustained, physically as well as aesthetically and spiritually. Though planted or created by God, the garden is given over to the human for care and keeping. Indeed, already in Genesis 2:5 we find that plants and herbs require human cultivation before they can exist. Gardens require cultivation and nurture. More will be said about the earth as wilderness in this book, but here earth as garden is in view. Here a symbiosis of human nurture and natural process is envisioned as the human vocation. It is not a vocation that has been revoked!

The Loss of a Theocentric Worldview

So what is the point of the biblical story about the human place in God's world? The primary implication I see is the threefold relationship that forms the core of our place in the world—our relationship to God, to one another, and to God's creation. Interestingly, the primary emphasis of the story thus far falls on our relationship to God's creation. Subsequent chapters of the biblical story explore our relationship with God and others in more depth, but the story thus far focuses on our place and our role within God's creation. We are not only intimately related to God's creation, deriving our sustenance and life from it. We are also responsible for God's creation, stewards called to represent God's character of love within the created order, among all the other forms of life God has created.

Such a way of describing the human relationship to creation stands in stark contrast to the way humans currently understand their relationship to the world. In the modern world, creation is seen as a reservoir of resources to be tapped for human use and consumption. Creation has value only in relation to its usefulness to humanity. Modern humans have been thoroughly secularized by the Enlightenment of the eighteenth century and the subsequent development of Industrialism, the growth economy, and technological advances. We no longer have a sense of being responsible to or for anyone other than ourselves and our needs. The theocentric point of view expressed in the biblical narrative is foreign to our thinking as modern people.

Of course, now that our unbridled greed and pride have begun to come home to roost in the ecological, economic, and energy crises of our time, a largely secular environmental movement has risen to challenge the assumptions that have resulted in the exploitation and wasting of the earth. Study after study, complete with the latest scientific documentation, bewails the dire consequences of our modern ways of living.[4] Helpful as these are for understanding our current crises, such studies often fail to challenge the underlying anthropocentric perspectives of the modern and postmodern worlds. Often political or technological fixes are proposed to correct current

---

4. Early alarms of this nature include the two reports to the Club of Rome, both published in the 1970s: Meadows, et al., *Limits to Growth*; and Mesarovic and Pestel, *Mankind at the Turning Point*. A more recent study with abundant documentation, as well as a biblical/ethical perspective is Northcott, *Moral Climate*.

abuses. Appeals are made to the survival of the earth, replacing the current anthropocentric perspectives with a bio- or geocentric perspective. Humans then become simply another of the many creatures at risk in the crises that beset us. Exactly how humans are related to the natural order remains a confounding puzzle. Are we to be valued more than any other species of life? What exactly is our responsibility for the natural order if we are simply part of it? How do we reconcile our obvious destructiveness with our presumed ability to remake the natural order in our own image?

What is missing in the current discussions about the human place in creation is the theocentric perspective central to the biblical story. It is what clarifies both our relation to and our responsibility for the natural world. It reminds us that we are a part of the earth, but that we also bear responsibility for the earth. While interpretations of the biblical story have certainly been used to justify the abuse and misuse of God's creation, classical Christian theology in both the Orthodox East and Catholic West has consistently reflected the kind of narrative I have shared here. Among Christians, Protestantism has perhaps had the hardest time accepting this narrative. Liberal or mainline Protestants have often been so influenced by Enlightenment assumptions that they may be uncomfortable with the theocentric assumptions of the Bible. Meanwhile, conservative Protestants have accepted a gnostic, otherworldly, dualistic view of life that makes concern for God's creation irrelevant, as I will argue in chapter 11. While both conservative and liberal Protestants are readjusting their thinking and discovering their Christian roots in the current crisis, these churches are playing catch-up to the traditional Christian perspectives of the biblical narrative. In recent centuries, biblical texts have indeed been used to justify the exploitation of the earth, but these misuses of Scripture buttress fundamentally Enlightenment anthropocentric assumptions about the human relation to the world rather than being intrinsic to the message of the Bible.

Still, I have to acknowledge that a repetition of the biblical narrative like that I have given here sounds quaint and anachronistic and parochial to our modern ears. We are looking for absolute truths, analytic studies, and universal statements. We want to see the documentation and the footnotes. What earthly good is a story about a God who wants to create one creature in God's own image? In particular, why should this one local and parochial story with Judeo-Christian roots be taken seriously?

I surely acknowledge that there are many other local and parochial stories that reflect the same theocentric concerns expressed in the biblical narrative. Local and aboriginal cultures the world over have seen and continue to see the world with these kinds of theocentric lenses. All of these local and parochial stories contribute to a fuller understanding of the human place within creation. Basic to the approach of this book is the notion that it is precisely the local and parochial stories of the human relationship to God, creation, and others, that have the wisdom we need to find our human place in the world. While scientific data, analytic studies, and universal statements can be helpful to our understanding, they paralyze us as much as they energize us. They make us irrelevant to the unfolding of life and creation, observers rather than participants. They place us outside the system instead of seeing us as integral to it. That is what sets the local and parochial theocentric stories apart, for in these stories, humans are always primary actors, subjects rather than objects.

This still does not answer why the particular Judeo-Christian story should be given priority. Dogmatic answers can be provided to justify such parochialism. But rather than assert the primacy of this story, it seems best to leave the jury out on this question, and to proceed with the story. If it is worth telling, it won't need dogma to enforce it. Furthermore, the validation of one story does not make another story invalid. It is not that there must be only one story. It is that every story contributes its own wisdom for us to embody. This is the local and parochial story in which I have sought to find my life, and it has given purpose and strength to my living.

The Missional Implications of the Anabaptist Mennonite Agrarian Heritage

North American Mennonites are heirs of the sixteenth-century Anabaptist movement, the left wing of the Protestant Reformation, or the Radical Reformation, as it is sometimes referred to. The Anabaptist movement began as an urban movement in Zurich, Switzerland, among the young radical intelligentsia of the Zurich elite, who were pushing the reformer Ulrich Zwingli to be more thoroughly biblical in his reforms. In particular, the radicals in Zurich wanted Zwingli to discard infant baptism as unbiblical. They eventually baptized one another on each other's confession of faith, initiating the Anabaptist movement and eventually the Mennonite Church.

While it began as a movement of the urban elite, it quickly became evident that the greatest appeal of the Anabaptist movement would be among the dispossessed and oppressed peasants of the European continent. So in less than a generation, the leadership of the Anabaptist movement shifted to peasants, whose stories of martyrdom are poignantly told in *Martyr's Mirror*.[5]

The reasons for the popularity of Anabaptist ideas among the peasant classes are obvious. Anabaptists stressed a radical egalitarian communalism that empowered rural peasants to resist the oppression under which they lived and enabled them to form alternative, local communities of faith that empowered their lives and their livelihoods. It is for this same reason, I believe, that Anabaptism still finds its growing edges among the oppressed and colonized people of the Third World. Meanwhile we North American Mennonites, the biological descendants of European Anabaptists, are not sure we really want to own the radical implications of our forebearers' faith. Why else is it that the Mennonite churches of Asia and Africa are now larger than the historic Mennonite churches of Europe and North America?[6] Surely our mission

---

5. Braght, *Bloody Theatre; or, Martyr's Mirror*.
6. Byler, *Mennonite*, 197; Huber, "World," 1–2.

efforts beginning early in the twentieth century must take some credit. Yet, truth be told, the version of the gospel proclaimed by Mennonite missions tended to owe more to nineteenth-century evangelical and missiological thinking than it did to Anabaptist theology. We largely left it up to our mission churches to discover for themselves the radical implications of the Mennonite churches they were. Once they made the discovery, they were eager to embrace these radical implications, which address so directly and so concretely the situations of oppression under which they live.

It is the missiological implications of the spread of Anabaptism among the rural peasantry of Europe that have not yet been explored. Scholars embrace the first Anabaptist movement as a powerful evangelistic movement, which indeed it was. They credit this to the vision of the urban elite who began this movement, and they tend to see the subsequent rural and quietistic history of the Mennonite Church as an abandonment of the evangelical fervor of the first generations of the Anabaptist movement. In the process, they overlook the social and environmental dynamics of Anabaptism's appeal among the oppressed peasants of central and northern Europe. Severe persecution surely played a role in the retreat of Mennonites into quietism as *die Stille im Lande* (the quiet in the land), known more for their agricultural expertise than for their social radicalism or their evangelical fervor.

The creation stories of Genesis about the human place in the world are pertinent in this context. Rather than seeing the Mennonite church of the seventeenth and eighteenth centuries abandoning a missiological vision, it is possible to see these European Mennonites embodying the vision of humanity's place within the world—the vision of caring for God's creation through the building of self-sustaining agrarian communities. These communities presented a stark alternative and contrast to the warring European nobility at whose largesse they lived. It was not that Mennonites could not find a haven. It was that they frequently rejected the conditions of citizenship, taxation, and conscription that would have enabled them to put down roots. So they were invited to revitalize the depleted soils of Europe, drain the swamps of East Prussia, and break the steppes of the Ukraine because rulers recognized their agricultural expertise and were willing to grant concessions to these eccentric pacifists in exchange for that expertise.

The point is not that our Mennonite forebears in Europe always made the right choices of faithfulness to God. They were at times overly eager to find safe havens, and were at times surely driven by economic motives as much as motives of faithfulness to God. They should probably have been much more thoughtful and wise about the rulers whose invitations for safe haven they accepted, and for the political and relational consequences that would come to them as a result. Likely they did not always make the best agricultural choices either, in terms of caring for the land. But clearly, the Mennonite diaspora of migrations from the seventeenth to the twentieth centuries reflects elements of attentiveness to God's call—the call of caring for the earth through the creation of alternative communities living in egalitarian, self-sustaining ways among the dominant cultures of the world.

As North American Mennonites who have acculturated to the dominant culture in many ways, we have been conditioned to think of the quietism of our Mennonite past as a sign of unfaithfulness, a turning away from the missiological implications of the gospel. At the same time, we can say in our confession of faith that "the church is called to live as an alternative culture within the surrounding society. . . . The church lives within the dominant culture, yet is called to challenge that culture's myths and assumptions when they conflict with Christian faith."[7] Despite their many failings, it is precisely this that the Mennonites as "the Quiet in the Land" endeavored to incarnate in the egalitarian, agrarian communities in which they lived. In the process, these European Mennonites came closer than we do today toward fulfilling God's first mandate for the human family, that of keeping and caring for the earth.

The establishment of agrarian communities living self-sustaining lives on earth in the midst of dominant cultures is not irrelevant to the mission of the church. It is in fact at the heart of God's will for the human family. It is how the earth can be kept and cared for in the best possible way. It is how the message of the gospel can most effectively be shared with the world. It is in the context of these kinds of communities that the threefold relationship we have as humans with God, creation, and one another can best be tended and nurtured.

---

7. *Confession*, 44–45.

Chapter 2

Our Original Sin

The Desire to Be Like God (Gen 3:5)

Our Refusal to Accept Our Mortality

FROM OUR FIRST AWARENESS of our human condition as mortal creatures made in God's image, we humans have been troubled by the ambiguity of our lives. While we were glad, even eager, to accept our role as stewards over the rest of creation, we were troubled by the awareness that we were mortal creatures.

While the tree of life was not proscribed, implying our access to the source of eternal life, we chafed under the restriction that we should not eat from the tree of the knowledge of good and evil. So when we were tempted to believe that this forbidden fruit would make us immortal, "like God, knowing good and evil" (Gen 3:5), it was too much for us to resist. Our original sin reflects our lack of trust in God, and our refusal to accept God's promise that we can share in the divine life through obedience to God and by observing the constraints of our creaturely existence. To put it another way, our original sin reflects our profound fear of mortality as a natural process. Our deepest anxiety was that by dying our unique personhood would be lost.

In the pursuit of a shortcut toward immortality, humankind was introduced to the knowledge of good and evil, the awareness that our human choices made selfishly outside the boundaries of God's intention for humankind have consequences we cannot foresee, threatening not only our own lives and the harmony of life, but indeed the future of life itself. The consequences of sin are not only personal (shame, guilt), but also relational (blaming, power struggles) and ecological (disharmony, unfruitfulness).

To protect humans from perpetuating themselves eternally in a sinful condition, God mercifully barred the way to the tree of life for humans until their sin could be addressed. Though called to represent God on earth and reflect God's image, we can do so only as mortal creatures. When we aspire to be like God, we threaten to undo all that is good in God's creation.

The Biblical Story

Living Within Limits: You Shall Not Eat (Gen 2:17)

We live in a culture that tends to reject boundaries and limitations of any kind. Moral proscriptions regarding sexuality and the sanctity of human life that were held for centuries as matters of wisdom are routinely broken. Economic affairs are carried out without regard for regulations of any kind or any concern for the common good, with the bottom line of profit being the only aim. Material resources of the natural world are routinely exploited as though they were unlimited. Money is spent as though there will always be more. People indulge their appetites for food, drink, stimulation, or sex as though their bodies were indestructible.

While this disregard for boundaries and limitations has been a characteristic of humans throughout history, there are eras when such disregard is phenomenal, and we live in such an era. Common sense would seem to suggest the obvious consequences of such a disregard for limitations. Our health industry deals regularly with the ill-health of self-destructive behavior. When ecosystems are stretched to the breaking point, they will collapse. When bountiful resources keep being exploited, they will run out in this finite planet. When profits are pursued without the public good in mind, the social order will collapse. When moral proscriptions are disregarded with impunity, the social fabric comes undone in individualism, tribalism, and a survivalist mindset.

The fact is that we are mortal creatures living in a finite world. Despite the obvious consequences of ignoring this fact, we humans have tended always to reject the notion of limitations and boundaries. Wise parents soon learn that if they wish to avoid entering a continual warfare with their children, particularly as they enter their teen years, they will make as few rules as possible, relying instead on loving relationships with their children. The more they rely on legalism, the more they either incite their youth to rebellion or risk an authoritarian regime that threatens the moral development of their children. For example, I remember virtually no explicit rules governing my behavior as a teen, though of course it was always very clear to me which behaviors were risky for myself and bound to incur the displeasure of my parents. Perhaps being the youngest of six children I was the beneficiary of years of trial and error on the part of my parents!

Thus, in calling attention to the limitations and constraints under which we live as mortals, God wisely gave only one prohibition: "But of the tree of the knowledge of good and evil you shall not eat, for in the day that you eat of it you shall die" (Gen 2:17). The whole world, everything in the garden, was available to us freely, even the tree of life (Gen 2:16). Only we must remember that we are mortal creatures, and live within the boundaries and constraints of our mortality. There is one forbidden fruit, and the consequence of disobedience is death.

Our Original Sin

Christian theology has struggled to understand what this means. Is this consequence of disobedience our physical death? Were we indeed created immortal, and is mortality a consequence of disobedience? Or is this *death* rather a more profound relational term having to do with our relationship with God? Do we *live* in relationship to God only when we observe the limitations and constraints of our creaturely existence, and do we *die* to God as soon as we grasp the forbidden fruit, that which goes beyond the limitations of our creaturehood?

Within the symbolic world of the creation story, it seems that the presence of the two trees in the garden, the tree of life and the tree of the knowledge of good and evil (Gen 2:9), holds the key to our understanding. The tree of life is freely available to the human (Gen 2:16), while the tree of the knowledge of good and evil is proscribed (Gen 2:17). This suggests to me that as humans, we have access to immortality when we live within the boundaries and limitations of our creaturehood. Despite the reality of our mortality and the certainty of our death, God created us to share in God's eternal life if we live within the limitations of our creaturely life. However, when we reach out to take the forbidden fruit, we lose access to this immortal life with God. As for the tree of the knowledge of good and evil, the forbidden fruit was itself the consequence of our refusal to live within the boundaries God had established for humans. When we eat the forbidden fruit, we gain the knowledge of good and evil. We know ourselves to be disobedient.

Thus it seems to me that from the first, it was our awareness of our mortality that has been the defining constraint of our lives. Though made in God's image, we saw that we are like the other creatures around us, subject to death. Though provision for our immortality was made by our access to the tree of life, we had no guarantees that the fruit of this tree would make us immortal. We questioned whether it would prevent us from dying, or enable us to survive beyond death. We feared that our mortal death would spell the complete extinction of our unique personhood, created in God's image. While we perceived our uniqueness in relation to God and the world that God had made, we chafed under the awareness that we were mortal like the other creatures God had made. We had to trust God's promise of immortality beyond this mortal life, made concrete in our access to the tree of life. We had to live within the constraint of the prohibition not to eat from the forbidden fruit. We had to remember our place in God's creation.

The Temptation of Shortcuts: You Will Not Die, You Will Be Like God (Gen 3:4–5)

In the Bible, temptations are typically portrayed as shortcuts toward a promised goal when the prescribed steps toward that goal are seen as too costly or impossible. In the pursuit of inheriting God's promises, Abraham and Sarah yielded to the temptation of resorting to surrogate parenting when the possibility of having a child of their own seemed to fade (Gen 16). In the pursuit of his vocation as God's Messiah, Jesus was tempted to resort to the use of miraculous powers when it was his submission until death to the powers of evil and sin that was required (Matt 4). I'm grateful Jesus resisted those temptations!

The reality is that God's promises are contingent on the completion of a divine order. We may ask why this must be. We may rebel against it. We may chafe under the restrictions and constraints this places upon our lives. We may doubt God's ability to keep God's promise according to God's plan. We may yield to the temptation of trying a shortcut in order to gain God's promise. None of this changes the fact that God's promises will be fulfilled only in the way that God has established within the divine purpose for creation.

God's promise that we may share in the divine life of God, which we intuitively perceive as creatures made in God's image, is contingent on our completing our creaturely life here on earth. We are called to do so as creatures who honor and serve God by choosing to fulfill the divine vocation ordained for us in caring for God's creation. As we have already noted, this requires us to trust God's promise, symbolized by our access to the tree of life. It requires us to accept the limitations and constraints of our creaturely existence, including our creaturely mortality itself. It requires us to accept the divinely ordained vocation of reflecting God's image in our lives. It requires us, in other words, to make choices that honor God's plan for human life.

Since God's promise of eternal life requires such a high degree of trust and obedience, it isn't surprising that temptations in the form of shortcuts should present themselves to us. As with our youth, the temptations begin whenever there is a proscription. Whenever we hear a *thou shalt not*, we wonder, *why not*? Surely something is being denied to us, something that might resolve the doubts and questions and fears we are feeling, something that might lead us toward the goal we desire more quickly and easily than the way laid out before us, which seems either impossible or difficult or at best doubtful.

The temptation begins with a question. Is there a proscription? *Can you eat from any tree in the garden* (Gen 3:1)? This highlights both our freedom and the constraint. "We may eat of the fruit of the trees in the garden; but God said, 'You shall not eat of the fruit of the tree that is in the middle of the garden, nor shall you touch it, or you shall die'" (Gen 3:2–3). The proscription and its consequence of death are not only repeated but heightened! The woman says it is not only forbidden to eat the fruit, but even to touch it (Gen 3:3)! Prohibitions always have a way of being exaggerated; such is their power.

The temptation here is twofold. The temptation, first, is to eat the forbidden fruit, and then, second, in this way to become like God. Here the fruit of the tree of the knowledge of good and evil is presumed to be the way for humans to become divine: "For God knows that when you eat of it your eyes will be opened, and you will be like God, knowing good and evil" (Gen 3:5). The assumption of the tempter is that knowledge of good and evil is what makes God divine. Whether this is a correct assumption or not, it links the prohibition with a desired end for mortal humans—the ability to be like God. *Eat from this tree of the knowledge of good and evil, and you will gain your objective of becoming divine*, the tempter says.

This is what made the temptation irresistible for the first humans, and so also for us. At the heart of our rebellion against God is our anxiety about our mortality, and our doubts about whether God's promise of immortality can be trusted in view of our obvious mortality. The forbidden fruit was not only nutritious; it was not only aesthetically pleasing; it also contained the promise of wisdom, the ability to distinguish between good and evil, enabling the one who partook of it to become wise (Gen 3:6)! With so desirable a shortcut to solving the human dilemma, is it any wonder that we could not resist the temptation of rejecting God's purpose for our lives, of refusing to live within the boundaries God had established for our mortal lives?

The story raises all kinds of questions, to be sure. For one thing, it might be presumed that the knowledge of good and evil is indeed desirable, even necessary, in order for us to become fully human. Can we imagine truly being free to choose our course in life if we cannot discern the difference between good and evil? Was not the divine prohibition in reality a limitation on our full maturation as free moral agents? However, we have to ask whether we as mortals can ever truly know the difference between good and evil. Can we ever be assured that we understand enough about ourselves, others, God's world, and God to adequately discern on our own the wise alternative? Must we not always rely on God for this discernment, as Scripture and the subsequent history of human tragedy suggests? The issue is not whether moral discernment is required for our full moral maturation, but whether we as humans are prepared to trust God for such discernment and to make our choices within the limitations and boundaries that God has set for us.

Another question we have about this story relates to the origin of temptation. In this story, the tempter is the serpent, which subsequent Christian history understands to represent the devil, or Satan. While doubts and anxieties about our mortality are inherent in our human condition as mortal creatures, the shortcuts of temptation are extraneous to our being. Temptation comes from outside ourselves, raising the specter of what we will choose to do. Will we resist the temptation in faithfulness to God's purpose for our lives, or will we choose to yield to the shortcut?

Still, we legitimately wonder about the source of these temptations. Where does the serpent come from? In this story it is clearly one of God's created life forms, but a creature that has already assumed a role in human thinking far beyond what the natural life cycle of snakes allows. What we confront here is a force outside or beyond the natural world, as God is outside and beyond the natural world, and yet in opposition to the divine purposes of God. If God's creation was good, as Scripture declares, then where does this sinister force of evil we call the devil come from? Do we indeed live in a dualistic world in which good and evil forces are battling it out? Is there a power of evil independent of a benevolent God that is threatening to undo the goodness of God's creation?

Yes, and no! There are powers of evil at work in the world threatening to undo the goodness of God's creation. Yet the Bible would be loath to say that such powers of evil are independent of God, seeing them instead as spiritual powers that had been created good by God but are now rebelling against God. While Scripture affirms that humans are the only mortal creatures with the capacity for making moral choices, Scripture also affirms a realm of created spiritual beings beyond or outside the universe visible to humans who also have the capacity for moral discernment.[1] Scripture affirms frankly that among these spiritual beings created by God, some have rebelled against God and do indeed seek to undo the goodness of God's creation.[2] The creation of a mortal creature with the capacity for moral choice, like that of the human being, presented these powers of evil with their best opportunity for undoing the good work of God. Indeed, it is unlikely that such powers had much opportunity to affect the unfolding of God's creation apart from influencing free moral agents like ourselves who are a part of this created order. Hence we see the source of the temptations or shortcuts that we humans continually experience.

We might also ask why God would permit such evil powers to exist, much less threaten to undo God's creation by tempting humankind with disobedience. This question must ultimately remain a mystery to human insight. However, we can imagine that God has God's own intentions about how to deal with rebellious spiritual beings other than the exercise of brute force. We might even imagine that God's intentions are that such powers should be undone by the faithful obedience of a mortal creature graced with moral choice, like ourselves! If we had resisted the temptations that came to us and fulfilled God's intention for our lives wouldn't that have spelled the ultimate defeat of these powers? Isn't that indeed what did happen in the life, death, and resurrection of Jesus Christ? But perhaps we are getting too far ahead of our story!

The Consequences of Shortcuts: Then the Eyes of Both Were Opened (Gen 3:7)

Eating the forbidden fruit did indeed enable us to know good and evil. Our eyes were opened. But what we saw was not beauty but shame: "And they knew that they were naked; and they sewed fig leaves together and made loincloths for themselves" (Gen 3:7). God's intention for the human family as male and female is that they might both be naked and not ashamed (Gen 2:25). Such is the beauty and mystery of the marital

---

1. See for example Job 1–2; also the visions of Isaiah and Ezekiel in Isaiah 6 and Ezekiel 1:5–14.
2. In the Old Testament, Isaiah 14:12–14 speaks of the Day Star (Lucifer) falling from heaven after having exalted himself above God, later alluded to also by Jesus in Luke 10:18. Compare also the account in Revelation 12 of Satan and his angels being thrown down to earth from heaven by the archangel Michael and his angels.

relationship at its best, which we sometimes experience. But once we had rejected God's purpose for our lives, the beauty and mystery was lost in shame. We saw ourselves in nakedness we wanted to cover up. We hid from God's presence (Gen 3:8). We were afraid to face God (Gen 3:10). Guilt and shame are the first consequences of our rejection of God's purpose for our lives. The fruit of the tree of the knowledge of good and evil, so desirable as a temptation, turns out to be a curse in reality, as temptations always are, based as they are on deception and distortions of reality. Thinking we can know good and evil apart from God is always disastrous.

The consequence of our disobedience in eating the forbidden fruit is the fracturing of all the relationships in which God intended us to live. Our relationship with God is marked by alienation, signified by our hiding from God's presence (Gen 3:8). Our relationship with one another is marked by a struggle for power and control, especially between the sexes, signified by the excuses and blaming given by the man and the woman for their behavior. The man blames the woman and the woman blames the serpent (Gen 3:12–13). Genesis 3:16 describes the power struggle between men and women in the ambivalence of their desires and the male assertion of dominance over the female. This obviously is not a prescriptive statement of how things should be, but a descriptive statement of how things are in a fallen world. Finally, our relationship with God's creation is marked by toil and the unsettling of the ecological order (Gen 3:17–19). This is not the origin of human labor, as humans have already been charged to care for the earth and tend it. But now our labor becomes toilsome and burdensome. Now the earth no longer responds fruitfully and without impediment to human labor.

Designed by God to reflect God's image within creation and to fulfill God's purpose in caring for creation, we instead bear into our history the burden of an image distorted by our disobedience and lack of trust in God. Designed to live in a relationship of trust and humility and obedience to God, a relationship of justice and peace and love with one another, and a relationship of harmony and care and respect for God's creation, our relationships instead are characterized by alienation from God, oppression between humans, and exploitation of the natural world. Now, having eaten from the tree of the knowledge of good and evil, we presume to have the wisdom to order our own lives apart from God, in our own interests, and at creation's expense. The brokenness of our world now reflects the brokenness of our own lives and relationships.

Worst of all, our disobedience precipitated not only our fall into sin, but also the fall of creation. Rather than serving to disarm the spiritual powers of evil by our obedience, if that was part of God's intention for the human family, our choice to mistrust and disobey God made us slaves to those very powers of evil. Our disobedience did what the powers of evil by themselves apparently could not do. It unleashed the powers of evil into the natural world. We have become the instruments of the evil powers in the desecration of the natural world, having become agents enslaved to the powers of evil. Our choice to disobey God resulted not only in our own fall into sin;

it also resulted in the fall of creation—the compromising of God's good creation. That is why it is not only humans themselves who need to be redeemed from sin, but why creation itself needs to be "set free from its bondage to decay" (Rom 8:21).

Then there is again the issue of our mortality. God's sentence for our disobedience concludes with the statement that we shall return to the ground from which we were taken, for "[we] are dust, and to dust [we] shall return" (Gen 3:19). Now indeed we risk mortality, but it is a mortality much more serious than the natural death of our bodies. Now, having separated ourselves from God, one another, and God's world, we are truly dead. Should we eat from the tree of life, the tree of immortality, in such a state, we would seal for all eternity our awful fate of being separated from God, others, and the world. We would truly become the disembodied spirits presumed to roam the ethers of creation with no home. So God, "who is rich in mercy" (Eph 2:4), aware of our peril, removed us from our access to the tree of life. "'See, the man has become like one of us, knowing good and evil; and now, he might reach out his hand and take also from the tree of life, and eat, and live forever'—therefore the LORD God sent him forth from the garden of Eden, to till the ground from which he was taken. He drove out the man; and at the east of the garden of Eden he placed the cherubim, and a sword flaming and turning to guard the way to the tree of life" (Gen 3:22–24).

What has often been understood to be a final punishment for human disobedience, our sentence of death through our removal from the tree of life, I understand instead to be an indication of God's loving and redemptive purpose for humanity. God understood the peril in which we stood, having separated ourselves to be alone. If we ate from the tree of life in such a condition, we would live forever in that state of death. So God mercifully acted to remove our access to the tree of life until God could provide a means for our redemption from the power of evil under which we were living. Only then, at the end of the Bible, is access to the tree of life once again possible, when God's new creation through Christ's life, death, and resurrection has begun. Then, on either side of the river that flows from the new Jerusalem, there will be the tree of life, with a different fruit for each month, and whose leaves "are for the healing of the nations" (Rev 22:2).

Dealing with the Reality of Evil in Human Life

As a teenager, I observed and sometimes shared with my peers a periodic fascination for what might be termed the dark side of reality. I noted the same interests and concerns among the youth who took our catechism classes at church. Ouija boards and books on the occult designed to provide access to the spirit world make periodic appearances in our lives and communities. Stories of ghosts and demons formed a part of the folklore of my rural community, as they do in local communities throughout the world. Most of these phenomena are fairly innocent and innocuous, but every now and then one might suspect that a more susceptible individual was being swept away and captivated by such phenomena. In contemporary culture, such phenomena have a genre all their own in horror movies usually involving nubile teenagers. It is the contemporary nod toward the reality of inexplicable forces of evil at work in the world.

In fact, however, such cultural expressions do little justice to the reality of evil at work in the world. They represent sensational distortions about the way in which evil forces have in fact insinuated themselves into the human fabric of life. These cultural expressions prove that contemporary culture really doesn't take the power of evil seriously, by trivializing and sensationalizing it.

Of course, contemporary culture must acknowledge the reality of evil. We live, after all, in a world of terrorists and other evil people out to get us. In other words, we externalize evil into whatever threatens our security and our way of life. In the good old-fashioned style of Westerns, our leaders can talk about going out to eliminate the evil guys intending to take over our town. The presumption, of course, is that evil exists only *out there* and not *in here*. It is a very convenient view of the world, for it excuses us from having to think that evil may in fact be as evident in our own lives and our own way of life as it is in our enemies.

We live in an empirical world, a world defined by our senses. Just as our contemporary world denies a theocentric perspective, so it is skeptical about the presence of evil as a spiritual, non-empirical reality that forms a part of the fabric of human life and the empirical world. Except for entertainment purposes, we demythologize and psychologize all the ancient language about demons and spirits and ghosts. We treat all paranormal phenomena as illusions of the mind, mental illness, or, if forced to give an explanation, we ascribe such phenomena to extraterrestrial agencies, aliens from another world. That way, we can continue to externalize evil and avoid confronting the reality of evil within our own lives and in our own culture. Contemporary society is a chronicle of our human coping with the consequences of our disobedience to God and our refusal to live within the limits God has established for human life.

What we refer to as the fall of humankind into sin is not just an ancient story about moral failing on the part of the first humans. It is instead a story about the way in which the world as we know it, including ourselves, has come under the influence of powers of evil external to ourselves, spiritual powers that inhabit the fabric of human and natural life on earth. The purpose of such a story is not to excuse the human choice to disobey God, as the first humans in Genesis 3 did when they blamed the serpent for their disobedience. The purpose of this spiritual view of reality is to understand the pervasiveness of evil within our own hearts and lives, as well as within our own culture and its institutions.

The biblical terminology for this spiritual realm that lies beyond the natural world of our senses is the language of cosmic powers, rulers ,and authorities in heavenly places. "For our struggle is not against enemies of blood and flesh, but against the rulers, against the authorities, against the cosmic powers of this present darkness, against the spiritual forces of evil in the heavenly places" (Eph 6:12). Colossians 2 speaks of us being captive to "the elemental spirits of the universe" (Col 2:8), "rulers and authorities" Jesus disarmed through his death (Col 2:15). So now we no longer should live as though we still belonged to these "elemental spirits of the universe" (Col 2:20).

A significant body of contemporary theological literature has examined this concept of cosmic powers in New Testament thought, beginning with H. Berkhof in *Christ and the Powers*, and more recently in the trilogy of Walter Wink devoted to the powers.[3] These works make it clear that these powers are not simply vague spiritual realities. Instead, they take on visible form in both personal and institutional manifestations. Both individuals and the institutions organized by humankind to order its life show evidence of being possessed by spiritual powers. Or, to put it a little differently, every moral agent, personal or institutional, manifests both a natural, social reality and also a spiritual reality. The spiritual reality is carried by a spiritual power, sometimes referred to in Scripture as the angel of that person or institution. It reflects the ambiguous mix of good and evil that resides in every moral agent, every person or institution capable of moral discernment. This is particularly a literary device of apocalyptic literature. In Daniel 10:13, the "prince of Persia"—angel? clearly not a human agent—opposes and delays the angel Gabriel's arrival to Daniel, and later, in verse 20, the angel Gabriel leaves Daniel to fight with the "prince of Persia" and later the "prince of Greece." In Revelation 2–3, the seven churches of Asia Minor are each addressed through their respective "angels." This is why evil is never something that resides only in the other. All of our lives and institutions are compromised by and subject to the powers of evil. By the same token, not only our lives, but also the institutions of society compromised by evil, can also be redeemed.

The presence of evil in human life and within human society has two primary practical implications. The first has to do with the question of limitations and constraints. This chapter began by noting the inability of people within contemporary society to restrain themselves, to live within any kind of rational limitations and constraints. Nothing indicates the extent to which humankind lives in subjection to the powers of evil so clearly as the inability to exercise restraint. We are driven to consume and accumulate because of the profound insecurity of our position vis-à-vis God. Having declared our independence from God and claimed to take God's place, we are profoundly anxious to provide for ourselves and make our own way in the world. The contemporary consumer-driven society reflects humanity's deeply rooted insecurity in relation to God, resulting in the pride and greed that drives so much of the modern world.

The other practical implication of the presence of evil in our lives and within human society has to do with our contemporary understanding of work. Our world has come to see the labor basic to the sustenance of human life as drudgery, work to be despised and avoided as much as possible. So we pay others to raise and preserve and prepare the food we eat and to dispose of the wastes we accumulate. Whether or

---

3. *Naming the Powers*; *Unmasking the Powers*; and *Engaging the Powers*.

not our work is truly creative and satisfying, we still believe that it is too important for us to be bothered with the daily tasks of caring for our needs as physical beings. We have by now nearly forgotten how to use our hands to sustain our lives. We have by now nearly lost the skills required by sustain our lives. Now that the ground is cursed because of our sin against God, we see every task necessary to sustain our lives as drudgery. This has profound implications for our lives as humans that we will return to in the course of this book.

The Constraints of Traditional Cultures

It is part of the thesis of this book that civilization, which represents the greatest achievements of humankind, also reflects most strongly the compromised character of the human story. The more civilized we become, the more difficult it is to live within the limitations and constraints of our humanity. This is not to say that traditional cultures are not subject to the powers of evil. The effects of the fall are universal, "since all have sinned and fall short of the glory of God," as Paul says in Romans 3:23. Still, the historical record suggests that traditional cultures have typically found ways to live in some type of harmony with the natural world. Traditional cultures have learned, perhaps through long and bitter experience, how to live within the constraints of their natural environment. Indeed, many traditional cultures have survived in a form of synergy with the natural environment for millennia, and are only now being threatened with extinction by the challenges the civilized world is placing before them.

Within the dominant cultures of the civilized world, there continue to exist both traditional cultures and significant subcultures that consciously set themselves against the excesses of the civilized world and choose to live within certain limitations and constraints. In twenty-first-century America, the Amish represent one such attractive subculture. To those of us outside the Amish community, the choices Amish make for their lives often seem arbitrary and absurd. Why pull an implement having a gas engine with horses? Why do extensive travel between Amish communities in vehicles but refuse to purchase automobiles? Why allow a telephone at the end of one's drive but not in one's home? With the rapid introduction of new energy and communication technologies, we can't imagine what types of challenges Amish communities will face and what kind of strange accommodations they might make.

In fact, however, the Amish response to new technologies is guided, ideally at least, by a very simple principle. What effect will this technology have on the quality of life in the community?[4] That's a quite different question from the utilitarian question that most often guides the introduction of new technology in the dominant culture. *If we can do it, why not do it? If it serves my interest, why not use it?* Yet it quickly becomes apparent that the Amish question might very well turn out to be the most pertinent question of all. We are only beginning to learn, within the dominant culture, about the

---

4. Nolt, *History*, 266.

destructiveness of new technologies to both community and the natural world, to say nothing of the health and welfare of human beings.

Living within the constraints and limitations of our creaturely mortality means learning to live with the interests of community ahead of self-interest. Sustainable communities require that members of the community put communal welfare ahead of self-interest. This is what differentiates traditional cultures from the dominant cultures of urban civilization. Again, it is important to observe that the impulse toward selfish behavior is just as evident in traditional cultures as it is in the dominant culture. Yet, traditional cultures rely on face-to-face relationships. Their survival, often against great odds, depends on people acting together for the good of all. Within the dominant cultures of urban civilization, such built-in constraints to selfish behavior become less and less operative.

This book is not intended as an apology for the Amish way of life. The Amish represent only one subculture that survives within the dominant culture. There are any number of communal enterprises that are able to live against the grain of the dominant culture, and many of these are emerging currently as the dominant culture of American civilization disintegrates. Still, these communal enterprises must all share several elements characteristic of Amish communities, such as evaluating new technologies by their effect on community, living close to nature in self-reliant communities, and putting communal welfare ahead of self-interest.

I represent an element of the Anabaptist Mennonite experience that has for the most part acculturated itself to the dominant culture of American society. The congregations of Mennonite Church USA and Canada struggle to maintain a unique identity of living against the grain of the dominant culture. Our effort to become a missional church represents our struggle. We want to see ourselves representing God's mission in the world. We emphasize the values of peace and justice. Yet we lack the communal cohesion required to really live against the grain of our culture. Our congregations are not characterized as centers of communal discernment, where communal welfare takes precedence over personal interests. The members of our congregations struggle to comprehend the need to live within the limitations and constraints of our mortal creaturehood. Our lives are shaped too much by the values of the dominant culture—values of unlimited economic growth, imperial power, and unrestrained consumption.

At the same time, I am a familial descendant of the Amish heritage. My great-grandfather, Christian Kaufman, was an elder of the Swiss Volhynian Amish community that came to the plains of South Dakota from the Ukraine in 1874. It was a community in transition from Amish to Mennonite, as the Amish community in the Ukraine was influenced by the Mennonites colonizing Russia in the nineteenth century. As I observe the struggle of my rural church and community for survival now in the twenty-first century, I wonder what we have lost by choosing to leave our Amish roots. We struggle to put communal welfare ahead of personal interests. How will we learn to live again within the limitations and constraints of our creaturely mortality?

Chapter 3

The Powers Unleashed

Cain Built a City and Named It Enoch (Gen 4:17)

The Matrix of Urban Civilization

HISTORICALLY, THE CITY HAS its origin in the surplus of settled agriculture. Once production exceeded consumption, the city was inevitable, as some people would begin to pay others to do the work of food production and preparation for them, so that they might busy themselves with other more creative enterprises. The city exists only on the surplus of agricultural production—that is, on the benevolent or harsh exploitation of rural human and natural communities of life.

Spiritually, the city is built out of human rebellion against God's protection and providence. It represents *Enoch* (a "new beginning"), where humans seek to live apart from God. It is often the anonymity of the city that people seek when they have a past they wish to evade.

Positively, the city is closely linked with the creativity of the human spirit, both in the development of the creative arts and in the introduction of new technologies. Negatively, the city represents the retributive and exploitative spirit of sinful humanity (Gen 4). In both respects, the city marks the emergence of *urban civilization*, the assertion of imperial control and cultural dominance by the city (metropolis) over the surrounding countryside.

The new technologies developed in the city inevitably lead to a renewed pride in human abilities and new efforts to play God or take God's place. In the face of human hubris, God mercifully acts to confuse and scatter the pretentiousness of human civilization, limiting to some degree human destructiveness and exploitation of the world (Gen 11). Hence we see the successive rise and fall of civilizations, each of which represents both some pinnacle of human achievement and some excess of prideful exploitation.

The Biblical Story

The Origin of the City

Our human forebears lived originally as small bands of hunters and gatherers, so far as we are able to determine. They hunted wild game and gathered edible parts of wild plants, and lived fairly nomadically in small bands, which were likely extended family units. Remnants of this kind of human existence have continued into the modern world, among the pygmies and other isolated tribes of Africa and the aboriginal people of Australia and the Americas. Though many of the folkways and practices of these peoples have been largely disrupted by the modern world, especially here in North America, the values and belief systems of Native American communities still bear witness to this earliest of genuinely human life here on earth.

About ten thousand years ago, at the dawn of the Holocene epoch, agriculture (the culture or cultivation of the field) began in the Near East with the domestication of plants and animals, a technological development that quickly spread wherever humankind lived on earth.[1] Nearly every habitat on earth has contributed to the range of plants and animals domesticated for human use. The development of agriculture made settled human habitation possible for the first time. Now it was possible for larger communities of humans to live together in settled villages. Indeed, it was not long before larger settlements (towns) developed, as can be discerned through archaeology. Jericho, in the Jordan River Valley of Palestine, and Çatal Hüyük, in the central plain of Turkey, are two such early towns, dating back as far as the eighth millennium BCE.[2]

The story of Cain and Abel in Genesis 4 highlights this era of the human story. These children of the first human couple are presented as tiller of the ground and keeper of sheep, respectively (Gen 4:2). They represent, in other words, the two major forms of agricultural pursuit—the domestication of plants and animals. Though these two forms of agricultural pursuit might best be kept together in a symbiotic relationship, they have often been in tension with one another through history. Ranchers (herdsmen) and farmers (tillers of the soil) have frequently been at odds with one another, as they are in this story, and as we know also from the settlement of the West in the United States and from popular musicals like *Oklahoma*.

It is tempting, though ill-advised, to read into the story of Cain and Abel a divine preference for herdsmen over farmers. What made Abel's sacrifice of a firstling of his flock more acceptable to God than the firstfruits of the ground had less to do with the source or worth of the offering than with the internal disposition of the one making the offering. The text is unclear about what ailed Cain, but his anger and subsequent behavior in killing his brother bears witness to the rivalries and jealousies that arise between siblings, perhaps even more than in other human relationships. Most of us

---

1. Barraclough, *Harper Collins Atlas*, 38–39.
2. Ibid., 40.

experience the most dangerous temptations of human relationships with those closest to us—those who share our own heritage. Here is evidence that sin is just as operative in the open country of God's creation as it is in the urban environment shaped by humans. The issue, as we shall see, is which environment provides the best context for helping us deal with our sinful nature.

While agriculture made possible permanent human settlements in towns and villages, it was the success of agriculture that led to the next stage in the human story. In the areas where agriculture was most successful—the river valleys of the Tigris and Euphrates in Mesopotamia, the Nile in Egypt, the Indus in Pakistan/India, and the Yellow in China—cities began to emerge about the middle of the fourth millennium BCE. The city is differentiated from the village and town not only by the higher concentration of population, but by the level of social organization operating in it, with a complex division of labor, a literate class, political and religious hierarchies, monumental building structures, and complicated technological developments.[3]

The city is characterized by its dependence on agriculture and on the ability of agriculture to produce enough surplus commodities to sustain urban life. In towns and villages there is a symbiotic relationship between the human community and the natural world that sustains it. Because of the concentrated human population and power of the city, the city takes more than it is able to give back to the human and natural communities that sustain it. Indeed, all it really gives back are wastes that cannot be readily recycled into the natural environment. This accounts for the success of archaeology in unpacking the story of urban life. Cities are currently making efforts to become more sustainable. But the concentration of population and the complexity of urban life as an environment shaped by humans continue to make cities dependent upon the surplus of agricultural production and natural resources garnered from distant places. Cities have an inevitably imperial character, imposing their rule upon the world in an exploitation of rural human and natural communities of life that may either be harsh or benevolent, but which is imposed nonetheless by virtue of the power inherent in urban centers.

A Biblical View of the City

Back in 1970, the French sociologist and theologian Jacques Ellul published his book *The Meaning of the City*. It is a biblical study of the city in Scripture, informed by Ellul's sociological training and perspectives, as well as his Reformed theology. It was and continues to be a timely and perceptive study of the city. It shouldn't surprise us that it is a work that has been virtually ignored by the church, as well as the world, given the fact that it speaks prophetically and critically in the face of the global trends toward urbanization that have characterized the modern world. It was for me as a young

---

3. Ibid., 52.

pastor a deeply formative book, shaping my view of ministry as the pastor of a rural congregation in a small rural community in southeast Iowa. While Ellul's book was formative for me, and while what follows reflects Ellul's thinking, I take responsibility for the way these thoughts are expressed here.

The city, in Scripture, has its roots in the story of Cain. After the murder of his brother Abel, Cain's act is discovered by God, who laments that human blood has been shed upon the ground (Gen 4:9–10). Cain's sentence is that he will be "cursed from the ground" he has tilled (Gen 4:11). If Cain now tills the ground "it will no longer yield to [him] its strength" (Gen 4:12). Cain himself will be "a fugitive and a wanderer on the earth" (Gen 4:12). Does this mean he is to be returned to the nomadic life of hunters and gatherers? In any case, Cain complained that this punishment was more than he could bear. He expected vengeance for having killed his brother, and feared being killed by anyone he met (Gen 4:13–14). God promised to mark Cain visibly, as a sign that he lived under God's protection, and to protect him from the vengeance he feared (Gen 4:15). But this assurance of living under God's protection was not enough for Cain. "Then Cain went away from the presence of the LORD, and settled in the land of Nod [wandering], east of Eden. Cain knew his wife, and she conceived and bore Enoch; and he built a city, and named it Enoch after his son Enoch" (Gen 4:16–17). Ellul points out that Enoch means "initiation" or "dedication"—a new beginning apart from God.[4] Thus is the city born!

Several things in this account are telling. Cain left the presence of the Lord (Gen 4:16). He was not comfortable living under God's protection. Perhaps he did not trust God's promise of protection from vengeance. He settled in the land of Nod, a land of wandering, east of Eden. Despite his rejection of God's sentence, Cain would in any case "settle" as a wanderer, but his wandering would be an internal wandering of not being content or at home where he was.[5] Next, Cain procreated! He had a son to bear his future, as we humans tend to do. If that were not enough, Cain built a city, and named it after his son (Gen 4:17). The city was the place of Cain's making, the place where Cain would live apart from God's presence, because to live in God's presence was too burdensome for him (Gen 4:13).

It is easy for rural people like myself to read into this story a tendency we observe. When someone in our communities wants to hide something they have done, when they want to get lost, they often seem to seek the anonymity of the city, an environment artificially constructed by humans. The subsequent verses of Genesis 4 confirm urban life as the setting for both escaping the past and pursuing retribution and revenge. It was Lamech, the fifth-generation descendant of Cain, who declared to his wives the principle of unlimited vengeance, with the threat of seventy-sevenfold vengeance toward anyone who struck him (Gen 4:23–24). This was surely in Jesus' mind when he proclaimed to Peter the divine principle of unlimited forgiveness,

---

4. Ellul, *Meaning*, 5–6.
5. Ibid., 3.

seventy-seven times, in Matthew 18:22. While vengeance is certainly common to all sinful humanity, as we know from the stories of the feuding Hatfields and McCoys in the hills, this emphasis on overkill (seventy-sevenfold retribution for a blow) seems characteristic of urban civilization.

Lamech's family also reveals the link of the city with the development of civilization. Among Lamech's children were Jubal, the ancestor of musicians, and Tubal-cain, the ancestor of metal workers (Gen 4:21–22). Fine arts and industry are the pursuits of urban life. They are the evidence of civilization, the greatest human achievements. Unfortunately, such endeavors have only been pursued at great cost and too often for the wrong purposes. Typically, the first implements of metal workers were weapons of war to be used for the protection of the city and the expansion of the city's influence. In the postdiluvian account of the city's expansion, Nimrod, portrayed as the builder of the first great cities and empires of history, is described as a "mighty warrior" (Gen 10:8–12). While conflict and even violence are endemic to the human experience as creatures in rebellion against God, war belongs to the history of the city—an evidence, ironically, of human civilization.[6]

From a biblical point of view, we may view the city from two perspectives. We may see what the city represents theologically, and we may describe the city historically or sociologically. Theologically, the city is rooted in an attempt to humanly reshape the natural environment. It is a place where humans can begin again to live apart from God in an environment artificially constructed by humans. There is nothing wrong with the human desire to exercise our creativity. It is part of our inheritance as creatures made in God's image. But when we use that ability to reinforce our separation from God and to prove that we don't need to live within the constraints God places upon us, then we can expect the result to have at best mixed and at worst disastrous consequences. This is only to say that while the human constructs of urban life can and certainly will be redeemed in some fashion, their character in history is deeply compromised by the intentions of their creators. In the making of cities, humans are typically not seeking to participate with God in the unfolding of God's creation. They are seeking instead an alternate, humanly constructed creation in which they can live apart from God.

Along with this, the city also represents the beginning of structured social inequities and injustices and the institutional exploitation of the natural environment. Sociologically and historically, the city represents the development of a distinctive class structure in human society. As production exceeded consumption in developing agricultural communities, some people began to pay others to do the menial tasks of daily living. This was probably not a consequence of laziness, but rather grew out of a desire to use human creativity for more engaging activities. Who of us have not looked for ways to maximize the time we can spend on activities that engage our creative energy? There is nothing wrong with this desire to use our creative energy on making

6. Ibid., 10–13.

a beautiful building or a work of art or the accumulation of wealth. It does become problematic when it cuts us off from the natural world on which our lives depend. It does become problematic when it involves the oppression of those who are paid to do the menial tasks associated with our livelihood for us—the preparation of our food and the disposal of our wastes. When the economic functions of production and consumption are separated as they are particularly in urban life, then the possibility of exploitation and injustice grows exponentially.

Sociologically, it is not only the economic separation of consumption and production that leads to class divisions within human society. It is also the hierarchy of power and control that leads to such distinctions within the human family. The high concentration and diversity of population in the city require a high degree of social organization and control, and some people are quick to use their creative gifts to supply this social need. Again, this is a necessary and useful function of human society, and such rule, however autocratically it may be exercised, may be benevolent and just. By the same token, given the fallen state of all humans, it is likely that those who exercise power will be tempted to use it for their own advantage and at the expense of those who are more vulnerable within the human community.

What I mean to say is that the city magnifies exponentially all the sinful tendencies found among humans anywhere. The loss of face-to-face relationships, the development of complex social organizations, and the withdrawal from the constraints of nature, to say nothing of the attempt to establish human life apart from God, expands the arena in which the powers of evil can be operative. In chapter 2, we spoke of how our rebellion against God unleashed the powers of evil, allowing them to keep us under their power. When in turn we sought a place where we could begin again away from God's presence in an environment of our own making, the realm in which these powers were free to function was exponentially increased as well. The development of the city does indeed represent a new arena in which the powers of evil are unleashed.

This is not to deny or minimize the universality of evil and sin within human history. The same forces of evil found in the city are operative in the more simply organized lives of humans in the countryside. However, rural communities most often involve face-to-face relationships and an accommodation to the constraints of the natural world, both of which mitigate the effects of sin and circumscribe the realm in which the powers of evil can be at work. By the same token, this is not to say that genuine human community cannot be formed in the environment and within the structures of urban life. Indeed, cities are generally composed of neighborhoods that replicate the characteristics of rural communities. These urban communities struggle against the dominant structures that govern urban life just as rural communities do. But it is easier in the city for individuals to avoid the accountability that comes from living in face-to-face relationships and with the awareness of both natural and divine constraints upon our lives.

God's Intervention to Curb Urban Pretensions

The story of the tower of Babel in Genesis 11 reveals again the theological dilemma of the city. Genesis 4–11 relates the primeval history of humankind. It is here that we see the consequences of our human rebellion against God, our discontent with the boundaries and constraints God had set for human activity. Here we see the human family becoming ever more deeply mired in forces of evil that are released to operate in the more highly organized life of humanity. Even after the judgment and new beginning of the flood, the reprieve of humankind is short lived. Noah's family gives birth to the Table of Nations in Genesis 10, reflecting a humanity divided into warring and hostile "families, languages, lands, and nations" (Gen 10:5, 20, 31). The matrix of urban civilization lies in the human discontent with the boundaries and constraints God had established for human life. Genesis 11 describes a humanity determined to make its own way to heaven, make a name for itself, and prevent its being "scattered abroad upon the face of the whole earth" (Gen 11:4).

There is much that is good and beautiful about urban life. As a "country boy," I enjoy walking city streets and observing the diversity of humanity that has come together in the city. The city attracts people of varied ethnic backgrounds to its streets, and in the city these diverse people live together. But though many languages are spoken, the city is united by speaking one language, a lingua franca. The people of the city are united by the common purpose of making a name for themselves, and in the process much that is good and beautiful is created. The problem is with the purpose or the intention of this human unity. It is to exalt humankind, not to glorify God! Indeed, the intention is to make God irrelevant. *The tower we build will reach to heaven! Then we won't need God anymore.* As Ellul says, "The cities of our time are most certainly that place where man can with impunity declare himself master of nature. It is only in an urban civilization that man has the metaphysical possibility of saying, 'I killed God.'"[7]

However, this points toward the other really attractive feature of urban life—the introduction of new technologies that enable humanity to create a humanly shaped environment. As we have noted, the city is marked by the construction of impressive public monuments and buildings. Who of us have not been awed by the public buildings of a national capital like Washington, DC, or other capital cities of our world? Indeed, it was the introduction of new construction technologies that made possible the pretensions of Babel. Previously, construction was limited by using shaped stones and mortar. With the introduction of baked bricks and using bitumen to bind them together, the famous ziggurats of ancient Mesopotamia became possible—towers that seemed to rise into the heavens (Gen 11:3)! In our own era, the skyscraper still marks the prestige of the city, though the events of September 11, 2001, have demonstrated that even the towers of the World Trade Center in New York City were not invincible.

---

7. Ibid., 16; the male noun is in this case an appropriate anachronism.

Nevertheless, it is an exceedingly dangerous adventure theologically for humans to embark on this project of anthropocentric aggrandizement. Given our God-given calling to serve and worship God, it is a form of idolatry. Given the human cost of such endeavors, it is the primary arena of human oppression and injustice. Given our mortality and our dependence upon the earth for our sustenance, it is suicidal. So we find God mercifully intervening in Genesis 11 to confuse the speech of the urban dwellers, so that they might not complete their ill-advised project and perish. Babylon was the city where the tower was built to reach the heavens. The name, which means "gateway to the gods," is reinterpreted by the Hebrew writer of Genesis as *Babel*, "the confusion of tongues" (Gen 11:9).[8] The project of building the tower to heaven and making God irrelevant was discarded (Gen 11:8). They were no longer able to make a name for themselves. The thing for which they banded together in the city—to avoid their scattering over the face of the earth—is the very thing that comes about as a consequence of God's intervention. It is only much later, with the advent of the Holy Spirit in power, that we can regain the ability to understand one another for the right reasons—to honor and glorify God for God's mighty deeds (Acts 2:1–13)!

In the meantime, may God continue to preserve us from the worst consequences of our urban pretensions! Indeed, in the march of civilizations over the past six thousand or more years, we do perceive this limiting, beneficent hand of God at work. We see in human history the rise and fall of great civilizations. Each brings its own glory and strength to the human story. Each reflects some pinnacle of human achievement. Each, when it has dangerously overreached its capacity to be sustained, has collapsed in upon itself. The pride and arrogance that create great civilizations also prove to be their undoing. So we always find ourselves being confused again, and scattered over the face of the earth, with our great projects left unfinished in the ruins.

Human Residences: Rural and Urban

The *World Christian Encyclopedia*, published in 1982, by David Barrett, estimated the world population in 1900 of 1.62 billion to be 85.6 percent rural; the population projection for 2000 was 6.26 billion with 49.5 percent being rural.[9] Clearly the last century has seen an exponential growth in the expansion of urban areas across the globe, along with the population explosion itself. The United Nations Department of Economic and Social Affairs put the 2011 world population at 6,974,036,000, and estimated the urban percentage to be 52.1 percent. Northern America (United States and Canada) is the most highly urbanized region at 82 percent urban, and Africa is the least urbanized continent at 39 percent, with Asia close behind at 45 percent.[10] A little over half the world's population lives in cities, but nearly half still lives in rural areas.

---

8. Ibid., 15.
9. Barrett, *World*, 780.
10. *Urban Agglomerations 2007*, 11.

Of course, the definition of rural and urban is notoriously difficult to resolve. Some definitions revolve around the population of a town or city. Others have to do with density of population in a given area. Still others include socioeconomic criteria. The 1990 United States Census Bureau found that by its definitions the US population was 75 percent urban and 25 percent rural.[11] The 1990 census defined "urban population" as places of five thousand inhabitants or more, usually but not necessarily incorporated as cities, villages, boroughs, and towns. Open or rural areas, even within urban boundaries, are defined as areas of at least five square miles with a population density of less than 100 persons per square mile.[12]

As I have reflected on rural/urban issues, I have found it helpful to work toward my own typology of the places in which the human family typically resides. The size of the place as well as its location forms one continuum. The character of the place in terms of its social structures and relationships and power arrangements forms another continuum. The sustainability of the place within the natural ecology forms still another continuum. Consider the size and location of the following places where humans reside in permanent homes.

Single family homesteads: farms and ranches established in open land / countryside / rural areas, typically with a population of *less than 10*. Such settlements were previously largely self-sufficient, but now are usually connected to public services for energy, water, and transportation. Such units are usually but not always engaged in agrarian pursuits such as farming and ranching. Often these are now residences for people who work in a nearby town or city.

Hamlets: small, multifamily settlements in open land / countryside / rural areas, with a population of *less than 100*. Residents are typically engaged in agrarian pursuits, and may sometimes but not always be composed of extended families. Sometimes these places are named locally, but usually they have little if any centralized or organized structures of communal life, though they typically are connected to public services.

Villages: small clusters of dwellings in open land / countryside / rural areas, with a population of *less than 1,000*. Residents are usually engaged in agriculture, but with a somewhat more diversified economic life and with a small organized bureaucratic structure. Villages retain strong face-to-face relationships and are often bound together by kinship ties. Villages may offer a few public services.

Towns: settlements in open land / countryside / rural areas, with a population of *less than 10,000*. Towns offer a diversified economy and a structured political administration, with a full range of public services, including health and education facilities. Towns have a symbiotic relationship with the surrounding agrarian homesteads and villages and with the natural ecology of the region, providing goods and services in exchange for food and raw materials.

11. *World Almanac, 2000*, 386.
12. *World Almanac, 1990*, 564.

Cities: places that are built up, in which people reside in an environment shaped by humans, with a population of *less than 100,000*. Cities are centers for pursuits related to technology, education and knowledge, the arts, health care, religious hierarchy, economic institutions of commerce and industry, and political administration. Cities typically consume more energy and resources than can be sustainably provided by the economy of the surrounding region, and produce more wastes than can effectively be distributed into the ecology of the region. Still, small cities of one hundred thousand or less can likely be sustainable and achieve a healthy relationship with the surrounding countryside if efforts are made toward that end.

The *metropolis*: a built-up urban area with a population of *less than 1 million*. As cities grow larger than 100,000, they begin to swallow up the surrounding open land, as well as surrounding towns and villages, to create urban areas (suburbs) larger than the city itself. Culturally, as well, the imperial character of the city becomes evident in the metropolis (literally, "mother city"). In his book *Empire as a Way of Life*, historian William Appleman Williams characterizes imperialism as "the loss of sovereignty—control—over essential issues and decisions by a largely agricultural society to an industrial metropolis."[13] Quoting Adam Smith, Williams says, "The city enjoys and exploits a structural advantage over the country. The metropolis routinely displays and occasionally uses its military power, and metropolitan advisors (official and private, academic and corporate) are always on guard as supervisory personnel, but the essence of imperialism lies in the metropolitan domination of the weaker economy (and its political and social superstructure) to ensure the extraction of economic rewards."[14] The metropolis is often composed of multiple political jurisdictions surrounding a central urban core.

The *megalopolis*: a built-up urban area with a population of *more than 1 million*. This is simply an expansion of the metropolis. Called "urban agglomerates" by the United Nations Department of Economic and Social Affairs, there were 434 megalopolises in 2011, with twenty-three having a population of more than 10 million. The largest megalopolis is Tokyo, with a population of more than 37 million. Delhi, Shanghai, Mumbai, Mexico City, Sao Paulo, and New York City all have a population of about 20 million.[15]

While this completes the range of human residences in terms of size and location, there are several other terms of residence that are important. *Suburbs* are satellite settlements to metropolises, with varied population and political structure. Suburbs are designed for residential use with access to urban areas. Sometimes suburbs develop from villages and towns in proximity to urban areas; sometimes they develop ad hoc on the edges of urban areas; and sometimes they are intentionally planned residential parks in formerly rural areas with consumer and public services available

---

13. Williams, *Empire*, 7.
14. Ibid., 7–8.
15. *Urban Agglomerations 2007*, 7.

to residents. Suburbs are typically the most common feature of urban expansion in the metropolis, often displacing agricultural pursuits and other natural resources.

In the typology I am describing, the rural/urban divide comes between the *town (1,000 to 10,000)*, and the *metropolis (over 100,000)*, with the *city* being an intermediate category. Towns of less than 10,000 are "rural" by nearly every measure, at least in the American Midwest. I can conceive of *cities (10,000 to 100,000)* being ecologically and economically sustainable in the context of their region. I find it more difficult to believe that the *metropolis* could ever be ecologically or economically sustainable, even if it were to deny its character as an imperial metropolis. Population concentrations of such immensity are simply unrealistic for the future of human life on earth. If a catastrophic future is to be avoided, the trend toward urbanization we have seen in the twentieth century will have to be reversed. Population centers will have to be decentralized, along with the concentrations of power inherent in them. Over time, people will need to take more responsibility to sustain their own physical lives and return to a way of life that recognizes and seeks to achieve natural constraints and ecological limits.

There are two other terms of residence that are important for this discussion—the *neighborhood* and the *community*. These are both terms of location and may sometimes be used synonymously. However, with the term *neighborhood* the focus tends to be primarily on residential proximity. It designates those who live together in close proximity, even though these neighbors may not always see themselves as part of the same *community*.

In the introduction to this book, where I presented the thesis I am working to defend, I spoke of *community* as the place where humans can best fulfill God's intention for the human family by living in just, equitable, participatory, interdependent, and sustainable relationships. That's an idealistic definition of community, but it highlights the face-to-face relationships that distinguish *community* from the impersonal and even anonymous relationships that govern human life in the urban context. Sociologically, community can be defined as the place or location where groups of people find their primary identity and fulfill their primary needs. "A *community* is a place or location where groups of people interact for mutual support."[16]

Regardless of where people live, whether in urban or rural areas, and regardless of their size or location, people generally find the most meaningful relationships of their lives in the community where they experience face-to-face relationships. Such communities may be intentional or may be the result of proximity (neighborhoods). Individuals may typically relate to a number of *communities*, perhaps one by virtue of their neighborhood, one by virtue of their faith (their congregation), one by virtue of their work or vocation, one by virtue of the school their children attend, and so on.

While modern transportation has stretched the concept of a community defined as a specific location or place, communities still require face-to-face relationships.

16. Flora and Flora, *Rural Communities*, 19.

The rural churches I have served have all had a regular active membership spanning a radius of from twenty to fifty miles—hardly a neighborhood or parish! Virtual or electronic communities would be non-specific to location or place, but that would also rule them out as true communities, in my view. After all, whether rural or urban, communities are concerned with the welfare of their place as a real place where real people live. Communities are inherently *local* in some concrete sense, not least in having regular face-to-face relationships. Communities are the contexts in which individuals, whether in rural or urban settings, take responsibility for their lives in ways that are just and sustainable. The imperial character of the metropolis utilizes individuals as distinct units of production or consumption. This is what makes it difficult for individuals to stand against the imperial policies of the city. Only as communities will the human family be able to move toward a just and sustainable future.

The Parameters and Fortunes of a Rural Mennonite Community

The most immediate community in which I grew up as a rural Mennonite was the Swiss Volhynian East Freeman community along the Turkey Ridge valley in southeastern South Dakota. This community comprised my home congregation, Salem Mennonite Church, and its mother congregation, Salem-Zion Mennonite Church, known locally as the South and North churches. This community interacted with two other Mennonite and a number of non-Mennonite communities, which together formed the larger rural area around Freeman, South Dakota. With variations, the story of my home community is characteristic of the Mennonite experience in the first centuries of Mennonite life here in North America.

All of these ethnic Mennonite communities (Swiss Volhynian, Low German, and Hutterisch Mennonite groups, as well as Reformed, Lutheran, and Catholic German groups) had come to the plains of South Dakota from the Ukraine in the 1870s. There were also Scandinavian and Czech immigrant communities in the larger area. In a treaty of 1858, the Yankton Sioux tribe had ceded a large portion of what was to become southeast South Dakota to the United States government in exchange for a reserve in Charles Mix County, some fifty miles southwest of Freeman.[17] This ceded land was then opened for settlement by white European immigrants.

When these immigrants first came to the plains of South Dakota, there was no infrastructure, not even railroads. My Swiss Volhynian community received some help from established Mennonites in the eastern United States,[18] and with that help, much hard labor, and much cooperation with the other local communities, a strong rural community was built. Over a dozen congregations were established, along with two parochial and many public schools, a hospital and nursing home, and an old people's home. Various cooperatives were developed to facilitate the economic life of

---

17. Sansom-Flood and Bernie, *Remember*, 47–52.
18. Unruh and Waltner, *Andreas Schrag*, 3–17.

the community, along with the small businesses, services, and infrastructure required to meet the needs of the community.[19]

The original pioneers were able to establish their children and grandchildren on small family farms, enabling the population of the community to expand rapidly. The two Swiss Volhynian congregations grew from an initial settlement of 71 families (about 175 members), to a combined membership of over 1,017 in 1970, with most of the growth occurring prior to 1940. Since 1970, these two congregations have lost a third of their membership (combined membership in 2008 was 716).[20] This decline of membership is probably less than the population decline of the counties in which these churches are located. Today the community struggles to keep its remaining parochial school open. Public schools in surrounding communities are struggling to survive. Services at the local hospital have been drastically reduced. The local business district of Freeman has struggled. The community is in many respects in survival mode.

The reasons for the decline of this rural community are not hard to find. With the industrialization of agriculture after World War II, dictated by the imperial needs of the American metropolis, machine energy and fossil fuel replaced human labor. Farm size increased exponentially, making people unnecessary and driving them from the land. The depopulation of our rural community was not the result of overcrowding in rural areas, or the inability of the land to sustain a larger population. Clearly, the land could sustain a community at least double our current size. Indeed, the population of Turner County in 1905 was 13,895, nearly twice the county's population of 8,237 in 2010.[21] It was not ecological or economic necessity that decimated the population of my home community. It was policies advantageous to the imperial culture of American society that made living in a rural community unattractive economically and culturally. These policies were implemented by the political power of the nation-state, the economic power of corporate entities, and the technical power of elite specialists.

In many places around the world, such policies literally make it impossible for rural communities to survive. In our community, we can hardly place all the blame for our decline on the forces of urbanization. We have been complicit in the process ourselves. The imperial city not only imposes its will on the surrounding region; it also seduces the rural population to serve its will. In our community, we were more seduced than coerced into abandoning our rural way of life. We were drawn by the lure of new technology and economic growth. In the process, we have lost a vision for how to sustain our community.

In the first generations of our congregational life, the mission of our members was the building of the infrastructure and institutions required for our rural way of

---

19. See Unruh, *Century of Mennonites*, for a good summary of the early history of the community.

20. See the Membership Chart in the author's thirteenth sermon, "Our Golden Age," in *Roots that Nourish*.

21. Kaufman, "Anatomy," 19.

life. No one articulated this in the missional language the church uses today. Still, our members invested their lives, their labor, and their resources in the building of a rural community as an expression of their Christian faith. Once the process of urbanization began in earnest in the years after the Second World War, we found ourselves with excess wealth and excess progeny. We could no longer absorb our children into the fabric of our rural community, so we caught the vision that our children, with proper training and education, could be of service to God's kingdom in the larger world. In the same way, we came to see that our mission was to give generously of our wealth for the church's mission, especially in foreign lands. Recent generations in our congregations have been generous with both their children and their finances. The mission of the church had become the support of missions with our financial resources and our children.

Now we are having to refocus our missional thinking toward the revitalization of our rural community. The repopulation of rural areas like ours is a very real possibility. In many ways it has already begun, aided by the economic, ecological, and energy crises our country is facing. While presenting us with many challenges, there are also great opportunities for the ministry of the church in the current crisis. But these challenges will require us to abandon the privatized and individualistic understandings of missions and relearn the missional aspects of building community. The forces of urban civilization remain very strong. It is only as we learn how to rebuild community that we will be able to help our culture make a peaceful transition to a post-petroleum, post-industrial, post-imperial way of life.

Part B

God's Covenants: Paradigms and Strategic Models of Human Experience

Chapter 4

The Call of Faith to Live as a Sojourner

Go to the Land That I Will Show You (Gen 12:1)

An Alternative Community of Faith Within a Dominant Culture

FROM THE BEGINNING, THE formation of alternative communities of faith living within the dominant culture has been central to God's plan for redeeming fallen humanity. It is not God's way, typically, to challenge the idolatries of the dominant culture directly. Instead, God calls persons into alternative communities characterized by radical faith and trust in God to live within the dominant culture, modeling (incarnating) lives of faithfulness to God's intention for the human family. Those in this alternative faith community are called to live as sojourners or resident aliens within the dominant culture. Far from calling those with faith to withdraw out of this world, God invites those who respond in faith to engage the world at its most vulnerable crossroads.

Hence it is no accident that it was to Palestine that God called Abraham and his familial community to sojourn with faith in God's promise. Palestine was the crossroads of ancient civilizations, the narrow land bridge between Mesopotamia and Egypt, the frontier between Persia and Greece, Parthia and Rome. It was precisely to the central, most vulnerable geographical setting of the ancient world that God brought the Abrahamic community to sojourn as resident aliens. So it is that Abraham is portrayed as traversing the entire Fertile Crescent, from Ur of the Chaldeans to Egypt.

While resident aliens may prosper, as Abraham did, they remain marginal outsiders in significant ways: by virtue of being an ethnic or religious minority within the dominant culture; by virtue of being landless or holding land only as tenants; by virtue of rejecting the civic powers inherent in being citizens of a realm; or by virtue of choosing technologies and patterns of life that enhance and enrich communal life. This very marginality enables a community of resident aliens to bear a considerable witness to the dominant culture in which it lives, as indeed Abraham is portrayed as having done during his long sojourn in Palestine.

The Biblical Story

A Pilgrimage of Faith

Perhaps it is inappropriate to speak of God in this way, but it seems to me that God had a dilemma! God could of course see and deplore the mess we humans had created for ourselves and for God's creation, by our sin and rebellion against God. God could see that our sin had unleashed the powers of evil upon the earth, and that we were helpless to set ourselves free from these powers of evil. In particular, God could see how we humans were trapped by the institutions and structures we had created. Necessary as these structures were, they also made it even more difficult for us to be faithful to God's intention for our lives, even when we sensed what that intention was.

Being the almighty Creator, God could simply have intervened to forcefully destroy the powers of evil, along with the evil people themselves. Indeed, this seems to have been God's strategy in the story of the flood. God set the divine hopes on this one faithful human, Noah, who "found favor in the sight of the LORD" (Gen 6:8). By calling Noah to build the ark and to preserve his family from the flood along with representative life forms of the earth, God hoped to achieve a new beginning. Yet after observing the devastation of the flood, this was God's resolve: "I will never again curse the ground because of humankind, for the inclination of the human heart is evil from youth; nor will I ever again destroy every living creature as I have done" (Gen 8:21). God seemed to realize that Noah himself would soon disappoint him, as turned out to be the case in Genesis 9:20–21, after Noah planted a vineyard and became drunk. But in the meantime, we have the wonderful promise of Genesis 8:22: "As long as the earth endures, seedtime and harvest, cold and heat, summer and winter, day and night, shall not cease," a promise that is sealed in Genesis 9:12–17 with the sign of the rainbow.

So with the forceful exercise of divine power as retributive justice being ruled out, at least for the most part, God needed to find another way to redeem an intolerable situation of human sinfulness. While the answer to God's dilemma is not spelled out explicitly, it is acted out in God's call to Abram in Genesis 12. God was resolved to work in and through the lives of those who were responsive to God's inner call, God's invitation to a pilgrimage of faith. For despite the grip of evil in which all of us as humans live, God's presence continues to touch the hearts of all but the most hardened of humankind.

Now and then, despite ourselves and however imperfectly, we respond to the inner prompting of God to a journey of faith and trust in God. Sometimes that journey carries us a long way, and sometimes it is quite short lived. Sometimes we are able to recognize and name the inspiration that leads us to live in accordance with God's intention for our lives, and sometimes we simply act on some inner compulsion we don't ourselves fully understand.

This call of God, this journey of faith, typically drives us to live against the grain of the dominant culture in which we live—a culture that has become oppressive and binding. After all, the worst tendencies of human rebellion against God are usually magnified exponentially in the structures and institutions of the dominant culture, as we saw in the last chapter. So when we find ourselves being responsive to the divine initiative, we typically feel compelled to live against the grain of the dominant culture. Since it is usually incredibly difficult to stand alone against the culture, we usually take such a stand only in the company of others. It may not be many. It may only be a small circle of friends. It may only be one's family and kin. But together, however fitfully and imperfectly, we engage in a community of resistance, a place where we take our stand against the injustices, exploitation, and idolatry of the culture around us.

So it is that Abram and Sarai, along with his nephew Lot and the persons associated with their households, responded to what they understood to be God's call and journeyed to the land of Canaan (Gen 12:1–9). They made this journey, as we all do in such adventures, on the strength of a promise, a new beginning. The Bible calls this promise a covenant with God. We embark on such adventures because we feel called to seek a place where God will bless us, where we can live out the vision we have from God for human life on earth. In Abram's case, the promise involved not just a personal blessing, becoming "a great nation" and having "a great name," but also becoming a blessing to "all the families of the earth" (Gen 12:2–3). In other words, we respond to what we perceive to be God's call upon our lives in the hope that our lives can make a difference—that we can minimize if not undo the oppression and exploitation and idolatry we see around us.

This is what makes any pilgrimage of faith both risky and rewarding. We do not embark on such a pilgrimage as disinterested beings. We want to make a difference with our lives, for ourselves if not for the world or history. But once self-interest enters into our adventure of faith, as it must, it is always easy to misread the divine intention. We may embark on the adventure deeply committed to reflect God's plan for a better world, but before we know it motives of self-aggrandizement begin to color and warp our perception of God's plan. Before we know it, we are no longer content with the promise. We carve out for ourselves a role much more grandiose and self-serving than what God had in mind with the promise. Yet how sad the human story would be if no one risked striking out on a pilgrimage of faith on the strength of the promise that our lives here on earth can make a difference for God!

Resident Aliens in the Land

In view of our tendency to exaggerate God's promise in self-aggrandizing ways, the question we need to explore is what God intended by calling Abram to the land of Canaan. Clearly a part of God's intention was to bless Abram himself: "I will make of you a great nation, and I will bless you, and make your name great" (Gen 12:2). But

God's blessing is not an end in itself, but the means toward an end: "so that you will be a blessing" (Gen 12:2). God's ultimate purpose in the divine promise to Abram is that through Abram "all the families of the earth shall be blessed" (Gen 12:3). The implication is that Abram is to be a model, the agent through whom God's blessing can flow to all the people of the earth. The personal blessing is contingent on becoming a blessing to "all the families of the earth."

We sometimes forget that the call of Abram in Genesis 12 comes in the context of a larger human migration. In the wake of the scattering of the nations at the Tower of Babel that we explored in the last chapter, Terah, a descendant of Noah's son Shem, pulled up stakes from the heart of Mesopotamian urban civilization, Ur of the Chaldeans (Gen 11:31). Perhaps the departure was prompted by the death of a son, Haran, in Ur (Gen 11:28), and by the barrenness of Abram's wife Sarai (Gen 11:30). Was there no future for this family in the context of urban civilization? Walter Brueggemann, in his classic study on land in the Bible, contrasts the barrenness of life in Ur with the promise of fruitfulness in the land of promise.[1] The destination for Terah's family initially was "the land of Canaan; but when they came to Haran, they settled there" (Gen 11:31). It is not said that this original migration came at the instigation of a call from God, but it is significant that Canaan was the original destination and that the journey was interrupted by the settlement in Haran. This settlement has the character of a false start, the acceptance of an easier resolution than the original plan.

In any case, it is in the context of this larger, earlier migration that Abram is called by God to complete the journey, to become a sojourner in the land of Canaan. It is crucial to emphasize that Abram was called to be a sojourner, a resident alien in the land of Canaan. In each of the theophanies Abram experienced in Canaan the land is promised, but only to Abram's descendants (Gen 12:7; 15:18; 17:8). Abram himself is called to live as a resident alien in the land. Several times in the Abrahamic narrative, it is said that Abram "passed through the land" (Gen 12:6), or "journeyed on by stages" (Gen 12:9) through the land. After sharing the land with his nephew Lot, Abram is invited by the Lord to "walk through the length and the breadth of the land, for I will give it to you" (Gen 13:17). This last verse might suggest the land will belong to Abram, but in fact that never happens. The land remains a place of reconnoitered promise, not a place of personal possession. An inveterate wanderer, Abram goes down to Egypt at the time of a famine in Canaan (Gen 12:10), and into the Negev toward the Wilderness of Shur in the northern Sinai peninsula (Gen 20:1). However, in each of these instances, Abram is drawn back into Canaan, the land of promise.

What we begin to understand is that it is as a *resident alien* in the land that Abraham is to fulfill his vocation of becoming a blessing to others. As Norman Habel points out in his book *The Land Is Mine*, Abraham is consistently portrayed as being respectful of those who lived in the land, who are his hosts.[2] "Abraham is portrayed

---

1. Brueggemann, *Land*, 18.
2. Habel, *Land*, 125–30.

as an exemplar of how to share the land, overcome conflict, and mediate blessing to the inhabitants of the land. The host peoples of the land live together with Abraham as a welcome immigrant in their midst."[3] In contrast to the other land ideologies of the Bible, in which the land is often conquered and possessed, the Abrahamic covenant portrays Abraham living as a resident alien willing and careful to share the land through a generous grant (as with Lot in Genesis 13), peaceful negotiations (as with Abimelech in Genesis 20 and 21), and limited purchase of the land for a burial plot (as with the Hittites of Hebron in Genesis 23). As the ancient stories of Genesis 14 indicate, Abraham was respectful of the religious heritage of the inhabitants of the land. "Here there is no denunciation of Canaanite worship, no condemnation of Canaanite inhabitants, no rejection of Canaanite rulers as oppressors, and no concern about acknowledging a Canaanite deity.... Instead, Abraham fosters a way of life in Canaan that mediates blessing and creates peaceful relations with the owners of the land."[4]

The point being made is that Canaan was inhabited land when Abram came to sojourn on it, as indeed all land on earth is inhabited land. "At that time the Canaanites were in the land" (Gen 12:6). Ever since the dawn of human history, it hasn't been possible for anyone to journey to a truly pristine land. All the land of the earth is land occupied by someone. In order to fulfill God's intention for our pilgrimage here on earth, we have to learn how to live among those who inhabit the land. In the Bible, Abraham is presented as a model for how to become a blessing to all the families of the earth, all the people among whom we live.

So Abram came to Canaan as a resident alien. He is portrayed as a herdsman, a man of the open country, who had no need of the city. Indeed, he is portrayed as "very rich in livestock, in silver, and in gold" (Gen 13:2). It is after all possible to prosper as a resident alien, not at the expense of but alongside those who inhabit the land. Though Canaan was even then a highly urbanized land, there was much open country, as there is still today, for people to make a livelihood from the land. As we recall from the last chapter, Canaan was among the first places to become urbanized, beginning with Jericho as a walled town more than six thousand years ago. The peoples inhabiting Canaan in Abram's time, listed in Genesis 15:19–21, were presumably urban dwellers, purveyors of urban civilization. Their way of life stands in contrast to the rural life of Abram who has no need to possess the land in order to prosper, though given Abram's tenuous status as a resident alien no negative judgments are made with regard to these inhabitants of the land. Repeatedly, Abram receives the blessings of the land as gift from God, to whom the land ultimately belongs.

One other observation needs to be made about the place of Abraham's sojourn as a resident alien, a geographical consideration that is often overlooked. We know that Canaan, or Palestine as we know it today, was the land bridge between the Egyptian civilization along the Nile river in Africa and the civilizations of Mesopotamia,

3. Ibid., 125.
4. Ibid., 127.

the land between the Tigris and the Euphrates rivers. I have come to see it as highly significant that it was in this land between the civilizations of the ancient world that God called Abraham to sojourn. Indeed, we see Abraham himself spanning the entire Fertile Crescent. He was born at Ur of the Chaldeans, in the heart of Mesopotamia, lived his settled life in Haran at the apex of the Fertile Crescent, and then sojourned in Canaan, with forays into Egypt as well.

If we were to extrapolate from the example of Abraham, we could say that God calls humans to live as resident aliens, sojourners in the midst of urban civilization. When we get sidetracked and want to put down roots, or when we leave the journey because it is too hard, God keeps calling us back to that vulnerable place where the clashes of urban civilization are most likely to occur. For if nothing else is true, the history of Canaan demonstrates how difficult it is to live in contested land, land that is caught between the forces of great urban civilizations that not only covet this land for themselves but also must cross it to challenge each other's hegemony. The call to live as sojourners in the land of promise is hardly a call for a withdrawal from the world. It is a call to engage the world at its most vulnerable and dangerous intersections, so that we might become the agents of God's blessing to all people, as Abraham was in his sojourn.

Living on the Strength of a Promise

Living as a resident alien requires a person to live as a marginal outsider to the dominant culture in significant ways. It requires a person to defer one's own desires or needs for the sake of a larger goal. It requires a person to live on the strength of a promise rather than to assume the right to have that promise fulfilled. It is in fact this marginality that makes the influence of the resident alien so effective within the dominant culture in which the resident alien sojourns. This may at times involve hardship, but it does not mean that one must be consigned to a miserable existence. After all, Abraham is portrayed as prospering greatly as a resident alien in Canaan. Abraham prospered not only materially as a herdsman; he prospered also in a rich relationship to the peoples of the land in which he sojourned, and he prospered in his awareness of the divine reality that pervaded his life and the land on which he sojourned.

Abraham was marginal in significant ways. First, he was a descendent of Noah's son Shem, with roots in the ancient civilizations of Mesopotamia, while the Canaanites were descendants of Ham (Gen 10–11). Abraham was a stranger ethnically in the land of Canaan. Second, Abraham was a nomadic herdsman in the context of the urbanized Canaanite city-states. Perhaps Abraham chose this type of life because it fostered the kind of communal life he felt called to model. Third, as a resident alien, Abraham was free from the constraints and obligations involved in owning land, of living as the citizen of a city-state. This enabled Abraham to relate to his neighbors in a more disinterested way, without being bound by duty or competition or obligation for the land, what we today might speak of as the obligations of citizenship. When these issues surface in Abraham's relationship to Abimelech in Genesis 21 and in his purchase of a burial plot from the Hittites at Hebron in Genesis 23, Abraham's independent status is not only protected and respected, but it is what also enables him to develop good relationships in these circumstances, becoming the blessing God had called him to be.

While marginality is central to the experience of being a resident alien and the calling of God to a sojourn of faith in which one can become a blessing to others, no one should imagine that it is easy to live as a sojourner on the strength of a promise! Consider the case of Abraham and Sarah. They came to Canaan when they were already old—seventy-five and sixty-five years respectively. They were not spring chickens anymore. The difficulty was not simply that they felt called to model a different kind of life in the midst of the Canaanite city-states among whom they sojourned. It was that the promises made to them, that they should become a great nation and have many descendants who would inherit this land from God, involved the existence of an heir. We were already informed earlier in the story, when they still lived in Ur of the Chaldeans, that they were childless (Gen 11:30).

Perhaps in the first years of their sojourn in Canaan, it was relatively easy to live with the dissonance between God's promises and their childlessness. Perhaps that's even why Abraham brought his nephew Lot along on this sojourn, as a potential heir, though after their peaceful falling out in Genesis 13, this became a fading possibility. However, with the passage of time the dissonance in which they lived became cacophonic. When God reappeared to Abraham some ten years into his sojourn in Canaan, Abraham desperately clutched at straws, saying that his only heir was the steward of his household, Eliezer (Gen 15:2–3). When God reaffirmed in a covenant renewal ceremony with Abraham that the promise would be fulfilled in the issue of his own body, he "believed the LORD; and the LORD reckoned it to him as righteousness" (Gen 15:6).

Still, the desperation of Abraham and Sarah is evident in Genesis 16, some ten years into their sojourn, when they attempted to take matters into their own hands. They resolved to have a child utilizing Sarah's Egyptian handmaid, Hagar, as a surrogate mother. It was not a happy experience, as is true of most attempts to shortcut God's promises. Sarah and Hagar were alienated from one another. Years later, amid the sudden laughter of Isaac's surprising birth to Sarah, Hagar and her son Ishmael were banished from the household (Gen 21). This was despite God's steadfast and expressed intention to bless Ishmael along with Isaac and without regard for the fact that Ishmael was the fruit of Abraham and Sarah's lack of trust (Gen 17:18–21).

It was Abraham's inability to manage his broken family, not God's intention, that resulted in the disinheritance of Ishmael! Abraham ended up not being sure that there would be enough blessing from God to cover both his sons. With both Arabic and Jewish people owning the patriarch Abraham as their father, making the most intractable conflict of the modern age a family feud, we must acknowledge again the fateful consequences of self-aggrandizing choices as we follow God's call. How incredibly hard it is to hear clearly God's call to become a blessing to all people and to be content to live on the strength of God's promise, without trying to force God's hand! This is true even for those like Abraham and Sarah, who in other ways model so well God's call to a sojourn of faith in the land of promise.

Human Wandering, Modern Immigration, and Urbanization

We humans are inveterate wanderers! It is a part of our biological inheritance. As we multiply, we expand the range of our habitation until we cover the earth. So it is that modern humans originating in Africa some hundred thousand years ago expanded across that continent and spread from Africa through the Near East into Europe and Asia, then into North and South America, and finally into Australia and Oceania.[5] In this expansion, we humans simply replicated the tendency found among all the creatures and forms of life God has made. It is a fulfillment, if you will, of God's mandate in Genesis 1:22 and 28 to "be fruitful and multiply," a mandate given to the creatures of both the sea and the air on the fifth day and the creatures of the land on the sixth day of creation.

This nomadic existence is the normative experience of the human family. Beginning with extended households and then growing to become clans and tribes, the human family spread across the earth. Humans migrated as family groups, clans and tribes, who intermingled but also took on unique characteristics as they lived in diverse geographical and ecological contexts. Occasionally, individuals might leave one group to migrate to a far distant place, but that was likely rare. The human experience was a communal experience of wandering nomadism.

This normative nomadic existence of the human family only began to change with the advent of agriculture some ten thousand years ago, as noted in chapter 3. As humans domesticated plants and animals in a specific region of the earth, they were able to achieve a more stable and permanent way of life. Later, the success of agriculture made possible the settlement of towns and cities, so that today we think of urban living as the normative human experience.

All this is to highlight the fact that God's call to a life of faith as a sojourner or resident alien in the land is not a call to a new experience for us as humans. Regardless of the location or the size of the settled place where we live, we have within our past if not within our own recent history or experience stories of living as immigrants.

On the other hand, modern human migrations tend to differ significantly from the earlier, traditional migrations of the human family. In his book, *Rethinking Holy Land*, Marlin Jeschke reminds us of how the concept of the *nation* has changed. In

---

5. Leakey, *Origin*, 79–99.

ancient and biblical times, the nation referred to "an ethnic or linguistic group that usually possessed a self-conscious identity but often did not have clearly defined boundaries."[6] By contrast, in modern times, the nation refers most often to a political state "that often has a pluralist ethnic and linguistic population within clearly defined borders."[7]

There are exceptions to this understanding. The First Nations of North America reflect the traditional or biblical definition of nationhood—a distinct ethno-linguistic group with a strong identity, but without clearly defined boundaries. But in the world at large, nation-states today have clearly defined boundaries, and most have a highly pluralistic population ethnically. This sometimes creates problems for the unity of the nation-state. In our day, ethnicity or ethnic heritage may have largely replaced what the Bible means when it talks about the nations.

This distinction is relevant to our discussion about human migration. In the traditional understanding of nationhood, human migrations involved the movement of fairly distinct ethno-linguistic groups, nations if you will, from one location to another. They brought with them to their new location the local customs, folkways, rituals, and practices they knew, adapting them as required to the new setting in which they found themselves. The migration, in other words, did not typically destroy the local communal life that they had shared, though over time that communal life itself might be shaped by the new environment.

This is in rather stark contrast to the more recent human migrations of the modern world, and particularly the rural to urban migration that is such a marked characteristic of our time. These tend to be individual migrations, in which individuals from a particular ethno-linguistic heritage leave their local community to enter the pluralistic environment of the city. Sometimes this involves also crossing the clearly marked and defended borders of nation-states, as in the migrations from Mexico to the United States, or from Asia to Canada. Sometimes this only involves leaving a local, rural community and culture for the dominant, pluralistic culture of the city within the same nation-state. However, in both cases, the migration tends to be individualistic rather than communal, the journey of an individual leaving his or her community for the pluralistic culture of the city.

This type of migration has two consequences. On the one hand, it isolates the individual from his or her moorings within a local community, creating a crisis of personal identity for the individual. On the other hand, it serves as an instrument of destruction for the local, rural community from which that individual has departed. As rural residents the world over know by now, the lure of urbanization spells the decline if not the destruction of rural communities, as more individuals leave the community for the supposedly lucrative opportunities of urban life.

---

6. Jeschke, *Rethinking*, 25.
7. Ibid.

To be sure, there is much that is attractive and compelling about the pluralistic ethno-linguistic character of modern cities and the nation-states they have spawned. (In my view, nationalism should be understood as an extension of the imperial claims of the metropolis, as described in chapter 3). One of the most trenchant criticisms of rural communities is their ethnocentrism and their inability to easily incorporate and include persons of another ethno-linguistic heritage. One of the major gifts of the modern world is the way it has broken down ethno-linguistic barriers between groups of people and enabled people the world over to see themselves as members of one human family.

Still, one must ask whether the personal dislocation of the individual and the destruction of local community merits the continuation of modern forms of individualistic migration from the country to the city. Does the pluralism of the dominant culture really reflect a respect for the unique ethnic heritage every person carries? Isn't the city primarily interested in the consumer and producer potential of the individuals that come to it? Is it really true that rural communities are inhospitable to strangers? Traditional rural peoples of nearly every culture hold sacred the duty of extending hospitality to the stranger, and many have experienced this. Our visit to the Palestinian village of At-Tuwani, south of Hebron, with a Christian Peacemaker Team delegation in 2008 was typical of the respect and care shown to the stranger in such cultures.

I am keenly aware of how the rural congregations I have served struggle to really welcome and include people of diverse ethno-linguistic backgrounds. My own suspicion is that this has to do with the history of migrations we have undergone as a minority community within dominant cultures, making us wary of strangers and fostering in our communal life a strange mix of ethnic superiority and personal inferiority. We tend to have a low image of ourselves and a strong sense of communal identity that makes it hard for us to relate to the stranger graciously.

Pluralism, understood as openness to those who have a cultural heritage different from one's own, is a value to be affirmed. I don't believe it can be accomplished by turning our backs on traditional rural communities in favor of the anonymous and impersonal structures of urban life. It can only be fostered communally, as local communities in rural or urban settings become places of welcome to the diverse people who come to sojourn in that place. Ideally these would be communities that respect and celebrate the unique cultural/ethnic heritage of each person. Conversely, pluralism can only be fostered when the migrations of the human family become communal once again, and when communities of local culture sojourn in diverse settings as alternatives to the dominant culture, as Abraham and his extended family sojourned in Canaan.

Mennonite Migrations and Life as a Sojourn

Mennonite history is replete with the story of migrations. Much of Mennonite wandering in the lands of Europe parallels the experience of the Abrahamic community, that of living as a community of resident aliens within a dominant culture. After the Mennonites were scattered by persecution and became known as industrious farmers, they were frequently invited by the local nobility among Europe's ruling class to manage their lands. In the case of my own family history, this meant frequent moves as a community of faith from one benefactor to another. Rarely did Mennonites become citizens of the state where they resided or come to own the land they worked on the behalf of the nobility. They were for the most part resident aliens, or at best second-class citizens. They moved about as small groups of extended families, congregations in some cases or parts of congregations. As they did so, they frequently modeled an alternative communal life to the dominant culture of European civilization, being known and respected or at least tolerated for their religious faith and pacifist convictions.

Most of the Mennonite migrations to the new world of North America were also communal in nature. That is to say, it was communities or congregations of people, whole villages, who emigrated to the United States and Canada, not individuals. My own forebears came from communal agricultural villages in the Ukraine. In these villages, the agricultural land extended out from a central street on which the residences were built. United States land settlement policies embodied in the Homestead Act of 1862 prohibited the village pattern of land use in favor of isolated farmsteads in which pioneers laid claim to a quarter section of land.

The very first Mennonite settler in my home community near Freeman, South Dakota, Daniel Unruh, who came from the Mennonite colonies in southern Russia, tried to establish a village life patterned on the Old World experience, but it was given up in a matter of a few years.[7] I am not aware that there was ever any serious discussion in my community about what harm this change in dwelling patterns might cause for the community. In this community, the damage was mitigated to some degree by the location and dominant geographical feature of my place—the Turkey Ridge valley—that tends to highlight visibly the neighboring farmsteads within a range of ten miles or so.

Just as the dominant culture of North America discouraged a communal pattern of residence, so it also spelled the end of communal migrations. There were a few early dispersals of settlers to various destinations north and west in the United States by small groups from the congregations that had been established. Still, the demise of rural Mennonite communalism in my setting came through attrition during the last forty or fifty years, as young people migrated one by one to urban areas to seek their fortune or to engage their chosen ministry or vocation.

---

7. Unruh, *Century*, 28.

To a large degree, we no longer see ourselves as an alternative community of faith sojourning within the dominant culture either. For one thing, we put down roots and settled in when we came to this land, like the children of Israel when they came into the promised land. We saw this as our promised land, a place where we didn't have to live at the margins of the dominant culture any longer. I'll have more to say about this later in this book. We also fairly quickly rejected the use of distinctive cultural trappings, such as dress or language, as marks of our identity, and perhaps this was a wise choice. So it has been hard for us to think about what makes us a distinctive, alternative community, much less to think of ourselves as a community of sojourners within this dominant culture.

Despite all this, the image of the church as a community of resident aliens in the world remains a central if not dominant image of Christian faith. A prominent symbol for the church through history has been that of a ship adrift upon the sea. First Peter speaks repeatedly of Christians as exiles and resident aliens (1 Pet 1:1, 17; 2:11; 3:13–16; 4:1–4). Hebrews also appeals to the example of Abraham in calling Christians to live as "strangers and foreigners on the earth" (Heb 11:13).

My own experience of life as a sojourn of faith was honed by the four-month sabbatical my wife and I embarked on in the winter and spring of 2008. We were taken out of familiar routines for that length of time, with specific spiritual objectives and goals. My sabbatical brought home to me the way in which the Christian life as a whole is a journey of faith. Of course, that may also be an experience more common to pastors and their families, who invest themselves deeply in the life of the community of the congregations they serve only to be uprooted and begin the process all over again in another setting when the time comes for a pastoral change.

One of the books I read on sabbatical was Arthur Paul Boer's *The Way Is Made by Walking*, describing his month-long sojourn on the five hundred mile pilgrimage route of El Camino de Santiago in Spain. In particular, I was drawn to his description of the elements of a pilgrimage:[8]

- Travel and dislocation to an unfamiliar place
- Suspension of regular responsibilities and routines
- Freedom from constraints to the media of the dominant culture
- Implementation of disciplines to focus on God
- Willingness to make sacrifices and to be inconvenienced
- Willingness to engage in physically, psychologically, and spiritually taxing activities
- Reaching remote destinations, or impossible goals
- Having a spirit of openness to God's leading

---

8. Boers, *Way*, 184–85.

Each of these elements was a part of my sabbatical experience. During this time of travel away from home I came to realize how comfortable and self-indulgent I had become and how pampered my life was in many ways. Engaging the disciplines of a spiritual pilgrimage had the effect of renewing my spiritual life.

We typically envision a pilgrimage in terms of a solitary and literal journey to a particular destination. It is how we typically understand Abraham's sojourn in Palestine, as well. However, it's important to remember that Abraham's sojourn was not a solitary journey but a communal adventure. It's important to consider that a pilgrimage is as much a state of mind as it is a destination. It has more to do with how we engage the dominant culture where we live than with either travel or a nomadic lifestyle. Indeed, a pilgrimage involves not just a spatial dimension, but a temporal dimension. We are called to live our lives with the mindset of being a pilgrim in a foreign land, a sojourner who walks by faith, a resident alien in the land where we reside.

Two thousand eight was the centennial year of the congregation I served as pastor, Salem Mennonite Church. During our centennial year, I reflected in a series of sermons on the sojourn of our congregation. I began not with our founding a century ago, but with the primordial roots of our Christian experience, reaching back to Abraham and Christ, even beyond the experience of our first ancestors who heard and responded to the gospel of Christ. I continued by exploring the pre-history of our congregation as our people came to an Anabaptist Mennonite understanding of Christian faith and sojourned through the lands of Europe before coming to the United States in 1874. Then I came to the founding of our own congregation a hundred years ago, and our own interaction with the dominant culture in which we live. This, for me, is our sojourn of faith as a congregation of God's people.[9]

Nothing expresses quite so clearly for me the call of God to be a community of resident aliens in the world as the fifth and sixth chapters of *The Epistle to Diognetus*, dated in the mid-second century of the Christian era.

> For Christians cannot be distinguished from the rest of the human race by country or language or customs. They do not live in cities of their own; they do not use a peculiar form of speech; they do not follow an eccentric manner of life. . . . Yet, although they live in Greek and barbarian cities alike, as each man's lot has been cast, and follow the customs of the country in clothing and food and other matters of daily living, at the same time, they give proof of the remarkable and admittedly extraordinary constitution of their own commonwealth. They live in their own countries, but only as aliens. They have a share in everything as citizens, and endure everything as foreigners. Every foreign land is their fatherland, and yet for them every fatherland is a foreign land. . . . They busy themselves on earth, but their citizenship is in heaven. They obey the established laws, but in their own lives they go far beyond what the laws require. . . . To put it simply: What the soul is in the body, that Christians are in the world.[10]

9. Kaufman, *Roots*.
10. Petry, *History*, 19–20.

Chapter 5

The Character of Empire

And the Land Became Pharaoh's (Gen 47:20)

Israel's First Experience with Imperial Reality

THE CHARACTER OF EMPIRE is revealed throughout the Bible in the various empires of the Fertile Crescent and the Mediterranean world that impacted God's people in Palestine. Empire might fairly be said to come into being with the exercise of dominant if not absolute power or control by a centralized metropolis over surrounding territories and populations. Most often, this domination or control is sanctioned by a religious hierarchy that in turn benefits from the exploitation and is exempted from domination.

With this exercise of imperial power, self-sufficient rural villages able to sustain their communities in relative comfort and prosperity are increasingly disenfranchised and made to be dependent upon the dominating metropolis, be that Ramses, Nineveh, Babylon, Persepolis, or Rome. First people's access to resources and land, and then their labor and progeny, become owned by the ruling power of the metropolis. In practical terms, this means ordinary people no longer have control over the decision-making most basic to their livelihood. People become de facto if not literal slaves to the interests and power of the state (Gen 47).

For its part, the centralized metropolis becomes increasingly oppressive and controlling as its power grows and expands, and it feels itself increasingly vulnerable to subversion and revolution. While the power of an empire will wax and wane as it interacts with other imperial powers, the seeds of an empire's demise are typically internal. Empires either deplete their natural resource base or lose control over the oppressed population, or both. In the process, empires disintegrate or implode. While imperial civilizations are typically credited with the greatest of human achievements artistically and technologically, these achievements are invariably accomplished at an incredible cost in oppression, suffering, and violence.

The Biblical Story

Seeking Security and Exercising Power

As humans, we face a basic and daily dilemma. How are we going to meet our basic needs for survival—our need for nutrition, reproduction, and safety? Where will we find the food, shelter, and clothing we need in order to pursue a secure future for ourselves and for our families? It was the dilemma Jacob and his family faced in Genesis 42, when they were suffering from a severe famine in the land of Canaan. Learning that grain was available in the land of Egypt, both through the land irrigated by the Nile River and through the wise policies initiated by Joseph, Jacob sent his sons to get food from Egypt as many other people were doing (Gen 42:1–5).

We humans believe that we can be more secure by gaining control over our environment. The domestication of plants and animals in agriculture represented an attempt by humans to gain control over their food supply, so they were not quite so subject to the vagaries of nature. The emergence of the city, as we saw in chapter 3, represented an effort by urban dwellers to gain control over the excess agricultural production of the surrounding rural area in order to engage in civilized pursuits. The emergence of the state out of the city as a centralized governing agency represented a further attempt to gain control over all the peoples within that area. With the emergence of the imperial state, we see the attempt to gain absolute control. Empire means absolute power, supreme rule, domination. Imperialism is the policy and practice of forming an empire, of exercising absolute control. Empire, by definition, is totalitarian and dictatorial.

All of these efforts to gain control over our environment involve the exercise of power on the part of individuals or communities. There was a time in my life as a young pastor when I unrealistically eschewed the use of power. Perhaps this was a consequence of being a product of the '60s generation with its rejection of authority. Perhaps it was a misguided understanding of what it means to be a nonresistant follower of Christ. More likely it was a consequence of my discomfort with my own unperceived power as a pastor. I think I have come to a more realistic and appropriate understanding of power and its use, both my own power as a person and a pastor, and the power of the community to shape its life and meet its basic needs.

There are for me at least two questions we need to ask about the use of power in human affairs. First, is the power exercised reciprocal, symbiotic, sustainable, and ethical? Or is it idolatrous, oppressive, and exploitative? Power always has to do with making choices for the future that affect not only ourselves but all others connected with us. Does the exercise of power in any given instance serve the interests and needs of all parties involved, all the natural and human and divine communities of life that form the context of our human life? Or does it only serve the interests and needs of those exercising power? In other words, is power exercised for the common good or is it exercised to gain a selfish advantage over others?

Healing God's Earth

The second, related question about the use of power has to do with the locus of power. Who is making the decisions that matter for the future, and on behalf of whom are such decisions made? Are the decisions being made by one individual who by force or charisma has assumed or been granted the authority to exercise power on behalf of the community? Is the power being exercised communally by a local community working together to assure a sustainable future? Or, has power been ceded by individuals and local communities to secondary institutions, so that these secondary institutions become the primary agencies of power and decision-making on behalf of both individuals and communities? These would be the cultural, political, and economic institutions thought to be necessary to organize human life on the large scale of a city or state.

It is the thesis of this book that the second question can be answered most appropriately when the locus of power for decision-making is exercised by the local community. Individuals acting alone on behalf of the community can too easily allow the exercise of power to dominate their lives in self-aggrandizing ways. The individual ego needs to be held in check by the constraints of face-to-face relationships within the community. While hardly ever done perfectly, I have seen in my ministry how local congregations work at curbing and diffusing power being exercised inappropriately by ambitious or dysfunctional individuals within the congregation.

On the other hand, when decision-making is ceded by individuals or communities to secondary institutions—whether they be denominational hierarchies, secular governing authorities, corporate powers, or technical experts and educated elites—the exercise of power is institutionalized in ways that effectively destroy local communities. Of course, not every exercise of institutional power is imperial, an attempt to gain absolute control over the community, but the tendency is always there. Even in a democracy, there is a hierarchical, top-down quality to the exercise of institutional power through the power granted to elected officials. So even when institutional power is exercised benevolently with the best of intentions for the common welfare, the result tends to be the disempowerment and destruction of the local community. Obviously, institutional power is necessary and required within human life. At the same time, local communities need always to resist the encroachment of institutional power and to assert the primacy of communal power if the common good is to be preserved.

Israel's Descent to Egypt

There is for me an irony in the traditional language used to describe the patriarchal saga of Israel's sojourn to Egypt as told in Genesis 46.[1] It does indeed represent a local community's *descent* into the grip of imperial power. We can envision Jacob's extended family as a local community, using the terminology of this book. However patriarchal

---

1. For the language of "going down to Egypt," see Gen 39:1; 42:2; and 46:3.

it was in structure, it is portrayed in Scripture as a local and communal gathering of people with a unique identity and history. It sought to hold itself apart from the dominant, mainstream cultures of Canaanite society and to live as an alternative community of faith within that context.

It was at the same time not a healthy community. Most (all?) communities struggle with some measure of ill-health, but this early Israelite community was exceptionally dysfunctional. It was ravaged by the rivalries that had given it birth—the struggles for power we see with the twin brothers Jacob and Esau, exacerbated by parental favoritism and deception (Gen 25:19-28). It was further compromised by the character of the patriarch Jacob, whose birth name means "the supplanter" (Gen 25:26), and whose given name, Israel, "one who strives with God," was earned only after a long struggle with God (Gen 32:28). Jacob's own family was riven with sibling rivalry, fostered again by parental favoritism, leading to the abduction of the favored son, Joseph, and his sale into slavery in the land of Egypt (Gen 37).

Not surprisingly, this local community was ill-prepared to meet the external stress of the widespread famine that struck the region during the later years of Jacob's life. By divine providence, the rediscovery of the favored son, Joseph, now the prime minister of Egypt, second in power only to the Pharaoh himself, provided a convenient escape for this beleaguered extended family. After the trials of the brothers who appeared before Joseph asking for food without being aware of his identity, Joseph revealed his identity to them and invited the community of Israel to come and dwell in Egypt (Gen 45). The family of Israel left their pastoral homeland in Canaan to live at the center of power in the land of Goshen, right under the eye of Pharaoh himself, responsible for the care of Pharaoh's own livestock (Gen 47:1-12).

I'm of course aware that there is a good deal of scholarly skepticism about these patriarchal stories,[2] and I respect that skepticism. Yet it seems clear that if there is any historical basis to these stories (and I want to believe there is), Joseph's ascent to power as the prime minister of Egypt and Israel's descent to Egypt would fit best during the Fifteenth and Sixteenth Dynasties of Egypt, during the century and a half from 1730 to 1570 BCE, when the Hyksos ruled Egypt. The ethno-linguistic history of biblical lands and times is complicated, to say the least. Yet it seems clear that the Hyksos who ruled Egypt in the first half of the second millennium before Christ were warlike Asiatic invaders with Semitic and Hurrian ethnic origins. The Hyksos were responsible for introducing horse-and-chariot warfare into Egypt, as well as improved bronze weaponry.[3] However, the point that interests me is that at least some of the Hyksos likely shared a common ethno-linguistic heritage with the patriarchal Israelites.

This ethno-linguistic commonality might account for the frequent patriarchal forays into Egypt described in Genesis, as well as the rapid rise of Joseph to his position as Egypt's prime minister. It might account for the welcome given to Jacob's family

2. Gottwald, *Tribes*, 32.
3. Lambdin, "Hyksos," 667.

at their descent to Egypt and their settlement in the land of Goshen, the heartland of Hyksos power and rule. Finally, it might account for the profound hostility manifested by native Egyptians toward the Israelites after they were able finally to oust the Hyksos invaders and establish "a new king" over Egypt, "who did not know Joseph" (Exod 1:8).

In terms of the development and character of empire, which is our theme in this chapter, the Hyksos rule in Egypt reveals the often-obscured role of ethnocentrism and racism manifested by imperial enterprises. Imperial power typically assumes the ethnic superiority of those exercising such power. Often this provides the justification for the disenfranchisement and colonization of those of other ethnic origins, which is the modus operandi, the standard operating procedure, of imperial power.

In an even more ominous vein, Israel's descent to Egypt reveals the way in which local communities are tempted to sell out their autonomy when they perceive that their ethnic identity provides them with an advantage. My hunch is that Jacob would have been much more reluctant to relocate to Egypt had his favorite son Joseph not been in power on behalf of Semitic invaders ruling over native Egyptians. Living as a community in a foreign land among rulers who share one's own ethnic heritage is surely easier than living in a foreign land where the community's survival depends on living against the grain of the dominant culture. This is what the patriarchal community had tried to do in Canaan for three generations. While it seemed to work for Abraham and Sarah, at least to some degree, it had become increasingly problematic. Already in Genesis 26, we see Isaac in struggle with inhabitants of the land over wells in a time of famine, and again in Genesis 42, Jacob's family is in crisis due to famine. Jacob was ready to exchange the precarious existence of his local community in Canaan for favored status as tenders of the Hyksos Pharaoh's livestock in Egypt (Gen 47:6)!

The Imposition of Imperial Control and Its Consequences

Ironies abound! No sooner do we read of Israel's favored settlement in the land of Goshen than we read the account of Joseph's role in the supreme manifestation of imperial control—the disenfranchisement of the native Egyptians! Joseph is often viewed in Scripture as the prototype of a savior for the way in which he understood his life as God's instrument for his people's salvation. "Even though you intended to do harm to me, God intended it for good, in order to preserve a numerous people, as he is doing today" (Gen 50:20). So declares the magnanimous Joseph to his brothers after they appear before him with trepidation following their father Jacob's death!

Far be it from me to sully Joseph's good name! Indeed, there are many who view Joseph's actions in Genesis 47 in a favorable light as a paragon of administrative ability enabling an entire region to withstand the challenge of a major famine. The dreams of Pharaoh interpreted by Joseph in Genesis 41 of seven fat cows devoured by seven lean cows and seven full stalks consumed by seven blighted stalks were coming to

The Character of Empire

fruition. The seven fat years in Egypt had passed, and now the seven lean years were devouring what Joseph had wisely stored up, even within the land of Egypt itself. This story opens with the bleak statement, "Now there was no food in all the land, for the famine was very severe. The land of Egypt and the land of Canaan languished because of the famine" (Gen 47:13). Now even the irrigated land of Egypt was suffering from the drought.

What troubles me is that Joseph's actions in responding to this crisis describe step by step the imposition of imperial control by a centralized power over a subjugated people. First, Joseph collected all the money of the people in exchange for food (Gen 47:14). Next, Joseph took all the livestock of the people in exchange for food (Gen 47:15–17). Finally, the next year, Joseph bought the land and bodies of the people in exchange for food (Gen 47:18–20). The people were willing to work the land as slaves of Pharaoh in exchange for food and seed. So it is that "Joseph bought all the land of Egypt for Pharaoh. All the Egyptians sold their fields, because the famine was severe upon them; and the land became Pharaoh's" (Gen 47:20). Only the land of the religious hierarchy, who presumably sanctioned these actions of the state, was exempt from this confiscation (Gen 47:22, 26). The people became tenants of Pharaoh, sharecroppers who must give a fifth of the produce to Pharaoh in exchange for the privilege of working the land and receiving food and seed (Gen 47:24). And the people were pleased! "You have saved our lives; may it please my lord, we will be slaves to Pharaoh" (Gen 47:25).[4]

Here is a blatant account of the complete disenfranchisement of a rural population by a central power! It is a story that has been repeated over and over again throughout human history. A crisis, whether ecological or economic or social or political, provides an occupying power with the opportunity to disenfranchise a local population. Of course, the whole procedure has a benevolent veneer! Lives are saved! Children are able to eat! Tragedy is averted! Yet the ugliness of what is happening can scarcely be concealed. A people who had previously lived independent, self-sufficient lives in local communities have now lost control over their communities, their lives, and their destinies. They are now wards of the state, and they owe their existence to the state! What makes this story doubly troubling is that this imperial control was exercised by a foreign people (the Hyksos and Joseph) occupying a land by force and disenfranchising the indigenous (Egyptian) population.

Here we see the character of empire most clearly revealed. It is the exercise of dominating power by a supposedly superior ethnic or social group over another presumably inferior ethnic group, often an indigenous community with historic claims to the land and with a history of sustainable living on the land. It should also not be overlooked that such an imposition of power usually finds sanction from a religious hierarchy that then also benefits from the oppression. The Hyksos who ruled Egypt

---

4. I first encountered this reading of the Joseph story in an article by Brueggemann, "Theses on Land," 8.

had adopted the Egyptian language and perhaps Egyptian religious traditions as well, finding in this way additional justification for their oppression of the people. Despite their physical domination and presumed superiority, those exercising imperial power are often culturally inferior to those they dominate.

It is of course ironic that people often welcome their enslavement, seeing in it their means to survival and salvation. We have already seen Jacob's eagerness to find security in the bosom of the Egyptian empire (Gen 47:4). In this story we see the gratitude of an enslaved people for the "salvation" granted to them (Gen 47:25). The same dynamic can be seen in the flight of rural people to the city in much of the modern era. People are often eager to abdicate responsibility for their local community in favor of the benefits and security offered to them by imperial power. After all, community is hard work! It is risky work! It pits a small group against the power of an empire. People can hardly be blamed for choosing the benefits and security of imperial power over the risks and struggles of building local communities.

There is also irony in the insecurity of imperial power, which grows in proportion to the degree of control exercised by that power. Empires at the peak of their power are typically most insecure and most oppressive. As competition grows for scarce resources and as a conquered population is oppressed, the empire becomes more and more vulnerable to the threat of subversion or revolution. As a result, imperial control becomes ever more firm, with a proportional decrease in security. The dynamic can be seen played out in the first chapter of Exodus when a new Egyptian Pharaoh turns the tables on the foreign Israelites and makes them his slaves occupied with building his supply cities (Exod 1:11). The more oppressive his policies become, the more resistant the population becomes.

Still another consequence of the exercise of imperial power is its overextension in terms of natural resources. While we are given no hints as to the reasons for the regional famine described in Genesis 47, history abounds with examples of the ways in which exploitation and abuse of natural systems lead to ecological collapse. As a writer on ecology has said, "Civilized man has marched across the face of the earth and left a desert in his footprints."[5] The authors of the work just quoted credit ecological collapse as a primary cause for the fall of empires. "The destinies of most of man's empires and civilizations were determined largely by the way the land was used."[6] The rise and fall of empires bears witness to the reality that empires fizzle out from being overextended at least as often as they are conquered.

Finally, empires and the civilizations they create represent many of the highest pinnacles of human achievement. They provide the context for extraordinary achievements in architecture, art, music, administration, commerce, technology, and industry. Witness the pyramids and the building of the storehouse cities of Pithom and Rameses by Israelite slaves as described in Exodus 1. However, the enslavement of the

5. Anonymous quote found in Dale and Carter, *Topsoil*, 6.
6. Ibid., 7; the use of the male nouns is an appropriate anachronism!

Israelites in Exodus 1 and the disenfranchisement of the Egyptian people in Genesis 47 remind us that these achievements come only at an immense cost in terms of human oppression, suffering, and violence. At some point, we need to ask whether the cost is justifiable. Might there not be another way for human creativity to be measured and released than the monumental building and artistic and technological endeavors characteristic of imperial power?

Imperialism and a Brief History of Empires

In his book *Empire as a Way of Life*, historian William Appleman Williams defines imperialism as "the loss of sovereignty—control—over essential issues and decisions by a largely agricultural society to an industrial metropolis."[7] We have already explored in chapter 3 the dynamics of metropolitan life and its effects on rural communities. While the tendency toward imperialism is already apparent in the development of urban life, in this chapter I am reserving the term *empire* for the totalitarian exercise of power by a centralized state over formerly independent populations or ethnicities. As Williams points out, such empires may be formed either by the "union of initially separate but physically and politically and socially related units of population under one central authority" or by "the forcible subjugation of formerly independent people by a wholly external power, and their subsequent rule by the imperial metropolis."[8] The United Kingdom of Great Britain and Northern Ireland is an example of the first case. In the second case, the "external power" may be either an invading/occupying force (as with the Hyksos in Egypt that we have been examining), or a colonizing force, (as was the case with European powers in Asia, Africa, and Latin America in the nineteenth century).

Whether or not the empire is established forcibly, what makes an empire an empire in this understanding is that one group, usually with a particular racial or ethno-linguistic identity, asserts its superiority over other groups, however large or small the historical differences might be. In other words, empire is an expression of ethnocentric power by one group over another or others. It is an attempt to exercise totalitarian power over other groups that are presumed to be inferior, of less value and worth, less powerful, and therefore exploitable.

In this respect, empire is something different than the process of urbanization, though it may be the logical result of urbanization. Empire represents the subjugation of one culture or ethno-linguistic group by another. So it is that historians typically speak of the emergence of empire only with respect to the Akkadian state that emerged in Mesopotamia under Sargon some twenty-three hundred years before Christ.[9] Humankind had by then been building cities for more than a millennium, and numerous

---

7. Williams, *Empire*, 7.
8. Ibid., 6.
9. Barraclough, *Harper Collins Atlas*, 55.

kingdoms and dynasties had been established as centralized governing authorities in these cities. Civilization was well underway. But the drive toward imperial control was inevitable.

As one reviews the annals of history, it becomes evident that the imperial drive is endemic to the human condition. From this first Akkadian Empire more than two millennia before Christ to our time, there are easily more than fifty imperial states, some lasting only a few decades, and others several centuries. Imperial power emerges on every continent and in every age of human history. Consider the Mali and Songhai Empires in Africa; the Mayan and Inca and Aztec Empires of the Americas.

More often than not, these empires are associated with the names of conquerors—Thutmose III of Egypt, Tiglath Pileser III of Assyria, Cyrus of Persia, Alexander of Macedonia, Augustus of Rome, Asoka of India, Justinian of Byzantium, Charlemagne of France, Genghis Khan of Mongolia, Adolph Hitler of the Third Reich, Joseph Stalin of the Soviet Union. Solomon of Israel might be added to this list, for though the Israelite Empire was short in duration, Solomon's reign in the tenth century before Christ represented an imperial adventure as well, with Israel subjugating surrounding states from the Euphrates River to Egypt.

On the other hand, imperialism is not just the result of despotic rule by imperial conquerors. Despite its espousal of democratic ideals, the United States of America expressed imperial ambitions from its founding in the Revolutionary War. These ambitions can be seen in its treatment of African slaves and its westward expansion on the North American continent and the subjugation of the peoples of the First Nations. In *Empire as a Way of Life*, Williams documents at the end of each chapter American interventionist activity in international affairs from the founding of the nation.[10] The founders of the United States were driven by a sense of manifest destiny, that it was the divine destiny of Americans to bring enlightenment to a benighted world. In this we also see the way in which religion is used to sanction and justify the use of imperial power on behalf of the state.

Colonialism and nationalism are both manifestations of imperialism in the modern era. The European colonization of Africa, Asia, and Latin America from the sixteenth to the nineteenth centuries represents the imperial ambition of all the major European powers—Portugal, Spain, Great Britain, France, the Netherlands, Belgium, Italy, Germany, and Russia. The emergence of the nation as an entity in the modern era with a geographically-defined boundary encompassing all the ethno-linguistic groups within that area has given every nation the character of an empire. Within each national area, we see one group seeking to dominate and exercise power over other less powerful (and supposedly inferior) groups. This is what makes the nation-states carved out by European colonialism in so much of the world so tension-filled and often untenable. The nation of Iraq, which has preoccupied the world for the past two decades, is a prime example, with Shiite, Sunni, and Kurdish factions all vying for dominance and control

---

10. Williams, *Empire*, 73–76, 102–10, 136–42, 165–67.

because Great Britain declared that territory inhabited by all three groups ought to be a nation-state. The colonial powers have made imperialism the dominant political system of the world, with every nation being an aspiring empire.

At the same time, the bankruptcy of the imperial use of power is also beginning to be evident. Within our lifetime, we have seen the relatively peaceful dissolution of a major imperial power—the Soviet Union. With the dissolution of that empire, we have seen small, independent, coherent states begin to emerge in Central Asia and Eastern Europe, many of which no longer have serious imperial ambitions. At the same time, the emergence of the European Union and the United Nations points the way toward new models of centralized power in which imperial ambitions can be curbed by respecting the uniqueness of each national and ethno-linguistic heritage representing in membership. While the exercise of imperial power will continue to dominate global affairs into the future, there is some hope that the drive toward the exercise of imperial power may be waning.

In the meantime, it is unfortunate that the exercise of imperial power continues to be the dominant force shaping the human story. It is true that empires inspire human creativity. They do so by providing the wealth and leisure presumed to be necessary for human creativity. Whether through forced labor or through sponsorship, imperial power has created impressive achievements in art and architecture, commerce, industry, and technology. At the same time, imperial power inspires human creativity in reaction to its oppression, as well. The writings of Alexander Solzhenitsyn and the music of Dimitri Shostakovich in the former Soviet Union bear witness to this, inspired by their resistance to Soviet power. However, rarely have we calculated the cost of human suffering in the production of these human achievements and sought to assess if imperial power is indeed required, necessary, or even advisable for these creative endeavors.

Personally, I prefer community-based artistic expressions to those sponsored by imperial power. The Southeast Iowa Symphony or the Sioux Falls Symphony, classical organizations that have nurtured our family life, are composed, at least in part, of non-professional musicians—public school teachers and the like—who are given the opportunity in this way to use and share their gifts. My own community sponsors Schmeckfest each spring, a fair of ethnic food that includes a major musical production, as well. Seeing the gifts of ordinary people used and shared in local communities far outweighs for me the technical excellence of professional ensembles sponsored by metropolitan and imperial power. Community-based arts and crafts may not have the visibility of those sponsored by imperial power, but they are more durable, continuing long after imperial power has faded from the scene.

A contemporary philosopher of technology, Albert Borgmann, in his book, *Technology and the Character of Contemporary Life*, describes the way in which the technological life of urban civilization threatens and overwhelms a more participatory and engaged approach to life, which he describes in terms of "focal things and practices."[11] It is the difference between eating out and having a meal prepared together around the family table, between listening to a compact disc and playing an instrument ourselves. "A genuine choice is made when a family decides to eat out more often. The practice of preparing a traditional meal, of setting the table, of saying grace, of conversing and eating thoughtfully is partly surrendered to the machinery of a fast-food chain and partly lost. . . . When parents decide to give their child a stereo set and receiver instead of a flute and instruction, they help to inundate the child with sounds and fail to encourage fully embodied and disciplined engagement with music."[12] These "focal practices and things" are precisely the product of local cultures and communities, in contrast to the products of urban civilization.

Mennonite Migrations in Imperial Contexts

At first it may seem that the history of the Mennonites is far removed from the life of empires and civilizations. It is true that Mennonites have rarely aspired to the exercise of imperial power. Throughout our history, we as Mennonites have usually seen ourselves as alternative communities of faith, far removed from the dominant centers of power and influence. Yet as I was reviewing the history of my own congregation (and family) for our church centennial in 2008, I began to observe that we benefited from the exercise of imperial power in ways very similar to that of Jacob and his family in their descent to the imperial power of Egypt.

The history of my people and my church is a history of migrations. Tracing our origins back to Switzerland, our forebears migrated to the Alsace-Lorraine area in France and the Palatinate in Germany, then east to Galicia and Poland, then further east to Volhynia in the Ukraine, and finally west to the Midwestern plains of Kansas and South Dakota.[13] These migrations began as attempts to escape persecution as Anabaptists. Frequently the migrations came about as the result of an invitation by a nobleman seeking the agricultural expertise of these peasant Anabaptists, despite their questionable beliefs and practices.[14] Rarely in any of these settings did our forebears own the land upon which they lived. They were often wards of the local nobility who had sought their services. Clearly they were marginal, second-class citizens at best. This status fit well with the Mennonite desire to avoid taxation and conscription for war.

But it is the last two migrations to Volhynia and the United States that interest me the most. Mennonites were first invited to Russia by Empress Catherine the Great, who ruled from 1762 to 1796. She was a German princess who had married into the Russian royal family and was an enlightened though thoroughly despotic ruler who

11. Borgmann, *Technology*, 196–210.
12. Ibid., 104.
13. Schrag, *European History*, describes these migrations.
14. See Ibid., 42–48, for a description of the Swiss Mennonite move from Montbeliard in France.

wanted to bring progress and prosperity to Russia. She continued the process of Europeanization that had begun in Russia with the rule of Peter the Great (1682–1725). She was also ambitious and ruthless, and soon become the sole ruler of Russia after the death of her husband, Peter III.[15]

Under Catherine's rule, Russia had pushed back the frontiers of the Turkish Ottoman Empire to the south, opening up a lot of empty crown land in the Ukraine. Rather than developing and encouraging the Ukrainian peasants indigenous to those areas, Catherine invited German agriculturalists to settle the Ukraine. Mennonites responded to this invitation, along with Lutheran, Reformed, and Catholic German people. These German people were given special privileges and allowed to keep the German language and culture and religious practices, becoming in many cases self-governing German colonies such as Chortitza and Molotschna in southern Ukraine.

Not surprisingly, the presence of these German colonists in their midst was deeply resented by the indigenous Ukrainian people, and it was only a matter of time before a "new king" would arise to change the fortunes of these German colonists. In 1870, the German colonists learned of Czar Alexander the Second's policy of Russianization. German colonists were given the choice of acculturation to Russian society or emigrating, and this led to the major Mennonite emigrations of 1874 to Canada and the United States.[16] Mennonites who were more rooted in the Ukraine and stayed into the twentieth century experienced the major upheavals and persecutions of the First World War and the establishment of the Soviet Union.

In this story I see a strong parallel to Israel's descent to Egypt.[17] Like Jacob and his family in their descent to Egypt, Mennonites went to the Ukraine at the invitation of an empress who shared their German language and culture, and whose policies amounted to the continued disenfranchisement of the local Russian population. Is it any wonder that the Mennonite presence was so resented by the Russian peasants? This is not to say that the Mennonites deserved the suffering they eventually endured in the Soviet Union. But it is to suggest that we as Mennonites have not always been discriminating in the choice of our migrations, and that we might have done more to consider the implications of these choices. While we did not exercise imperial power for the most part, even within the Mennonite colonies of the southern Ukraine, we surely benefitted from imperial policies that guaranteed the disenfranchisement of the Ukrainian people, just as Jacob and his family benefitted from the imperial policies of Joseph and the Hyksos rulers he served.

Some of the same dynamics were at work, unfortunately, in the migration of the Mennonites from Russia to America in 1874, and we as a people have still not really come to terms with the implications this has for our lives and relationships with the

---

15. Dyck, *Introduction*, 126–28.

16. Schrag, *European History*, 78.

17. This parallel is described in "Mistaken Direction," sixth in the author's sermons, *Roots that Nourish*.

First Nations people whom we displaced. Through the Yankton Treaty of 1858, the Yankton Sioux ceded their claims to the area where my forebears settled in exchange for a reserve in Charles Mix County. Our forebears were led to believe by the United States government that this was empty, uninhabited land. The First Nations population had become invisible to most white settlers. My mother, growing up at Avon, South Dakota, just across Choteau Creek from the Yankton Sioux reserve, remembers friendly visits with Indian neighbors, but few serious relationships were established with the first inhabitants of this land. Turner County, where my home church is located, was surveyed and laid out for white settlement beginning in 1859, and the first white settlers laid claim to land under the Homestead Act of 1862 in 1869, just five years before my Mennonite forebears came to this county.[18]

The Mennonite migrations to the United States in 1874 represent another occasion when we as Mennonites benefitted from the exercise of imperial power. I don't believe there was conscious racism involved in the decision of my forebears to come to the United States. Still, I have to wonder if Mennonites would have been so eager to come to the United States if Anglo-Saxon people had not been in power. As Mennonites, we have not been immune to the temptation of seeking our fortunes with powers that share our ethno-linguistic and racial heritage.

Are we to blame for the imperial policies of Catherine the Great or the United States of America because we took advantage of opportunities to benefit from their policies? I don't have an answer to this question, but it does seem to me we have not grappled adequately with it. At the very least, it behooves us to revisit our relationship with the people displaced by our coming. The First Nations population here in South Dakota was 8.3 percent of the total in the 2000 census.[19] The people we displaced, the invisible people who had vacated this land and made it empty, are very much among us. They are trying to put together the broken pieces of their rich local culture. We still have the opportunity to learn to know these neighbors of ours and to see what they can teach us about living on this land. Their generations of living in America dwarf the 100-year history of my church and the 135-year history of my people living on this land. We might at least learn to know them well enough to thank them, so belatedly, for ceding to the United States the land upon which we live, however coercive and deceptive that ceding was on the part of the United States. We do know how destructive that ceding was to their local culture and way of life, but we also see the perseverance of the human spirit in the way Lakota culture continues to be preserved and renewed in our own time.

---

18. Stoddard, *Turner County*, 10–13, 20.
19. "Turner County, South Dakota."

Chapter 6

On Wilderness and Promised Land

The Israelites Ate Manna Forty Years (Exod 16:35)

The Tension between Being Landless Sojourners and Landed Settlers

As fallen humans, we live in a kind of tension between wilderness and promised land, between landlessness and landedness, between being settled and uprooted, between sojourning and citizenship. We long for the rootedness and stability of a settled life, symbolized by the promised land. At the same time, being settled represents the greatest internal threat to our spiritual well-being. It is when we are settled that we cease to trust God—relying on ourselves, worshipping idols, abusing one another, and exploiting the earth.

On the other hand, it is in the wilderness that we learn to trust God. It is in the wilderness that we are at the mercy of nature and need to fit into the limitations of natural systems of life. In the wilderness we are not in control of our lives. We experience ourselves as finite beings, at the mercy of forces beyond our control. It is in the wilderness that character and peoplehood are formed. Wilderness experiences of life shape both our character and our identity as a people.

When we are settled, there is something that draws us with both compulsion and revulsion back to the formative experiences of wilderness. When we experience the terror of being dependent upon God and at the mercy of forces beyond our control, we long for the security of being landed, even if landedness means loss of freedom and slavery.

Socially, psychologically, and spiritually, as well as physically, we live as humans in the tension between wilderness and promised land. We struggle to trust God and resent being dependent upon God. Yet we know what happens when we fail to trust God and rely instead on ourselves—we worship idols, abuse one another, and exploit the earth! So as humans and even more as God's people we live with one foot in the wilderness and one foot in the promised land. We move back and forth from landedness, where we exercise some control, to landlessness, where we are at the mercy of forces beyond our control.

The Biblical Story

Deliverance from an Oppressive Landedness: God Heard Their Groaning (Exod 2:24)

The book of Exodus opens with the tables being turned on the people of Israel. They had gone to Egypt several generations before as resident aliens granted favored status in the land of Goshen by Pharaoh, the Egyptian ruler. They were put in charge of his livestock (Gen 47:6)! Then, a new Pharaoh came to power in the land of Egypt, likely a native Egyptian ruler. During the reign of Ahmose (1570–1545 BCE), the first king of the Eighteenth Dynasty, the foreign rule of the Hyksos was finally overthrown. While the "new king" referred to in Exodus 1:8 is not named, it might have been Ahmose or one of his successors. During the Eighteenth Dynasty, Egypt succeeded in establishing a significant empire through Palestine into Asia, which reached its height under Thutmose III (1490–1436 BCE).

The next century was the time of the Amarna period, during which there was a strong movement toward monotheism in Egypt under Amenhotep IV (1369–1353 BCE), who changed his name to Akhenaton.[1] I've often pondered the significance of the presence of the Israelites in Egypt during a period when an Egyptian Pharaoh flirted with monotheism. Did they have some influence on this movement? Yet it was likely not until the Nineteenth Dynasty (1303–1202 BCE) that "God heard their groaning, and God remembered his covenant with Abraham, Isaac, and Jacob. God looked upon the Israelites, and God took notice of them" (Exod 2:24–25).

We know nothing about the way in which the fortunes of the people of Israel changed during these centuries. We only know that from their favored status as resident aliens in Genesis 47 they became a feared and despised and exponentially growing foreign population that was oppressed and ultimately enslaved in Egypt (Exod 1:9–11). The account itself notes the relationship between being an oppressed people and a people who multiply rapidly (Exod 1:12), a phenomenon I noted when we visited the Palestinian communities in the West Bank, living under Israeli occupation. Early in the Nineteenth Dynasty, Sethos I (ca. 1309–1290 BCE) and his son Ramses II (1290–1224 BCE), moved the Egyptian capital to the Nile delta and engaged in the building of the supply cities of Pithom and Ramses, as noted in Exodus 1:11. While the date and even the fact of the Israelite Exodus from Egypt is much in debate, the reign of Ramses II has traditionally been seen as the time for the events recounted in Exodus.[2] So whether suddenly, under the rulers of the Nineteenth Dynasty, or

---

1. Wilson, "Egypt," 2:47–51.
2. Wilson, "Ramses," 4:10–12; Bright, *History*, 110–13.

more likely gradually, beginning in the Eighteenth Dynasty, the people of Israel found themselves marginalized as a foreign population. By the time of Ramses II, they were ruthlessly oppressed, conscripted into the labor force of the Pharaoh of Egypt. At the end of Exodus 2, we are told that "the Israelites groaned under their slavery, and cried out. Out of the slavery their cry for help rose up to God" (Exod 2:23).

It is in this context that we read the dramatic story of Israel's Exodus from Egyptian slavery in Exodus 3–15. Through the calling and reluctant agency of Moses, himself an Israelite raised in the royal court of Egypt as the adopted child of Pharaoh's daughter, Pharaoh was challenged to "Let my people go" (Exod 5:1)! When Pharaoh refused to accede to this demand, the land of Egypt was struck with the ten plagues, ending with the striking down of all the firstborn of Egypt. While at first agreeing to release the Israelite slaves after each plague, Pharaoh always hardened his heart and changed his mind until after the final plague, in which the firstborn of Israel were "passed over" because of the sacrificial blood of the lambs painted on the doorposts and lintels of Israelite homes. But after the release of the Israelite slaves, Pharaoh hardened his heart and changed his mind one last time, sending his army with its chariots in pursuit of the Israelites who were trapped by the waters of the sea. His army was destroyed as the chariots became mired in the waters of the sea while the Israelites passed through the waters. This in brief is the pivotal salvation story of the Old Testament, with God credited in Exodus 15 as the mighty warrior who delivered the people of Israel.

As humans we experience landedness either as oppressors or as the oppressed. The Israelites entered Egypt as foreign oppressors of the local Egyptian population, if Joseph's role in the disenfranchisement of the native population is to be credited. The Israelites ended their sojourn in Egypt as an oppressed and enslaved foreign population. Either way, being landed provides a certain degree of security. Even when they are oppressed and enslaved, a landed people experience a degree of security, which is what made the Israelites long for the "fleshpots" of Egypt after they found themselves as landless wanderers in the wilderness (Exod 16:3). At the same time, the supposed security of landed oppressors is always tenuous, as the anxiety expressed by the Pharaoh in Exodus 1:9 indicates. Still, being landed, either as oppressors or as the oppressed, has become the normative experience for the human family.

Only rarely do human groups occupy land as free people for any length of time without becoming either oppressors or the oppressed. A part of the intention of this book is to explore the conditions that make such an option possible. In the next chapter, we will explore the early Israelite experiment with being a free and landed people in promised land, being neither oppressed nor oppressor.

Most commonly, landed people who have become oppressed experience their loss of freedom as a burden and a curse. They groan, and justly so, under their slavery. In desperation, they cry out to God for deliverance. Eventually in the historical process, though it often seems to us from a human point of view after all too much human suffering, God hears the cries of the oppressed and acts to deliver them. "God heard their groaning, and God remembered his covenant with Abraham, Isaac, and Jacob" (Exod 2:24). As it is, the tables keep turning. The witness of Scripture is that God is at work in the vindication and release of those who are oppressed. We may think God acts all too slowly. On the other hand, perhaps we should be careful what we cry out about! It just might be that God will hear our cries, and then we are in for the ride of our lives—an exodus that takes us from an oppressive landedness in the empire to the exhilarating and frightening landlessness of the wilderness!

The Character of Landlessness: You Have Brought Us Out Into This Wilderness (Exod 16:3)

Only six weeks into the wilderness, the people of Israel are longing to return to the security of landed slavery in Egypt. *Why didn't you just strike us dead while we still lived in Egypt?* the Israelites are asking God in Exodus 16:3. *At least there our stomachs were full* "when we sat by the fleshpots and ate our fill of bread; for you have brought us out into this wilderness to kill this whole assembly with hunger" (Exod 16:3). They'd rather have the quick death of being struck down by God in Egypt while their stomachs were full than this slow and tortuous death by starvation in this God-forsaken wilderness. Except that it wasn't God-forsaken! Indeed, it would be there that they would really learn to know this God who had delivered them from slavery in Egypt and brought them into this wilderness.

So what is it about wilderness? Why does God lead this redeemed people deep into the foreboding wilderness of Sinai when the easy coastal road from Egypt to Canaan beckoned? Why is this sojourn so prolonged? What is God's intention with this wilderness sojourn?

Wilderness represents the antithesis to settled land. As humans, we have come to view settled occupation, landedness, as the norm for human life. When we live in settlements, we order nature to fit our needs. We domesticate plants and animals for our use. As landed people we assume some measure of control over our natural environment. We put nature to our use to provide for our needs and our security. Of course, there are always vulnerabilities we cannot control, even in settled occupation, but being a landed people provides some measure of stability and security for human life. We no longer feel at the mercy of forces we cannot control.

Therein lies, for us as modern people, the lure and attraction of the wilderness! Why do we value and cherish wilderness areas in the way that we modern people do? I think it is because as humans we thrive on the challenge of living on the edge. There is something in the human psyche that needs the challenge and thrill of being vulnerable to forces larger than ourselves. The wilderness—whether we construe that in terms of mountains or deserts or polar regions or equatorial jungles or deserted islands or the vast sweep of the sea itself—draws settled people. Of course, we may not wish to live there, although there are always those like the monastic orders of early

Christianity who do so. But we relish the opportunity to escape to the wilderness for a week or two, especially if we can do so from the safety and security of civilized lodging, which gives us the illusion of being in the wilderness without the risks.

Being truly at the mercy of the wilderness without anything other than our wits and our experience for survival is another matter, and yet this is what the wilderness truly represents for settled humans. To be in the wilderness is to be at the mercy of forces beyond our control that threaten our very survival on every hand. In the normal experience of wilderness, these are the natural forces of cold or heat, sun or storm, water or height or depth, and life forms and creatures that endanger our lives either by their size and ferocity or by their ability to poison us. To be in such a harsh and inhospitable environment for any length of time demands that we use our wits to provide the shelter and sustenance our own bodies require. Such, I suppose, is the attraction of the many television reality shows that dwell on such themes.

Of course, we may construe wilderness not only in terms of forces of nature. As we pass through life, many of us have wilderness experiences of relational or emotional or mental or physical or spiritual instability. Sometimes these wilderness experiences are occasioned by accidents or tragedies or losses that come to us in life. Many people experience the wilderness of living as refugees, driven from their homes into refugee camps by the forces of violence and war, or forced by economic necessity from the security of their lives into the anonymity of urban life as "the homeless." Wilderness becomes the antithetical human experience to the secure and settled and harmonious life we have all come to expect as the normal human experience. Being in the wilderness forces us to realize our mortality and our dependency as humans. It confronts us with our vulnerability. It forces us to live within the limits of the natural system. It forces us to realize that if our wits and experience are all we have to depend on, we will not survive. We are going to need some help here. And in our desperation we call upon God! The wilderness forces us to realize our dependence upon God our Creator, for we have no other help!

This is why God led the people of Israel deep into the wilderness of Sinai, so that God might enter into covenant with this people at Mt. Sinai, as they realized their dependence upon and need for God! This is why throughout the Bible, those who were experiencing a crisis in their lives retreated to the wilderness, as Elijah did (1 Kings 19) and as Jesus did after his baptism (Matthew 4), to learn again what it means to depend upon God and to be led by God. This is why the people of Judah found themselves in the wilderness of Babylonian exile after their years of settled life in Canaan. At its root, wilderness signifies not just human vulnerability to forces and circumstances beyond our control, but ultimately, our dependence upon God.

What we have found, as humans, is that God does not disappoint! Indeed, it is in the wilderness that we meet God. It is in the wilderness that God is to be found! It is in the wilderness that God supplies our needs. It is in the wilderness that God leads us when we cannot find the way. It is in the wilderness that God makes our course clear.

It is in the wilderness that our character and our identity as people of God is shaped and molded. Before the people of Israel could enter the promised land, they needed to learn their dependence upon God and to have their life as a people shaped by the wilderness, and by God!

Exodus 16 presents us with a divine economy—an economy of abundance and adequacy, even in the hostile environment of the wilderness.[3] The divine economy is revealed in God's provision of manna in the wilderness. It can be summarized in five brief points:

- Everyone needs to participate in God's provision by going out every morning to gather the manna needed for that day. There is no such thing as a free lunch in God's economy. Everyone is required to work for their daily bread (Exod 16:16).

- Everyone, regardless of ability, will always have enough. Though some are able to gather much and others little, in the end everyone has just what they need for the day. Daily provision is the right of all, regardless of their ability (Exod 16:17–18).

- God's provision cannot be hoarded or "commodified." Perhaps some quick workers figured they could avoid the daily chore of gathering manna if they gathered enough for several days. Other Israelites may have seen the possibility of profit by gathering and hoarding manna and then selling it to others. But in God's economy, commodification is not an option; manna kept over from one day to the next spoiled (Exod 16:19–20)!

- God's provision is adequate for a trusting observance of the Sabbath. A double portion of manna could be gathered on the sixth day for use on the Sabbath, and on that day the manna did not spoil (Exod 16:22–26).

- God's provision depends on trusting obedience to God's instructions. Those who may not have gathered enough for two days on Friday thinking the manna would spoil anyway went hungry on the Sabbath when they went out to gather manna and found none. Obedience to God, observing the limitations God establishes for human welfare, is the bottom line in God's economy (Exod 16:27–30).

Human economies typically are based on the premise of scarce goods and services. Human economies assume that there will *not* be enough for all, so everyone is forced to compete for scarce resources. Some have more than enough while others go hungry. Human economies thrive on the commodification of all essential goods and services, so that a profit can accrue to good managers and fast workers. Human economies recognize no limit on the production of goods and services other than their profitability. Those involved in production in human economies can be driven to hunger and despair. Human economies thrive on the disparity between rich and

---

3. See Brueggemann, *Land*, 28–35; and Brueggemann, "Exodus," 1:809–16, both commentaries on Exodus 16.

poor. Indeed, advanced economies may be said to require an underclass of hungry, malnourished poor people to sustain the wealth of the minority.

The premises outlined for God's economy above are as true for those who are landed and settled in promised land as it is for those living in the wilderness. Indeed, in promised land these blessings require no miraculous bread from heaven! They require only a social order willing to abide by the provisions of God's economy. The bounty of God's earth will always provide more than enough for all. However, it isn't until we are in the wilderness that we discover the provisions of God's economy. It isn't until we need to depend upon God directly that God can enable us to see and trust God's provision. It is in the provisions of God's economy that we see the extent to which the wilderness shapes the life of God's people, down to the roots of their economic life. Is it any wonder that God took the people of Israel on this detour into the wilderness? Is it any wonder that it took more than a whole generation for the people of Israel to learn this lesson of dependence upon God? Is it any wonder that neither they nor we ever really learn these lessons, despite repeated wilderness experiences?

The Lure of Landedness: When You Have Built Fine Houses (Deut 8:12)

Israel's struggle with God's provisions in the wilderness was only beginning in Exodus 16. Adequate and abundant as the manna was, the Israelites longed for the provisions of the human economy, even if it was mediated to them by an oppressive empire, as it had been in the land of Egypt. So in Numbers 11, in the second year after the exodus from Egypt, as they stood on the brink of being able to enter the promised land, we find the Israelites still complaining about God's provisions even after the covenant-making ceremonies had been concluded at Mt. Sinai. Still they suffered the consequences of their distrust and unhappiness with God. They longed for the meat and fresh vegetables they had in Egypt, so God gave them meat until they were sick and died of it, being buried in "Graves of Craving" (Num 11:4–6, 18–23, 31–34).

Throughout the wilderness sojourn, the people of Israel were reminded that the wilderness was not their home. They were on the way to Canaan, the promised land. Spies were sent out to reconnoiter Canaan for forty days, and returned with extravagant stories about both the richness of the land and the strength of the people who inhabited the land (Numbers 13). Not trusting God's leadership, the people of Israel were ready to return to Egypt. For his part, God was ready to abandon this faithless people, as well, and only the intercession of Moses on behalf of the people before God kept this disaster from happening. However, because of this faithless behavior, the wilderness sojourn was continued for an entire generation (forty years), perhaps in the hope that eventually the people would learn the lessons of the wilderness (Numbers 14).

At the end of the forty-year wilderness sojourn, the people of Israel are reminded again about the provisions of God's economy, in Deuteronomy 8. The book of Deuteronomy is presented as farewell sermons by Moses on the eve of the people's entry into Canaan. In the eighth chapter, Moses reminded the people how God had provided for them throughout their long sojourn in the wilderness. Not only did God feed them with manna, teaching them that humans do not live by bread alone but by God's word (Deut 8:3), but God provided all the other necessities of life, as well. "The clothes on your back did not wear out and your feet did not swell these forty years" (Deut 8:4). Then Moses spoke about the bounty of promised land, describing the richness of Canaan as a land watered from heaven, "a land where you may eat bread without scarcity, where you will lack nothing" (Deut 8:9). Here we have the echoes of the provisions of God's economy outlined in Exodus 16. God's economy is one of abundance, not scarcity!

There is no difference between wilderness and settled land when it comes to the provisions of God's economy. Both are adequate and bountiful in their own way. Both require human initiative. Both depend on a social order that rejects the commodification of life's necessities. Both require human dependence upon God and a willingness to observe the limitations God places on human behavior for human welfare. Indeed, both depend on God's gift from heaven—the miraculous gift of manna in the case of the wilderness and the gracious gift of rain in the case of settled land.

Still, it isn't any wonder that we humans prefer the blessings of settled land. It is somehow easier to be dependent upon natural forces than to depend on a daily divine handout, even if God's handout still had to be gathered every morning. We feel a bit more in control of things when we're on our own in settled land. Why, we can even begin to feel that we might have something to do with our success in settled land. It might be our good management that gives us an advantage over our neighbors, or it might be the introduction of new technologies, or it might be our manipulation of nature. We can even begin to say, "My power and the might of my own hand have gotten me this wealth" (Deut 8:17). When we "have eaten [our] fill and have built fine houses and live in them, and when [our] herds and flocks have multiplied, and [our] silver and gold is multiplied, and all that [we] have is multiplied" (Deut 8:12–13), it is hard to remember our dependence upon God.

This is the lure of the settled life. This is why, despite our fascination with the wilderness and our occasional voluntary excursion into the wilderness, we usually avoid the wilderness like the plague in favor of settled land. We don't really like to be reminded daily of our dependence upon God, despite the fact that Jesus teaches us to pray for our daily bread—not bread for tomorrow or next week or our retirement: just bread for today! We prefer an economic system that provides for long-term security, old-age security!

So perhaps the best we can do until we are led kicking and screaming into our next experience in the wilderness is to keep rereading the warnings of Moses in Deuteronomy 8: "Then do not exalt yourself, forgetting the LORD your God, who brought you out of the land of Egypt, out of the house of slavery, who led you through the great and terrible wilderness" (Deut 8:14–15). "But remember the LORD your God, for it is he who gives you power to get wealth.... If you do forget the LORD your God and follow other gods to serve and worship them, I solemnly warn you today that you shall surely perish" (Deut 8:18–19). The consequence of not heeding the provisions of God's economy in settled land is a return to the wilderness!

Reflections on Contemporary Landedness and Landlessness

Our early human forebears must have experienced the earth only as wilderness, for there was as yet no settled land. Surely their lives were vulnerable to natural forces in a way we simply cannot imagine today. Surely many of them suffered and died from natural disasters, accidents, violent attacks by predators and enemies, and diseases. Yet they also learned to cope with wilderness. Indeed, wilderness can be more fruitful and abundant than settled land to those like our early human ancestors who had learned to make their home in the wilderness. Still, it is no surprise that one of the marks of early human life is the emergence of the religious sensibility—the sense that our lives are dependent on spiritual powers and forces beyond our control. Nor is it surprising that the gods and goddesses of early humanity were seen as personifications of the natural forces found in the wilderness. Who of us still today, when our houses are shaken with the rumble of a close lightning strike, do not feel in this power the presence of God?

It is not surprising to me, then, that the more settled and sophisticated and civilized human life becomes, the more secular it becomes, as well. Not only do we learn that the powers of nature have ostensibly natural causes. We also learn to insulate and protect ourselves from the effects of these powers. God—and indeed every form of spiritual power—becomes more and more irrelevant to human life. Who, in twenty-first-century North America, needs God? Most of us have become invulnerable behind the imposing, impregnable fortresses of modern life we have created for ourselves. Those who deplore the secularization of modern life should look not to a secular humanist ideology but rather to the settled character of civilization for the cause. I find it ironic that those who rail against secular humanism often have no more real use for God than those who frankly acknowledge the secular character of the settled life.

On the other hand again, we rarely consider how truly vulnerable we are in the security of our insulated homes. We can hardly function "off the grid" for more than a few hours. My wife and I felt this especially keenly as she needed to do peritoneal dialysis every night. And if a catastrophic natural disaster strikes, as it did in New Orleans a few years ago, or if those who wish to harm us could undo our access to power, there would likely be mass chaos. Petroleum or food shortages might have the same effect on a population that no longer knows anything about fending for oneself. We are perhaps much closer to wilderness than we suppose!

Of course, there are already millions of people living in the wilderness of poverty and urban homelessness, even here in the United States. Indeed, throughout history since earliest times, there have likely been many more humans subject to the wilderness of being driven from their homes due to oppression and the violence of war than for any other cause. Remember that at its root wilderness means having to leave all forms of security behind in order to face the vicissitudes of life. This is what illegal immigrants to our country seeking economic opportunity regularly do. It is what refugees from war are forced to do. It is what the poor farmers described in John Steinbeck's *The Grapes of Wrath* did in the 1930s in the midst of the dust storms of the Great Depression. It is what desperate humans have done throughout history when driven to survive, whether by oppression, warfare, or natural disaster.

These are people who still have need for God on a daily basis, in a way settled people simply do not. Indeed, these are people who cry out to God as the Israelites did from their slavery in Egypt. So we confront the dilemma of landedness—that it radically undermines our need of God and what belief in God provides, an ethic by which to order human life. Perhaps it is this central dilemma of landedness that accounts for the repeated movement we find in the human story—the movement from landedness to landlessness, and back again. The story of Israel moving from the landlessness of resident aliens in Canaan, to the landedness of foreign oppressors in Egypt, to the landlessness of the wilderness sojourn, to the landedness of promised land, to the landlessness of Babylonian exile, becomes a paradigm for the human experience.

I'm grateful to Old Testament scholar Walter Brueggemann for first formulating this realization in his seminal work *The Land*. "Israel's faith is essentially a journeying in and out of land, and its faith can be organized around these focuses. This subject is worth our attention because contemporary problems are quite parallel. We know in our time about the hunger for rootage and the yearning for turf. We know about the destructive power of coveting and the anxiety of displacement. And we know from time to time about gifts given and promises kept."[4]

It may be a stretch to presume, as Old Testament scholar George Mendenhall does, that this movement from landedness to landlessness occurs with some regularity in the human family every 250 to 300 years, or every tenth generation. However, as a matter of fact, this movement from landedness to landlessness occurs quite often, precipitated by "the deification of productivity and power."[5] When a people abandon an egalitarian communal life of trust in God in favor of the centralized power and organized productivity of being settled in the land, we can predict that it will not be too long before they lose the land.

The movement from landedness to landlessness and back to landedness provides one of the fundamental dynamics for understanding the human story. There may seem to be a sense of inevitability about the loss of land within the life of a civilization.

---

4. Brueggemann, *Land*, 14.
5. Mendenhall, *Tenth Generation*, 224.

In fact, the only thing that is inevitable is the consequence of abandoning the provisions of God's economy. When a social order begins to rely on human ingenuity and systems of domination, people make an idol of human power, begin to abuse one another, and exploit the earth for selfish ends. The consequence of idolatry, oppression, and exploitation is the loss of land. This is of course a historical process. Landlessness is an ultimate rather than an immediate consequence of abandoning the provisions of God's economy.

In the movement of this historical process, it is wilderness that is God's training ground for humanity. God's desire for us is promised land, settled land, a planted garden! But when being settled leads us into idolatry and oppression and exploitation and we find ourselves in the wilderness, God is there to teach us again what it means to rely on divine providence.

It is tempting to ascertain where in this historical process we are as a society here in North America. One might note that the United States of America is soon 250 years old. One can surely observe the patterns of idolatry and oppression and exploitation operating in the structures of the domination powers that govern our land. One can observe that the economic and energy and ecological crises of our time are harbingers of an approaching wilderness experience. However, it seems to me that the point of the biblical story is not to engage us in how to condemn or to save our nation. The point of the biblical story of landedness and landlessness is to engage our own commitment to the provisions of God's economy, so that we will be living already as landless sojourners in the land, even if we seem to be settled.

Mennonite Experiences with Landedness and Landlessness

The history of Mennonite people may seem to be an extended excursion into the lives of oppressed landless peasants. These were in any case the people in sixteenth-century Europe that were most open to the theological and ethical views of Anabaptism. The early centuries of Mennonite history were characterized by migrations within Europe and then to North America in search of social settings where these communities might live and practice their distinctive faith in the midst of the dominant cultures in which they lived.

Though respected by the European nobility who invited them for their agricultural expertise, the Mennonite communities of Europe usually did not own the land they worked and improved for their noble overlords. I wonder what motivated them to care for land they did not own or possess? It is deeply engrained in our American psyche that people will not care for what they do not own. Yet I observe that both my father and my father-in-law were renters. My father owned only eighty acres, and raised his family on that land and by renting an adjacent quarter section of land. My father-in-law never owned the land he worked for most of his life, moving his family to several farms as a tenant farmer through the years. Yet I noted that both these men took special care of the land entrusted to them. Why? Perhaps it was precisely because they did not own it, but were accountable for its use to the owner.

When it comes to Mennonite wilderness experiences, I think of the Mennonites exiled to Siberia in the era of the Soviet Union, and perhaps the Mennonite settlement of the Chaco in Paraguay, one of the only places open to their settlement as refugees from World War II. These were both wildernesses, extreme climatic and ecological environments into which an oppressed population was thrown and left to survive. The interesting thing is that in both cases, Mennonite communities did survive and even thrive, making of those wilderness environments a fruitful land. Though Mennonites in Siberia have now largely emigrated to Germany, they had before they left established what seemed to be sustainable and fruitful communities in that harsh land.

My own sense is that these Mennonite communities in Siberia and Paraguay thrived because they lived in these harsh environments as communities who depended on God and accepted the provisions of God's economy. If they had gone to these places as adventurers seeking their fortune, I doubt if the outcome would have been the same. Perhaps the land would have been exploited for personal gain, but sustainable and fruitful communities spreading to the original inhabitants of the land would likely not have been the result.[6]

Of course, Mennonite history also has examples of Mennonites coming into landedness. Though I don't know this history well, the story of the Dutch Mennonites in the eighteenth century may be an example, as well as the Low German Mennonites who remained in Prussia after many of their compatriots emigrated to Russia in the eighteenth century. The Russian Mennonite colonies of Molotschna and Chortitza are another obvious example.

I also think of my own family and congregational history in relation to coming into landedness. When Czar Alexander II in 1870 began revoking the special privileges previously granted to German settlers in Russia, the Mennonites there began to look for another home. Those interested in going to North America chose a delegation of twelve men to spy out the Great Plains of North America, which were just then being opened to European settlement. These twelve spies were chosen to represent the diverse Anabaptist communities in the Ukraine, including the Hutterite colonies and the scattered Low German and Swiss German communities of western Ukraine. For instance, Tobias Unruh and Andreas Schrag represented these scattered Low and Swiss German communities of the western Ukraine, and those communities ended up settling near each other in South Dakota, at Avon, and at Marion and Freeman.[7]

The whole notion of sending twelve men to spy out the land is reminiscent of the Israelite experience recounted in Numbers 13 and suggests to me that the Russian Mennonites were looking for their promised land. Indeed I have the impression that my forebears had a fairly clear sense that the United States was going to be their

---

6. See Dyck, *Introduction*, 243–48, for a description of the settlements in Paraguay.
7. Unruh, *Century*, 16–18; Waltner, *Banished*, 188–90.

promised land. Through the 1862 Homestead Act, the United States was offering to give a quarter section of land to those willing and able to settle on the land and make it their home. So after the spies returned from their expedition in 1873, some 18,000 Mennonites emigrated to the United States and Canada in the next decade, including, as in the case of my forebears, complete villages.[8]

Of course, there was a great challenge in settling what was then still virgin prairie—a wilderness, but my forebears worked together to establish their homes, and they also appealed for and received help from established Mennonite communities in the eastern United States. Indeed, my people may not have survived the harsh South Dakota climate had it not been for a grain shipment of wheat from eastern Mennonites, and the $50 loans subsequently made to quite a number of these impoverished Swiss Volhynian Amish Mennonite families.[9]

The fact that our people saw the United States as their promised land is corroborated for me by the rapidity with which we acculturated to American society. We accepted citizenship in the United States without objection, as well as the pattern of living on isolated farmsteads instead of in agricultural villages. Though we intended to retain our German language and culture, two World Wars with Germany sealed the fate of our cultural heritage. German services were abandoned shortly after World War II in the Salem congregation, and today the Schweitzer dialect of this Swiss Volhynian community is spoken by only a handful of individuals. Acculturation led to the dispersal of traditional Mennonite communities into the larger US society. For instance, my mother's home congregation at Avon, South Dakota, today has only a handful of descendants from the original Mennonite immigrants.

More telling is the nationalistic spirit that quite soon infiltrated these new Mennonite communities, leading to service in the armed forces of the United States on the part of a good number of Mennonite young men beginning especially in the Second World War. Of course, this was the very thing our forebears were seeking to avoid when they came to this land only a few decades before. More than anything else, it was the dilution of our commitment to the nonviolent way of Jesus that confirms for me the way we have succumbed to the lure of landedness. Now that we own the land, we feel we have both the duty and the right to protect our land (country). Indeed, many of us even succumb to the notion common in conservative Christian circles that the American way of life depends on maintaining American dominance in the world through preemptive warfare.

Of course, this degree of acculturation is not true of all Mennonites in the United States, and perhaps it is not characteristic of the church as a whole. Many of our churches, including those I served, struggle valiantly with the demands of following Christ, or what I referred to earlier in this chapter as accepting the provisions of God's

---

8. Unruh, *Century*, 23.

9. Unruh and Waltner, *Andreas Schrag*, 3–10; see also the author's eighth sermon, "Adjusting to a New Land," in his series, *Roots that Nourish*.

economy. As Christians, we are torn between the lure of landedness and the risks and vulnerability of landlessness. The problem is we've let it become each person for him or herself. We've lost the sense of being an alternative community of faith within the dominant culture. As a result, we have no base from which to challenge the dominant culture. We no longer see ourselves as part of a community that stands against the grain of the dominant culture. We don't always like what we've become, but we've lost the tools of a cohesive local community that could empower us to change and to regain our identity as people of God. Perhaps we need some time in the wilderness! Perhaps we need to allow God to reshape our character and our identity as God's people.

CHAPTER 7

The Call to Rural Community

So Now I Bring the First of the Fruit of the Ground
(Deut 26:10)

The Mandate for Extended Kinship Groups Living on the Land

WHILE THE DETAILS OF Israel's origin and entry into Canaan remain unclear, the biblical witness is that God intended Israel to form decentralized, egalitarian, rural communities of extended kinship groups living on the land as the basic social structure. The promised land in which Israel came into existence as a people was highly urbanized, with the presence of many Canaanite city-states. However, the Ten Commandments and the body of legal documents that form the basis of Israel's life as a people clearly assume an agrarian context for their life.

In obedience to God's will revealed at Mt. Sinai, the Israelites deliberately chose to organize their life in Canaan as egalitarian, decentralized rural communities. This was a deliberate alternative to the hierarchical, exploitative, and oppressive way of life characteristic of the Canaanite city-states among whom the Israelites settled. Around the core of pastoral redeemed slaves who are portrayed as being delivered from Egyptian slavery and encountering God at Mt. Sinai before entering Canaan, there likely gathered other related people in Canaan who came to share Israel's vision of rural community as an alternative to urban civilization.

Israelite life was structured around seasonal festivals that were to continually remind the Israelites of their dependence upon God, who alone retained ownership of the land as the primary resource of the community. The observance of the weekly Sabbath, the seventh year sabbatical for the land, and the fiftieth year of Jubilee, as well as the seasonal festivals of Passover, Firstfruits, and Booths, were all to be frequent reminders for the Israelites of their dependence upon God, despite their settled life on the land.

Healing God's Earth

These Israelite communities, organized into clans and tribes, were not intended by God to be ethnic enclaves withdrawn from the world. On the contrary, they were to be a "priestly realm" and a "holy nation" among the people of the world (Exod 19:6), a beacon of hope in a world increasingly dominated by the values of urban civilization. They were to be a people who reflected in their life together on the land God's intention for human life here on earth.

The Biblical Story

Israel's Journey into Landedness

Human life depends upon the fruitfulness of the earth. We may have illusions about that, and sometimes the modern diet of supplements and artificial, manufactured, highly processed foods obscures the connections between human life and the fruitful earth. But for the foreseeable future, at least, our lives are bound to the earth. So as we think about the relationship between human life and the land upon which human life depends, two land tenure questions are central. Who controls access to the land, deciding how the land and its bounty is to be used? And who, and under what terms and conditions, actually tills the land and harvests its bounty? Ideally, of course, it would be the same people in both cases. In other words, the people who till the land and harvest its bounty should also be the people who control access to the land and make decisions about how it and its bounty will be used. As we know from history and experience, that is often not the case!

As we read the story of God covenanting with the people of Israel in the Old Testament, it seems that God's intention was that Israel should be a people who had access to the land, made decisions about its use, tilled the land, and themselves enjoyed its bounty. As we read the foundational documents of Israel's life, God's covenant with Israel seems to assume an agrarian context and way of life. While this may seem too obvious, its significance has rarely been appreciated. After all, it isn't as though there weren't other forms of human life available to the people of Israel! The promised land of Canaan already had an urban history of several millennia by the time Israel became a people and settled in the land in agrarian communities. As Norman Gottwald says, "At the time of Israel's appearance, centralized government had existed in the ancient Near East for at least two thousand years and probably for a great deal longer."[1] In Canaan, this urban presence was manifested in the "Egyptian-Canaanite imperial-feudal blend spread over several centuries from about 2000 B.C. to about 1200 B.C.," which is well documented in the correspondence of the Amarna Age (ca. 1410–1350 BCE).[2] The Israelites wouldn't have had to "regress" to become farming communities unless they felt that that was what God was calling them to do!

1. Gottwald, *Tribes*, 449.
2. Ibid., 390.

The Call to Rural Community

The circumstances of Israel's emergence as a people are the subject of a great deal of scholarly debate. The general consensus continues to be that the people of Israel emerged as a distinct people in and after the thirteenth century BCE, the era we refer to as the period of the judges. The dominant biblical portrayal of Israel's origins envisions a group of Semitic peoples newly redeemed from slavery in Egypt meeting God at the foot of Mt. Sinai and being shaped into the people of God through the covenant based upon the Ten Commandments (Exodus 19–24). Following the forty years of wandering in the wilderness of Sinai, the people of Israel entered Canaan under the leadership of Joshua and proceeded to conquer the land. So Joshua 21:43–44 declares, "Thus the LORD gave to Israel all the land that he swore to their ancestors that he would give them; and having taken possession of it, they settled there . . . not one of all their enemies had withstood them, for the Lord had given their enemies into their hands."

This dominant "conquest model" of Israelite settlement of Canaan has been challenged by a number of other models. One is the "immigration model" advocated by scholars in the early twentieth century, notably Martin Noth, who saw Israel's entry into Canaan as a peaceful immigration of Israelites, particularly into the more sparsely settled highlands of Canaan.[3] Still another is the "revolt model" proposed especially by Norman Gottwald in *The Tribes of Yahweh*. This model sees Israel emerging from the dominant Canaanite city-states themselves in a revolt against the hierarchical, feudal oppression of these city-states. Amidst the social unrest already underway in Canaan in the post-Amarna era, the core of redeemed Israelite slaves entering Canaan provided a catalyst for the formation of a new social order.[4]

The biblical witness itself warns us not to settle on one of these models as the only option. The conquest model is challenged by Judges 1:1, where, upon the death of Joshua, the first question is, "Who shall go up first for us against the Canaanites, to fight against them?" And in Judges 2:20–23, God is portrayed as deliberately allowing the nations left in Canaan to remain there as a test of Israel's faith. Clearly there was no final and complete conquest of Canaan by the Israelites. On the other hand, there is evidence for the destruction of some Canaanite city-states by the Israelites. It also seems fairly clear that the early Israelite settlements tended to be in the hill country of Canaan, where there was opportunity to organize new communities on the land somewhat apart from the domination of the Canaanite city-states.

I am most intrigued by the possibility that "Israel" was not a strictly biological or ethnic designation but also and perhaps even primarily a religious and political designation. Already at the exodus from Egypt we have the hint of a "mixed crowd" fleeing Egypt along with the Israelites (Exod 12:38). It does seem credible to me that, following Gottwald's "revolt model," disaffected social classes of Canaanites and others of mixed origins should be attracted to the social and religious program being initiated by the "Israelites" after their formation as God's people at Mt. Sinai and in the

3. Ibid., 204–9.
4. Ibid., 214.

wilderness. Obviously, there isn't much evidence of such a process in the current Old Testament canon, but then that canon was the result of the triumph of an ethnocentric narrowing of the vision proposed at Mt. Sinai, the vision of being for God "a priestly kingdom and a holy nation" (Exod 19:6).

In any case, I find it credible that around the core of descendents of the patriarchs redeemed from Egyptian slavery there should gather people of diverse background who were drawn to the agrarian vision of the Israelites. I observed in the churches I served how quickly (relatively speaking) new family names were incorporated into the fabric of a closed ethnic community through marriage or conversion. Several of the current dominant names in these congregations are foreign to the dominant ethnic identity of these congregations.

In any case, what we discover is that sometime around 1200 BCE, Israelite communities begin to emerge in Canaan. What we are fairly sure about is that these communities became landed. They assumed responsibility for specific tracts of real estate, not perhaps on the crowded and contested coastal plain, but surely in the more marginal hill country of Canaan. They found, somehow, the freedom, however tenuous it might always have been, to claim the right to manage the land, till it, and enjoy its bounty. Whether they did this through violent revolt or conquest or through a nonviolent and strategic withdrawal from the centers of political power or through a combination of these tactics is less clear. But it is clear that the Israelites became a landed people in the promised land of Canaan.

The form of social organization adopted by these early Israelite communities is also quite plain. Early Israel in the period of the Judges was a tribal confederacy. As described in the book of Joshua, the land of Canaan was divided among tribes. Within the tribal territories, land was divided among clans (*mishpāʻāh*) referred to by Norman Gottwald as "protective associations of families,"[5] and called "kin groups" by Christopher J. H. Wright.[6] Within the clan, the land was further divided among extended families (*bēth-ʼav*, the father's house), which then were the most basic social units of Israelite society.[7] It was extended families who tilled the land and enjoyed its bounty, and who within the structures and constraints of the clan and the tribe had the right to determine how and by whom and for whom the land would be used. As patriarchal units, the extended family would include both several related generations and associated dependents and resident aliens. As Gottwald says, "The *bēth-ʼav* was the basic economic unit in the Israelite social system. It formed a self-sufficient unit in the sense that it produced the basic means of subsistence for all its members and consumed all, or nearly all, of what it produced."[8] Likely these extended family units functioned as hamlet or village entities scattered throughout the territory of the clans and tribes.

5. Ibid., 257.
6. Wright, *God's People*, 49.
7. Gottwald, *Tribes*, 285–92.
8. Ibid., 292.

This social system is described by Gottwald as "sociopolitical egalitarianism," in which a "self-governing association of economically self-sufficient free farmers and herdsmen" hold "common ownership of the means of production vested in large families."[9] This type of social organization stands in stark contrast to the "hierarchic centralized rule of the city-states in the same general area, from which Israel broke away."[10] This social organization was characterized by strong "political decentralization" and strong "sociocultural cohesiveness."[11] In other words, while maintaining a strong degree of political decentralization and economic egalitarianism, Israel also exhibited a strong sense of communal identity and cohesiveness that enabled it to stand against the hierarchical rule of the surrounding city-states.

Israel's Constitutional Foundation

If sociopolitical decentralization, socioeconomic egalitarianism, and sociocultural cohesiveness are the marks of early Israelite society, what accounts for this remarkable confluence of attributes? It sounds too good to be true! How can any society maintain a strong sense of communal identity and cohesiveness without hierarchical political authority being exercised? How can socioeconomic egalitarianism be maintained without that same resort to hierarchical political authority? And as if the internal pressures were not enough, how is such a society to live in the midst of power-broking, imperial, militaristic urban centers?

As the next chapter will recount, it was precisely these pressures that led Israel into monarchical nationhood. So the answer is that it is very, very difficult for a social order to maintain sociocultural cohesiveness and socioeconomic egalitarianism without resorting to hierarchical political power. Still, before we write off early Israel's attributes as unrealistic, unworkable, and too idealistic, we do well to remember that early Israelite society managed to survive for nearly two hundred years (as long as the United States has been a nation) with something approximating these attributes. Perhaps this is not all as impossible as we would like to assume. But in order to understand how it is possible, we have to understand what made it possible for early Israel.

Israelite society was shaped by the relentlessly theocentric constitution described in Exodus 19–24. The account begins with the theophany, God's appearance to the band of recently redeemed slaves gathered at the foot of Mt. Sinai in Exodus 19:1—20:21. Inserted into this theophany are the Ten Commandments (Exod 20:1–17). Following the theophany is the Covenant Code of Exodus 20:22—23:33. This code of miscellaneous laws reflects a settled agricultural society, with laws governing worship (Exod 20:22–26) and rhythms of worship (Exod 23:10–19). The code also addresses situations likely to occur in small, agricultural communities, particularly when livestock

9. Ibid., 613.
10. Ibid.
11. Ibid., 614.

are involved (Exod 21:28—22:4), and when people experience property losses involving crops and animals (Exod 22:5—23:9). While there is a recognition that inequalities will exist and members of the community may even fall into servitude, there are limitations on slavery (Exod 21:1–11). Special care is to be shown to vulnerable members of the community, especially the poor, resident aliens, orphans, and widows (Exod 22:21–27). This Covenant Code is followed by an elaborate covenant ceremony in Exodus 24, in which the covenant of God with Israel is ratified and sealed.

I referred to this as a theocentric constitution rather than a theocratic constitution. It isn't so much that God was understood to be actively ruling. It was rather that God's presence was understood to permeate the life of the community, and the community was to order its life in a way that reflected and respected God's presence. The same kinds of legal documents underlying Israelite society can be found in the Holiness Code of Leviticus 17–26, and the Deuteronomic Law Code of Deuteronomy 12–26. Having been redeemed by God from the oppression of political hierarchies in Egypt, the people of Israel were to live in a way that reflected God's holiness (Exod 20:2). Here we find the basis for the strong sociocultural cohesiveness that bound Israelite society together in the absence of a sociopolitical hierarchy.

What is remarkable about the Covenant Code is the promise of land on which to live it out and in which God will dwell with God's people. Concluding, or as some might say, attached to the Covenant Code is the remarkable promise of God in Exodus 23:23–33 to bring the people into Canaan, the promised land. The people of Israel are to worship God alone, and to avoid the idols of hierarchical power worshipped in Canaan. They are to live among the peoples of Canaan—the Amorites, Hittites, Perizzites, Canaanites, Hivites, and Jebusites—and allow God to overcome them in God's own way and God's own time (Exod 23:27–30). The point is that God's covenant with Israel is grounded in promised land. There is the context in which to live out this theocentric constitution—the promised land, where God will dwell in the midst of God's people.

In addition, we can observe that the socioeconomic egalitarianism of Israelite society was based on Israel's understanding of the land as belonging to God. The principle is baldly stated in the Holiness Code of Leviticus. "The land shall not be sold in perpetuity, for the land is mine; with me you are but aliens and tenants" (Lev 25:23). This part of the Holiness Code concerns the provisions for the Sabbath observance. Leviticus 23 enunciates the basic weekly observance of the Sabbath and then proceeds to outline the three annual thanksgiving festivals to be observed by the people of Israel—Passover and Unleavened Bread, Weeks, and Booths. The first and last of these were week-long observances. In this chapter we see evidence for an ancient pentecontad calendar in which the year consisted of a cycle of seven fifty-day periods (seven weeks plus one festal day equals fifty days, times seven equals 350 days, plus the two festal weeks equals 364 days, plus one new year's day equals 365).[12] The basis for this

---

12. Morgenstern, "Week," 4:826.

whole calendar and for the weekly Sabbath observance was rooted in the rhythms of agricultural life, a concern that draft animals and people all needed a weekly day of rest (see Exod 20:10, 23:12), and a sense that the whole community should regularly throughout the year observe days of worship to celebrate God's good provision in the gift of the land.

Leviticus 25 extends the sabbatical principle further, mandating a seventh year of rest for the land, as well as a fiftieth year of Jubilee following a cycle of seven sabbatical years. It is in the context of the sabbatical and Jubilee legislation that we see the basis for Israel's socioeconomic egalitarianism. In the Deuteronomic Law Code, the sabbatical year legislation in Deuteronomy 15:1–11 provides for the remission of debts incurred by one Israelite to another. Both Deuteronomy 15:12–18 and Exodus 21:1–11 mandate the release of Israelites who have become enslaved to a neighbor. Finally, under the Jubilee legislation of Leviticus 25:8–55, we see that while *use* of the land could be purchased by an Israelite from a neighbor in need, land should be redistributed to all within the community in the year of Jubilee.

In all of this, we see that the Israelites understood themselves to be tenants of land (the earth) that belonged, finally, to God. Extended family units were the primary holders and caretakers of the land that was entrusted to them by God. At the same time, there was a frank recognition of human variability in this arrangement. Some family units might have more productive land. Some family units might have better managerial skills and entrepreneurial abilities. Over time, it was likely that some families might prosper while others would struggle, fall into debt and even servitude, losing their land in the process. Yet the Sabbatical/Jubilee legislation ensured that the basic socioeconomic egalitarianism of the system would be preserved. Debts can be remitted; slaves can be set free; family units that have lost their land have the opportunity for a new beginning. And all of this is possible only because the land belongs to God! It is for this reason that the Israelites were to regularly bring to God the first fruits of the land in worship at the appointed festivals. "So now I bring the first of the fruit of the ground that you, O Lord, have given me" (Deut 26:10).

I acknowledge that the assertion here of Israelite egalitarianism is undercut by the fact that the extended family unit was a patriarchal construct, under the presumed authority of the patriarch and head of the family. Women, children, and resident aliens working in the household might very well not have felt that there was anything egalitarian about this system. Christopher Wright devotes the third and last part of his book *God's People in God's Land*[13] to an examination of the place of women, children, and slaves in Israelite society. While the basic structures of patriarchy and slavery cannot be denied, the legal provisions calling for the protection of widows, orphans, slaves, and resident aliens mitigate the lack of status these persons have within the social structure. It is also important to note that it was to the "father's house" (*bēth-'av*) that certain rights and privileges were given, and not to the patriarch alone. What this

---

13. Wright, *God's People*, 181–259.

means is that the rights of women, children, and other dependents were assumed in the rights and privileges given to the *bēth-'av* as a unit.

So how are we to understand the land tenure pattern of early Israel? Contrary to common thinking, it was not a pattern of private property, for the Israelites understood themselves to be tenants of land that belonged to God. Though they were responsible for its care and use, the Israelites had no illusion about owning the land, and it was, in any case, entrusted not to individuals but to extended households. While this gave a communal cast to Israel's land tenure practices, the land was still entrusted to extended households who were expected to care for and nurture the land autonomously, on their own initiative and according to their own creative insights. Since the land was thus entrusted to extended households who might prosper or languish, as the case might be, care was also taken to build into the land tenure-system guarantees through the provisions of the sabbatical legislation to preserve egalitarian access to the land for everyone within the community. The fruits of the land were in particular to be made available to the disenfranchised members of the community, in the injunctions regarding gleaning (Lev 19:9–10; Deut 24:19–22; Ruth 2). Land was understood by early Israelites to be the gift of God entrusted to the whole community for the welfare and blessing of the whole community.

Israel's Mission: A Priestly Kingdom and a Holy Nation (Exod 19:6)

Before leaving the topic of Israel's land tenure policies so basic to the life of Israel as the covenant people of God, we must remember again that the land and community of Israel did not exist for itself. In other words, God's covenant with Israel was not intended to create a special people who would live unto themselves, enjoying God's favor and blessing for themselves alone. Indeed, God makes it clear to the Israelites that it was not because of their greatness (Deut 7:7) or their goodness (Deut 9:4–7) that God entered into covenant with them. Instead, it was God's purpose through this covenanted people to model for the world God's intention for all humanity.

Noting the hierarchical oppressiveness that had taken shape within the human family, God's purpose for Israel was to model a different kind of life, an alternative with a more promising future. That is what it means when God says, "Now therefore, if you obey my voice and keep my covenant, you shall be my treasured possession out of all the peoples. Indeed, the whole earth is mine, but you shall be for me a priestly kingdom and a holy nation" (Exod 19:5–6). To be a "priestly kingdom" is to become a community that mediates between God and humanity. To be a "holy nation" is to become a community that represents God's intention and God's holiness before the whole world. While these are political terms, they don't imply "kingdom" and "nationhood" as commonly understood in the world, for "priestly" and "holy" modify both terms. What is in view is the formation of a faith community, not the formation of a nation understood ethnically or geographically or a kingdom understood as the realm of a human king.

Of course, it's difficult to know the extent to which this vision forming the basis of Israel's covenant with God took root within the early Israelite community. However, we have noted several things in this chapter that suggest at least some ownership of this vision. First of all, we have seen that early Israel took its place within and among the urbanized civilization present in the land of Canaan. While Scripture presents a variety of perspectives about Israel's coming into Canaan, there are enough passages like Exodus 23:23–33 and Deuteronomy 7:17–26 to suggest that early Israel lived among the Canaanite city-states, avoiding both the oppressive hierarchy evident in these contexts and the pagan worship that legitimized this oppressive use of power. In this sense, early Israel was indeed a "priestly kingdom" and a "holy nation," modeling before a skeptical and hostile world an alternative, egalitarian social order.

We have also noted the possibility that early Israel understood itself not primarily in ethnic terms, but as a community of faith open to all who were prepared to receive the vision of God's purpose for humanity. In other words, it is possible that around the core of redeemed slaves descended from the patriarchs Abraham, Isaac, and Jacob and empowered by their encounter with God at Mt. Sinai, there gathered many others, a mixed company of people disillusioned with the power politics, inequality, exploitation, and oppressiveness of life in the mainstream. If this occurred, these diverse people were likely incorporated into the formal tribal structure that defined the largest social organization of early Israel. If this was not indeed the case, it does in any case seem to be a part of God's intention in entering into covenant with this people. The exclusivity of an ethnic community hardly fits with being a "holy nation" and a "priestly kingdom," important as it always is to own and cherish the ethnic heritage that belongs to each person as a birthright.

This missional aspect of Israel's life as a covenant community was undoubtedly very difficult to express and live out, as most of us know from our own struggle to become communities of witness and welcome in the world. Clearly, Israel failed often and even abandoned the missional vision altogether, although prophets, especially in the exile, reclaimed this vision, as we shall see. However, my point here is to highlight the fact that Israel's mission was to incarnate and model egalitarian, agrarian communities of faith in the midst of a highly urbanized environment, thus presenting the world with a viable alternative to the hierarchical, exploitative, and oppressive way of life around them.

Perspectives on Land Tenure Patterns through History

Land tenure, how land is held and used in human communities, is a complex issue. In our time, real estate as private property is assumed to be the norm. Land use ethics assume the right of private landownership, and appeals are made for how individuals with exclusive claim to the land are to care for the land. In a system of private landownership, the local community has very little say or control in the use of land. The only constraint on what an individual may do with the land he or she owns is the legal constraint of public policy. Rarely in current discussions is the abuse of land ascribed to a faulty system of land tenure. The principle of private property in which the owner has exclusive claim to the land and its use is currently unchallenged.

Anthropologists helpfully identify the range of social relations in regard to objects or land that define the emergence of private property. "Property" is defined as the "network of social relations that governs the conduct of people with respect to the use and disposition of things."[14] Objects or things that can be used by anyone at any time are regarded as a "commons." Here there is no property claim. Objects to which all members of a particular community have equal access or use and in which the community as a whole decides on the use are "communal property." Objects whose use is limited to members of a particular group within the community, such as a family or clan or association, are considered "joint property." (The land tenure pattern described earlier in ancient Israel might fit best in this model.) Finally, objects whose use is limited to one individual alone is "private property." "If the status of an individual in relation to the object is such that he alone has predominant priority in its use and disposition, then we are confronted with *private property*."[15]

The dominance of the current pattern of private landownership is of course a fairly recent human innovation. In most traditional societies, land was accepted as a "commons," a resource that, like the water and the air, was simply there to be used to meet the needs of the community. The idea of "owning" a specific tract of real estate was foreign to this way of life, and indeed repulsive. We see this in the response of Native American communities when white European men came to North America with the intention of claiming or purchasing the land. Chief Joseph of the Nez Perce said, "The country was made without lines of demarcation, and it is no man's business to divide it. . . . I never said the land was mine to do with as I chose. The one who has the right to dispose of it is the one who has created it."[16] Or, in the famous words of Chief Seattle, "How can you buy or sell the sky, the warmth of the land? The idea is strange to us. If we do not own the freshness of the air and the sparkle of the water, how can you buy them? This we know. The earth does not belong to man; man belongs to the earth."[17]

In many traditional societies, land was held communally in the sense that a particular territory was the turf of a specific community or tribe, but even here the notion of "national sovereignty" over a specific territory was foreign. It was simply that certain tracts of land were understood to be the area certain groups used for the purpose of sustaining their communal life. Both a "commons" and a "communal" view of land in traditional societies see the land as the gift of the Creator for the benefit of the

14. Hoebel, *Anthropology*, 424.
15. Ibid.
16. Quoted in Hart, *Spirit*, 43.
17. Quoted in Granberg-Michaelson, *Worldly*, 29.

community, as in Leviticus 25:18–24. "The land will yield its fruit, and you will eat your fill and live on it securely.... The land shall not be sold in perpetuity, for the land is mine; with me you are but aliens and tenants" (Lev 25:19, 23).

On the other hand, even within traditional societies it is likely that some individuals with entrepreneurial ability saw the advantages of claiming specific land for their own use. Though perhaps not formally sanctioned or recognized within the societal structure, private property held for personal enrichment has a long history. This is not altogether a negative reality. The community as a whole often benefits in the long run from entrepreneurial innovations made by gifted individuals within the community, even when those innovations initially only benefit the entrepreneur and his family. Still, land as private property seems to come with land perceived as a source of wealth. When land becomes an investment instead of being a life-sustaining gift, land comes to be viewed as private property. It is this tendency toward private ownership and the accumulation of resources that makes provisions like the Sabbath and the Jubilee legislation in the Old Testament necessary, if land is to be valued as a commons and as a communal asset.

Quite early in human history, as we have seen in earlier chapters, centralized governments or states developed in urban centers, eventually extending imperial control over the surrounding countryside. In such situations, we often see the ownership of land devolving to the imperial state through taxation, colonization, or outright conquest. We saw the process at work in chapter 5, where the land of Egypt "became Pharaoh's" and the people worked the land as tenants of Pharaoh. Throughout much of history, ordinary people more often than not worked the land as tenants for the monarchs and noblemen and agents of imperial power.

At the same time, throughout most of human history, there was simply too much land for even the largest and most greedy empire to manage. There was always room for squatters to live at the margins or edges of imperial control. Such people and communities had no title to the land, but used it as a commons to sustain their lives. Their lives were necessarily precarious, both in the sense of living from hand to mouth, but more importantly because of the constant threat of coming under the jurisdiction and control of the empire where they lived. It was not until the twentieth century that essentially all the land on earth has been claimed by one or another nation-state, making all the people within each territory subject to the policies of that state, and with the state claiming ultimate jurisdiction of the land. With the exception of Antarctica, is there a square kilometer of earth that is not claimed by some nation-state?

Still, it was not just the emergence of the nation-state that led to the triumph of private ownership of land. It was, at least in Western civilization, the emergence of capitalism as an economic system that confirmed the triumph of private property. Ironically, this has undercut the viability of holding land as private property. While the fiction of private ownership of land continues, the reality is that land holders, particularly in the United States, are beholden to the corporate powers that work hand in glove with the nation-state to guarantee an economy of unlimited growth. Indeed private landowners are exceedingly vulnerable to the constraints of corporate and state power structures. It is this, I believe, rather than any true loyalty to the principle of private property, that accounts for the resistance toward any communal patterns of land tenure. Corporate and state powers recognize communal forms of land tenure as the primary threat to their control over the land and its resources.

To be sure, our world has recently seen, as well, the disaster of organized state communalism with the emergence of the Soviet Union in the twentieth century. While the impetus toward communism was a trenchant analysis of the injustices of capitalist imperialism, the attempt to organize communal ownership of land on the basis of the imperialism of state communism was a tragic disaster, both for the land and for the people living on the land.

Within the United States, private ownership of land became the dominant pattern of land tenure, and indeed was the basis for citizenship itself. In the states that became the United States of America, voting was granted only to those men (males) who owned property.[18] While this was a democracy of sorts, it was hardly universal suffrage! What happened in North America is that the colonial powers, and later the United States itself, made claim to the land without regard for the First Nations living in the land, and then proceeded to distribute that land to colonists as private property, subject of course to the taxation and regulations of the state. The Homestead Act of 1862 is an example of this, as are the concessions granted to railway companies to make land available to settlers along the newly established rail lines.

It sounds like a good deal! The land is deeded to individual owners, who use the land on their own initiative and pass it on to their descendants, while the state benefits from the taxation and controls the use of the land through state or federal policies. In fact, it is a clever though perhaps unintentional prescription for imperial control over all the land. Individual landowners are extremely vulnerable to the corporate and state powers that grant access to the land as so-called private property. Individual landowners find it very difficult to do what they may know is best for their land because they are bound both by economic pressures imposed by corporate and state powers and by competition from their neighbors who face those same pressures.

The "rural crisis" that has characterized rural America at least since the oil embargo of the 1970s testifies to the untenability of private ownership as a system of land tenure for rural communities within an imperial context. Farmers depend for their survival on government subsidies and controls. Farmers are at the mercy of corporations that control both agricultural inputs (seeds and fertilizers and machinery and fuel) and agricultural output (commodities for a global market). Decisions for how the land is to be used are made by a technical elite in the service of the state and the corporations. The intention of the system is to extract wealth from the land in the form of global commodities for the benefit of the state and the corporation. While

---

18. Zinn, *People's History*, 82, 95.

The Call to Rural Community

maintaining the fiction of private ownership of land, farmers are in fact only laborers on behalf of the imperial powers of the state, the corporation, and the technical experts. They make no significant decisions about how the land will be used, and they and what is left of their community extract little benefit from the produce of the land, other than personal wealth for those who know how to work the system best. All the while, individual landowners are in competition with one another for land and survival on the land, which make cooperative or community efforts to resist the power of the corporate state almost impossible.

While land as private property was probably not established with the intention of maintaining imperial control, it has in fact been an incredibly effective tool in ensuring imperial control over the land by the corporations and the state. The concept of private property continues to be an almost sacred mantra in rural America. In fact, it is only when *communities* regain control over the land and decision-making about land use that the power of the corporate state can be thwarted. If we believe it is desirable for communities of people to live on the land, benefit from its use, and decide how the land and its bounty is to be used, then some form of community control over the land is required. Within the current structures of social life in North America, nonprofit community land trusts seem like the most promising vehicle for such community control over the land. In a land trust, land deeded to the trust is used for the production of the food and fiber required to sustain the local community, and its bounty is made available to meet the needs of the maximum number of people.

Land Tenure Patterns in a Traditional Mennonite Community

Like many other immigrant communities, the Mennonite pioneers, my forebears, who came to Dakota Territory in 1874 from the Ukraine benefited from the Homestead Act of 1862. Settlers laid claim to a quarter section (160 acres) of virgin prairie, which was more than they could conceivably utilize with hand labor and draft animals. After incredibly brutal and trying initial years dealing with a harsh climate, an unbroken wilderness, and an absence of any social infrastructure, these pioneers established a thriving rural community through their hard labor and the productivity of the prairie environment. Then they established the infrastructure required for community life—roads, trading centers, marketing cooperatives, schools, churches, medical services, and so on. The community originally was largely self-sustaining. Farmers worked together in the production of the food and fiber required for their families. They sold eggs and cream and some unneeded grain and animals for cash income to buy the few goods and services they could not provide for themselves.

Initially, these Mennonite settlers were not the only people laying claim to the land. A 1908 map of Turner County, South Dakota, shows that many quarter sections were claimed by non-Mennonites between the scattering of Mennonite claims.[19] By

---

19. The map can be found in Heritage Hall Museum and Archives, Freeman, SD.

the time I was growing up in the 1950s, however, almost all that land was claimed by Mennonite families, and the Mennonite East Freeman community was spreading beyond its original boundaries. I'm not sure how to account for this. I suspect it had to do with the fact that Mennonites had a strong communal, mutual aid history and identity, and that this communalism proved no match for the interspersed "English" settlers who were gradually bought out and displaced.

The pattern of land tenure in my own extended Kaufman family was as follows. My immigrant great-grandfather, Christian Kaufman, settled on a quarter section. He had three sons and three daughters. A quarter section was provided for two sons, including my grandfather, in adjacent sections, and the third son inherited the original farm. The daughters married settlers from other nearby families. My grandfather had six sons, and while all began as farmers, only one inherited the home place and only four farmed all their lives, though all stayed in the community. When my father married in 1925, he was able to purchase eighty acres within the community, which he nearly lost in the Great Depression. My father had three sons, and only one of my brothers stayed in the community, inheriting a farm from his wife's grandfather.

The problem with land as private property for the survival of the community is that a community rapidly runs out of available land. My immediate community, the East Freeman Schweitzer churches of Salem and Salem-Zion, had an initial membership of about 175, some seventy families, in 1874. This community grew rapidly until 1940, when the two churches together had about 900 members, and the membership of these churches peaked in 1970 with 1,017 members before dropping back to about 1930 levels in 2008, with about 700 members.[20]

While the situation is complex, I believe two primary factors have been at work in the decline of my home community. The first is that our farmers as private landowners fell prey, especially in the post–World War II era with the industrialization of agriculture, to the pressures of the corporate state described in the previous section. They had to compete with one another for economic survival and keep enlarging their agricultural enterprises. Those who could not compete sold out and left the community or found other employment.

But I believe that private ownership of land itself is also a factor in the decline of my community. When each new generation requires two or three additional farms to provide for the heirs, it is inevitable that the community will quickly run out of land, as happened in my community, or expand to the point where a new community must be established. This last option is the one that seems to be chosen by the Amish and conservative Mennonite communities of various types that continue to expand throughout North America, settling new rural communities, as land in established

---

20. From a membership chart in the thirteenth sermon, "Our Golden Age," in the author's series, *Roots that Nourish*.

communities becomes scarcer. Now it is these traditional Anabaptist communities that are the fastest growing segment of the Anabaptist presence in North America.[21]

In my community, what happened as the land became scarce and the community became larger is that the focus of the community shifted. Whereas the missional energy of the congregations was devoted to building the infrastructure of a strong rural community during the early decades of the twentieth century, once those institutions were established and land was becoming scarce, the churches encouraged their youth to seek an education and enter (preferably) a service profession out in the world. While this contributed greatly to the mission of the church in the world, it spelled trouble for the rural community itself. With our people becoming more and more dependent on the practices and policies of corporations and the state, the community has effectively lost control over the use of the land, just as private landowners themselves have. Currently, land in our community is often deeded to heirs who sometimes live outside the community and rent it out on terms most favorable to themselves. When land does come up for sale, it is often sold at public auction to the highest bidder, who more often than not represents the strongest competitor for corporation and state control of land.

An alternative to the private ownership of land is communal ownership, a pattern well-established in the Hutterite colonies that dot the James River valley throughout South Dakota. This communal, sectarian ownership of land has been effective in keeping the control of the land and its use in the hands of the community. However, the communalism of the colony may represent too radical a pattern to be acceptable to most people. Conflicts with neighboring communities and civil authorities as colonies expanded and multiplied reveal the threat such a pattern of land tenure represents to the dominant culture.[22]

I believe that a nonprofit, faith-based community land trust might represent the best option for a land tenure policy that could stand against the pressures of corporations and the state. It may also in our North American context be the closest we can come to the land tenure pattern described in the Old Testament. With the formation of a community land trust for agricultural purposes, individuals would be able to deed private property to the trust, guaranteeing a life income to the donor, if necessary. The land trust would specify how the land is to be used for the welfare of the community and would lease the land to those who would use it on those terms and make their livelihood from it. In this way, the community would regain access to and control over the land and its use for its own welfare and survival, while at the same time allowing opportunity for individual entrepreneurial activity on the part of those given access to the land.

This model of land tenure would have several significant consequences:

---

21. Kraybill and Hostetter, *Anabaptist World USA*, 75.
22. Ibid., 99.

- It would remove land from the speculative market as a source of personal wealth.
- It would provide a mechanism for distributing access of the land to those who need it and are willing to work it in keeping with the common good established by the land trust.
- It would remove the land from the control of corporations, the state, and its technical elites.
- It would allow communities (via the trustees of the land trust chosen by the community) to determine the best use of the land for the welfare of the community and its members.
- It would be a way of providing for the food and fiber required by the local community in sustainable ways, and also be a source of food and fiber for nearby urban residents in cities close to the land trust.

Chapter 8

Rural Community and Urban Civilization in Conflict

A King Like Other Nations (1 Sam 8:5)

The Challenge of Being an Alternative Community of Faith in God

THE ANCIENT ISRAELITES HAD the misfortune of entering Palestine about the same time that the Philistines settled on the coastal plain of Palestine. The people from whom the term Palestine was derived, the Philistines, were a military aristocracy with superior iron technology bent on being the overlords of Palestine. The Philistines became Israel's persistent thorn in the flesh, harassing them and making the Israelites dependent upon them for iron agricultural implements. The feudal hierarchy of the Philistines was characteristic of the Canaanite city-states dominating the landscape of Palestine.

Developing and sustaining an egalitarian, agriculturally-based counter-culture in this context was a major challenge for the Israelites. Not only had they to contend with their own propensity to compete with one another for scarce resources, but they had also to contend with the continual depredations of the city-states among whom they lived. At last the Israelites were ready to give it up! "Appoint for us, then, a king to govern us, like other nations," they pleaded with Samuel, the last of the judges (1 Sam 8:5). Samuel was loath to accede to this request knowing that it represented an abandonment of trust in God. He warned them of the taxation and conscription inevitably associated with the royal system of governance. But it seemed an acceptable trade-off for the Israelites—their freedom in exchange for order and security, the rule of law to curb their own greed, and the power of a standing army to deal with external threats.

Assured that God would allow these people to make this choice despite the betrayal of trust it represented, Samuel acquiesced to the request, and the Israelite monarchy was initiated. Within a generation, a dynastic empire in the line of David effectively made Israel a regional power dominating all of Palestine, and under Solomon, Israel itself reached imperial status for a time, a power to be reckoned with in the world of the Fertile Crescent.

The Biblical Story

The Challenge of Living as an Alternative Community of Faith in a Dominant Culture

In this book, I am putting forward the thesis that God's intention for humankind, as reflected in the biblical witness, is to live as dispersed rural communities across the face of the earth, caring for creation, living justly with one another, and worshipping God the Creator. This original intention of God was frustrated by human sin, our refusal to live within the limitations and constraints of our mortal creaturehood and our attempts to be like God. The result of human sin was the development of urban civilization, in which powers of evil were unleashed more intensely upon the earth. We have seen how the sinful human tendencies towards idolatry, oppression, and exploitation are increased exponentially within urban civilization with the hierarchical power arrangements, economic domination, and dynamic technological innovations that enhance the human ability to shape the natural world of God's creation.

Not content to abandon this good creation of planet Earth, God began remedial efforts to redeem this world and the human family now itself subject to the domination powers of evil. In the biblical framework, God's first effort in the flood involved the forceful destruction of a world caught up in evil powers (Genesis 6–8). But after beholding the devastation of the flood, God resolved never again to resort to this arbitrary use of divine power. The rest of the Bible is, if you will, the story of God's next and current plan to redeem the earth and its life. By making the divine presence and intention known to ordinary people, God called out local communities to a sojourn of faith and trust in God, living within the context and structures of the dominant cultures of idolatry, exploitation, and oppression that had come to rule the world. In this way, it seems, God hoped to mitigate the destructive character of urban civilization and provide a model of God's intention for the human family.

The first efforts to form alternative communities of faith living within the dominant culture, as recounted in the Old Testament, were necessarily tentative and experimental. It is no easy thing to be a countercultural community that lives against the grain of the dominant culture in which it lives. This chapter will explore the dynamics and challenges, both internal and external, of living as countercultural communities of faith within a dominant culture.

Israel's entrance into Canaan and emergence as a distinct community of faith took place around 1200 BCE. The next century, as the Israelite tribal confederacy took root in the hill country of Canaan, saw a dramatic decline of Egyptian imperial power in Canaan. Egyptian territory was being invaded by "Peoples of the Sea," including Philistines, and though Ramses III (ca. 1175–1144) succeeded in repelling invasions into Egypt proper, Egypt was left exhausted and weak. Egyptian hegemony over Canaanite city-states waned, and these small city-states were left to feud among

Rural Community and Urban Civilization in Conflict

themselves. Egyptians allowed some of the invading sea peoples, the Philistines, to settle on the southern coastal plain of Canaan in the five city-states of Ashkelon, Ashdod, Gath, Gaza, and Ekron, as nominal Egyptian vassals. This was about a generation after the Israelites themselves entered Canaan and began to settle there and emerge as a people.[1]

The Philistines, who gave their name to Canaan in the form of Palestine, were probably an Indo-European people "displaced from their original homelands as part of the extensive population movements of the latter half of the second millennium B.C. in the E Mediterranean and SE European area."[2] The Bible notes that they came from Crete (Caphtor) (Amos 9:7; Jer 47:4). Cherethites and Pelethites (Cretans and Philistines) appear in 2 Samuel 8:18 as part of King David's mercenary army under the leadership of Benaiah. If this seems strange, we must remember that David himself served for a time as a military captain to the Philistine lord of Gath, Achish, before he became king and while he was fleeing from King Saul (1 Samuel 27–29).

The Philistines might best be described as a military aristocracy. After entering Canaan, they rapidly adopted the Canaanite language, culture, and religion. What they brought to Canaan was their "superb military technology."[3] They fought using chariots and horses, as well as heavily armed infantry, some of great stature. Remember Goliath (1 Samuel 17)? Most of all they brought to late–Bronze Age Canaan the technology of ironworking, which made weapons highly superior to the bronze weapons of Canaan.[4] Once again, a new technology is introduced, and introduced first as a weapon of war! Indeed, having a monopoly on ironworking guaranteed that the technological edge it gave to the Philistines in battle remained with them. The Israelites had to go to their enemies, the Philistines, in order to purchase iron agricultural implements for their daily labor, as we are told in 1 Samuel 13:19–22.

Though the Israelites settled in Canaan a generation or two before the Philistines, and were perhaps the stronger group culturally, the Philistines turned out to be the major threat to the fledgling Israelite presence in Canaan. The Philistine threat emerges most strongly in 1 Samuel, where beginning in chapter 4 the Philistines attacked Israel in the mid–eleventh century BCE. Initially Israel was defeated and the ark was captured. Later, in chapter 7, under the leadership of the last judge, Samuel, the Philistines were defeated, only to reappear as a major threat to Israel during the reign of Israel's first king, Saul.

However, though the Philistines emerged as the strongest external threat to Israel's early existence as a people, they were by no means the only threat. The period of the judges is filled with stories of conflicts with Israel's new neighbors—the Canaanites on the coastal plains of Canaan, and Israel's neighbors to the east and south and north,

---

1. Bright, *History*, 152–53.
2. Greenfield, "Philistines," 3:792.
3. Gottwald, *Tribes*, 414.
4. Ibid., 415.

as well. Many of these were peoples assumed to be related to Israel. The Amalekites (Judg 3:13; 6:3) were descendants of Esau (Gen 36:12); the Moabites (Judg 3:12–30) and Ammonites (Judges 10) south and east of Canaan were descendants of Lot (Gen 19:36–38); and the Midianites (Judges 6–8) were descendants of Abraham through his wife Keturah (Gen 25:2). Once again the primary threat from the Midianites was the result of a new technological innovation—the development of camel domestication, which allowed for mobility and swift striking power in military excursions.[5]

The book of Judges describes the people of Israel's encounters with these various peoples, and outlines Israel's response. With the extended family/clan/tribal structure of Israelite life, when a particular tribe was under threat or attack, the other tribes were rallied in the defense of the tribe, usually by a charismatic leader, such as Gideon (Judg 6:33–35). However, the responses to these threats were not necessarily military, at least as conventionally understood. In Gideon's case, the troops were cut from 32,000 to 300, and the Midianites were routed through a nonviolent nighttime demonstration (Judges 7).

Nevertheless, the continual threat to Israel's existence from her neighbors was serious and ongoing and debilitating for the Israelites. They were being asked to live in a very vulnerable way, even in their highland enclaves in the hill country of Canaan. They were called, indeed, to trust God for deliverance, rather than to rely on tribal alliances or military might. In the view of the compilers of Judges, therein lay the crux of the matter. For instead of trusting God, the people of Israel kept resorting to the idolatrous worship of their neighbors, which sanctioned the power politics of the day. That was the reason they were always being threatened. The pattern is described in Judges 2:16–23. God left Israel's neighbors in place as a test for Israel's faith, to see "whether or not they would take care to walk in the way of the Lord as their ancestors did" (Judg 2:22).

So we find that the real threat to Israel's existence was not Israel's hostile neighbors. The real threat was internal. Did the Israelites really believe in their own revolution? Did they really believe that decentralized local communities can thrive in the midst of urban civilization? Could they trust that God would show them the nonviolent strategies to stand against the dominant cultures around them? Their resort to pagan idolatry, the worship of the dominant culture's gods of power, boded ill for their future as an alternative community of faith.

This does not even consider the other internal struggles they had as decentralized communities of faith—struggles within and between extended families, clans, and tribes over access to the land, and struggles over political and religious leadership for the symbols of the "sociocultural cohesiveness" that had marked their emergence as a people in the thirteenth century BCE. It required an immense investment of time, energy and sacrifice to maintain their life as an alternative community of faith amidst the dominant cultures of their age.

5. Landes, "Midian," 3:376.

Compromises with the Dominant Culture

In the previous chapter, we saw that the marks of early Israel were sociocultural cohesiveness, socioeconomic egalitarianism, and sociopolitical decentralization. Israel's struggle as an alternative community of faith was how to maintain the first two characteristics without resorting to the centralization of political power. It isn't easy for a community to keep its unique identity and to share resources equitably without resort to the hierarchical use of power.

So it's no surprise that late in the eleventh century BCE, as the judge Samuel was aging and his own sons were shown to be corrupt in the exercise of justice (1 Sam 8:1–3), the Israelites came to Samuel demanding a king—centralized political power. "Appoint for us, then, a king to govern us, like other nations" (1 Sam 8:5). It is no surprise that Israel's compromise with reality came in the area of political hegemony. However skeptically Samuel or we might view this request, it was not intended to be an abandonment of Israel's core identity and commitment to an egalitarian rural economy. The Israelite elders who made this request of Samuel had no intention of abandoning their faith in God. It was just that they had grown exceedingly weary of the struggle to maintain their way of life without a centralized political authority.

So it may be that the real compromise the Israelites were engaged in when they asked for a king was a loss of understanding their core identity as decentralized autonomous communities of faith. It was not their intention to abandon their worship of God, though Samuel was right in seeing that as the practical result. It *was* their intention or wish to become like the nations around them. Starting as subversive cells of revolt against the exercise of coercive political authority in the city-states of Canaan, the Israelite had by now, two centuries later, achieved a sense of national (ethnic) identity that overshadowed their radical roots. Once they had only been interested in establishing viable communities of faith in the marginal land of the hill country of Canaan. Now they were interested in establishing and maintaining a national (ethnic) identity as a large, politically self-conscious people. They wanted to become "like other nations" around them. They wanted to become one of the *goyim* (nations) among whom they lived, and in the process they risked losing the sense of being God's *am* (God's holy people).[6]

When the preservation of cultural identity, understood as ethnicity or nationality, becomes more important than the concrete life of the community as the face-to-face, local network of relationships, then the transition is being made from a rural to an urban mindset. So far as we can tell, Israel in the period of the judges had no interest in the building of cities, although many undoubtedly worked and traded and lived in the Canaanite cities around them. Israel did maintain shrines in this period at Gilgal (Josh 4:20), Shechem (Joshua 24), Bethel (Judg 20:26–28), and ultimately,

---

6. Hamlin, "Nations," 3:515.

in Samuel's time, at Shiloh (1 Sam 1:3).[7] However, none of these cities emerged as a capital for Israel, and indeed, it isn't even clear that they ceased being Canaanite cities. Norman Gottwald sees Shechem as a neutral Canaanite city, with a Canaanite shrine within the city wall and the Israelite shrine outside the city.[8] However, this was soon to change, as a king requires a capital from which to reign. Israel's request for a king indicated that Israel was ready to move from being an agrarian movement to an urban power. The rural towns Israel had built up over two centuries now had to be defended by the power of an urban center.

Israel's first king, Saul, had his very modest seat of power at Gibeah, his home town just north of Jerusalem.[9] But Gibeah was a rural town, not an urban center. Furthermore, Saul functioned in a kind of transitional manner between the judges and the monarchy. His administration had little centralized bureaucracy, and the small personal band of armed retainers Saul gathered around him hardly qualified as a standing army. Despite some initial military successes against the Philistine threat, the reign of Saul ended in tragedy, both for Saul himself and for the Israelite people, in war with the Philistines (1 Samuel 29–31).

It was under the much more gifted political leadership of David that Israel emerged as a nation, fulfilling the people's desire. After Saul's tragic death in battle against the Philistines, David was proclaimed king over Judah in Hebron (2 Sam 2:1–4). Seven years later, after the death of Ishbaal, Saul's son (2 Samuel 3–4), David was anointed king over all Israel (2 Sam 5:3). Early in David's reign, David succeeded in capturing the Jebusite city of Jerusalem, and he made this city his capital (2 Sam 5:6–10). Eventually David brought the ark of the Lord into Jerusalem, transferring to his political capital the religious sanction previously dispersed in a number of religious sanctuaries (2 Samuel 6). David's desire to build a permanent temple in his capital was frustrated by God and the prophet Nathan (2 Samuel 7), but was fulfilled in the reign of his son Solomon (1 Kings 5–6). Now Israel was not just a nation like other nations, but through King David's military victories and King Solomon's administration, Israel became an empire in her own right, ruling over nations from the Euphrates River in the north to the border of Egypt in the south (1 Kgs 4:20–21). The tenth century BCE can well be called the age of the Israelite empire!

The Cost of Compromise

Deuteronomy 17 anticipates the possibility that God's people will want to have a king after they have "taken possession of it [the land] and settled in it" (Deut 17:14). Already in that passage God granted the people the freedom to choose a king, so long as he belonged to the covenant community (Deut 17:15). However, the to-be king is

---

7. Gottwald, *Tribes*, 348–49.
8. Ibid., 563–67.
9. Bright, *History*, 169.

warned not to enslave the people as happened in Egypt by acquiring a large military and a large court. Instead, the king is to be given a copy of the covenant code (Deut 17:18), and he is to spend all his days studying the *torah* (Deut 17:19). Frankly it is hard to imagine a king worthy of the name who would devote himself to this task. Yet were such a political ruler to emerge, what a blessing it would be!

In the same vein, Samuel is instructed to warn the people, in 1 Samuel 8, about the consequences of their desire to have a king. There will be conscription of both sons and daughters for military as well as court service (1 Sam 8:11–13). There will be confiscation of land and taxation for the support of the royal court and its officials (1 Sam 8:14–17). But, God says, when all this happens to the people and they cry out for deliverance, they shouldn't expect God to answer (1 Sam 8:18)! When you choose to have centralized political power, there is no turning back! You have to live with the consequences of that choice!

Of course, what this really means is the loss of local control over the land and its use. Taxation and conscription radically challenge local sovereignty over the land. The local community, or in Israel's case the father's house (*bēth-'av*), which had been the primary arbiter of land use in ancient Israel, would no longer have that autonomy. It would now be subject to the dictates of the central political authority. The needs of the nation (*ethnos, goy*) are placed ahead of the welfare of the community. National or ethnic (cultural) identity would now take precedence over communal welfare.

However benevolently exercised, local communities would experience the dictates of centralized power as an oppressive force in their lives. The central bureaucracy will always extend its power and influence into the decision-making and the functioning of the local community. Local communities will always find themselves in a struggle for survival as they seek to provide for their welfare. Not only will they be in a possibly healthy competition with each other, but they will together be required to support a larger cause. For that cause, local communities will yield up their offspring and their wealth, all for the welfare of the nation.

Of course, a major consequence of the centralization of power is also the co-optation of the symbols of religious faith to the service of political authority. The very faith that had been the inspiration for resistance to the dominant culture of centralized authority now is used to sanction that power. Perhaps this is the reason God professes a reluctance to answer the people when they cry out under the oppression of their king (1 Sam 8:18). It is explicitly the reason God is reluctant to have David build him a house in Jerusalem, in 2 Samuel 7:5–7. God understands that David's intention in building a temple for God, however nobly expressed, is to institutionalize and confine God's presence and influence to the service of the state.

What we've been describing in this chapter is the emergence of the dominant culture of urban civilization within the life of a people who had previously eschewed the political hierarchy of urban civilization and indeed had seen resistance to that system as their reason for being a distinct community of faith. Urban civilization emerged in history as the consequence of the development of urban centers reliant upon the surplus agricultural produce of their settings. It is fascinating to see how urban civilization is rationalized and sought after among the very people who had previously based the reason for their existence on resistance to such a way of life. They thought that in exchange for security from their enemies and for the benefits of a centralized hierarchical system to curb their own internal conflicts over land and resources, it was justifiable and even necessary to adopt the ways of the dominant cultures of the nations among whom they lived. Indeed, such has been the conclusion of many people of faith, not only in the Bible, but throughout human history. The struggle between rural community and urban civilization is also a religious struggle between those who believe that hierarchical power is required for the survival of the nation and those who stake their existence on resistance to that power.

The emergence of Israel as a nation marks a distinct turning point in the unfolding of God's plan to restore the human family to its original divine purpose. There is no turning back from this point for people of faith. People of faith will henceforth live in the tension between those who own the radical roots of their religious faith in resistance to the dominant culture of urban civilization and those who appeal to those same symbols of religious faith to sanction their resort to political power and domination.

What sets these two perspectives apart is the ultimate objective each aims to preserve. The counterculture radicals seek to preserve the welfare of the local community in the face of the dominant culture of hierarchical power. Those who choose the hierarchical power of the state place the value of the nation or *ethnos* as a large group over the independence of the local community. If nationhood—whether defined in terms of ethnicity, religion, race, or nationality—is valued more than community, then the resort to centralized hierarchical political power (i.e., urban civilization) is inevitable. If the welfare of the local community is valued more than the survival of the nation, then it is possible to maintain alternative communities of faith living in resistance to the dominant culture.

Establishment Faith versus Alternative Community of Faith

In 311 CE, the Roman emperor of the east, Galerius, grudgingly proclaimed an edict of toleration for Christians after the persecutions he was visiting upon them failed to have much effect. Two years later, Constantine and Licinius, caesars in their own right, proclaimed another edict of toleration for Christians in Milan. A bit earlier, on October 28, 312 CE, Constantine continued his rise to power in a decisive battle with his main rival, Maxentius. In that battle, Constantine is alleged to have placed the Greek symbol for Christ (*chi/rho*, the first two letters for Christ) on the helmets and shields of his soldiers as a result of a dream that declared, "By this sign you will conquer." Constantine credited Christianity with his victory and rise to power, and increasingly became the benefactor of the church. Finally, in 323 CE, Constantine defeated his former ally, Licinius, and emerged as the sole emperor of Rome.[10] Christianity was now not only a legal religion within the Roman Empire, but increasingly the favored and official religion of the empire. Indeed, Constantine became the sponsor for the First Ecumenical Council of the church at Nicaea in May 325 CE, which resulted in the Nicene Creed, defining orthodox Christian faith in the face of the Arian heresy.[11]

Like early Israel, Christian faith emerged as a countercultural movement of subversive communities challenging the hierarchical power of the Roman Empire, as we shall see later in this book. This accounts for the sometimes severe persecution visited upon some Christians in the Roman Empire during the first three centuries. Yet in less than three centuries, Christianity became the official religion of the Roman Empire, with its primary symbol, the cross, co-opted to bless the endeavors of those seeking imperial power.

It would be easy to conclude, as Mennonites have often done, that the Constantinian synthesis of church and state—political power backed up with religious sanction—represents the fall of the church. It is easy to conclude that David and Constantine represent the cynical co-optation of religious symbols in the service of imperial power, and to question whether either had a genuine religious sensibility. However, in the case of David we are led to believe that he was "a man after God's own heart" (1 Sam 13:14), and the same man who co-opted the faith of early Israel for the establishment of the Israelite empire is credited with the inspiration if not the authorship of many of the Psalms! And while Constantine delayed receiving baptism until he was on his deathbed in 337 CE,[12] the piety and benevolence of his mother, Helen, in exploring and restoring the sites associated with Christian history in Palestine are legendary.

The conflict here is between two disparate visions of religious faith, one a subversive movement seeking to be an alternative community of faith, and the other an establishment faith designed to sanction and bless the established order of hierarchical power. As indicated earlier in this chapter, it is counterproductive to frame this conflict as one of true versus false faith. Not just the leaders who co-opt religious symbols, but more importantly the religious faithful who favor the establishment of religion, genuinely desire to be faithful to God no less than those committed to the subversive countercultural vision of religious faith.

Of course, early Israel and early Christianity were not the first religions to be co-opted to serve the interests of imperial power. It is inherent in imperial power itself to co-opt the religious symbols of its culture to sanction and bless imperial aims. One of the first instances of this blending of "church and state" is found in Genesis 47, as we saw in chapter 5. There, the land of the priests was exempted from royal control

10. Walker, *History*, 99–102.
11. Ibid., 108.
12. Ibid., 110.

and the priests themselves lived under Pharaoh's beneficence in exchange for their sanctioning of imperial power (Gen 47:22).

What makes this so chilling in the case of early Israel and early Christianity is that these two religious traditions both had their origin as specifically alternative communities of faith, countercultural movements designed to bear an alternative vision of God's intention for the human family. That's why in both cases there is such a strong sense of "being sold out" when they turn into an establishment faith sanctioning imperial power. So if it isn't helpful to see this as a true versus a false expression of faith, how are we to understand it?

What has often been overlooked in each case is the question of the character and identity of the community itself. This is not a struggle for who holds the right faith in God. It is a conflict about the nature of the communal entity with which one identifies. The imperial church defines and understands peoplehood in terms of ethnicity or nationality—those large groups that comprise one's cultural identity. The subversive church defines and understands peoplehood in terms of face-to-face communal groups united by a common vision of commitment to divine reality (God) and resistance to imperial power.

The rub comes in the fact that the subversive church can rarely divorce itself from the imperial church. However committed persons or communities may be to the communal vision of faithfulness to God and resistance to imperial power, ethnic or national group identity continues to be or to become a part of their identity. They rightly value their ethnic heritage and their national identity as factors in their identity. When that ethnic/national identity is threatened, it is very difficult to resist rising to its defense. When a religious movement such as early Israel or early Christianity becomes established and begins to form an ethnic or national identity, the communal identity based on faith commitments and resistance to imperial power is undermined.

Consider if you will the various possible ways we can define our identity. I reside in the rural community of Freeman, South Dakota, where I was born and raised. I am a son and brother, a husband and father and grandfather. I am a member of a local congregation by virtue of Christian baptism. I am an ordained pastor credentialed by Central Plains Mennonite Conference to serve congregations in Mennonite Church USA and Canada, and I hold a Master of Divinity degree preferred for pastors credentialed in this way. I have a Swiss and Low German ethno-linguistic heritage. I am a citizen of the United States of America. I am a human being of the species *Homo sapiens*. I am one of many life forms on planet Earth, made of the stuff of the earth, the matter (atoms and molecules and chemicals) of which all things consist. The planet on which I live is part of the solar system, with the sun being one of many stars in the Milky Way galaxy, which is one of many galaxies that comprise the universe. These statements define my identity by origin and residence (community), family roles, religious affiliation, ethnic heritage, vocational/educational credentials, citizenship, and biological origin, as well as planetary and solar and galactic location.

Given the limitations of our mortal creaturehood, only the first three statements are relevant in terms of daily, face-to-face relationships. The other definitions of my identity are cultural constructs. While they shape my identity in profound ways, they are largely beyond the scope of my daily activity. Whenever I devote myself to any of these larger cultural constructs, I uproot myself from the local community where I reside. This is why I, for instance, have lived and worked in four different congregations in four different communities, because my life was devoted to a career in Christian pastoral ministry. It is why, for instance, those who devote themselves to the nation-state find themselves fighting purportedly in its defense in Iraq and Afghanistan far from the communities where they and their families reside. This doesn't mean people don't have local communities and families. We all live somewhere for as long as we live. But there is a huge difference between devoting yourself to the welfare of the community in which you reside and devoting yourself to your ethnic or national or vocational or religious identity. In modern, urban civilization, the daily lives of most people are devoted to the cultural constructs that define their identity, and they seem oblivious to the welfare of the community in which they reside.

When you devote yourself to the local community where you reside, you devote yourself to the welfare of those you love. You devote yourself to the welfare of all the members of your community, for your welfare is bound up with theirs. Indeed, you devote yourself to the welfare and sustainability of the whole natural order where you live, for if you destroy the ecology that sustains the life of your community, you destroy yourself and those you love.

On the other hand, when you are devoted to any of the cultural constructs that define your identity, you will inevitably be required to damage and harm local communities somewhere, including likely your own. The perpetuation or defense of your ethnic or religious or national or vocational identity separates you from those of other ethnic, religious, national, or vocational identities. Those with other identities become threats to your own identity. In defense of your own identity, you will be required to act in ways that harm or damage others.

I have no desire to eradicate or annul any of the markers of my identity. Each of them is important in defining who I am. But whether I am the pastor of the church or the president of the nation, the only way I can keep those culturally constructed forms of identity from visiting harm or damage on others is to remain committed to the welfare of my local community. Think how such a consideration would affect the decision-making of a president of a corporation producing weapons or a senator considering foreign policy or a national president responsible for the deployment of troops to a foreign land. Or, closer to home, think how such a consideration affects the decision-making of pastors of congregations, superintendents and teachers of local schools, farmers caring for their land, or mayors of towns and villages. Whenever the welfare of the community to which one belongs or in which one resides is the priority, the decisions one makes are quite different than if one considers only the institutional identity itself. Choices that serve the welfare of one's own community will also serve the welfare of other communities near and far, while choices made in the interests of one's cultural identity will be destructive of both one's own community and that of others.

I long for a world in which the unique cultural identity of each person is valued and respected and honored as much as I value and respect and honor my own cultural identity. I long for a world in which local communities value and respect and honor the cultural identity of everyone who resides and chooses to live in that locality, and in which everyone in that community regardless of their cultural identity works for the welfare of the community. I long for a world in which persons responsible for maintaining the markers of cultural identity, beginning with pastors like myself, make decisions based on the welfare of the local community where they live instead of being governed by allegiance to their particular cultural identity.

The Struggle of Mennonite Churches to Be Countercultural Communities of Faith

Christianity began as a strongly communal movement. In the letter to Titus, Paul wrote to his young coworker on the island of Crete, directing him to "appoint elders in every town" (Titus 1:5). Here we see a process of "Christianization" in which a Christian presence was established in every town and village with the intention of bringing the good news of Jesus into the daily life of every local place. The central place of the Greek Orthodox Church and priest in every village and parish of Crete today still bears witness to the pattern of Christian presence apparently envisioned by Paul in the book of Titus. This pattern of Christian presence demonstrates the subversive character of the church as a local presence planted in every local community, in contrast to the later imperial presence of the church imposed upon the population by the powers that be.

Anabaptist Mennonites have retained the strong communal heritage of early Christian faith, but it took on a slightly different character in the Anabaptist Mennonite experience, at least after the initial decades of Mennonite history. Instead of bringing the Anabaptist presence into every town and village, which may have happened in the original movement, Mennonites have typically became absorbed in establishing internal communal boundaries over against "the world" outside. In other words, the congregation became the primary, face-to-face community for Mennonites. Mennonite migrations tended to be migrations of congregations, who together moved from one setting to another. Mennonites tended to settle and live as congregations. They built community by establishing the institutions and infrastructure required for communal life. This is in contrast to the model outlined by Paul in Titus, where community is built by bringing the Christian presence to bear on existing communal structures and institutions.

This model of communal life has been effective and strongly missional in subcultural groups like the Amish and the Hutterites, who established countercultural communities within the dominant society. The results have been much more ambiguous in mainstream rural Mennonite communities that acculturated to the dominant culture. In these communities, the church came to have primarily an exclusive ethnic identity. These churches became absorbed in defining and defending their institutional identity alongside the competing identities of the dominant culture. In doing so, these congregations themselves lost the sense of being a subversive, countercultural presence either as a congregation or within their communities.

My perception is that urban congregations of the Mennonite Church in North America are today the most effective models of subversive, countercultural community formation within the Mennonite Church. Today's Anabaptist Mennonite urban congregations tend to draw together diverse people into tightly knit congregations. Not having the built-in support structures of a traditional rural community, urban congregations form a surrogate community for mutual care and support. Members are not withdrawn from the world, but instead become the subversive leaven of Christian transformation within the existing structures and institutions of the city. People are drawn into the congregation not primarily for ethnic reasons but because of the desire to participate in the communal life and relationships engendered by the congregation and to affiliate with the values of the community.

Rural Mennonite congregations like those in the community where I live can learn from their urban cousins about becoming a subversive, countercultural presence in their context. Within the context of shattered rural communities, where the institutions and the infrastructures of communal life are all but dead, a good bit of rural redevelopment or revitalization is required. However, it would be a mistake for rural congregations like these to rebuild infrastructure focused on their own institutional life. Instead, rural congregations should invest their lives in the subversive re-creation of self-sustaining rural communities in the midst of urban imperialism. This may not lead to the growth of rural congregations, but it will lead to their revitalization. Indeed, rural congregations like those in my community have the entrepreneurial skills, the material resources, and the traditional wisdom to become effective agents of change within their rural communities, if they choose to do so.

It is difficult to say what shape this may take practically speaking, but we can predict some directions. It will mean congregational involvement in local food systems, both to sustain the rural community itself and as a source of food for nearby urban centers. It will mean ecumenical participation with other Christian and traditional communities in the formation of faith-based land trusts and other ventures designed to regain local control over local land and resources. It will mean developing practical rural/urban congregational partnerships designed to strengthen the communal life of both rural and urban congregations. It will mean becoming communities of welcome for new rural residents who are driven out or opting out of urban centers. While this may involve the loss of traditional "ethnic Mennonite" identity, it can be seen as a means of enriching the cultural identity of the local congregation!

The dominant North American Mennonite experience in the twentieth century paralleled the experience of the Israelites in the time of Samuel. Rural Mennonite congregations began to feel that it was too difficult to maintain a countercultural, subversive stance vis-à-vis the dominant culture. They wanted to become a "nation" (church) like the others around them. Yes, even the movement toward a professional pastor for every church reflected the Israelite desire for a king. They wanted to become an acceptable Protestant denomination with professional pastors to lead them. It's not all bad! It surely has given me a good life, as one of those professional pastors. At the same time, it has led congregations like those I have served into the stagnant pool of institutional maintenance, where the preservation of the institution takes precedence over the transformation (welfare) of the community. There is no future for the community in maintaining cultural identity alone! The only future we can hope for is the transformation of the community.

CHAPTER 9

The Triumph of Empire and the Persistence of the Rural Vision

The LORD Forbid That I Should Give You My Ancestral Inheritance (1 Kgs 21:3)

The Prophetic Challenge to Urban Civilization

WHILE THE IMPERIAL AMBITIONS of the Davidic dynasty foundered with the rebellion of the northern tribes of Israel against the rule of Solomon's son Rehoboam (1 Kings 12), the die was cast. The ancient Israelites would henceforth live under the rule of imperial ambitions and pretensions, with the northern kingdom of Israel becoming the primary heir of those ambitions; ironically, in view of its separation from Judah as a peasant-inspired rebellion. Meanwhile, the kingdom of Judah began its long journey toward exile under the truncated Davidic dynasty.

Yet the rural vision persisted, inspired and inflamed by the prophetic movement, a call to preserve the local, agrarian communities of faith in the face of royal demands. The incident of Naboth refusing the sale of his ancestral land at Jezreel to King Ahab in 1 Kings 21 is a prime example. Who does Naboth think he is, refusing to submit to royal whims? Doesn't he realize he is in a position to drive a hard bargain with the king to his own advantage? But Naboth is driven by the ancient notion that the land on which he lived had been entrusted to his ancestors and to him by God, and that he was responsible for the welfare of this land. He could no more sell this ancestral land for personal profit than betray his own kin into slavery!

Though Naboth paid for his stubborn adherence to the rural vision with his life, he was vindicated by Elijah's subsequent pronouncement of judgment upon Ahab and his queen Jezebel. The story reflects the tensions that arise when people in local communities are confronted by the imperial demands of the dominant culture. It is possible for a local culture to survive "beneath the radar" of the empire, with some accommodation to imperial power and pretensions. But when push comes to shove, the empire has its way—at least until God's way and the word of the prophet prevails.

Healing God's Earth

The Biblical Story

The Triumph of Empire

The previous chapter described the formation of the Israelite empire through the military conquests of David, the establishment of Jerusalem as a political capital, and the cooptation of Israelite worship to the service of the state. The opening chapters of 1 Kings describe the flowering of the Israelite empire under the administrative rule of David's son Solomon. Solomon's administrative structure for the united kingdom of Israel is described in 1 Kings 4:1-19. Although there were twelve administrative districts, these twelve districts no longer conformed to the old tribal structures and boundaries. While ordinary people surely still identified themselves by tribal lineage, this identification was largely irrelevant to their citizenship in the kingdom of Israel. Imperial identity always trumps local, communal identity. The summary statement of 1 Kings 4:20-21 describes the ideal conditions and extent of Solomon's empire. "Judah and Israel were as numerous as the sand by the sea; they ate and drank and were happy. Solomon was sovereign over all the kingdoms from the Euphrates to the land of the Philistines, even to the border of Egypt; they brought tribute and served Solomon all the days of his life."

Such an empire can be sustained only at great cost. The first two chapters of 1 Kings describe Solomon's succession to the throne, complete with the intrigue of displacing the more rightful heir, Adonijah, who was eventually put to death (1 Kgs 2:25) along with David's general Joab and other remnants of the royal court loyal to David. Though the empire had been established largely through David's military conquests, the empire was held together by a series of alliances with the vassal petty kingdoms over which Solomon ruled. These alliances were usually sealed by the marriage of princesses from these kingdoms to Solomon, most notably the Egyptian Pharaoh's daughter (1 Kgs 3:1). But Solomon also married princesses of Moab, Ammon, Edom, Sidon, and Hittite city-states (1 Kgs 11:1), a practice seen as the reason for God's judgment on the united kingdom of Solomon (1 Kgs 11:4-13).

Perhaps Solomon's most significant alliance was with the Phoenician king of Tyre, Hiram, from the Lebanon, who provided the cedars for Solomon's immense building projects in Jerusalem (1 Kgs 5:1-12). We are told that it took Solomon a mere seven years to build the magnificent temple in Jerusalem, and an additional thirteen years to complete his own palace (1 Kgs 6:37—7:1)! Of course, these building projects could not have been accomplished without forced labor. Solomon conscripted a force of 30,000 men to build the temple (1 Kgs 5:13). First Kings 9:20-22 tries to soften the blow by insisting that the conscripted laborers were only from the conquered Canaanites incorporated into the kingdom and did not include Israelites themselves, but such a distinction is not made in the fifth chapter. First Kings 4:22-28 lists the daily provisions needed to sustain the royal court in Jerusalem, along with the standing army.

The army of chariots and horses is described in 1 Kings 10:26–29, which were housed in the fortified cities built and listed in 1 Kings 9:15–19. Clearly the maintenance of the empire placed a major burden on the people of Israel, while also securing their security and prosperity.

It is then no surprise that the united kingdom of Israel would be difficult to sustain. Indeed, immediately after Solomon's death, his son Rehoboam failed to hold the empire together. The united kingdom was always a fragile alliance of Judah with the northern tribes of Israel, and after the death of Solomon, the northern tribes of Israel rejected Rehoboam as their king when he failed to lighten the load of taxation and conscription they had endured under Solomon. So Rehoboam was forced to rule only over Judah, the traditional base of the Davidic dynasty. Meanwhile Jeroboam, one of Solomon's officials who had been exiled to Egypt, was made king over the northern tribes of Israel. This story told in 1 Kings 12 is replete with irony, as Rehoboam could not believe his rule was being rejected until the people of Israel stoned Rehoboam's taskmaster of forced labor to death. Only then did Rehoboam flee to Jerusalem in ignominy (1 Kgs 12:18).

The division of the united kingdom also was the death knell for the Israelite empire, which pretty much disintegrated.[1] Israel and Judah would thenceforth continue as more typical small kingdoms in Canaan, sometimes in alliance with each other against larger threats, but more often in competition and at odds even with each other over power and territory. Ironically, though it was the peasants and landowners of Israel who rebelled against Rehoboam, it was the northern kingdom of Israel that aspired more often to an imperial presence in Canaan, especially during the years of the Omride Dynasty of the mid–ninth century BCE, and again in the mid–eighth century BCE during the reign of Jeroboam II (786–746 BCE).[2]

We might think that with Israel's empire disintegrated, the small kingdoms of Israel and Judah would have lost their imperial character. But imperial identity and character as a system of domination and control is not so easily relinquished. You might say, "Once an empire, always an empire," at least as long as the kingdom or political entity that was an empire survives. The habits and practices and methods of empire persist even when the political entity in question no longer has anything more than a pretension of imperial reality.

So it is that imperial reality continued to be the experience of the northern kingdom of Israel, even after Israel's peasants threw off the yoke of the Davidic dynasty. The first king of Israel, Jeroboam, first established his capital at Shechem, an ancient cultic center in Canaan (1 Kgs 12:25). However, Jeroboam's main claim to fame, and the occasion for God's displeasure according to 1 Kings 14:4–16, was the establishment of shrines for the worship of Yahweh in Dan and at Bethel as alternatives to the worship of Yahweh at Solomon's temple in Jerusalem (1 Kgs 12:25–33). Jeroboam surely had

1. Bright, *History*, 211.
2. Ibid., 237–39.

no alternative politically than to do this. But the lack of an established dynasty that marked Jeroboam's reign was indicative of the shaky start that the kingdom of Israel faced. There were five Israelite kings between 928 and 882 BCE, including Jeroboam I, but none were able to establish a dynastic succession, and there was continual political upheaval, with coups and counter-coups being the story of the day (1 Kings 15–16).[3]

That began to change when Omri became king in 882 BCE, the founder of the Omride Dynasty in Israel. Though his reign was relatively short, just twelve years (1 Kgs 16:23), it was a very able and effective reign.[4] Omri purchased the hill of Samaria and built his capital there (1 Kgs 16:24). Omri and his son Ahab, who ruled from 873 to 852 BCE, made an alliance with the Phoenician king of Tyre when Ahab married the Phoenician princess, Jezebel (1 Kgs 16:31). A princess from Omri's family, Athaliah, married into the royal family of David in Jerusalem, making an alliance between Israel and Judah (2 Kgs 8:18, 26). Ahab was also able to forge an alliance with the Aramean (Syrian) king, Ben-hadad, who had been his arch enemy, after defeating the Aramean army in battle and capturing Ben-hadad (1 Kgs 20). In this way the Omride kings were able to confront the threat of the emerging power of the Assyrian empire.[5]

The Persistence of the Rural Vision

This long excursion into the political situation of the kingdom of Israel before and after the dissolution of the united kingdom under Solomon reminds us that the annals of history are dominated by the exploits of imperial power and the kings who are the agents of that power. But it also sets the stage for an exploration of how the rural vision that inspired the origins of Israel as a people persisted, even under this imperial reality. Thankfully, every now and then, the Bible and other annals of history give us glimpses through recorded stories for how ordinary people in local communities lived and coped in the midst of the dominant culture of imperial rule.

One such story is related for us in 1 Kings 21—the story of Naboth of Jezreel. Naboth had the misfortune of owning land next to a palace King Ahab of Samaria had built in Jezreel, the town overlooking the Valley of Jezreel dividing the hill country of Ephraim from Galilee. It was for Naboth a fruitful vineyard, but King Ahab wanted it for a vegetable garden. So King Ahab proposed to buy the vineyard from Naboth, or to trade it for an even better vineyard. What a stroke of luck for Naboth, we are tempted to say! What an opportunity to "trade up", and to do so with the royal court, no less! So Naboth's reply is as shocking to us as it likely was to King Ahab. "The Lord forbid that I should give you my ancestral inheritance" (1 Kgs 21:3).

Walter Brueggemann, in *The Land*, helps us understand the strange world Naboth inhabits. For King Ahab (as for most of us), the land is a *"tradable commodity."*

3. Dates from "Chronological Table of Rulers," in Coogan, ed. *New Oxford Annotated Bible*, 530–33.
4. Bright, *History*, 222.
5. Ibid., 223–26.

The Triumph of Empire and the Persistence of the Rural Vision

For Naboth, land is an *"inalienable inheritance."*[6] As Brueggemann says, "Naboth is responsible for the land, but is not in control over it. It is the case not that the land belongs to him but that he belongs to the land."[7] "The relation of Naboth and land is not owner/property but heir/gift, and that is true even in the face of the king, not to say the queen."[8] In other words, Naboth is heir to the ancient Israelite view of the land, which understands it as the gift of God entrusted to humans for its care and passed on as an ancestral heritage from one *bēh-'av* (father's house) to the next.[9]

This stands in stark contrast to the royal view of the land, in which land is commodified, made into a commodity that can be bought and sold and traded with impunity. Ownership, not stewardship, is the prevailing paradigm for the use of the land in the royal court, and ownership gives the owner the right to use the land as the owner pleases, without regard for tradition or fidelity or divine intention. Actually, to be fair, this seems to be the view of Ahab's Phoenician queen, Jezebel. King Ahab himself simply went home and sulked after his offer to trade land with Naboth was rejected, until Jezebel inquired why he was so depressed. It was Jezebel who raised the ante! "Do you now govern Israel? Get up, eat some food, and be cheerful; I will give you the vineyard of Naboth the Jezreelite" (1 Kgs 21:7). Jezebel understood better than Ahab the ethos of royal power. If you are the king, you simply take what you want! So she arranged for two "scoundrels" to bear false testimony against Naboth, saying he "cursed God and the king" (1 Kgs 21:13). So Naboth was stoned outside the city wall, and Jezebel informed her husband that he was now free to take possession of Naboth's vineyard. Ahab wasted no time in doing so (1 Kgs 21:15–16).

What may surprise us is that still in the mid-ninth century BCE, more than a century after Israel's entry into imperial reality under David and Solomon, the formative, covenantal constitution of ancient Israelite society was still alive, and perhaps even well! All the intrigues and exploits that make up the dominant imperial story of Israel's kings have failed to obliterate the ancient understanding that the land belonged to God, and that the people were tenants called to care for God's land. The land was still being passed on from generation to generation, from one *bēth-'av* (father's house) to the next, as an "ancestral inheritance" (1 Kgs 21:3).

But perhaps this shouldn't surprise us. The fact is that within every dominant, imperial culture there continue to be innumerable local subcultures—the local communities where ordinary people live and work. Despite the professed power of the empire, the actual extent of imperial power is limited. To be sure, local populations need to pay lip service, and likely taxes as well, to the central power, the royal court. But in fact, local communities will always operate to a large extent on the basis of local tradition. In part, this is due to the conservatism and inertia of local communities

---

6. Brueggemann, *Land*, 93.
7. Ibid.
8. Ibid., 96.
9. See chapter 7 above.

that only reluctantly and gradually adjust to the changes being imposed upon them by imperial power. But in part, this may also be due to the wisdom and the faith commitments that govern the lives of such communities, as in the case of Naboth.

So there is always a subversive quality that characterizes the relationship of local communities to the power of the dominant, imperial culture. People will always find a way to assert the interests of the community, the requirements of justice, and their allegiance to the fundamental faith convictions that have shaped their community, in the face of imperial demands. Local communities will always have an uneasy relationship with the centralized power of the imperial court. They will live "beneath the radar" of imperial power for the most part, and when the empire does impinge its presence into the local community, the people will often find nonviolent strategies of resistance to the empire's power. A classic contemporary example might be the rural Muslim Palestinian villages of South Hebron who nonviolently resist the incursions of Israeli settlers and military personnel into their communities, as we saw firsthand during our Christian Peacemaker Team delegation to the village of At-Tuwani in 2008.

Of course, this is always a costly resistance. When push comes to shove, the empire always has its way in the short term, as it did in the case of Naboth, who was put to death for his resistance to the commodification of his land. Indeed, Naboth's community was enlisted to assist in the facade of his "trial." The elders of Jezreel surely knew they were being used by Queen Jezebel, and that Naboth was innocent of the false charges made against him. But likely they could not risk openly defying the queen's ploys and bringing royal retribution down upon their whole community.

Still, the case might be made that it is the nonviolent resistance of local community to the incursions of imperial power that sustain the dominant culture. It is obvious that the values of commodification and arbitrary power serve personal interests. But they always contravene the common good. A society predicated on greed and the arbitrary use of power is destined for a rapid fall. Such a society can only be sustained when local communities, acting for their own welfare, resist the imperial power and continue to seek the common good of their community. When many local communities engage in this resistance, even in an uncoordinated fashion, it allows an unsustainable, imperial, dominant culture to survive beyond its just deserts.

The Prophetic Challenge to Urban Civilization

The story of Naboth does not end with his unjust death, of course. The exercise of imperial power has its own consequences, which may take some time to unfold, but which are as certain and sure as the injustices themselves! So it is that the prophet Elijah met King Ahab right there in Naboth's field, at the very time Ahab had come to take possession of it. Ahab knew very well why the prophet was there. "Have you found me, O my enemy?" he said to Elijah. And Elijah responded, "I have found you" (1 Kgs 21:20).

Elijah proceeded to detail the consequences of Ahab and Jezebel's actions. Ahab's blood will be licked up by the dogs at the same place where Naboth was stoned to death (1 Kgs 21:19). This particular consequence was deferred to Ahab's son, King Joram, killed in battle in a military coup led by Jehu and instigated by the prophet Elisha (2 Kgs 9:24–26). The reason for this deferral was that Ahab repented when he heard this consequence (1 Kgs 21:27–29). In addition, all of Ahab's house will be exterminated (1 Kgs 21:21–22), which Jehu accomplished in 2 Kings 10, killing all seventy of Ahab's sons, as well as forty-two relatives of Judah's royal court visiting in Israel who were descended from Ahab. Finally, Jezebel herself would be eaten by the dogs at the royal palace in Jezreel, next to Naboth's vineyard (1 Kgs 21:23). Again, it was Jehu who instigated this consequence in his coup, as related in 2 Kings 9:30–37. Jezebel had decked herself out in all her finery to meet Jehu, standing on a balcony of the palace. Jehu ordered her eunuchs to throw her down from the balcony and then he and his company rode over her before going into the palace to eat and drink as the dogs licked up her blood.

What we learn from these bloody stories is that there are certain consequences that follow or attend the exercise of imperial power. Those consequences may be deferred, sometimes even for generations, by God's grace. But the bitter fruit of injustice and oppression will come home to roost. This is the message that the prophets of Israel and Judah were called to announce on behalf of God, as the prophet Elijah does with Ahab in this story. Whenever imperial agents, in this case the royal court and those allied with it, abused their power by exploiting, oppressing, and disenfranchising the people living on the land, the prophets of Israel swung into action, denouncing these abuses in the name of God.

As Brueggemann points out in *The Land*, the prophetic vocation in Israel is closely tied to landedness—living in the land.[10] Right after envisioning the rise of royal power in Deuteronomy 17, the writer of Deuteronomy declares that when the people "have come into the land" (Deut 18:9) God will raise up for them prophets like Moses, in whose mouths God will put his words so that they will speak to the people everything that God commands (Deut 18:18). Thus the vocation of a prophet in Israel is closely tied both to the situation of landedness, and to the exercise of imperial power, in this case the institution of the king. "It is probably the potential power and danger of the king which evoke the guarantee of a prophet. . . . Prophets are intended precisely to address kings. It is because of kings that prophets appear."[11]

Elijah and Elisha, along with Micaiah (1 Kings 22), are the first of the classical prophets to appear in Israel in the ninth century BCE. But the prophetic vocation can also be seen earlier during the reign of David and his interactions with Nathan the prophet, where Nathan is called to restrain and to expose the royal pretensions and abuses (2 Samuel 7, 12). The era of classical prophecy in Israel continues with the

10. Brueggemann, *Land*, 91.
11. Ibid.

canonical prophets Amos and Hosea in the mid-eighth century BCE, active in Judah and Israel respectively, followed by Micah and Isaiah, both active in Judah late in the eighth century and in the case of Isaiah into the seventh century BCE.

Zephaniah and Jeremiah were prophets of the late seventh and early sixth centuries BCE during the last days of Judah, followed by Ezekiel as an exilic and Haggai and Zechariah as post-exilic prophets, along with Second Isaiah. We are led to assume that these canonical prophets are simply the enduring figures, but that the life of the Israelite kingdoms was shaped by many more unknown and unnamed prophets and prophetesses.

A striking feature of the prophetic writings of the Old Testament, and a reason why they are difficult for modern readers, are the long sections of judgments denouncing the nations. Not just Judah and Israel, but their neighbors, as well as their enemies—the large imperial powers that threatened their existence—are denounced in the strongest terms. Examples of this literature are Isaiah 13–23, Jeremiah 46–51, Ezekiel 25–32, and Amos 1–2. While the prophets are most concerned with the social and political conditions of their own country, these diatribes against the "nations" make it clear that they were not seditious or traitorous people intent on the destruction of their own nation and loyal to the enemy. It was the institutions of domination and control and oppression represented by the kingdoms, nations, and empires of the world that troubled them. While "judgment" as the destruction and dismantling of oppressive powers at the hand of God are the dominant theme of these prophetic materials, it is important to realize that God's judgment simply involves the natural consequences of unjust and oppressive policies and institutions. Direct supernatural intervention may occur, but typically judgment will become evident in the natural unfolding of the historical process.

Another striking feature of the prophetic writings is the way they portray God's agony over the fate of humanity and creation. The prophets often express a kind of proto-apocalyptic view of the future, in which creation itself is de-created, as in Jeremiah 4:19–28 and Isaiah 24. Hosea 4:1–3 declares: "There is no faithfulness or loyalty, and no knowledge of God in the land. . . . Therefore the land mourns, and all who live in it languish; together with the wild animals and the birds of the air, even the fish of the sea are perishing." Such passages are striking for their ecological implications. The prophets reflect a covenantal understanding of human life in which we as humans are called to live in relationship with God, receiving the blessings God desires to share with us while holding us to live in relationships of wholeness and well-being with God, one another, and creation. It has often been noted that Micah 6:8 expresses most succinctly this covenantal understanding of life. "He has told you, O mortal, what is good; and what does the Lord require of you but to do justice, to love kindness, and to walk humbly with your God?" Here the trifold relationship we have with one another, God's creation, and God is addressed.

The Triumph of Empire and the Persistence of the Rural Vision

When this covenantal relationship is broken, it means oppression and suffering for humanity and creation, and this breaks God's heart. This type of covenantal relationship, and God's agony over the suffering of creation and humanity, is poignantly expressed, for example, in Hosea, whose marriage to a prostitute becomes a paradigm for God's relationship with Israel (humanity). Despite the fickleness of Israel in abandoning his care, God can scarcely bear to give Israel over to the consequences of idolatry. "How can I give you up, Ephraim? How can I hand you over, O Israel? ... My heart recoils within me; my compassion grows warm and tender. I will not execute my fierce anger; I will not again destroy Ephraim; for I am God and no mortal, the Holy One of Israel in your midst, and I will not come in wrath" (Hos 11:8–9). Indeed, one can gather that judgment is frequently delayed by God until long after what might seem a natural process to us, and this is portrayed as God's mercy for humanity at work.

It is characteristic of the prophets to denounce leaders and others in society who oppress and take advantage of weaker and more vulnerable members of the community, and to announce vindication for those who are oppressed. This denunciation is frequently expressed as a "woe" to those who oppress others, as in Isaiah 5:8, "Ah, you who join house to house, who add field to field, until there is room for no one but you, and you are left to live alone in the midst of the land!" One can imagine that in this way, the prophets gave courage and strength to local communities resisting the depredations visited upon them by the oppressive powers under which they lived, as Naboth was able to resist the royal confiscation of his land with the price of his life. Local communities were not alone in their resistance to the idolatrous powers that preyed upon their lives. They had a powerful, if unseen, ally in the presence of God, who would in the end set things right! The prophetic movement in Israel might best be seen as an effort to inspire and encourage and facilitate the continuing resistance of rural communities to the domination and oppression of imperial power. Things are not what they seem to be. The history being made by the dominant culture is bound to yield to the persistence of those who choose "to do justice, and to love kindness, and to walk humbly with [their] God" (Mic 6:8).

What, and Who, Makes History?

We've noted a number of times in this book that *history* is generally the story of the exercise of power and domination and force—the story of urban civilization. What make the history books are the power plays of charismatic military and political leaders who reshape the political configuration of the globe. What makes the history books is the expansion of empires as they conquer and subjugate minorities within their domain and colonize lands near and far to sustain their imperial presence. What make the history books are the great works of architecture and art and music and literature produced by those who work on behalf of those who patronize and sponsor these endeavors. What make the history books are the great technological achievements that reshape the natural environment to configure to the human presence. What make the history books are the workings of institutionalized religion designed to bless and sacralize the status quo of power and domination, oppression and exploitation.

What the history books omit, for the most part, is the story of ordinary men and women living in local communities within these spheres of imperial power. What the history books omit is the record of sustainable living on the land by local cultures the world over. What the history books omit is the record of the everyday arts and crafts by which people live in sustainable ways—the growing and cultivation and preservation of food, the making of candles and soap and tools and artifacts. What the history books omit is the local wisdom acquired through generations of communal experience about what is required to make this particular land fruitful, what it is most suited to produce, how it can best be kept productive. What history books omit is the folk art by which local communities are sustained. What the history books omit are the rhythms of life tuned to the natural cycles of life. What the history books omit is the loyalty and fidelity of ordinary folks living in local communities to the traditions and faith perspectives that inform their lives and make their communities sustainable. What the history books omit, in other words, are all the characteristics that comprise agrarian society—local communities living in intimate relationship with one another, the natural world, and the Creator.

There are exceptions, to be sure. There are excellent historical monographs describing everyday life in particular periods of history, and examining the folkways and artifacts of ordinary people. The best books of this genre, like Howard Zinn's *A People's History of the United States*, describe the lives of ordinary people in the context of the forces of the imperial culture in which they are living. Archaeological studies in particular shed light on such matters, and often it is these studies that now inform our understanding of ancient Israel as an agrarian society living within the dominant cultures of urban civilization.

Every morning as I get up, National Public Radio reminds me that the news is brought to me in part by the Gates Foundation, "dedicated to the idea that all people deserve to live healthy and productive lives." What a noble sentiment! I have no doubt that Microsoft founder Bill Gates is sincere in his desire to improve the lot of humankind. However, the sentiment is contradicted by the fact that all of us, along with Bill Gates, expect someone else to do what we perceive to be the drudge tasks of providing us with the food we eat and of disposing of the wastes we create. As noted in the second chapter, one of the implications of our fall into sin is our belief that working with our hands to sustain our lives and our world is drudgery, work to be despised and avoided as much as possible. So every time we buy processed food or eat in a restaurant or have the garbage truck pick up our wastes or flush the toilet, we are paying other people to do the work we perceive to be drudgery.

If all people "deserve to live healthy and productive lives," it follows that everyone, including presumably Bill Gates, should be involved on a daily basis in the routine tasks required for the sustenance and maintenance of their lives. Only in this way will all the people now doing our drudge labor have enough time to engage in a creative and fulfilling life. For what most people in the world need in order to have a creative and fulfilling life is not a handout from Bill Gates, but the opportunity to be free enough of exploitation so that they can provide for themselves and their families and still have some time left for creative and fulfilling activities.

It is of course open to debate how much time would be left for creative and fulfilling activities if everyone shared equally in the daily tasks needed to sustain and maintain our lives. Perhaps it would have limited or curtailed Bill Gate's creative technical feats in providing us with his Microsoft products, to say nothing of the billions of dollars in profits he now is burdened to divest. And surely, as indicated on the last few pages, the greatest works of art, technology, material culture, and social manifestations of power and wealth are only possible when a lot of people support the most gifted and creative individuals like Mozart and Michelangelo in their creative endeavors. Surely the world would be poorer had it not been for the freedom these gifted personalities had to pursue their creative talents. But if the aim is to provide *everyone* with a healthy and productive, creative and fulfilling life, then perhaps a curtailment of creative work by the affluent and powerful will be required as they engage the real work of providing for their lives through the daily tasks required for living. The popular perception that apart from the modern conveniences and consumption we currently employ life would be an unrelenting grind of hard labor is contradicted by the rich and full lives of agrarian communities throughout history.

But more to the point, we need to do an honest appraisal about what work is drudgery. Since the Industrial Revolution, when for the first time ordinary people could aspire to a creative and fulfilling life, the work of providing the necessities of life in its daily tasks has been supplemented by truly drudge work of factory assembly lines and office cubicles. We have replaced what is in fact creative and fulfilling work—providing for our lives through the work of our hands—with drudge labor measured by the clock and the salary. It is not that everyone hates their eight to five job, and aspects of this work are also fulfilling, I'm sure. But for the most part, the highly specialized and repetitive work in our society is something people endure for the sake of the income and presumed leisure it purchases.

What a contrast to the work of a household in an agrarian society! Here the labor is varied and open ended. One task leads naturally to another, and all of them are tied together by the necessity of eating and sustaining our lives. An agrarian household is deeply rooted on the land and in the ecology of the land. Here there is a direct relationship with the plants and animals upon which human life depends. Here there is a profound connectedness to the Creator, a daily awareness that life is God's gift we can only gratefully receive through the bounty of nature and the work of our hands. Here everyone in the household works together for the sustenance and welfare of all. There may be some division of labor within and between households, but labor is typically shared together. Here the home is the setting for one's work, and one is not driven away from the home for the better part of the day in order to "make a living." Here production and consumption are brought together. Here food is produced, preserved, and prepared on site, and the minimal wastes are returned to the earth. Here households live in productive and creative and healthy proximity to one another, making genuine community possible.

Growing up on a farm and living among farmers all my life, I am always amazed at the range of skills the typical farmer exhibits. He must be a horticulturalist, a soil scientist, a meteorologist, an animal husbandman, a pathologist, a naturalist, a cultural historian, a neighbor, a carpenter, a metalworker, a mechanic, and in our day also be computer literate, and much more. In the same way, a typical farm wife (though in our day the gender rules are thankfully no longer rigid) not only cooks "from scratch" using the produce of the farm, but also knows how to make gardens and preserve the produce through canning or freezing or drying, how to sew (and in some cases to spin wool), and so much more. Both husband and wife share the tasks of making the home and raising the children.

One of the things I discover over and over again among the farmers I have known is how excited farmers are about the creative challenges of their work. Every hour and every day there are new challenges that call for a creative response. It turns out that nothing is so satisfying for us humans than to live in the nexus or matrix that sustains our lives. This is hardly the life of drudgery often depicted by the dominant culture, though of course the work is often brutally hard and demanding of both men and women. These are families that are both self-reliant and also interdependent. They do what they can for themselves, but they also are quick to help each other out. And usually, such families have ample time to engage creative endeavors in the form of handicrafts, writing, nature exploration, building relationships, engaging educational projects, making music together, supporting community festivals and events, and worshipping together.

Of course, such agrarian households and communities do not live on isolated islands separated from the mainstream of society and the dominant imperial culture. Always a portion of the bounty they produce is given, or in less healthy settings taken, to support the urban centers and imperial powers among whom they live. When such exchanges can be made freely and with some adequate compensation, it is a willing and generous trade. And as long as the agrarian community itself remains strong, even in the face of adverse relationships with the surrounding culture, the agrarian community can thrive and prosper, for it is self-sustaining. It needs in the end very little from the dominant culture.

So what if Bill Gates had to give up his current presumably creative and productive life in order to provide for his own food and the disposal of his own wastes? What he would learn would be the myriad skills and practices required for human life to be sustained here on earth—the skills and practices of an agrarian culture. Given the current energy, economic, and ecological crises the dominant culture is facing, these are not bad skills to have! Indeed, if the food and energy and economic systems upon which the dominant culture depends collapse suddenly, it will be the remnant of agrarian communities who will be able to help our society move toward more sustainable and sensible ways of living. Much as I appreciate the convenience of the hi-tech laptop on which I am writing, I much more value the creative skills of the agrarian life I have inherited and still am able to utilize.

The Anabaptist Movement and the Peasant Revolt

When I was a theology student in the 1960s, Anabaptist historiography was dominated by Harold S. Bender and his "rediscovery" of the Anabaptist vision. In 1944, Bender published an essay, "The Anabaptist Vision," in the journal *Church History*, and later that year reprinted it in *Mennonite Quarterly Review*. In this essay, Bender identified three distinctive principles of "pure" Anabaptism exemplified in the early Anabaptist reformers of Zurich, Switzerland—George Blaurock, Conrad Grebel, and Felix Manz. These three principles—Christianity as discipleship, the church as an accountable community, and an ethic of love and non-resistance—came to be the measuring stick for an authentic Anabaptism.[12] Bender was concerned to define genuine Anabaptism over against the many other streams of the radical movements for social and religious reform being spawned in the sixteenth century. However, the effect of this historiography was largely to cut off the socioeconomic and political context in which the Anabaptist movement emerged.

More recent Anabaptist historiography has insisted on the "polygenesis" of Anabaptism's emergence in the sixteenth century.[13] In his book *Anabaptist History and Theology*, Arnold Snyder seeks to accommodate this "polygenesis" view of Anabaptism's origins by discussing Andreas Karlstadt, who moved beyond Martin Luther in advocating reforms, the revolutionary Anabaptism of Thomas Muntzer, the spiritualism of Casper Schwenkfeld, and (the influence I find most fascinating) the Peasants' Wars of 1524 and 1525.[14]

The Peasants' Wars represented a widespread agrarian revolt against the secular and religious lords and nobles to whom the peasants were beholden, involving as many as 300,000 peasants throughout central Europe in Germany, Switzerland, France, and Austria. These violent uprisings of the peasants were quite easily put down by the authorities at the cost of an estimated 100,000 casualties.[15] Occurring during the very months of the emergence of Swiss Anabaptism in Zurich, the relationship between these agrarian movements for reform and Anabaptism are clear. Snyder notes that the

---

12. Bender, "Anabaptist," 13–23.
13. Snyder, *Anabaptist History*, 3.
14. Ibid., 25–39.
15. Ibid., 32.

peasants demanded against the clericalism of both Catholic and Reformed churches that local communities be able to elect and hold accountable their own pastors, which the Anabaptist movement carried forward. The peasants also called for just economic relationships among Christians and opposed usury, and again Anabaptism carried forward this demand in the communal forms of their life together. In addition, the peasants articulated an egalitarian social ideal, which again was carried forward in the Anabaptist movement.[16]

With the violent suppression of the peasants' movements for reform, it might be said that their concerns were carried forward in the ongoing life of the Anabaptist congregations. The slaughter of the revolting peasants represented once again the triumph of the empire and the forces of domination and oppression the empire represented. However, the formation of sustainable, agrarian communities of faith driven by Anabaptist nonviolent beliefs represented the persistence of the rural vision. These early Anabaptist agrarian communities in the years following 1525, far from representing a retreat from a missional perspective, represent the incarnation of the rural, missional perspective—the formation of sustainable, egalitarian communities of sharing, living against the grain of the dominant culture while also serving the needs of that dominant culture.

To be sure, as Snyder notes in his history, the subsequent Anabaptist movement transferred the concern for the reformation of the whole society evident in the peasants' revolts to the formation of holy communities of nonresistant, egalitarian, communal living: "Reform principles came to be applied by the surviving Anabaptist groups only to the 'regenerated' who 'separated from the world,' as Schleitheim would state unequivocally in 1527. Insofar as the separatist principle was accepted, economic reform was directed inward, to the church, and society was left to its own devices."[17]

At the same time, the reform was thoroughgoing! As Snyder notes, "the Anabaptists were critical of the poverty they saw around them."[18] "Anabaptists were extremely suspicious of trade and commerce as a means of earning one's livelihood."[19] They advocated instead "honest hand labor,"[20] in other words, the life of an agrarian community working the land. And finally, Anabaptists rejected usury, "the charging of interest on money at loan."[21] With all this, the Anabaptists were simply living out in their communities the sabbatical and jubilee principles consistently taught in the Scriptures.

Of course, it could be argued that this was too little. Why did the Anabaptists not seek to change the whole social order? Why were they "content" to "withdraw"

---

16. Ibid., 33.
17. Ibid., 227.
18. Ibid., 247.
19. Ibid.
20. Ibid.
21. Ibid., 248.

from the world in order to create a "pure" community of believers? Why didn't they pursue a missional vision for the transformation of the dominant culture as a whole? But of course, who is to say that this wasn't their intention? After all, they were living, as God's people nearly always have lived, in the context of the triumph of imperial power. They knew this from observing the slaughter of their peasant compatriots at the hands of the lords and nobles. The best way they could find to transform society was to remake it from within, through the formation of nonviolent, egalitarian, agrarian communities caring for the earth and making it fruitful, serving the welfare of the whole society, and bearing witness through their life together of a different way of living.

Was this a failure of vision or a failure of nerve? Was this the abandonment of a missional vision for the transformation of society and the redemption of the world? Given the slaughter of their peasant compatriots, the early Anabaptists surely saw how futile violent resistance to the powers was. Their acceptance of the gospel's nonviolent resistance with the formation of alternative communities of faith in the face of the triumph of empire was a missional accomplishment of the highest order. Indeed, it remains a model for the calling of the church as an alternative community of faith living against the grain of the dominant, imperial culture. It is how God's kingdom comes on earth, as it already is in heaven.

CHAPTER 10

Exiles and Aliens

Seek the Welfare of the City (Jer 29:7)

Living at the Margins of the Empire

FROM THE LARGER PERSPECTIVE of history, it was only a matter of time before the independent kingdoms of Israel and Judah would be erased from the land of Palestine. Palestine was too strategic to be left alone by the major powers and too small to be a player on the world scene. So with the demise of the northern kingdom of Israel in 722 BCE and the Kingdom of Judah in 586 BCE, God's people became once again a pilgrim people living at the margins of the great empires of the world as exiles and aliens.

The counsel of Jeremiah in the waning days of the Judean monarchy to those already exiled to Babylon was to become the prevailing counsel for God's wandering people. "But seek the welfare of the city where I have sent you into exile" (Jer. 29:7). Wherever you find yourself, in whatever city or empire, make your home there. Settle down, not as citizens, but as resident aliens whose own welfare is bound up with that of the dominant culture in which you live. Form communal patterns of life; cultivate the land; even assimilate with the dominant culture through marriage! Allow the subversive local culture of God's community to grow in the midst and at the margins of the empire, so that the light of God's way may shine and be seen by all the nations!

The last prophets of Israel and Judah were at pains to emphasize the demise of national and ethnic hopes. The exile was no temporary miscue on God's part. Even the promised return from exile would not inaugurate a new national identity but instead broker a new community living in promised land, but under imperial patronage and domination. In Isaiah, the returned exiles were called to be "a light to the nations" (Isa 42:6), but in the process they would be in some way aliens in their own land.

The Biblical Story

The End of a National Identity (Summary of Old Testament Paradigms)

The chapters in the second part of this book have been exploring models or paradigms for God's people living in the midst of the powers that rule the world. Before continuing with the biblical exploration of the exile, it might be helpful for us to review the various options that have emerged in our review of biblical history. Each of these options represents a particular historical or cultural era and a particular human experience in relating to a dominant culture, but taken together these models or paradigms reflect a fairly full range of responses to the reality of living in the midst of structures and powers of the world. The list that follows includes also the two options that will be explored in this chapter.

1. Resident aliens living in promised land as guests in the midst of a dominant culture. (Chapter 4: Abraham and Sarah, the patriarchs.)
2. Collaborators with imperial power in foreign land working (ostensibly) for the common good. (Chapter 5: Joseph and Jacob's family living in Egypt.)
3. Landed slaves in foreign land subject to and oppressed by imperial power. (Chapter 6: The children of Israel in Egypt.)
4. Wandering sojourners in wilderness dependent upon God. (Chapter 6: Israel's wilderness wandering for forty years.)
5. Landed settlers in promised land as alternative communities of faith. (Chapter 7: Israel in the years of the tribal confederacy.)
6. Established communities in promised land seeking to become a dominant culture. (Chapter 8: Israel establishing a national identity through kingship.)
7. Alternative communities of faith living against their own dominant culture. (Chapters 8 and 9: Israelite resistance to the imperial ambitions of the kingdoms of Israel and Judah.)
8. Exiles and aliens in foreign land seeking the welfare of the city. (Chapter 10: The people of Israel during the Babylonian exile.)
9. Pilgrims living in promised land under imperial power as a light to the nations. (Chapter 10: The post-exilic community in Palestine.)

The models and paradigms listed here are those that might be construed in some way to be positive or constructive communal responses to the domination systems. Not included are the options of violent resistance like the Zealot uprisings against the Romans in first-century Palestine, the blatant imperialism of David and Solomon and their successors in both Israel and Judah, or the ethnocentric and nationalistic post-exilic endeavors of Ezra and Nehemiah. Taken together, the nine options listed reflect a fairly full range of possible constructive communal approaches to living as God's people in the midst of a hostile world. Perhaps the option of withdrawal (the Essenes of New Testament times or the Amish today) is not clearly represented, although options 5 and 7 would come close to fitting.

The typology developed here seeks to identify two variables—the setting of the community, and its relationship to the structures of power and domination. The settings for these options are wilderness, foreign land, and promised land, and reflect the community's self-perceived relationship to the land where they find themselves. Does the community understand itself to be in wilderness, in foreign land, or in land promised in some way by God? This self-understanding is basic to how the community perceives its relationship to the dominant culture in which it finds itself. Does it stand "outside" the dominant culture, or is it addressing the dominant culture from "within"?

The community's relationship to the structures of power and domination is more complex. Sometimes the community flirts or even collaborates with imperial power, as in options 2 and 6. Sometimes the community stands "over against" imperial power, as in options 5 and 7. Sometimes the community finds itself oppressed and dominated by imperial power, as in options 3, 8, and 9.

However, regardless of the community's setting and its relationship to imperial power, several options are already ruled out and not listed here. The community cannot engage in violence either in resistance to imperial power or in support of itself. To do so contradicts the fundamentally nonviolent character of God's response to the powers of domination, a response that will be fully documented in the next two chapters. Additionally, the community cannot understand itself primarily in ethnocentric or nationalistic terms. While the community will always have an ethnic character to be celebrated in terms of its origins and membership, it cannot be a community of God's response to the domination powers of this world and define itself ethnocentrically or nationally. Both of these self-understandings contradict God's response to the powers of domination, which insists on an inclusive and welcoming community in which all have a place, including especially those who are most marginal and vulnerable.

Israel's experiment with national and ethnocentric identity should have come to an end with the destruction of the temple in 586 BCE and the Babylonian exile. Nevertheless, such idolatrous self-understandings always die hard within every community. The ministries of Ezra and Nehemiah in the formation of a post-exilic Jewish community in Palestine, the years of Hasmonean independence established through the Maccabean revolt against the Seleucid empire in the second century BCE, and the current State of Israel, conceived in extreme Zionist form as a homeland for all Jewish people (but only for Jewish people), are examples of how this self-understanding has persisted among the Jewish people. Many other examples of the same persistence of ethnocentric and nationalistic communal identities can be found within a Christian context. The most extreme example might be that of the Third Reich in Hitler's

Germany. But it creeps into the self-understanding of nearly every congregation, including those of disestablishment Anabaptist heritage, which yields to the idolatry of ethnocentric and nationalistic self-understandings.

Hence it is all the more important to understand the particular callings of God for God's people in exilic and post-exilic times, revealed in the prevailing prophetic insights of this period. Ironically, the biblical prophets cannot easily be construed to be defenders of the kingdoms of Israel and Judah as ethnocentric or nationalistic institutions of power. Whether in prospect or in retrospect, the prophets understood the catastrophes of their kingdoms as the consequence of the abandonment of their people's covenant with God, and consequently as God's judgment upon their land for its injustices and exploitation and idolatry. They may have talked about the renewal of a Davidic kingship, or the renewal of a covenantal community in promised land, and such language could easily be read ethnocentrically or nationalistically. But it is difficult if not impossible to fairly read the prophets honestly as justifying ethnocentric or nationalistic understandings of God's covenant with community.

The futility of an ethnocentric or nationalistic understanding of God's covenant for the people of Israel is obvious when we remember the geopolitical situation of Canaan or Palestine as the land bridge uniting the two major centers of ancient civilization at either end of the Fertile Crescent—Egypt to the south along the Nile River and Mesopotamia to the north and east along the Tigris and Euphrates Rivers. Palestine was too strategic to the aims of imperial power to be left alone, and too small to compete on the world stage. In retrospect, it was sheer folly for the people of Israel to imagine that they could be a nation "like other nations" around them (1 Sam 8:20). It was an impossible dream in a world of imperial power. It was only a matter of time before their national identity would be challenged and then destroyed by the much larger imperial powers around them. Ironically, Israel's choice to become "like other nations" around them planted the seed of their national destruction, for it involved at its root the abandonment of their identity as a covenant people of God. Once again we can see the purpose of God in choosing Palestine at the center of the civilized world as promised land, but also the supreme difficulty of being God's covenant people in such a strategic geopolitical environment.

The northern kingdom of Israel was the first to meet its fate, at the hands of the Assyrian Empire under the ascendant power of Tiglath-Pileser III (745–727 BCE) and his successors Shalmaneser V (727–722 BCE) and Sargon II (722–705 BCE).[1] The sad tale of the fall of Samaria, the deportation of the people of Israel to the regions of northern Mesopotamia, and the importation of a mixed population who later became the Samaritans is told in 2 Kings 17.

The southern kingdom of Judah survived for another century and a half, perhaps because being much smaller, Judah was much less a threat to the dominant imperial powers. Ironically, this only led the people of Judah deeper into the illusion that

---

1. Bright, *History*, 252–58.

because they were the heirs of a Davidic dynasty and Solomon's temple, God would never allow their nation to be destroyed. The mindset is described by Jeremiah. "Do not trust in these deceptive words: 'This is the temple of the LORD, the temple of the LORD, the temple of the LORD.' . . . Here you are, trusting in deceptive words to no avail. Will you steal, murder, commit adultery, swear falsely, make offerings to Baal, and go after other gods that you have not known, and then come and stand before me in this house, which is called by my name, and say, 'We are safe!'—only to go on doing all these abominations?" (Jer 7:4, 8–10).

The mighty Assyrian empire was destroyed by the New Babylonian or Chaldean Empire, with the Assyrian capital of Nineveh falling in 612 BCE.[2] An Egyptian attempt to challenge rising Babylonian power, a source of great hope to the Judean kingdom, was defeated in the Battle of Carchemish in Northern Mesopotamia in 605 BCE.[3] After repeated provocations by Jehoiakim, the Babylonians invaded Judah in 598 BCE. Jehoiakim conveniently died before the Babylonian invasion, leaving his young eighteen-year-old son, Jehoiachin, on the throne. Jehoiachin surrendered to the Babylonians after a three-month siege of Jerusalem, leading to the first deportation of Jews to Babylon. The Babylonians placed Jehoiachin's uncle, Zedekiah, on the Judean throne, but Zedekiah again rebelled against Babylon in 589 BCE, leading to the final destruction of Jerusalem in 586 BCE, and the second deportation to Babylon.[4]

The story of Judah's last days is chronicled in 2 Kings 24–25, repeated in Jeremiah 52. Second Chronicles 36:20–21 reports that the exile would last seventy years, "until the land had made up for its sabbaths" (2 Chr 36:21), which the people of Israel had failed to properly observe during their 490-year sojourn in promised land. God's covenant people were now consigned to live at the margins of the great empires of the world as exiles and aliens.

Seeking the Welfare of the City to Which You Have Been Exiled!

It is the first reference to urban gardening that I can find in Scripture! After the first deportation of the Judean elite in 597 BCE, those exiles began to imagine that they might soon be allowed to return to Judah. As related in Jeremiah 27, rumors were rife between the Davidic court in Jerusalem and the community of exiles in Babylon. Popular prophets were announcing the imminent return from exile. Jeremiah 28 relates a dramatic encounter between the prophets Jeremiah and Hananiah. Jeremiah had taken to wearing a yoke to symbolize the necessity of Judah's submission to Nebuchadnezzar, the Babylonian king, and it did not endear him to the establishment. Hananiah confronted Jeremiah in the temple in Jerusalem, announcing that within two years the yoke of Babylon would be broken and the exiles could return home.

2. Ibid., 294.
3. Ibid., 305.
4. Ibid., 305–309.

To prove his prophecy, Hananiah tore the yoke from Jeremiah's neck and broke it in pieces, announcing that in that way God would break the Babylonian yoke on Judah. For this false prophecy, Jeremiah announced that Hananiah would die within a year, and he did (Jer 28:12–17)!

Following these events, Jeremiah wrote a letter to the exiles in Babylon, reminding them that their exile would not be brief but last for seventy years (Jer 29:1–10). In view of this, God's word through Jeremiah to the exiles was this: "Build houses and live in them; plant gardens and eat what they produce. Take wives and have sons and daughters; take wives for your sons, and give your daughters in marriage, that they may bear sons and daughters; multiply there, and do not decrease. But seek the welfare of the city where I have sent you into exile, and pray to the LORD on its behalf, for in its welfare you will find your welfare" (Jer 29:5–7).

What an astounding mandate! This is a prescription for the building of community in exile; indeed, in the heart of the enemy empire—its capital city! This is not just a blueprint for survival, a strategy for surviving the trauma of exile. This is a missional mandate! Essentially it says to these exiles, *Do where you now live what you have always been called to do! Begin building self-sustaining communities of nonviolent resistance in the heart of the city that has taken you into exile far from your homeland. But do this not just for your own sakes! Do it for the sake of the enemy among whom you have been taken by force to live! Indeed, pray for the welfare of the city—the enemy city that has been the instrument of your exile, the instrument of the loss of all you have held dear!* This runs counter to every normal human response to enemies and the trauma of exile, but that is the point! God doesn't make it easy to be God's people!

This also ran counter to all that the people of Judah had come to understand about their life as God's people. It meant that their community of faith did not depend on owning and possessing promised land. It meant that their community of faith did not require the existence of a temple as a focal point and center for the worship of God. It meant that their community of faith was not limited to the existence of a national identity expressed in the rule of a king in the line of David. It meant that their life as a community of God's people was not over with the loss of land and temple and national identity. It meant that God still had a purpose and a mandate for them in the midst of the disaster that had overtaken them because of their reliance on the idolatries of land and temple and national identity. It meant that God still wanted them to fulfill the purpose for which God had shaped them and brought them to promised land—the purpose of being an alternative community of faith in the midst of the empires of the world, even within the heart of the enemy empire that had been the agent of their losses!

They were to do this by settling down in the place of their exile, even in the heart of the enemy city to which they had been taken by force, first by building houses and making homes, then by planting gardens, and finally by having families. This final point is interesting. Living in exile always places a community in the midst of another, likely hostile, ethnic context. While the marriages envisioned in Jeremiah 29:6 are not explicitly described as mixed marriages with the local Babylonians among whom the exiles lived, this possibility is not ruled out either. As every Romeo and Juliet story confirms, the attraction of sons and daughters to the originally forbidden other is universal! Ethnic purity is again confirmed as myth! Alternative communities of faith grow as they intermarry with the local populations where they find themselves, despite the resistance to such growth on the part of these alternative communities of faith, which are always tempted to guard their unique identity on the grounds of ethnic purity.

Then there is that mention of *urban gardening*. Babylon had one of the wonders of the ancient world in its hanging gardens, fed by the waters of the Tigris River. But in Jeremiah 29:5, it is vegetable gardens that are envisioned in the mist of the city. These alternative communities of faith in exile no longer have promised land to work and on which to live. But they are still called to engage in the production of food, both in order to be self-sufficient communities and in order to sustain the city to which they have been sent as exiles. It is part of how they are to seek the welfare of the city, for they have the skills and the ability to till the land even in the city and to make it fruitful. It reminds me of the immense food production encountered in the immigrant communities of North America—the Hispanic and Hmong communities among many others. Alternative communities of faith are called to be engaged in caring for the earth and tilling the land, even in the midst of the cities to which they might be exiled.

It turns out that the exile functions much like the wilderness in human experience. Indeed, exiles are as often sent to the wilderness (as in Siberia) as they are to the city. But regardless of the locale (urban or wilderness), the experience of exile is the counterpoint to promised land. Exile, like wilderness, is the experience of being stripped of the crutches of the settled life and thrown upon the mercies of God. Through the loss of land, temple, and national identity, God's people discover that God is faithful, and they (re)discover their calling of being alternative communities of faith. For those seeking to be faithful to God, wilderness is the place where humans encounter natural forces that strip them of all the securities of promised land, while city is the place where humans encounter spiritual forces of power and pride that also strip them of all the securities of promised land. In both settings, those who seek to be faithful to God are cast upon God's providence and mercy.

For the exiles of Judah, the exile in Babylon taught them that they could function as God's people without at least two of the three losses of land, temple, and national identity that they had prized. It was during the years of the Babylonian exile that the synagogue characteristic of later Judaism was possibly born.[5] Stripped of both land and temple, the Jewish people discovered that they could still maintain their identity and practice their worship in small groups.

---

5. Sonne, "Synagogue," 4:478–79.

The idol of national (ethnic) identity was more difficult for the exiles in Babylon to shed. Ezra and Nehemiah's efforts to establish a "pure" community among the exiles who returned to Jerusalem shows the struggle (Ezra 9–10; Neh 13:23–31). Indeed, this may be the idol most difficult for God's people in every age. For in fact, ethnic identity, however illusory it is as a concept of ethnic purity, remains a strong expression of a community's and individual's heritage, something to be valued and celebrated. As humans we struggle to know how to do that without forming exclusive communities in conflict with other communities.

In any case, it is instructive to realize that land, temple, and national (ethnic) identity represent the key losses of those sent into exile. While each of these are aspects of life in promised land, each of them also embody idolatrous temptations that can divert us from our calling as God's people. So it is that we move from wilderness to settled land, and from settled land to exile, in our human experience. For when land and temple and national (ethnic) identity become for us idols to which we cling, then they must and will be taken from us, whether we understand that loss to be God's judgment or simply the ongoing consequence of the historical process. What does not change for us is God's calling to be alternative communities of faith living within the imperial powers of the world, whether in exile or promised land. Always we are called to "seek the welfare" of the cities among which we are living, whether as settlers, resident aliens, or exiles, for in the welfare of the city we will find our own.

A Light to the Nations (Isa 42:6)

The exile nearly broke the spirit of the people of Judah. Their condition is described in Ezekiel's vision of the dry bones in Ezekiel 37, where God declares that the valley of dry bones Ezekiel has just had occasion to visit are "the whole house of Israel. They say, 'Our bones are dried up, and our hope is lost; we are cut off completely'" (Ezek 37:11). Only the wind of God's Spirit was able to breath new life into the despairing dry bones of the exiles (Ezek 37:9).

Ezekiel was the prophet of the exile, a member of the priestly elite who was taken to Babylon in the first deportation of 597 BCE. Perhaps the strange and even weird images of his prophecies bear witness to the trauma of being torn from his homeland. In any case, he was also the prophet of the return from the exile. Not content to simply revive the hope of a defeated people as in Ezekiel 37, Ezekiel also held out the hope for a return to promised land for the exiles in Babylon. This was not for the sake of the people of Israel, Ezekiel makes clear, but for God's sake, so that God's honor among the nations might be upheld (Ezek 36:22–24). This return to promised land would be based on a renewed covenant of God with God's people, in which God would give the people a new heart, a heart of flesh to replace the heart of stone they had because of the injustice, exploitation, and idolatry of their former life in promised land (Ezek 36:25–27).

But not only would Israel return to promised land, but promised land itself would be renewed! The land of Israel had gained the reputation of being a devourer of those who lived upon it (Ezek 36:13). But when the exiles returned to promised land, it would be to a land renewed. God would make "the fruit of the tree and the produce of the field abundant" (Ezek 36:30). The desolate land would be tilled again, so that it will appear as "the garden of Eden" to those who pass by. In this way, too, God's honor would be restored (Ezek 36:34–36).

As though this were not enough, Ezekiel also held out the promise of a reunited Israel, the northern and southern kingdoms of God's people brought together as one under the leadership of a Davidic king (Ezek 37:15–28). This new Davidic king would not be a ruler of conquest, but a shepherd; not a ruler who exploits the people for personal gain, but a ruler who cares for the most vulnerable (Ezek 34). And of course, the book of Ezekiel ends with the vision of a restored temple, as one would expect of a prophet of priestly lineage (Ezekiel 40–48).

So there you have it—a restored people of God returning to a renewed promised land in a unified kingdom with a Davidic king and a new temple to boot! It sounds like a return to the status quo ante of the first Israelite kingdom under David and Solomon. Surely it was and is often read and understood that way, particularly by Jewish people bent on returning to promised land and by Christians with a Zionist bent. But I think those who read Ezekiel this way miss the nuances. Ezekiel does indeed hold out the promise of a return to promised land renewed as a unified people with a Davidic king and a new temple. But the whole vision is premised on a new covenant with God, where "hearts of stone" are replaced with hearts of flesh and blood. All the terms of identity—land, temple, peoplehood/ethnicity/nationality—are placed in the context of this new covenant with God, which precludes an Ezra/Nehemiah-like enclave of ethnic purity.

Still, for me, the clearest expression of God's purpose for the post-exilic community of God's people in promised land is found in the book of Isaiah, and particularly in the second part of Isaiah that likely dates from exilic and post-exilic times. But already early in Isaiah we find the vision that informs and unifies the book of Isaiah as a whole, the vision of "the mountain of the Lord's house" being "raised above the hills," with "all the nations" streaming to it (Isa 2:2). It is the vision of Zion (Jerusalem with its temple) being the destination for all the peoples of the world in order that the God worshipped in Jerusalem "may teach us his ways, and that we may walk in his paths" (Isa 2:3). It is the vision of a universal reign of peace, in which God will judge between nations and peoples, in which the weapons of war will be transformed to agricultural implements. Violence and domination and force will be renounced, so that as Micah adds in his version of this vision, "they shall all sit under their own vines and under their own fig trees, and no one shall make them afraid" (Mic 4:4).

It is a rather astounding vision for the ethnocentric, nationalistic, imperial-minded, exclusionary-temple-functioning era of the prophet Isaiah in the days of "Uzziah,

Jotham, Ahaz, and Hezekiah, kings of Judah" (Isa 1:1). This is not the stuff designed to make a prophet popular or profitable. This is a call for a return to the ancient vision of God expressed in the formation of Israel as a distinct people—that they should be for God "a priestly kingdom and a holy nation" (Exod 19:6). There is nothing particularistic about this vision for Zion. It envisions Jerusalem as a city open to all the nations. It portrays God as the teacher and arbiter among all the nations and peoples of the world, not simply for the Israelites themselves, who are merely servants of this God. It is geopolitical in scope, encompassing all nations and peoples, the whole earth. And, by the way, it is a vision for Jerusalem renewed by John in Revelation 21:22–26. Would that the Jerusalem of our day was declared to be an open and international city, sacred to all the three great monotheistic faiths for whom the city is a holy place!

This missional theme keeps being repeated throughout the book of Isaiah as its unifying leitmotiv. It is especially prominent in the Servant Songs of Isaiah 42:1–9 and 49:1–13. Here the symbols of city and temple recede and the role of Israel as God's redeemed community is highlighted. The servant called by God in Isaiah 42:1–4 to "bring forth justice" (Isa 42:1) with persistent gentleness is commissioned to be "a light to the nations" (Isa 42:6), the vindicator and healer of those who are oppressed (Isa 42:5–9). God's people are still called to be that "priestly kingdom and holy nation" that brings light to all the nations and peoples of the world, and to do so nonviolently and with the persistent, gentle practice of justice for the most marginalized and oppressed members of the human community.

The vision is stated even more explicitly in the second servant song of Isaiah 49, both with respect to the identity of the people as a post-exilic community of redeemed exiles and with respect to the global and universal aspect of this mission. The song opens with Israel lamenting the misspent years of her kingdom while also confirming God's call given before birth and being secretly prepared for ministry (Isa 49:1–6). Isaiah 49:5 speaks about the servant's role in bringing Jacob and Israel back to God, presumably from exile. But verse 6 is again explicitly universal when God asserts of God's servant, "It is too light a thing that you should be my servant to raise up the tribes of Jacob and to restore the survivors of Israel; I will give you as a light to the nations, that my salvation may reach to the end of the earth" (Isa 49:6). This is the most explicit statement of Israel's mission as a post-exilic people. They are not called to return to a closed, restored, ethnic kingdom under an exploitative Davidic king. They are called to be "a light to the nations," the messengers of God's salvation to the ends of the earth.

Practically speaking, this meant for the returned exiles that they were called to live as pilgrims in (their own) promised land, under what turned out to be Persian imperial power. It was the Persians who conquered the short-lived Babylonian Empire and assumed sovereignty over Palestine with Cyrus' victory over Babylon in 539 BCE.[6] Persian rule seems to have been more efficient and benign that the imperial

---

6. Bright, *History*, 341–42.

rule of most empires of the ancient world. But the fact remains that despite Cyrus' decree of 538 BCE allowing the exiled Jews of Babylon to return to Judah and his reputation as a "truly enlightened ruler,"[7] Palestine remained a colony of the Persian Empire, and the people of Israel had no independent national existence. While the first leaders of the returned community of exiles were Davidic heirs—Shesh-bazzar and Zerubbabel—and were commissioned as "governors" by Cyrus, they were hardly "kings" in any real sense.[8] The post-exilic community of God's people in Palestine lived as resident aliens in their own promised land, much as Abraham had done. They had come "home," but "home" was not theirs to claim. Their calling was to be "a light to the nations" among whom they were living, the same calling that had brought their forebears to Palestine in the first place some seven centuries earlier.

Learning to Live with(in) Urban Civilization

The basic premise of this book assumes a fundamental conflict between local/rural communities and urban civilization. Dependent as they ultimately are upon rural communities for their sustenance—humans in the city do have to eat food grown from the earth or taken from the sea, after all—urban civilizations tend to relate to rural communities through oppression, domination, and exploitation. Rural communities struggle to maintain their autonomy, independence, and vitality in the face of urban domination. Their traditional way of life and their access to the land and resources required to sustain their own communal life, as well as that of their urban neighbors, are always threatened by the dominant culture of urban civilization.

But then along comes the key verse of this chapter. "But seek the welfare of the city where I have sent you into exile, and pray to the Lord on its behalf, for in its welfare you will find your welfare" (Jer 29:7). This seems to contradict the basic premise of this book. It suggests a much more complicated relationship between local community and urban civilization—a mutual interdependence and indeed a willingly assumed servanthood role of local community on behalf of urban civilization, despite the oppression and domination exercised all too frequently, benevolently or malevolently, by that dominant culture of imperial power. It suggests that the development and revitalization of local communities is not only necessary in rural areas, but is also urgently needed in urban areas. This is not exactly where I had wished to arrive when I began writing this book!

The fact is that urban civilization is not going to go away anytime soon, if ever. The fact is that however necessary it might be for the future of life on earth to decentralize megalopolises and metropolises, a majority of the human family will continue to live in cities and metropolitan areas for the foreseeable future. The fact is that rural people from agrarian and local cultures will continue to find themselves pushed or

7. Ibid., 343.
8. Ibid., 345.

pulled into these urban centers, whether by the illusion that there they might escape the poverty of their rural towns and villages or by virtue of losing their land and being displaced by the forces of the dominant culture. With urbanization currently continuing, urban areas are filled with formerly rural people from traditional cultures, only one or two generations removed from their agrarian roots.

It would be fascinating to discover what percentage of urban residents are only one or two generations removed from their agrarian roots, but I'm not aware of any studies or statistics that measure populations in this way. The stories of Garrison Keillor on *Prairie Home Companion* often focus on people from the country who have moved to the city and their interaction with the folks back home as they seek their fortunes in the city. Clearly, the ad hoc, so-called slum areas (e.g., the *favelas* of Brazil) common to most urban areas, especially in the global South and Third World countries, might be made up almost exclusively of agrarian people, peasants recently dispossessed from their lands. These recent immigrants to urban areas see the world quite differently from those who are truly urban, who have lived in urban areas for several generations and have no memory of their agrarian roots, no desire to experience nature, and no knowledge of how to fend for themselves outside the humanly constructed urban environment. This would be especially true of rural peasants dispossessed from their land; perhaps less so for those lured to the city by the promise of a better future.

I was alternately fascinated and repelled by the truly urban mindset I discovered in David Owen's book *Green Metropolis*, which one of my urban daughters recommended to me. It was most strikingly evident in Owen's chapter on "The Great Outdoors," where he describes walking in Manhattan with his infant daughter. She was born in Manhattan, and he describes how she seemed content and fascinated with their walks on the city streets. When their daughter was a little over a year old, Owen and his wife moved to an acreage in a small town in northwest Connecticut. He describes a walk with his daughter on a spectacular autumn morning at the peak of New England's leaf season. Now his daughter was fussy and squirmed in her backpack almost the whole way. "As far as she was concerned, there was nothing to look at. The absence of urban commotion along our route made the walk seem long and boring. And it usually has the same effect on me, although I hate to admit it."[9] That a toddler might find nature boring after the chaotic stimulation of urban streets is understandable. That a parent shares the sentiment discloses a person with no sensibility for the natural cycle of the seasons upon which all human life ultimately depends. Here is someone who can only feel comfortable in the humanly constructed urban environment.

Of course, I accept and affirm the central thesis of Owen's book that densely populated urban cores with high-rise apartments sitting above the required shops are infinitely more sustainable and efficient than the spread-out suburban sprawl of McMansions and shopping malls requiring private automobiles to go anywhere, which

9. Owen, *Green Metropolis*, 178.

he repeatedly critiques.[10] But it is equally clear that Owen has absolutely no conception of the agrarian way of life and the natural cycles of life upon which not only rural communities but urban centers depend.

One of my urban daughters lives conveniently on the edge of the urban core of Minneapolis, and I have found great pleasure in walking all through downtown Minneapolis across the Mississippi River and back again in just a couple of hours. But there, my attention is focused on the bustle of city streets, the dominating skyscrapers, and the impressive bridges and buildings that master even one of nature's masterpieces—the Mississippi River! It's quite different than my walk today (January 6, 2012) around a section of agricultural land outside Freeman, South Dakota, lying in fallow winter rest, and pondering not only the vast sky beneath an early winter's sun but also the watersheds that these farmers struggle with in order to make this flat section tillable, as well as the lack of measurable precipitation for the past four months!

Urban centers are currently doing a lot to become more sustainable, not only in energy use, but also in terms of food production. I applaud the way in which vacant land within urban centers is being returned to food production. I also see the way in which urban gardening itself builds community in an urban setting. I think of the ad hoc community formed around my daughter's community garden in Minneapolis, where twenty or thirty urban gardeners share a community garden with the incessant sound of Interstate 94 traffic in the immediate background beneath them, each with one or two small plots planted to vegetables or flowers.

Still, it seems to me that the best hope of urban centers in the continuing economic, ecological, and energy crisis we are facing in America and around the world lies with all those recent agrarian immigrants to the city. They are the heirs of a communal way of life. They still possess the skills needed to till the earth and make it fruitful, even in the unlikely environment of the city. I'm always struck by the definite neighborhoods that define urban centers like Chicago, with its Hispanic and Polish and African American and Greek and Asian communities. These people, exiled to the city as they are, whether by their own desires or by dispossession from the land they once knew as their own, are those most likely to heed Jeremiah's counsel to build houses and plant gardens, if not in response to God's directive then by desire and necessity. It is they who seek the welfare of the city to which they have been exiled, for in its welfare they find their own (Jer 29:7). Yes, even this city that has been the agent of their dispossession, their uprootedness from the land that they had known as their home, they will now serve.

David Owen speaks disparagingly in his book about the local food movement, asserting that California raspberries he purchases in the city "have a smaller carbon footprint than the local raspberries I picked recently at a farm just a couple of towns away."[11] The reason? He and his wife drove thirty miles to pick those raspberries,

10. Ibid., 8–13.
11. Ibid., 300.

because they preferred the locally grown produce, and it is more sustainable to ship California raspberries in bulk across the county than to drive thirty miles to pick them locally. All this is very well, as long as there is fuel to produce and transport the California raspberries. Owen cannot apparently imagine a time when energy prices will reach a point where he will be glad for local producers who know how to raise raspberries. Indeed, what will he and the myriad other urban dwellers who have no use for nature and find it boring do then? Their only hope is that a community with agrarian roots and knowledge will provide for them until they, too, learn the skills of producing locally grown food, even in the gardens of the city.

In the meantime, I'm puzzled about people like David Owen, persons so irrevocably shaped by the urban environment for so long that they have no sense of rootedness in the earth, no sense of where they have come from. Such people themselves are clearly not oppressors, however much their dependence on urban structures contributes to the oppression of rural communities. They may be functionaries in the institutions that exploit and oppress and dominate—the corporations and universities and governmental agencies and denominational headquarters. But most often they are victims of these institutions as much as are those who live in the surrounding countryside. They are clearly and often well-meaning people who have formed their own communal ties focused around work or neighborhood or apartment building or church affiliation. Still, I find it hard to imagine so many people being so cut off from the natural world upon which their lives depend that they are bored by it and alienated from it.

Meanwhile, back in the country, rural communities like my own also need to surrender their preoccupation with the production of agricultural commodities for a global market (especially the pipe dream of raising corn for ethanol), and get back to the business of raising food for themselves and their nearest urban neighbors. We, too, need to seek the welfare of the city with which our agrarian lives are irrevocably bound up. That means developing local markets that are efficient and deliver food to urban residents without the waste of energy Owen describes. It means reengaging in the hard manual work of nurturing food crops. More importantly, it means establishing relationships with local communities of all kinds within the urban environment and partnering with them in ways that bypass the imperial structures of domination and exploitation under which both rural and urban people live.

Mennonite Urbanization and Rural/Urban Connections

Mennonite Church USA, to which I belong, was a predominantly rural, agrarian denomination until two or three generations ago, at least through the Second World War. Immigrants to North America, Mennonite people came to the United States as agrarian communities. While they adapted their agrarian cultures to the North American landscape and environment, they remained a deeply agrarian culture and church through the first half of the twentieth century. The typical church was a simple building on a rural road, the center of life for the surrounding rural families. In this respect, Mennonites were like other immigrant communities and denominations. Drive through rural North America, and the landscape is dotted with Lutheran, Catholic, Reformed, and Mennonite church buildings, representing German, Scandinavian, Czech, and many other ethnic heritages.

Today, many of those same church buildings are still there, most nearly empty with only a remnant of farm families left on the land. Or they are now thriving suburban congregations, with perhaps a very small number of farmers, but with a strong majority of members coming from commercial, industrial, and professional work realms and either living on an acreage in the country or commuting out to the church from the city. In their book *The Mennonite Mosaic*, J. Howard Kauffman and Leo Driedger indicate that from 1972 to 1989, the number of urban Mennonites living in population centers of more than 2,500 in five Mennonite denominations grew from 35 to 48 percent.[12] Looking more specifically at the farm residence of Mennonites, Conrad Kanagy in his book *Road Signs for the Journey*, found that in 1972, 36 percent of Mennonites lived on a farm, and that figure had shrunk to 26 percent in 1989 and 12 percent in 2006.[13] While 40 percent of Mennonites in Kanagy's study grew up on farms, only 23 percent remained on the farm in 2006.[14] Except for what Kanagy refers to as racial/ethnic members of Mennonite Church USA, most Mennonites live in small and medium size cities; less than 10 percent of Mennonites live in urban centers of more than 250,000.[15] By contrast, 39 percent of racial/ethnic members of Mennonite Church USA live in urban centers of 250,000 or more.[16]

These statistics document the growing urbanization of Mennonite Church USA. But they also reveal that many urban Mennonites are only one or two generations removed from the farm. Such is the case with my own children, two of whom live in large urban centers. While I forsook the farm I grew up on to become a pastor, I served rural congregations, and we lived in rural villages and small cities and towns, the environment of my children's youth. Now as urban dwellers, they hardly fit the "urban mindset" described in the previous section. They are interested in gardening and are knowledgeable about the processes and cycles of nature.

In the same way, the rural revitalization group I meet with in the Freeman, South Dakota, community, Rural Revival, is driven in part by young urban Mennonites with roots in the Freeman community who have returned with the intention of being engaged in local food systems and communal endeavors. These young adults indicate

---

12. Kauffman and Driedger, *Mennonite Mosaic*, 36.
13. Kanagy, *Road Signs*, 58.
14. Ibid.
15. Ibid.
16. Ibid.

that many of their peers in the city also desire to return to their agrarian roots, if only it seemed economically feasible to do so.

On the other hand, urban congregations are also realizing the potential of their agrarian roots in reaching out to their urban environment. The November 2011 issue of *Mennonite Creation Care Network* carried the story of the Berea Mennonite Church in a depressed area of Atlanta, Georgia, which is opening doors to its neighbors with a large three-acre urban garden. On the church blog, entitled "Holy Manure," the pastor, John Wierwille, says, "the model of church-as-farm is a radical witness in a world slave to bad food, big industry, individualism and apathy."[17] The December 2011 issue of *The Mennonite* also highlights congregations in Kansas City, Kansas, Elkhart and Goshen, Indiana, and Stryker, Ohio, who are developing church and community gardens as ministries of their congregation.[18] In this way, these congregations are fulfilling God's call to work for the welfare of the city by building houses and planting gardens. At the margins of the empire, these congregations are remaking sustainable communities that carry the potential of transforming the larger communities in which they live.

In one important respect, Mennonite Church USA is missing an important missional opportunity. It involves the racial/ethnic congregations that are currently the only growing segment of the denomination. Many of these urban congregations are recent immigrants to the United States. For instance, my own Central Plains Mennonite Conference has a Hmong congregation in the Twin Cities. From my visits to farmer's markets in the Twin Cities, I know that the Hmong people are avid and prolific gardeners, as their produce stands attest. Yet we as a recently agrarian denomination have not found ways to assist Hmong communities in the Twin Cities to become landed, or to find settings near urban areas where they might perpetuate their agrarian culture in this new North American setting.

Obviously, the traditional culture of the agrarian Hmong people would take on new features here in North America, just as the Low and Swiss German agrarian cultures of traditional Mennonites did when their communities moved to North America. Still, it seems it would be a missional priority of the highest urgency to enable new immigrant groups from Latin America, Asia, and Africa find places where they might preserve their unique agrarian cultures and at least slow if not halt their rapid assimilation into the dominant imperial culture of North America. Given the number of empty farmsteads (and church buildings) in most rural Mennonite communities like my own, it should not seem impossible for small farms to be made available to new immigrant communities who share both our Anabaptist faith and our agrarian heritage. But thus far, neither we as traditional Mennonites nor our new racial/ethnic fellow believers in these urban congregations have been able to connect on such a vision.

17. Schrock, "Featured," 2.
18. Groff, "Church Harvests," 44.

Part C

The Divine Intervention

Chapter 11

God Made Flesh in God's Own Self

The Word Became Flesh and Lived Among Us (John 1:14)

God Acts to Deliver Humanity and Creation from the Domination Systems

THE CALL OF GOD upon humanity is consistent and persistent. We are to participate with God in fulfilling God's purposes for creation and history. We are to represent God, so that God's character and nature can be seen in us. While the covenantal character of God with humankind described in the Old Testament reveals and illuminates very clearly facets of this divine purpose for humankind over against the domination forces unleashed by human sin, it also highlights a fundamental reality—we are subject to these domination forces!

A study of the Old Testament reveals God's purpose for humanity, the human rebellion against God, the development of the domination systems that control our world, and the various strategies and paradigms and models by which God intends humanity to fulfill the divine purpose within the domination system. But it also highlights the reality that we are captive to the domination systems unleashed by our sin.

It took a dramatic yet unobtrusive divine intervention at a specific time and place in history embodied in a concrete person bearing the divine image to change this reality—God in God's own self made flesh in the person of Jesus of Nazareth. Our redemption from the power of the domination systems was effected by this one man, who in his life embodied the life God intends for each person and all humanity. His life of humble obedience to God, loving service to others, and gentle care for creation, persistently followed to the point of death in the face of the domination systems of first-century CE Palestine, broke the power of those systems over humankind.

In this, Jesus was no victim of forces beyond his control. He chose to "lay down [his] life" (John 10:15) in nonviolent love in the face of these powers, trusting that if he did so, God would vindicate and redeem his life in resurrection. In the process, Jesus, fully human and mysteriously God-enfleshed, has made it possible for us humans

Healing God's Earth

to fulfill God's purpose for our lives, releasing us from the power of the domination systems in which we live.

The Biblical Story

Jesus the Divine Savior

I grew up with the highly gnosticized understanding of Jesus characteristic of the evangelical Christianity of North American culture. In this understanding, Jesus is seen as the divine savior who has come to deliver us out of this world, save us from hell, and bring us to heaven. In this understanding, Jesus has very little if anything to do with this world, other than perhaps to comfort and strengthen the believer until he or she can be delivered out of this world through death. There may be some personal moral/ethical implications involved in being a Christian, but there are virtually no social/political implications, and certainly no ecological implications. After all, the concern here is not with this world, the real world in which we live, but almost exclusively with the world to come. Our physical bodies and the physical world are after all in this view a fallen if not evil sphere destined for destruction after our souls are delivered from these bodies and this material world in death.

While this is the dominant view of Jesus within North American evangelical Christianity, it has dominated much of Christian thought to a greater or lesser degree since the second century after Christ. It is not altogether to be discounted, for it answers in a powerful way that profound human anxiety that led us into sin and rebellion against God described in chapter 2—our human anxiety about our mortality. Observing ourselves to be mortal creatures subject to death like all the other creatures around us, we humans have found it hard to trust God's promise that we are created in the divine image and destined to share an eternal life with God. It was our uneasiness with and mistrust of God that led us to seek shortcuts toward immortality—eating the forbidden fruit, thereby subjecting ourselves to the powers of evil and sin unleashed by our rebellion against God. So we do need a divine savior to be redeemed from the powers of evil and sin. We do need a divine savior to be granted the eternal life with God denied to us by our sin.

Still, the gnostic framework of religious thought in which much of contemporary evangelical Christianity expresses the idea of Jesus as the divine savior is a profound betrayal of genuine Christian belief in Jesus Christ as God's Son. Gnosticism as a religious philosophy arose in the Hellenistic/Roman world contemporaneously with Christian faith, but with much broader roots, including Greek philosophy and the Greek mysteries, and the eastern religious thought of Babylon and Persia. Already inclined toward syncretistic modes of thought, gnostic thinkers found much they could borrow in the Christian story of Jesus. Though exceedingly diverse, gnostic thinkers had in common a dualistic view of the world that denigrated the natural world and viewed it as evil. They affirmed a spiritual world of light ruled by a high God, and believed that humans were fragments of this spiritual world imprisoned in this visible world of darkness. Through various media of special *gnosis* (knowledge), humans could be delivered from this material world on a solitary journey toward the light. Aspects of Jesus' life and teachings became part of this esoteric *gnosis* for some of the gnostics, but they denied that Jesus truly became a mortal human. For them, Jesus was a spiritual being, only apparently human in form.[1]

M. C. D'Arcy, in *The Mind and the Heart of Love*, gives this evaluation of gnostic thought: "Gnosticism seems to have been one of those unfortunate forms of thought for which human beings have a chronic appetite. That is to say, it was a syncretistic philosophy and religion; it made an apparent lofty unity of the various systems known, and by picking out what it liked and eviscerating the doctrine of its true meaning within the original system, it pretended to be the highest and most spiritual of religions and the key to all others."[2] This is a typically harsh Christian assessment of Gnosticism, but it describes the subtle way in which gnostic thought undermined Christian faith. Christians, following Old Testament teaching, saw this creation and our bodies as good, though compromised by human sin and by the powers of evil unleashed by human sin. They affirmed the incarnation, that in Jesus Christ, God in God's own self became embodied in the flesh to dwell with us. They believed that Jesus came not to deliver us out of this material world into some spiritual realm, but to redeem this world to reflect the good creation of God through the formation of a human community living in justice and peace and love with one another in a relation of care and harmony and respect for the natural world.

Gnostic thought undercut the communal, socioeconomic, political, and ecological implications of Christian faith. For the gnostics, Jesus was irrelevant to the socioeconomic and political order and to the natural world in which we live. Jesus was useful only as a divine savior able to deliver spiritual humans trapped in this evil, material world into the sphere of spiritual enlightenment. In Gnosticism, there is no effort to build or maintain communal patterns of life. Each spirit is on his or her own individual journey toward the light.

I'm of course aware of the current popularity of gnostic thought in American culture, reflected for instance in Dan Brown's novels. I also have read with appreciation scholarly reviews of recently discovered gnostic literature, as in Elaine Pagels's *The Gnostic Gospels*. I appreciate Pagel's view that the development of the creedal, hierarchical institutionalization of the church effectively silenced and distorted gnostic forms of thought.[3] Nevertheless, I continue to view the dominant, privatized, and spiritualized Christianity of our popular culture as the triumph of gnostic thought. This view of Jesus as the divine savior who has come to save us out of this world and

---

1. Walker, *History*, 51–53.
2. D'Arcy, *Mind*, 57.
3. Pagels, *Gnostic*, 149–51.

bring us to heaven owes more to Gnosticism than it does to the person of Jesus Christ revealed in the gospels.

In my own case, this gnosticized Christianity of the popular culture was ameliorated to no small extent by the Anabaptist Mennonite theology of my upbringing. Rural Mennonite congregations throughout much of the twentieth century found themselves having an unresolved bifurcated theological understanding. On the one hand, Mennonites were drawn toward the conservative, evangelical tenets of a gnosticized Fundamentalism. At the same time, they sought to cling to the more radical Anabaptist perspectives of their heritage, which called them to engage with and care for this world in a transformative socioeconomic and political challenge to the dominant powers bent on oppressing, dominating, and exploiting both the human community and the natural world. While this bifurcation of theological thought sometimes led to conflicts within congregations and institutions of the Mennonite church, these two streams of theological thought tended to reside uneasily together within the psyches of many Mennonites and many Mennonite congregations throughout the twentieth century.

I'm aware, in any case, of my own uneasiness as a pastor in speaking of the more radical, transformative message of the Christian gospel. I remember feeling the need to apologize for saying or implying that perhaps Christian faith had something to do with how we live in this world. Yes indeed, Jesus came to save us from hell and to bring us to heaven. But perhaps Jesus also came to transform how we relate to creation and how we live together with one another. Still there is something incredibly satisfying about feeling that we are helplessly trapped in this evil and wicked world, but that we have a divine savior who has come to deliver us out of this world. It allows us to have hope for the future while also not intruding very deeply into our conformity to and complicity with the dominant culture of domination, oppression, and exploitation. We can go on living as we are in this life, since there isn't anything we can do to change it and since it is in any case on its way to destruction, all the while being assured of our divine deliverance for the life to come—truly, in the minds of many, the best of both worlds! As D'Arcy says in his evaluation of Gnosticism, "Not so many grasp the truth that a too spiritual ideal which despises the body and this earth is also anti-Christian."[4]

The points at which my preaching ministry was both most effective and most abrasive were those times when I was able to challenge the Gnosticism of popular Christianity, but it took me many years of trial and error before I could find the language to do this effectively. Not surprisingly, the more effectively I was able to communicate this challenge to a Gnosticized Christianity, the less popular I was with segments of the congregations I served, even though this message usually resonated well with most parishioners.

---

4. D'Arcy, *Mind*, 60.

So yes, indeed, Jesus was and is the divine savior! But Jesus came not to deliver us out of this world but to redeem us from the powers of evil and sin to which we had become enslaved because of our own sin and rebellion against God. Jesus came not "to condemn the world, but in order that the world (*cosmos*) might be saved through him" (John 3:17). Divine savior that Jesus was and is, Jesus came among us not as a spiritual being untouched by this material world. Instead, Jesus came among us, most improbably, as God in truly human form. As John says in his gospel, using terms familiar to the gnostics but as a direct challenge to their worldview, "The Word became flesh and lived among us, and we have seen his glory, the glory as of a father's only son, full of grace and truth" (John 1:14). In contrast to gnostic thought, Christians affirm that Jesus was truly and fully a mortal human like ourselves.

It is indeed a scandalous proposition, this Christian affirmation that "God so loved the world that he gave his only Son, so that everyone who believes in him may not perish but may have eternal life" (John 3:16). But nothing else would do. If humans were to be delivered from their slavery to the powers of evil and sin, if God's creation was to be restored to its original goodness, if God cared that much for this good creation God had made, then God must come to us in fully human form. Or to express it from the other side, this man Jesus, who was the Word and was with God and was God, the one through whom all things came into being and in whom there is both life and light, had now been born into the human family as a unique human being at a particular time and place in history (John 1:1–5). The language of incarnation, the enfleshment of God, fails to adequately describe the mystery that lies at the heart of genuine Christian faith. God took on human being fully and truly in the person of Jesus Christ!

Jesus the Cosmic Lord

One of the most striking elements in a reading of the gospels is the amazement or astonishment Jesus engenders in the people around him. Again and again people are astounded by the things Jesus says or does. Often, as in Mark 6:1–6, the astonishment rises out of the incongruity of Jesus' humble origins and appearance as an ordinary human and the extraordinary authority and activity of his words and actions. As Jesus returned to his hometown (presumably Nazareth), the people were "astounded" (Mark 6:2) by Jesus' teaching in the synagogue. After all, they knew his origins. He was a carpenter, the son of Mary. His brothers and sisters were well known. And as sometimes happens, the people's familiarity led in this case to "offense" (Mark 6:3) at Jesus. Who does he think he is?

Sometimes, as in Mark 1:22 and 6:2, it is Jesus' words or teaching that astound people, primarily because of the wisdom or authority of his words. Often, such teaching is accompanied by healings or exorcisms, and Jesus' power over unclean spirits engenders amazement (Mark 1:27). Jesus' assumption of divine prerogatives also engenders both amazement on the part of the people and consternation on the part of the religious authorities. This is the case with Jesus' presumption to forgive the sins of the paralytic (Mark 2:1–12), his assumption of authority over the sacred Sabbath (Mark 2:27–28), and his healing on the Sabbath, which led to the first conspiracy to destroy him by the unlikely alliance of Pharisees and Herodians (Mark 3:1-6).

Jesus' unique identity as "God made flesh" not only astounded humans, but also was recognized by the demons and evil spirits inhabiting and enslaving humans (Mark 1:34; 3:11; 5:7), who also submit to his authority. The disciples were also in "great awe" and "utterly astounded" by Jesus' authority over the natural forces of wind and wave in twice stilling the Sea of Galilee (Mark 4:35–41; 6:47–52). The recognition of Jesus' unique character as a human being is also affirmed by Gentiles outside the boundaries of Israel, as people are "astounded beyond measure" by Jesus' healing of the deaf and mute man in the Decapolis (7:31–37). Clearly the gospels intend to portray Jesus as a person of extraordinary authority and power despite his humble vocation as a carpenter and origin in obscure Nazareth.

The words and actions of Jesus that inspire such awe on the part of those who lived with him have often been used to prove the divinity of Christ. *See, no mere human could do such deeds or speak in this way, so Jesus must have been God incarnate.* While this may be true, and while these stories may help us to accept that Jesus the man was God incarnate, such a formal and rational use of these stories is far removed from the experience of those who lived with Jesus. They had no intention or desire to prove Jesus' divinity as a rational proposition. They just wanted to know how they were going to cope with all the powers and forces that were dominating and oppressing their lives.

As has been the case with peasants in rural communities throughout history, the peasants who lived in the villages of Galilee where Jesus carried on his ministry faced incredible pressures from the dominant culture in which they were living. Of course, they had to deal with the physical illnesses and diseases of life exacerbated by the poverty in which they lived and unrelieved by a working health care system. They faced the same vagaries of storms and natural forces rural people always confront. They endured the heavy restrictions placed upon their lives by the religious authorities, as for example, Sabbath restrictions that crippled their freedom to observe the intent of the Sabbath. They experienced the oppression of living under Roman occupation, either directly or through Herod Antipas, the proxy for Rome in Galilee. Through both religious and secular authorities who milked the fertile Galilee to support the urban elite, they confronted immense indebtedness and disenfranchisement from their land due to high taxation. In addition, they lived with the frustrations of a polarized, diverse society, divided ethnically between Jew and Gentile and by class between rich and poor, which meant that they were always in competition with other downtrodden groups for scarce resources.

Of course, the people likely did not experience all these forces as direct causes for their dire plight. They shared many of the same values and prejudices of the dominant culture in which they lived, and so may have willingly endured, for instance, the temple taxation, and despised their non-Jewish neighbors as heartily as the religious authorities despite the fact that they were as oppressed as their Gentile neighbors. At the same time, people lived under the oppression of their failure to live up to what they felt God had called them to be. They couldn't imagine their lives as worthy even if they were free. Forgiveness seemed an impossibility to them, and they felt trapped in a way of living from which there was no escape.

The reality is that the rural peasants of Galilee were indeed *occupied* or *possessed* by spiritual powers, which manifested themselves in the various forms of oppression just described above. They experienced this as *demon possession*, which rendered them incapable of improving their lot or breaking free of their oppression. They were held captive in Satan's household, as Jesus described it in his saying about the strong man (Mark 3:23–27). Accused of casting out demons as the ruler of demons, Jesus pointed out the absurdity of the charge, and declared that if Satan's house was being plundered, if people were being delivered from the evil powers holding them captive, then Satan himself (the strong man) must first have been bound. I am indebted to Ched Myers's *Binding the Strong Man*, both for these insights into Mark 3 and for this reading of the significance of Jesus' ministry.[5]

Here we see the immediate reason for the awe in which Jesus was held by those among whom he lived. Jesus kept revealing himself by his words and actions as someone capable of redeeming the people from the oppressive forces under which they were living. By his words and actions, Jesus demonstrated that he both assumed the authority and had the power to release people from the oppression under which they lived. By releasing people from their demons and by calling them into a new kind of relationship with one another, God, and creation, Jesus was engaging in a process of community formation that would enable them to live as alternative communities of faith within the dominant, oppressive culture in which they were living.

This was in part an educational venture, enabling people to identify and name the oppressive forces to which they were subject. It was in part a community-enablement project, facilitating the emergence of an alternative community. But more than all that, it was a spiritual empowerment in which Jesus was engaged. Due, as Christians confess, to God's presence in his life, Jesus proved himself stronger than the forces of evil and oppression that were operating within the human and natural world of God's creation. In any case, Jesus assumed the authority and demonstrated his power to neutralize and overcome the forces of evil.

A key part of Jesus' calling and ministry, demonstrated again in his words and his actions, was to reveal the true nature of God and God's intention for humanity. More often than not, people understood the oppressive forces under which they lived as God's punishment upon them for their sins. Whether manifested in terms of disease or natural forces or human agency, people imagined that they were only getting

---

5. Myers, *Binding*, 164–67.

Healing God's Earth

what they deserved. In contrast, whether through his teaching or healing ministry or through nature miracles, Jesus assumed the authority to indicate God's benevolent character and intention for humanity and creation. God makes the sun shine and the rain fall on just and unjust alike (Matt 5:45). God provides a bountiful catch of fish after a long night's labor (Luke 5:1–11). God intends for people to be whole. God not only expects people to be treated justly and fairly, but God is a God of unlimited mercy and forgiveness, who forgives "seventy-seven times" (Matt 18:22).

In all these ways, Jesus functioned as the *cosmic Lord*, the one with the authority and the power to conquer all the forces of evil and sin under which humanity and creation are bound. He did so as the "Son of God," who fully shared the divine being of God, even as a humble human being. Was Jesus himself always aware of his uniqueness? Was he self-consciously aware of being the "God/man"? The gospels seem to portray him that way, but hardly in the psychologizing manner in which we moderns ask these questions. In any case, despite the power and the authority Jesus assumed, Jesus never presumed to be anything other than the humble man of mortal flesh he also was. If he had a special relationship with the divine that enabled him to work wonders, it was never something Jesus presumed upon, and surely not with reference to any selfish interests of his own. Jesus functioned as "the cosmic Lord" only for God's sake and for the sake of God's reign here on earth.

Jesus the Suffering Servant

The central struggle of Jesus' life, as in each of our lives, was how to fulfill God's intention for his life. As do we all at our best, Jesus had a desire to do God's will and some notion about what that entailed. We all desire at some level a better and more harmonious world. We all want justice to prevail and for everyone to be able to live "healthy and productive lives," as the Gates Foundation ad declares.[6] It isn't for lack of understanding or comprehension that we humans fail to live out God's purposes for our lives. Where we go astray is in choosing the means to pursue God's intention, and in the will to follow the way that best reflects God's purposes. In other words, we might all theoretically agree that we should live in a social order of justice and peace and love in which everyone is so treated, but it is in the means used to achieve that end that we go astray. Or if we do perceive the appropriate means, we lack the will to follow that path if it requires us to change our behavior or values. The common refrain, "We don't have any choice," indicates that we feel powerless to do what is required to achieve God's purposes with the appropriate means. So we keep on seeking justice through the use of domination, force, violence, intimidation, and exploitation—all the "shortcuts" we humans have devised that are supposedly more effective and efficient than the appropriate means God has laid out for us.

---

6. See the reference to the Gates advertisement in chapter 9.

God Made Flesh in God's Own Self

The Gospels of Mark, Matthew, and Luke all present Jesus struggling as a young man with all these issues before embarking on a public ministry on behalf of God's rule, the ministry to which Jesus already felt called. The Synoptic Gospels describe a forty-day sojourn of Jesus in the wilderness being "tempted by Satan" (Mark 1:13). This sojourn occurred immediately after Jesus had been baptized by his cousin John in the Jordan, an experience in which Jesus was confirmed with divine blessing in the descent of the Spirit as a dove and the heavenly words, "You are my Son, the Beloved; with you I am well pleased" (Mark 1:11).

Several things are notable about this temptation experience of Jesus. It occurred immediately after Jesus came into a full acceptance of God's call upon his life and a full realization of his relationship with God as "God's Son." It occurred during a forty-day fast "in the wilderness," which as we have repeatedly seen is the place where we humans are thrown beyond our own capabilities to depend fully upon God. The significance of a sojourn of forty days or years in the wilderness as the setting for a formative experience of learning to depend upon God has multiple Old Testament precedents.[7] It came at the instigation of the same Spirit that had just descended upon him as a dove, who "drove" Jesus out into the wilderness (Mark 1:12). But it also involved an encounter with Satan, the embodiment of all the forces of evil and domination and the source of the same temptations to find shortcuts in doing God's will that had led the first humans and all of us into bondage to the powers of evil (Genesis 3).

The Gospels of Matthew and Luke provide us with a description of the nature of the temptations that came to Jesus from Satan during this forty-day sojourn in the wilderness. They revolved around economics, turning stones into bread to feed the people (Matt 4:3–4; Luke 4:3–4); religion, throwing himself from the pinnacle of the temple in order to assume religious authority for a reformed religion (Matt 4:5–7; Luke 4:9–12); and politics, receiving political dominion over all the kingdoms of the world (Matt 4:8–10; Luke 4:5–8). In each case, Jesus responded to the temptation with quotes from the book of Deuteronomy. "One does not live by bread alone, but by every word that comes from the mouth of the LORD" (Deut 8:3). "Do not put the LORD your God to the test" (Deut 6:16). "The LORD your God you shall fear; him you shall serve" (Deut 6:13). For his part, Satan demonstrated his own knowledge of Scripture by quoting Psalm 91:11–12 in the second temptation, promising the protection of God's angels who will "bear you up, so that you will not dash your foot against a stone." But Satan's hand is called in the last temptation, when it is revealed that all the kingdoms of the world will belong to Jesus if only he will "fall down and worship" Satan! After all, as Satan says in Luke, all the glory and authority of the kingdoms of the world "have been given over to me, and I give it to anyone I please" (Luke 4:6). Political dominion is Satan's realm!

Notice that none of these temptations involves seeking something wrong. Each of them involves a good and positive end—full bellies for the people, the establishment

---

7. See the discussion on wilderness in chapter 6.

of a reformed religion, and a political order of justice and peace. The strongest temptations for Jesus, as for us, came in the realm of means, not of ends. This is not to say that some people are not also tempted to pursue wrong ends, and yield to those temptations. But it is to recognize that the strongest and most subtle temptations involve the means toward a good end. Jesus was tempted to take shortcuts to desirable ends. He was presumably capable of using and choosing these shortcuts, given his unique character as the "God/man." Instead, Jesus chose to remain true to his human character, to observe the limitations of his mortal humanity, and to be obedient to the divine calling that was his—to be God's suffering servant of love.

Jesus was clearly a person immersed in the Scriptures of his tradition. Not only was he quick to quote from the book of Deuteronomy in resisting the temptations that came to him. He was also deeply immersed in the Psalter, the prayer/hymn book of his people. When it came to choosing the means of fulfilling the divine vocation, Jesus turned to the descriptions of the prophetic vocation voiced by the book of Isaiah. Isaiah 61:1–2a, with its call to proclaim God's year of Jubilee, became the text for Jesus' inaugural sermon at Nazareth, according to Luke 4:14–30. Indeed, it seems to have been the Servant Songs of Isaiah 42–53 that most clearly informed Jesus' perception of his mission and its method. Jesus felt himself called to confront the powers of evil and sin binding his land and its people with unconditional love—self-sacrificial, vicarious, suffering love involving persecution and death.

It is noteworthy that there is nothing new about either this mission of confrontation or this method of vicarious, suffering love. The intention of God for humankind was and had been known for centuries, repeated by the prophets again and again. Indeed, it formed the core of Israel's calling as a people of God, the call to be for God "a priestly kingdom and a holy nation" (Exod 19:6) in the midst of the nations of the world. So Jesus hardly introduced anything new to the world through his life and ministry. What Jesus succeeded in doing, where humanity has always failed, was to resist the temptations to choose shortcuts in the pursuit of this calling. What Jesus succeeded in doing was to remain faithful to God's way of suffering love in the fulfillment of his mission even to the point of death.

There was, to be sure, nothing inevitable about Jesus' suffering and death. Jesus was not trapped in circumstances that led inevitably to his suffering and death. Throughout his life and ministry, Jesus made it clear that both his confrontation with the powers of evil and his ultimate death at their hands were matters of his own choosing. This becomes most clear in Jesus' words in John 10 about being the good shepherd who "lays down his life for the sheep" (John 10:11). "No one takes it [my life] from me, but I lay it down of my own accord. I have power to lay it down and I have power to take it up again" (John 10:18). It should also be said that Jesus had no death wish. Jesus loved this world and this life as much as and more than any of us do. In the Garden of Gethsemane the night before his death, Jesus prayed that some other way might be found to accomplish God's purpose (Mark 14:32–42). He would have loved to have lived out his life in the quiet obscurity of home and family, as portrayed in Nikos Kazantzakis' marvelous novel *The Last Temptation of Christ*. This is what gives Jesus' choice to "lay down his life" its authenticity and integrity as a vicarious sacrifice.

In any case, Jesus' ministry brought him into early deadly confrontation with the religious and political authorities. Already in Mark 3:6, we find the sworn political and religious enemies of one another, the Herodians and Pharisees, conspiring together about how to destroy Jesus. Throughout the gospels, Jesus never had any illusions about the cost of following his vocation as God's Messiah. Indeed, in three successive chapters of Mark, 8–10, Jesus spoke openly to his uncomprehending disciples about his impending suffering, death, and resurrection at the hands of the religious and political authorities.

If Jesus himself was quite aware of the costs of following in God's way, his disciples demonstrated that they were still under the sway of the tempting shortcuts—religious and political and economic power—as revealed in their incomprehension and internal power struggles after each of these three announcements of Jesus' passion and death. At least in Mark's gospel, Jesus spent the better part of his ministry trying to lay the ground work so that when he was gone the deluded disciples might finally come to understand the significance of his life, his death, and his resurrection.

Ultimately, Jesus precipitated the crisis that led to his voluntary death by bringing his announcement of God's rule to Jerusalem at the Passover festival, likely in the year 30 CE. His staged demonstration of popular support in the "triumphal entry," his action of shutting down temple operations, and his direct confrontations with the religious authorities (Mark 11–12) demonstrated that Jesus was engaged in a carefully orchestrated challenge to the religious authorities. The religious authorities responded by collaborating with Roman officials to have Jesus executed. Throughout these actions, Jesus never presumed to be anything other than the mortal human he was. At every turn, temptations to take shortcuts, such as calling on legions of angels for deliverance (Matt 26:53), were resisted. Jesus remained true to his vocation of fulfilling as a mortal human God's intention for the human family.

So we ask, what made Jesus efficacious as a redeemer of creation and humanity? It was surely not just his sacrificial death, as in so many understandings of the atonement in Christian theology through the years. It was instead the totality of his life, the choices he made that led to his death, his willingness to give his life in self-sacrificing love for God, others, and God's creation. In his submission to God's will, his love for others, and his care for God's creation, Jesus lived the life God intended for all humankind. In accepting the limitations of his mortal humanity and refusing to accept shortcuts of power and domination, Jesus thwarted the powers of evil. When the powers of evil conspired to cut short his life, Jesus continued to live in love until his death, even as he hung upon the cross. Throughout his life, until his very death, Jesus continued to trust God's promise of sharing in eternal life, despite and beyond the death of his mortal body. And in the end, God vindicated Jesus' trust by raising him from the dead and granting him a new order of existence, which anticipates God's new creation, a redeemed world.

Jesus was able to do all this, we Christians confess, because in him God in God's own self had come to dwell. But just as importantly, Jesus was able to do all this because he remained resolutely a mortal human being, despite having genuine shortcuts of God/manhood available to him. It was finally that God became human, assuming our mortal humanity and submitting to the powers of evil, that made our redemption possible. In Jesus, God in God's own self came to redeem us from the powers of evil, by assuming mortal human nature fully, even unto death.

What Jesus' life, death, and resurrection reveals above all is the means by which God intends to conquer the forces of evil and sin that hold humanity and creation in their grip. That means is self-sacrificial love, the ἀγάπη (agape) described in the New Testament and modeled for us so well in the person of Jesus Christ. While the forces of evil and sin rely on domination and oppression and exploitation, being the embodiment of the shortcuts we humans chose in our attempts to become like God, God remains true to God's character of self-giving, relational love in addressing these forces of evil. In the person of Jesus, through his life, death, and resurrection, God overcame the forces of evil and sin with this self-giving love, and thereby redeemed humanity and creation from the grip of these forces. Now we no longer are bound by these powers, the shortcuts of domination and exploitation and oppression we had chosen. Now we are free to relate to God and others and creation with the same self-giving love we see in Jesus, thereby participating with God in the redemption of the world. Through Jesus' life, death, and resurrection we are able to represent the true character of God, which is our human calling.

The triumph of love over the forces of evil is nowhere more aptly described than in the final lines of the third sonnet, "Nor to avenge any wrong," in Kenneth Boulding's *There Is a Spirit: The Nayler Sonnets*, based on a statement of faith by the British leader of the Society of Friends, James Nayler, in 1660. The sonnet begins with the doubt we all have about the efficacy of love:

> Now am I veined by an eroding doubt,
> Insidious as decay, with poison rife,
> Is love indeed the end and law of life,
> When lush, grimacing hates so quickly sprout?

But after exploring the ways in which revenge so easily does "my sword of reason flout," Boulding points out that though hate "rises in enfolding flame," it soon dies out, while "love's small constant light burns still the same." Then come the final, concluding lines of the sonnet:

> Know this: though love is weak and hate is strong,
> Yet hate is short, and love is very long.[8]

---

8. Boulding, *There Is a Spirit*, 3.

The Myth of Redemptive Violence Exposed

Since September 11, 2001, the American public has been subjected to a daily barrage of violent, retributive, vindictive, and militaristic images and rhetoric. Within months of that awful attack on targets in New York City and Washington, DC, using passenger airliners as weapons, the United States invaded Afghanistan, the presumed origin and sanctuary of those responsible for the attack, and the war in Afghanistan has continued unabated since then. In addition, the United States staged a preemptive attack on Iraq in 2003, and the last US troops were only withdrawn in December, 2011. Meanwhile, the United States has waged attacks using drone missiles throughout these years on presumed terrorist targets in South Asia, often at the expense of collateral damage involving the death of innocent civilians. George W. Bush, the US president of those years, used language reminiscent of Western movies and books, claiming that the US will search out and destroy the enemy, bringing them to "justice" dead or alive. Bush's successor, Barack Obama, the winner of a Nobel Peace Prize, completed that threat in March 2011 by ordering a Navy Seal attack on the compound of Osama bin Laden in Pakistan, killing him in cold blood with no effort made to exercise due process—hardly a just act.

Of course, there is nothing new about the mindset reflected in the attitudes and actions of the United States in the aftermath of 9/11. We are daily reminded that we owe our freedom to the courageous sacrifice of United States men and women who have fought in past wars and who are serving now in the armed forces, though the connection between our freedom and those military actions is hardly examined carefully. One need not disparage the courage or the sacrifice of military men and women and their families to ask whether the militaristic policies and actions of the United States are indeed making us more secure and free as a society.

The more fundamental question has to do with the efficaciousness of violent retribution as an instrument of either justice or security. This is simply assumed within the ethos of the myth governing the actions of the dominant society, which Walter Wink refers to as the "myth of redemptive violence."[9] The staple of virtually every entertainment product of the popular culture, as one would expect for the myth governing the most fundamental values of the culture, the myth of redemptive violence assumes the efficacy of violent retribution in dealing with evil. We must be stronger and more powerful than our adversary, and we must be prepared to exterminate our adversary to preserve our freedom. So whenever the community faces an external threat, we wait for the hero to ride in, six-guns blazing, to redeem the community from the threat by the extermination of the enemy.

But as Wink points out, neither the adversary nor the hero ever learn anything from their encounter.[10] They simply replay over and over again the same destruc-

---

9. Wink, *Engaging*, 13–17.
10. Ibid., 18.

tive story, with only the stakes growing larger with every destructive encounter, in an unending cycle of retributive violence. Far from resolving threats to our security or making us more secure, the myth of redemptive violence only perpetuates the cycle of violent retribution. Despite the claim, there is nothing redemptive about violence, and violence leads neither to justice nor to security.

Walter Wink finds the roots for the myth of redemptive violence in the creation myth of ancient Mesopotamia, the *Enuma Elish*, in which the world is created out of the murdered body of the goddess Tiamat.[11] "War, conquest, plunder, rape, and enslavement are all ordained in the very constitution of the universe, which itself is formed from the corpse of a murdered goddess. 'Civilization' is a condition of periodic or perpetual warfare, 'peace' the achievement of warfare, 'prosperity' the fruit of warfare successfully accomplished. If human beings are created from the blood of a slaughtered god, how can one expect from them anything but violence?"[12] And, as Wink aptly points out, the myth of redemptive violence is rooted in the subjugation of women through the establishment of patriarchal order. Women are the first and primary casualty of the attempt to maintain power through domination and force.[13]

What isn't clear, and is perhaps unanswerable, is the question of whether we humans are violent by nature. Is aggression and violence endemic to the human condition, as many scientists in the 1960s suggested?[14] Is violence indeed constitutive of the very creation of the universe and life itself, as we often assume when we talk of nature? Alfred Tennyson, in the 56th canto of his poem, *In Memoriam*, responding to the myriad newly discovered but now extinct forms of life from eons past and contrasting evolutionary life with the life of the human, speaks of "Nature, red in tooth and claw."[15]

In view of this common perception, I've been fascinated with this statement by Fritjof Capra, the German physicist, in his book *The Web of Life*: "The recognition of symbiosis as a major evolutionary force has profound philosophical implications. All larger organisms, including ourselves, are living testimonies to the fact that destructive practices do not work in the long run. In the end the aggressors always destroy themselves, making way for others who know how to cooperate and get along. Life is much less a competitive struggle for survival than a triumph of cooperation and creativity. Indeed, since the creation of the first nucleated cells, evolution has proceeded through ever more intricate arrangements of cooperation and coevolution."[16] Perhaps violence and aggression are not after all endemic to the nature of life! Perhaps after all it is possible for humans to live together in communities where cooperation and mutual care are the operating principles.

11. Ibid., 14.
12. Ibid., 33.
13. Ibid., 17.
14. See Morris, *Naked Ape;* Lorenz, *On Aggression;* Ardrey, *African Genesis*.
15. Tennyson, "In Memoriam," 146.
16. Capra, *Web*, 243.

In the end, Wink roots the rise of the domination system and the myth of redemptive violence to the emergence of the *powers*, the spiritual manifestation of those institutions and structures characteristic of urban civilization as I have been describing it in this book. "But Satan, demons, and the Powers are rather late arrivals. Humanity was slow to perceive the spirituality of complex institutions and forces. These spiritual realities are the peculiar distillate of domination, and they only became discernible after human societies had reached a certain threshold of density, complexity, and conflict."[17] A little later, Wink goes on to describe how both leaders and people become slaves to the powers in such systems. The decisions of leaders "are determined not by what would enhance the quality of human life but by what will increase competitive power. . . . People have thus become the slaves of their evolving systems, rather than civilized society being the servant of its members."[18]

I conclude that the myth of redemptive violence has its origin in the development of urban civilization and imperial powers. As noted in chapter 2, violence itself is endemic to the human condition and often most evident in the most intimate relationships of life. But it is in the structural and institutional dynamics of civilization that the myth of redemptive violence achieves its oppressive power, binding leaders and people together in the cycle of violent retribution and ultimately leading to their destruction. It is from these powers that we humans need to be redeemed, if we are to recover the life for which God has created us.

Walter Wink's mantra in *Engaging the Powers* is "the Powers are good, the Powers are fallen, the Powers will be redeemed."[19] By this Wink means that the powers are part of God's good creation, those authorities that "have been instituted by God" (Rom 13:1) for the welfare of the human family. His book is a description of the fallenness of the Powers, attested both by human experience and the fall.[20] Wink makes the faith affirmation, which I too share, that the powers can and will be redeemed by God through the life, death, and resurrection of Christ.

In speaking about the redemption of the powers, Wink contrasts a socio-political approach that envisions structural and institutional changes on the part of governments, universities, corporations, and denominations with personal changes and the transformation of individual lives through conversion.[21] Wink eventually and expectedly comes down on the side of "social entities," in which the institutions of society live up to their own positive role and potential as powers authorized by God.[22] I would concur with Wink that Jesus came and lived and died and rose again not just to change and transform individual lives, but also the structures and institutions of human life.

17. Wink, *Engaging*, 39.
18. Ibid., 42.
19. Ibid., 65.
20. Ibid., 69.
21. Ibid., 73–85.
22. Ibid., 84.

In Colossians 2:13–15, Paul affirms that it was by his death on the cross that Jesus "disarmed the rulers and authorities and made a public example of them, triumphing over them in it [the cross]" (Col 2:15). By Jesus' sacrificial death, the vicious and ever-expanding cycle of violence is broken and exposed for the sham that it is.

However, in this book I also posit another sphere for the transformative work of God in Jesus Christ. I am not optimistic about the historical redemption of the Powers. It is for me, as it is to some extent also for Wink, an eschatological affirmation, rather than a historical one. It is not that I think institutional change is impossible or completely unachievable. Efforts toward positive changes in governments, corporations, universities, denominations, and other organized structures of civilization should be hoped for and worked toward. But I don't think we as humans can afford to wait around for the redemption of the powers! We need to get on with God's work by forming and re-forming sustainable, local, face-to-face communities that reflect God's transformative redemption in Christ.

The redemption of community seems more plausible historically than the reformation and redemption of the powers. Indeed, as we shall see in chapter 13, it is the communal manifestation of the church as local congregations of believers that turns out to be primary creation of Jesus' life and ministry, and then also the agent of God's redemptive work on behalf of creation and the powers, as well as humanity. Of course, Jesus came to save and redeem individuals, as the gnostic myth of salvation affirms. And of course, Jesus came to redeem the powers, and with them all creation, as well, as Wink affirms. But it is impossible for individuals to be delivered from the powers individually. None of us have the strength, even as persons redeemed by God in Christ, to be truly free from the oppressive cultures of domination in which we live. We can only be delivered from the powers by becoming a part of a local community that understands itself as a new creation, an alternative to the systems of domination and oppression and exploitation in which it lives. And on the other hand, the powers can hardly be redeemed by individuals. Movements for radical social change led by charismatic individuals consume those individuals. It is only as local communities emerge as alternatives to systems of domination and oppression and exploitation that significant societal change is possible.

So it turns out that God's primary vehicle in bringing redemption to the world through Christ is neither the individual nor the state, or society as a whole. In this sense, Jesus didn't come (just) to save you and me, nor did he come (only) to effect societal change. Jesus came, in the first instance, to bring into reality local, face-to-face, redeemed communities of faith as alternatives to the dominant cultures of the world, communities in which individuals can be saved and through which societies can be reformed from the bottom up.[23]

---

23. See Yoder, *Politics*, 149–53, for a similar argument.

Mennonites and the Nonviolent Atonement

The narrative of the salvific nature of Jesus developed in the final biblical section of this chapter, "Jesus the suffering servant," portrays Jesus' life, death, and resurrection as an integrated whole. Jesus lived in obedience to God's intention for the human family, reflecting God's image most clearly in the manner of his life. Jesus died as a consequence of the way in which he lived in challenging the powers of domination and exploitation. God raised Jesus from the dead to vindicate Jesus' faithfulness and reveal the triumph of sacrificial love in breaking the cycle of retaliation and violence that had held humanity in its grip.

This is the *Christus Victor* way of speaking about Jesus' saving work on the cross, in contrast to Anselm of Canterbury's *satisfaction* theory of atonement, and the *moral influence* theory of atonement formulated by Abelard in response to Anselm's satisfaction theory.[24] The Christus Victor motif is the classical Christian view of the atonement, but it "fell out of favor," Walter Wink asserts, following J. Denny Weaver, "once Christianity became the religion of the empire."[25] The "*preservation of the empire became the decisive criterion for ethical behavior.*"[26] Now that Christianity was required to justify the retributive cycle of violence by the empire, the Christus Victor motif was no longer acceptable: "it was subversive to the church's role as state religion."[27]

Emerging as it did as a countercultural, pacifist sect in the sixteenth century, Anabaptism should have had no problem with the classical Christus Victor motif of the atonement. Indeed, it would seem to have been a justification for the Anabaptist opposition to the domination, oppression, and persecution they suffered at the hands of the states and official churches of the Reformation era, empowering their nonviolent resistance to their persecutors. The tension, for the early Anabaptists, was not with the satisfaction theory of atonement, but with the role of discipleship in relation to atonement, as I explored in one of my major papers during seminary studies, entitled "Christ In Us or Christ For Us?" What does it mean that Christ died for us when we find ourselves required to die for him?[28] Anabaptists, in other words, focused their theological energy not on academic theories of atonement but on the basis for their commitment to communal discipleship.

While I'm not aware of historical studies of the development of atonement theory in subsequent Mennonite history, I would hazard that Mennonites began to buy into satisfaction theories of atonement of classical Protestantism only when we had settled into life in our promised land, the United States. It was here in the twentieth century that we began to borrow significantly from the conservative theological currents of

---

24. Weaver, *Nonviolent*, 14–19.
25. Wink, *Engaging*, 150; see also Weaver, *Nonviolent*, 85.
26. Wink, *Engaging*, 150 (italics in original).
27. Ibid.
28. See Yoder, *Politics*, 120–28.

the dominant culture around us. The individualistic, gnosticized theology of personal salvation began to replace the communal theology of corporate discipleship we inherited from our tradition.

This accounts, I think, for the controversy surrounding the restatement of classical narrative Christus Victor theology made by J. Denny Weaver in his book *The Nonviolent Atonement* in some Mennonite circles. What should have sounded familiar and sound in a tradition committed to discipleship and a redeemed community suddenly seemed suspect to many in the pew. Where is the comforting assurance that Jesus paid the price for me, that my sins are covered by Jesus' blood, and that I am therefore saved to go to heaven? All that classical narrative Christus Victor theology gets me is a ticket to costly discipleship as I join with others in the formation of a redeemed community that puts us in opposition to the dominant culture around us!

So I am grateful to the recent generation of Anabaptist theologians who have articulated for us the classical narrative Christus Victor theology. It is this narrative, rooted in Jesus' life, death, and resurrection, that has the power to deliver us from our bondage to the dominant culture and to shape a redeemed people as an alternative community of faith to the dominant culture of oppression and exploitation in which we live.

But I'm grateful also to those many communities within the Mennonite world today who, however theologically unsophisticated they might be, still embody these kinds of alternative communities of faith. The authors of the book *Amish Grace* emphasize again and again that the Amish people of Lancaster County were able to forgive the family of the shooter who killed their daughters because they were immersed in the words and example of Jesus, their heritage of martyrdom and self-sacrifice, and the self-denial of living in an intensely close community of faith.[29] No wonder a culture steeped in the myth of redemptive violence and retribution stood in amazement and disbelief at this community, which in Jesus and like Jesus broke the cycle of retribution and revenge with forgiveness and love!

---

29. Kraybill, et al., *Amish Grace*, see especially the chapters in Part Two.

Chapter 12

The Restoration of Rural Community in the Person of Jesus Christ

The Time Is Fulfilled, and the Kingdom of God Has Come Near; Repent, and Believe In the Good News (Mark 1:15)

God's Rule in Person

JESUS GREW UP IN the highly urbanized and dynamic society of first-century CE Galilee. A few miles from Jesus' hometown of Nazareth, the Roman city of Sepphoris was being rebuilt, and on the Sea of Galilee, Herod Antipas was building his new capital of Tiberias. Perhaps as the son of a carpenter Jesus did work in these growing urban centers. Yet when it came time to fulfill his calling, Jesus inaugurated his ministry by seeking baptism from John the Baptist, who stood lonely resolute against the trends of Herodian urbanization.

As he contemplated his mission, Jesus intentionally turned away from the political, economic, and religious manifestations of the domination systems in which he lived. He chose instead to be an itinerant teacher and healer who announced the imminent appearance of God's rule to the dispossessed and threatened rural people and villages of Galilee. Jesus' itinerant ministry was designed to empower the rural Galileans to stand together as communities of faith in God's rule against all the depredations of the domination systems under which they lived.

But Jesus not only challenged the foreign domination of the Romans, the Herodians, and the Judeans in Galilee. He also challenged the temple system itself, which dominated the religious life of the Jewish people in an oppressive way. God's rule was to be written on the heart, not in the keeping of external, formal religious practices and rituals, however meaningful and helpful these practices were designed to be. The rule of God was to be evident in the justice and peace and love characterizing life together in the faith community, in the humility and trust and obedience characterizing life with God, and in the harmony and care and respect shown for the life of

Healing God's Earth

God's creation. In this way, these rural communities would undermine subversively the values of the dominant, imperial culture that was oppressing the people.

The Biblical Story

Jesus as the Proclaimer of God's Realm

We noted in the last chapter the authority with which Jesus spoke and acted, and the awe that inspired among those with whom he lived. That authority is nowhere more evident than in the first words attributed to Jesus in the Gospel of Mark. "The time is fulfilled, and the kingdom of God has come near; repent, and believe in the good news" (Mark 1:15). This is the announcement of a new order, the realm of God, as an alternative to the current order and structure of the world. Jesus' world was governed by a patchwork of religious and political authorities, some ostensibly in competition with one another but all acting in self-interested collusion to maintain the status quo guaranteeing their own power within the social order.

The Galilee of Jesus' day, the scene of Jesus' earthly ministry, was a dynamic society. It was ruled by Herod Antipas, son of Herod the Great. Herod Antipas was one of the tetrarchs to whom the rule of the kingdom of Herod the Great was divided after his death in 4 BCE. Like his father before him, Herod Antipas was a loyal client ruler for his Roman overlords, who had occupied Palestine since Pompey conquered the area in 63 BCE. During Herod Antipas' reign (4 BCE–39 CE), he engaged in major urbanization projects, rebuilding the city of Sepphoris a few miles northwest of Nazareth and building a new capital on the Sea of Galilee he named Tiberias in honor of his patron the emperor. Sepphoris, such a near urban neighbor to the tiny village of Nazareth just four miles to the southeast, was on major trade routes through Galilee. The city had been destroyed by the Romans as the center of a revolt after the death of Herod the Great in 4 BCE. Under Herod Antipas, Sepphoris was rebuilt as a Roman city, and had as many as 30,000 residents.[1] If Jesus was indeed a craftsman with his father, Joseph, they surely were employed by the rapidly growing urban elite in nearby Sepphoris.

Recent decades have seen an explosion of scholarly studies about the life of Jesus, many of them seeking to describe the socioeconomic conditions of Galilee itself, the scene of most of Jesus' active ministry.[2] I find it particularly appropriate and helpful for this to be the case. If God becoming human (the incarnation) is significant, then it is also important to understand the specific time and place of such an event, both in terms of its natural and geopolitical setting and in terms of the socioeconomic condition of the people among whom this stupendous event unfolded. One of the most

---

1. Crossan, *Historical*, 15–19.

2. In addition to the Crossan book already referenced, I would add: Wright, *Jesus and the Victory of God*; Freyne, *Galilee and Gospel*; Horsley, *Sociology and the Jesus Movement*.

The Restoration of Rural Community in the Person of Jesus Christ

striking features of the gospel narratives about Jesus is that except for Jerusalem, they are almost all set in the rural environment of the villages of Galilee. Despite the urbanization programs of Herod Antipas at Sepphoris and Tiberias and their proximity to the scene of Jesus' activity, Sepphoris is never mentioned in the gospels, and Tiberias is mentioned only in passing but not in relation to Jesus' ministry.

The composition of the rural population of Galilee is difficult to ascertain, and has been the subject of some controversy.[3] However, archaeological evidence suggests that the population of Galilee was predominantly Jewish, surrounded by predominantly Gentile areas and urban centers to the west (Tyre and Ptolemais), north (Caesarea Philippi), and east (the Decapolis, Beth-shan or Scythopolis).[4] To the south was the territory of the Samaritans.

The character of the Jewish population of Galilee is also fraught with controversy.[5] There may have been a remnant of old Israelite stock that remained in Galilee following the Assyrian conquest of the northern kingdom of Israel in 722 BCE.[6] There may have been colonies of Itureans (from Syria) who settled in Galilee during the Hellenistic era and were forcibly converted to the Jewish faith, according to Josephus.[7] But perhaps the bulk of the Jewish population of Galilee came with Hasmonean (Judean) colonization of Galilee following the Maccabean revolution of 167 BCE and the period of Jewish independence.[8] Of course, it is likely that many non-Jews lived in Jewish areas and that many Jews lived in Gentile areas.

As for the urban centers of Tiberias and Sepphoris within Galilee proper, the evidence suggests that despite being centers of Herodian power, they were also predominantly Jewish in character.[9] While Herodian urbanization represented the political reality in these cities, it was also true that the Jewish elite of these urban centers contributed to the oppression of the rural people and villages of the countryside. The Gospel of Mark portrays the Herodians (representing the Roman political economy) and the Pharisees (in this case describing the agents of the Jerusalem priestly aristocracy) conspiring together to do away with Jesus, despite their antipathy for one another (Mark 3:6; 12:13). In other words, both the Herodian market economy and the theocratic religious economy of the Jerusalem aristocracy were agents in the exploitation and oppression of the rural population of Palestine in the Roman era.

Ekkehard and Wolfgang Stegemann, in their book *The Jesus Movement*, describe the economic situation in Palestine during the Roman period.[10] "The economic

---

3. Freyne, *Galilee*, 67.
4. Ibid., 176–82.
5. Ibid., 67, 177.
6. Ibid., 67.
7. Ibid., 247.
8. Ibid., 179–80.
9. Ibid., 190–91.
10. Stegemann and Stegemann, *Jesus Movement*, 104–25.

changes in Palestine under Roman rule can therefore be characterized . . . as an acute lack of land, that is, as a shortage of agriculturally usable land per capita of population. More and more people had to earn their living from less and less land. . . . Confiscations and the oppressive tax burden narrowed the possibility for self-sufficiency, and thus more and more small farmers lost their land. *Therefore the indebtedness of small farmers and expropriation of their land are the hallmarks of this Roman epoch.* Hence one can indeed speak of a regular process of pauperization. The decline of free small farmers to small leaseholders, then day laborers, and even beggars was nothing unusual. . . . Property was increasingly concentrated in the hands of the few. In this way, whole villages became dependent on large landowners, while, conversely, a few individual farmsteads become agglomerations of many smaller houses."[11] The Stegemanns go on to describe in detail both the state and the religious taxation imposed upon the population, leading to the "pauperization" of the people.[12]

It was in the context of this kind of socioeconomic environment that Jesus appeared after his baptism by John the Baptist, announcing the imminent presence of God's rule. It is perhaps difficult for us to fathom how Jesus' announcement would have been heard and perceived, both by those to whom he spoke and by the political and religious authorities. We have been conditioned to hear Jesus' words as an eschatological pronouncement about the future, not as a statement about present reality.[13] However, the gospels endeavor to impress upon us that Jesus understood his words to have import for the present in which he saw himself. "Once Jesus was asked by the Pharisees when the kingdom of God was coming, and he answered, 'The kingdom of God is not coming with things that can be observed, nor will they say, "Look, here it is!" or "There it is!" For, in fact, the kingdom of God is among [or within] you'" (Luke 17:20–21).

Jesus meant his announcement as a prophetic statement about the presence of God's rule in the lives of his listeners within the specific context of the injustices of the Galilean countryside. That is why Jesus' announcement was met with both popular acclaim and official alarm and opposition. Jesus was announcing the inauguration or at least the possibility of a new local social order structured around the old principles of the Sabbath and Jubilee, as indicated in his inaugural sermon in Nazareth in Luke 4 based on Isaiah 61:1–4.

"The time is fulfilled" (Mark 1:15a). Now is the time! The era of Jubilee is now! Don't wait any longer for proclamations from Jerusalem or Rome! You don't need official permission to live under God's rule. You don't need a permit from imperial powers or their lackeys to receive God's rule. It is a present, available reality!

"The kingdom of God has come near" (Mark 1:15b). The realm of God (space where God's rule is available or evident) is here! It does not depend on official endorsements or violent revolutions or state-imposed sanctions! It does not require the

---

11. Ibid., 112, italics in original.
12. Ibid., 113–23.
13. Freyne, *Galilee*, 222.

presence of imperial structures or leaders. In fact, it operates within the workings of the natural world and in the lives of ordinary people, in contrast to the domination and oppression and exploitation of imperial rule.

"*Repent, and believe in the good news*" (Mark 1:15c). All that is required for anyone to experience and live in the realm of God is repentance and trust—a turning away from preoccupation with imperial reality and a corresponding turning toward (trust in) God. If God's realm, seen in the bounty of the natural world and the human community of justice and peace and love, sounds like good news, all that is required for it to be a lived reality is a turning away from domination and oppression and exploitation and a turning toward God in trust.

Jesus as the Healer of Every Ill

Standing as he did in the prophetic tradition of the Old Testament, Jesus not only proclaimed the rule of God as a present reality. Jesus also incarnated that rule of God in his own life. Jesus lived out the reality of God's rule, and in that way invited others to place themselves under that rule of God as well.

Again, as with the prophets of old, the primary manifestation of God's rule in the life and ministry of Jesus is to be seen in his healing ministry—the signs and wonders he performed, which inspired such awe in his contemporaries. These signs and wonders were never designed to call attention to himself and to his own power. Indeed, Jesus never claimed to be able to do anything his followers could not do themselves. "Very truly, I tell you, the one who believes in me will also do the works that I do and, in fact, will do greater works than these" (John 14:12). These signs and wonders were always designed to reveal the presence of God's rule in the (re)formation of genuine community. God's rule, in Jesus' understanding, is never simply a matter of individual or personal salvation. It is always a matter of individuals finding their place within a redeemed human community of justice and peace and love. Indeed, the focus is not really on the individual as such, in Jesus' ministry, but on the community as a whole, and the way in which the community embodies the context where every human person can be whole and creation can be restored.

This is obvious in the accounts of Jesus' healing ministry. It has been helpfully noted that Jesus was a healer, not a doctor. Doctors, when they are able, cure diseases. Healers heal illnesses. Disease is a biological/physical condition of infection or disability or accident. "Illness includes secondary personal and social responses to the primary malfunctioning (disease) in the individual's physiological or psychological status (or both). . . . Viewed from this perspective, illness is the shaping of disease into behavior and experience. It is created by personal, social, and cultural reactions to disease."[14] So, approached by a leper begging for healing, Jesus heals the man pro-

---

14. Arthur Kleinman, *Patients and Healers*, 72, quoted in Crossan, *God and Empire*, 119.

claimed by the culture to be unclean by touching him, demonstrating the wrongness of ostracizing people based on skin afflictions. In addition, Jesus did not consider the man to be healed until he had been certified clean by the religious authorities, thus also reincorporated into his community despite the absurdity of the conventions that had declared him to be unclean in the first place (Mark 1:41–44).

Within traditional cultures around the world, it is customary to think of health in this holistic sense rather than to focus solely on the physical symptoms of disease, as we do in the (over)developed world. On a Mennonite Central Committee economics study tour to Mexico and Honduras in the 1990s, my wife, a registered nurse, was struck with the way people in indigenous villages would ask about the relational health of the community when someone became ill. This is not to deny the physical causes of disease, but is simply an acknowledgment that ill-health is a social and cultural reality as well. What Jesus intended with his healing ministry was not just the healing of individuals suffering from disease, but the healing of relationships and communal patterns of life, enabling the (re)formation of local communities.

Another related aspect of dis-ease and ill-health is the spiritual dimension. Traditional cultures ascribe illness to spiritual powers, as seen in the prevalence of shamans instrumental in healing, but also in the case of witch doctors causing ill-health. It is in this context that we can fruitfully understand the role of exorcism so common in the healing ministry of Jesus. The gospels speak of demons or "unclean spirits" inhabiting certain persons (Mark 1:23–26; 5:1–20). Note also the frequent summary statements in Mark describing the casting out of demons as a feature of the healing ministry of both Jesus and the disciples (Mark 1:34; 3:11–12; 6:13).

Sometimes, as in the case of the Gerasene demoniac in Mark 5, the symptoms of demon possession seem to be clearly related to the socio-political-economic realities of Palestine under Roman rule. Ched Myers, in *Binding the Strong Man*, describes how details of the healing in Mark 5 point to the fact that the demons in this man represent the colonial military occupation of Palestine by the Romans. His demons are "legion," Jesus "dismisses" the demons into the herd of pigs, and the pigs "charge" into the sea—all military terms and images.[15] So in healing this man, Jesus was releasing him from the oppression of Roman occupation that had possessed his life, enabling him to "go home to [his] friends, and tell them how much the Lord has done for [him], and what mercy he has shown [him]" (Mark 5:19).

In Mark 3, when accused by the scribes from Jerusalem of casting out demons by the "ruler of the demons" (Mark 3:22), Jesus responded by declaring himself to be stronger than the "strong man" himself—Satan. Jesus declared that he had bound the strong man, broken into "the strong man's house" and was now engaged in "plundering his property," by releasing those who had been held in Satan's grip (Mark 3:27). In no way was this more evident than in Jesus' ability to cast out the demons that were occupying both the individuals and the rural communities of Palestine. Jesus, and by

---

15. Myers, *Binding*, 191.

extension his disciples, had the power by God's spirit to cast out the demons of oppression and greed and exploitation that have bound the world.[16] In this way not only individuals (like the Gerasene demoniac) who manifested the evidence or symptom of the illness afflicting communities were redeemed, but the communities were, as well, enabling them to be (re)formed by God's grace.

In contrast to other healers and to the consternation of the disciples, Jesus did not set up shop in Capernaum at Peter's house after a day of healing, but intentionally maintained an itinerant ministry (Mark 1:32–39). In this way Jesus prevented his healing ministry from being "brokered" by a healer from an office.[17] Instead, Jesus emphasized that this healing ministry was not his but the property of the people, any and all who put their trust in God.

It should also be noted that this ministry of healing was not limited to Jewish Galilee, but was extended to the predominantly Gentile areas surrounding Galilee, as already evidenced in the healing of the Gerasene demoniac in the region of the Decapolis east of Galilee. Local (rural) communities throughout the region were suffering from the same demons of oppression, greed, and exploitation that the Jewish villages of Galilee were experiencing. In addition to Jesus' invasion of the Decapolis in Mark 5, the Gospel of Mark describes other expeditions into Gentile territory—the region of Tyre and Sidon and the Decapolis (Mark 7:24, 31, extending to 8:10), the Gentile feeding of the 4,000 in Mark 8:1–10 and another expedition to the "villages of Caesarea Phillippi," beginning in Mark 8:27. The Gospels of Luke (9:51–56) and John (4) also describe Jesus' passages through and ministry in Samaria.

As indicated in his inaugural sermon, with its description of God's grace being shed on foreigners like the widow of Zarephath in Sidon and Naaman the Syrian, and like the prophets before him, Jesus had no intention of limiting the realm of God's rule to geographically or ethnically or politically or religiously defined boundaries (Luke 4:14–30). What does seem to be clear is that the field of Jesus' ministry was the local (and in his case) rural community, distinct from the urban centers dominating the life of the rural people. In all the gospels, Jesus is found in an urban environment only in Jerusalem, and then in clear opposition to the domination emanating from the city. Even in his excursions into foreign territory, Mark is careful to say that Jesus went to the "region" of Tyre and Sidon (7:24, 31), and the "villages" of Caesarea Philippi (8:27), and not to those significant urban centers themselves.

What explanation can be found for this exclusively rural focus of Jesus' ministry? Sean Freyne is insistent about the rural character of Jesus' ministry. "I have repeatedly contended that the Jesus movement was rurally based."[18] Did this come from the kind of aversion to the city common among rural folk like myself? On the contrary, Freyne indicates that "Jesus is not critical of the city, just as he does not romanticize

---

16. Ibid., 164–67.
17. Crossan, *Historical*, 346.
18. Freyne, *Galilee*, 57.

rural life, but I do believe that the silence about a visit to Sepphoris or Tiberias is not accidental. His opposition is not to places as such, but to certain values that are associated with city dwellers, especially among the elites who shaped and dominated their ethos, especially as this was viewed from the distance of the peasant. . . . The Herodian foundations [cities] of Galilee represented alien values as far as 'country' Jews were concerned, that is, the Jewish population of the Galilee living in towns and villages."[19] Those "alien values" had the character of economic domination by urban residents over their country cousins. "The intensification of the market that is represented in the emergence of Sepphoris and Tiberias as administrative centres within an agrarian economy brought about considerable changes in the lives of Galilean peasants. In such a climate it is the small landowner that is most vulnerable since there is no protection built into the system against the failure of a bad harvest, illness or some other catastrophe."[20]

I see the picture emerging here as a confirmation of the central thesis of this book. The development or emergence of the city as a spiritual power represents an imperial presence of domination, oppression, and exploitation over both urban residents and the surrounding countryside upon which the city depends for its sustenance. So when we consider how humanity and creation are to be redeemed from the spiritual powers of evil holding the world in thrall, a key aspect of that redemption revolves around the question of how the imperial domination of the city can be broken. There is the usual option of violent revolution, an option attractive to a number of Jesus' contemporaries. Yet that only feeds the cycle of violent retribution.

So apparently Jesus chose another route. Jesus reverted, if you will, to the ancient covenant of God with the people of Israel. "The inspiration of the Jesus movement was scriptural and rooted in the Israelite tradition, as indicated by the selection of the core group of the Twelve, symbolizing the league of the twelve tribes."[21] "The value system of the Jesus movement . . . proposed an ideal in the name of the God of Israel that was the antithesis of prevailing norms, in religious as well as social terms. From this perspective, both Herodian and Jerusalem values were under attack and both were regarded as distorting and alienating."[22] In short, Jesus called "for a transformation of human relations not on a global or even national scale at first, but within the village life of Galilee."[23] Jesus' strategy was, in the terminology of this book, to reconstitute or (re)form rural (local) communities as alternative communities of faith in the midst of the dominant political, economic, and religious culture of his day.

This strategy was, to be sure, subversive. It undercut the values and the power of both the Herodian political and Jerusalem hegemonic establishments, to say nothing

19. Ibid., 71.
20. Ibid., 195.
21. Ibid., 56.
22. Ibid.
23. Ibid., 55.

of Roman colonial occupation. But it was not a frontal attack on these institutions, except perhaps we might say in Jesus' final challenge to Jerusalem that led to his death. Jesus was not out to do away with these institutions, even in his final confrontation with them in Jerusalem. He only didn't want local, rural communities to wait around for their demise, which of course was also sure to come. He insisted that the (re)formation of strong local communities was the antidote to the domination and exploitation that rural and urban people alike were experiencing at the hands of imperial urban spiritual powers. He insisted that these powers were powerless when local communities of nonviolent resistance declared their independence and began to function outside the structures of domination and exploitation that were their modus operandi.

In the next section, we will explore the nature of this alternative community of resistance. Here it is important to note again the centrality of Jesus' healing ministry in the (re)formation of this alternative community. The healing ministry is what demonstrated Jesus' power over the domination forces of imperial power. It was the means by which Jesus set people free to imagine the reconstitution of alternative communities of faith, releasing them from the spiritual powers that kept them in thrall, oppressed by demons and ill health and broken relationships and the disintegration of their local community and culture.

Jesus as the Catalyst for an Inclusive Community of Resistance

If Jesus' primary concern was the (re)formation of local communities in both rural and urban settings, what would or did those communities look like? If Jesus' strategy was "the transformation of human relations . . . within the village life of Galilee,"[24] what kind of village life did Jesus want to see? What were the characteristics of this alternative community of faith living in the midst of the dominant imperial culture? From the teachings of Jesus throughout the gospels, it is not difficult to sketch some of the principle characteristics of the kind of local community Jesus had in mind.

1. *A central theme of Jesus' teaching is the call to trust God implicitly.* This is seen in Jesus' call for non-retaliation and love for the enemy (Matt 5:38–48), his insistence on corporate prayer as a way of fostering trust in God (Luke 11:1–13), his warnings regarding anxiety and greed (Luke 12:22–34; Matt 6:19–34), his insistence on forgiveness as integral to communal life (Luke 7:36–50), and his assurance of God's provision of daily bread from the bounty of God's (nature's) economy. "Give us this day our daily bread," Jesus prays in Matthew 6:11.[25]

These are not teachings primarily addressed to individuals for their personal edification, although they need to be practiced by all the members of the community. These are the foundations for those who have covenanted to live together in a

---

24. Ibid.
25. Compare also the conditions for God's economy given to the Israelites in Exodus 16 and described in chapter 6.

community of trust and dependence on God. These are principles that guard a community from the hazards of exploiting the earth and oppressing one another through covetousness and greed and insecurity. These principles call for a return to the covenanted communal trust in God's protection characterizing Israel living in the midst of the nations. They are also a protection against the kind of violent resistance to injustice and oppression that seems so efficacious to humans conditioned as we are by the myth of redemptive violence.[26]

2. *A community of egalitarian power sharing.* One of the most frequently repeated sayings of Jesus in the gospels is, "But many who are first will be last, and the last will be first" (Mark 10:31). The community of Jesus involves a reversal of status and rank in which those who are great become the servants of those who are least. What this represents is a radical egalitarianism of power, in which the weakest and most vulnerable persons in the community are empowered to be full members, despite whatever limitations or statuses have made them weak and vulnerable. In this, Jesus was in tune with the covenantal community of Israel, in which the Israelites were always admonished to make provision for the poor and the alien, as well as widows and orphans.

Jesus extends this even further to include children generally. Children are held up as models for life in God's realm, and adults are told that they must "become like children" (Matt 18:3). "Whoever becomes humble like this child is the greatest in the kingdom of heaven" (Matt 18:4). And in Mark 10, when the disciples order children to get out of the way, Jesus rebukes them and invites the children to come to him. "Whoever does not receive the kingdom of God as a little child will never enter it" (Mark 10:15). It is perhaps the trusting character of children Jesus is asking adults to emulate, but the point is that children have as much to teach us about God's realm as theologians. Indeed that is true for every member of the community, however vulnerable or weak or dispensable he or she might seem. That is why every member of the community must be empowered to take his or her share in the life of the community.

This was for the disciples, as it is for us, one of the most difficult of Jesus' teachings to grasp and practice. So much of life in community revolves around establishing our place in the pecking order, the way a herd of cows can be seen jockeying for position as the lead cow presumes the right to be first at the water and in the prime place at the feed bunk. It frankly runs counter to what we perceive as nature to look out for the most vulnerable members of the community. Indeed, this may be the distinguishing characteristic of the human community in distinction from animal societies. We have the ability and obligation to care for the most apparently dispensable members of our community.

But we find the disciples continually falling back into the pattern of the world. Right after Jesus' second and third predictions of his passion, death, and resurrection, the disciples are found to be quarreling about or seeking to claim the first place (Mark 9:33–37; 10:35–45). In both instances, Jesus insisted that "whoever wants to be first

---

26. See again the essay on the myth of redemptive violence in chapter 11.

must be last of all and servant of all" (Mark 9:35). "Whoever wishes to become great among you must be your servant, and whoever wishes to be first among you must be slave of all" (Mark 10:43–44). Here Jesus contrasted the way of this new community with the way things are in the world. "You know that among the Gentiles those whom they recognize as their rulers lord it over them, and their great ones are tyrants over them. But it is not so among you" (Mark 10:42–43). This last instruction must be repeated again at the Last Supper, the night before his death, when the disciples at this "first communion" are arguing with one another about "which one of them was to be regarded as the greatest" (Luke 22:24). There Jesus pointed to his own servanthood role as the model, as he did also at the Last Supper in John 13, when he washed the disciples' feet.

3. *A community of spiritual kinship / surrogate familial relationships.* This aspect of community will be explored more fully in the next chapter, but it is clear that Jesus envisioned and practiced communal relationships modeled on spiritual kinship or surrogate family arrangements. This aspect of community challenged the dominant patriarchal familial relationships of ancient Israel and Jewish society. It was also designed to militate against the rivalries and jealousies that riddle and threaten communal life in village settings, especially in light of the economic pressures experienced by villagers living under imperial domination.[27] Evidence of this kind of rivalry can be seen in the family dispute that evidently ushered in Jesus' parable of the Rich Fool in Luke 12:13–21, and also in the parable of the Prodigal Son (or more appropriately, the Resentful Brother) in Luke 15:11–32. "Tell my brother to divide the family inheritance with me" (Luke 12:13). "When this son of yours came back . . . you killed the fatted calf for him" (Luke 15:30).

The positive model of spiritual kinship or surrogate familial relationships as the basis for Jesus' new community can be seen most clearly in Jesus' encounter with his own biological family that brackets the parable of the Strong Man in Mark 3:20–35. The passage opens with Jesus' family coming to take Jesus home. After all, the crowds were pressing so upon Jesus that he couldn't even eat, and the rumor was going around, "He has gone out of his mind" (Mark 3:21). So his family set out to bring Jesus back home to the carpenter shop in Nazareth. *It's been a good ride, but it's over, Jesus*, they might have been saying. *This ministry business will come to no good end for you*, an insight confirmed by the delegation of scribes from Jerusalem who arrived to examine Jesus for possible demon possession (Mark 3:22). But when his family finally arrived at the house to take charge of him, Jesus has what seems like harsh words for his family. When he was told that his mother and brothers and sisters were outside asking for him, Jesus replied, "'Who are my mother and my brothers?' And looking at those who sat around him, he said, 'Here are my mother and my brothers! Whoever does the will of God is my brother and sister and mother'" (Mark 3:33–34).

---

27. Freyne, *Galilee*, 112, 205–6.

Healing God's Earth

This is not a denial of physical kinship and biological family, as we might think. It is not a call to abandon ties of blood kinship, though sometimes answering the call to follow Jesus might result in being rejected by one's own family, as Jesus also reminds us (Matt 10:34–39). It is instead a call to extend to all present and potential members of the community the same love, consideration, and respect that is felt for and shown to one's own family. This can also be seen in Jesus' teaching on love that transcends reciprocity and extends to those who are unworthy or undeserving, even to one's enemies (Matt 5:43–48; Luke 6:32–36).[28]

This surrogate kinship model of community was a particular challenge to the patriarchal structures of family life in Jesus' day. So it is no surprise to find that women formed an integral part of Jesus' community from the outset. Luke names a number of women "cured of evil spirits and infirmities" who formed a part of Jesus' community—Mary Magdalene (almost always named whenever women followers of Jesus are named), Joanna (the wife of a retainer in Herod's court), Susanna, and many others. Luke says these women "provided for them [Jesus and his disciples] out of their resources" (Luke 8:2–3). Mark also notes the community of women who watched the crucifixion of Jesus "from a distance" (Mark 15:40). He highlights their role as those who "provided for him when he was in Galilee" (15:41), and their presence both at Jesus' burial (15:47) and as the first witnesses of Jesus' resurrection (16:1–8). We should begin to observe that this was a highly controversial and non-conventional community that was gathered around Jesus—one truly based on the surrogate kinship model designed to challenge and replace the patriarchal system and to place women on an equal footing with men in the new community.

4. *A community of economic sharing / shared resources*. We have already seen this dimension of Jesus' new community emerging in the women who supported Jesus. The principle of economic sharing is found in Jesus' admonition to "Give to everyone who begs from you, and if anyone takes away your goods, do not ask for them again" (Luke 6:30). But the community of shared resources is most clearly articulated in Mark 10, in the story of the Rich Young Ruler. There a man approached Jesus asking what is required to "inherit eternal life" (Mark 10:17). Jesus affirmed the terms of God's covenant with Israel. When the man protested that he had kept all these from his youth, Jesus looked at him with love and said, "You lack one thing; go, sell what you own, and give the money to the poor, and you will have treasure in heaven; then come, follow me" (Mark 10:21). The man turned away "grieving, for he had many possessions" (Mark 10:22).

This encounter led to an extended discussion with the disciples. Jesus observed how hard it was for the wealthy to enter the kingdom of God. The disciples were perplexed by this, and Jesus asserted again, "It is easier for a camel to go through the eye of a needle than for someone who is rich to enter the kingdom of God" (Mark 10:25). Finally Peter observed, "Look, we have left everything and followed you" (Mark 10:28),

28. Ibid., 206.

for once getting it right. Then comes this astounding assertion of Jesus, "Truly I tell you, there is no one who has left house or brothers or sisters or mother or father or children or fields, for my sake and for the sake of the good news, who will not receive a hundredfold now in this age—houses, brothers and sisters, mothers and children, and fields, with persecutions—and in the age to come eternal life" (Mark 10:29–30).

This has always seemed to me a crucial text for understanding discipleship and community. Jesus clearly envisioned a shared community of trust, one in which those who are willing to give up family and home and land (fields) for the sake of God's kingdom are promised a new community, home, and family through surrogate kinship and yes, fields a hundredfold. All this is promised *in this age*, along with persecutions, and in the age to come eternal life. Jesus here belies those who claim that the gospel only has eternal rewards, as he does also in the third Beatitude, "Blessed are the meek, for they will inherit the earth," not heaven (Matthew 5:5)! This is clearly a community that requires of its members an incredible trust in God, a trust the rich young ruler found himself unable to broach. But it is also a community that discovers the truth that God always provides for all. In the sharing of what one has, the needs of all in the community are met, both the need for intimate relationships and the need for sustenance.

Jesus apparently takes the view that wealth beyond one's daily needs always represents a theft from the welfare of the community as a whole. Jesus lived in an era, as we do, in which the earth was being exploited for profit rather than simply providing sustenance to the people of the land.[29] The result was that private landowners in the peasant villages of Galilee were being pressured and taxed. This led to "intra-family feuding about property and inheritance rights" and "a downward spiral of options—from landowning to leasing, to day-labouring, to slavery or banditry."[30] This was the dilemma from which Jesus was attempting to deliver the rich young ruler, but for his part, the rich young ruler still could not see beyond his many possessions.

Jesus' encounter with the tax collector Zacchaeus in Luke 19 confirms the principle of shared resources in Jesus' community. We don't know what Jesus said to Zacchaeus over dinner after inviting himself to Zacchaeus' table. But Zacchaeus came out a changed man. "Look, half of my possessions, Lord, I will give to the poor; and if I have defrauded anyone of anything, I will pay back four times as much" (Luke 19:8). This is the counterpoint to the story of the rich young ruler—the story of someone ready to engage Jesus' community of shared resources.

5. *A community of the common table—open commensality*. Perhaps the most striking and consistent picture in the gospels is that of Jesus as the host. The pattern is consistent. Jesus takes what is gathered for the meal. He blesses it. He breaks it. He shares it with all at the table. At the last supper, Jesus "took a loaf of bread, and after blessing it he broke it, gave it to them, and said, 'Take; this is my body'" (Mark 14:22).

29. Ibid., 204.
30. Ibid., 205.

Taking, blessing, breaking, giving! This is the pattern of the host. It was how Jesus was recognized after his resurrection by the disciples from Emmaus. "When he was at table with them, he took break, blessed and broke it, and gave it to them. Then their eyes were opened, and they recognized him" (Luke 24:30–31).

This is also what Jesus does at the miraculous feedings of the multitudes recorded in all the gospels. Jesus looks for those willing to share their food, however little or much it might be. He takes it, blesses it, breaks it, and breaks it, and breaks it, until there is enough to feed the multitude. The meal is shared with everyone who is with him—no questions asked, no requirements established, no registration required. If you're there, you are a part of the table!

Jesus staged two mass feedings, one for his Jewish followers in Mark 6:30–44 and one for the Gentiles in Mark 8:1–10. We should note the significance of the strange dialogue of Jesus with his disciples about the baskets of leftovers and the yeast of the Pharisees and the Herodians in Mark 8:14–21. As Ched Myers points out, Jesus was trying to convince his disciples that they only needed one loaf. They had twelve baskets of leftovers at the feeding of the five thousand, enough for the whole people of God. They had seven baskets of leftovers at the feeding of the four thousand, enough for the whole world. But all are able to eat from one loaf. Only one loaf is needed! There is one new people of God, encompassing both Jew and Gentile.[31]

Indeed, Jesus seemed to be indiscriminate about those with whom he shared a table. He ate as guest in the houses of Pharisees who were his enemies (Luke 7:36–50), and he was accused of being "a glutton and a drunkard" for eating in the houses of tax collectors and sinners (Matt 11:19; Luke 7:34). When he sent the disciples out on a mission, he ordered them to go empty-handed and to accept the hospitality of the first house to welcome them in each village (Mark 6:7–13). So Jesus was not only a gracious host who welcomed everyone into the circle of his table fellowship. He was also a guest who never refused an invitation to the table, either from rigidly religious enemies or from socially suspect outcasts. You might say Jesus never turned down an invitation, and always welcomed everyone to his table.

Food indeed is one of the key ways in which community is established. Anthropologists note the significance of food as the way differences among social groups are distinguished.[32] But giving and receiving food is also one of the key ways in which community is established. Those who share our table become our friends and neighbors. They are related to us. Sharing a table establishes a communal relationship for both hosts and guests. A community defines itself in terms of who is welcome at the table, and a community is defined by all those who sit at the table, either as hosts, regulars, or guests.

It is this that makes Jesus' behavior both as host and as guest so remarkable. Jesus refused to draw boundaries for the new community he was establishing. All who

---

31. Myers, *Binding*, 225–26.
32. Crossan, *Historical*, 341.

would come are welcome. If some refuse the table out of pride or negligence, others are welcomed in their place, as in the parable of the Great Dinner (Luke 14:15–24). The table is always prepared and there is always room for all who would come. The table is never too small! There is always room for more and enough for all! No one is ever turned away from Jesus' table, not even the sinful woman who intrudes to wash Jesus' feet with her tears (Luke 7:37–38).

There are of course significant implications in this understanding of community for the church's practice of holy communion. As a pastor, I know that there are good and significant reasons, not only for the practice of open communion, but also for limiting communion to those who know the Lord Jesus as their Savior. But it is significant that Jesus himself drew no such boundaries at the Lord's table. Even on the eve of his death, even after Judas had already agreed to betray Jesus, even with the hollow protestations of allegiance on the part of the other disciples who would soon deny and desert him, Jesus invited this flawed group of disciples to receive the bread and the cup as the symbols of his body and his blood, broken for them and poured out for many. It is hard to conceive of Jesus denying anyone participation at his table for any reason. That, in the end, is what the church's celebration of the Lord's table is intended to convey.

"Open commensality" is the technical term for Jesus' practice.[33] Crossan makes the point that "commensality was, rather, a strategy for building or rebuilding peasant community on radically different principles from those of honor or shame, patronage and clientage. It was based on an egalitarian sharing of spiritual and material power at the most grass-roots level."[34] What Jesus envisioned was a community in which every member and guest, everyone present, is valued and affirmed and accepted and given a place at the table, in which no one is left out or overlooked or rejected. In this community, everyone is invited to bring his or her heritage and identity and gifts to the table, and everyone is expected to value the history and identity and gifts of every other person around the table. This is the community that God intends! This is the community that can stand against the depredations of the dominant culture of urban civilization.

The Failure of the Industrial Food System

The table forms the community. At the center of the community is the table, where all gather to eat together. Whether it is the daily or weekly or monthly or annual family dinner, the senior citizen potluck, the Sunday school class dinner, the corporation banquet or workplace Christmas party, the class party, or the Lord's Supper, community becomes visible and tangible around the table. One of the most satisfying and intriguing features of the TV show *Blue Bloods* is the weekly intergenerational Sunday

33. Ibid., 341–44.
34. Ibid., 344.

dinner of the Reagan family, which everyone is required to attend and no one will willingly miss. (Yes, I too succumb to the drama of the myth of redemptive violence, now that I in my old age have a TV!)

Just as the table forms the community, the food on the table defines the community. The food should most often reflect the land/climate/ecology of the specific and unique setting of this face-to-face community. But it should also reflect the identity and diversity of the community's members. It should reflect the uniqueness in taste and texture and flavor of the heritage of each member of the community, as they bring their offering to the table to be shared with all for their own and the community's sustenance and well-being and health. The annual heritage festival of the Freeman, South Dakota, community, Schmeckfest (taste feast), includes the Low German grüne schauble suppe (green-bean soup) and zwiebach (twin buns), the Hutter dampfleisch (stewed beef) and nudel suppe (noodle soup), and the Swiss German gebratene kartofflen (fried potatoes) and mach kuchen (poppyseed rolls), plus many other delicacies![35] Food is often the most intimate and unique way of identifying both the specific cultural identity and the specific ecological context of a particular community.

Currently here in North America, we are nearly all locked into an industrial food system that destroys local cultures and communities in so many different ways. It is a food system with profit as the bottom line. The existence of local food systems and cultures are the prime threat to the current industrial food system. In keeping with the imperial character of the dominant culture, the industrial food system cannot abide the existence of foods and cultures outside the system. It is virtually impossible to opt-out of the current industrial food system. A few families here and there produce and consume virtually all their own food on the land, a few more communities are seeking to preserve or move toward local food systems, but the effort is daunting and is met with huge resistance by the dominant culture, both in attitude and in regulation. It is important to note some of the primary ways in which the industrial food system militates against local communities and food systems.

1. The industrial food system makes the people who work the land (farmers in particular, and by extension agriculture itself) into the producers of commodities instead of people who raise food. The commodification of food is essential for the industrial food system—food products have to be commoditized, made uniform, and sold with the ubiquitous product code carefully attached to every apple! But even more seriously, in the American Midwest, farmers are led to produce grain commodities for a global market, most of which is not for human consumption at all and much of which (40 percent of corn production, according to a National Public Radio report I heard on January 17, 2012) is currently used to inefficiently produce ethanol, thereby putting an intense strain upon the land. Though they are no longer raising food in any real sense of the term, the rhetoric persists that American farmers are feeding the world. In the

---

35. Waldner and Hofer, *Many Hands*, 191.

meantime, local communities are diminished and destroyed as farmers are led to seek the required economies of scale for an industrialized agricultural system.

2. The industrialized food system destroys the culture of local food reflecting the promise and limitation of a particular place and the particular agriculture that derives from that place. In place of a local food culture, we are offered the substitute of a global marketplace, with restaurants and food products that specialize in Chinese or Greek or Italian or German or Mexican or any of the many other cultural cuisines that comprise the global marketplace. However genuine or fake such offerings might be, they can never replace local food cultures that reflect the ability of human communities to cultivate the earth sustainably in the most varied environmental contexts and with the most amazing gastronomical results. Yet these local food cultures are fast disappearing, along with the long agricultural knowledge that has made them fruitful and unique. Someday, perhaps in the not too distant future, we will rue that loss.

3. The industrial food system creates a consumer dependency on an unsustainable food system, resulting in a culture in which farmers often raise none of their own food, not even so much as a backyard garden! The industrial food system requires an enormous supply of energy in equipment and machines required for the production and processing and transportation of food from a few prime agricultural food producing areas (e.g., California's Central Valley) to consumers across the country. While this food system has so far been successful, it is only because of the availability of cheap fossil fuels and at the cost of global warming. As we move into the era of peak oil and as the climate changes caused by global warming disrupt current agricultural production regions, we will no longer be able to depend on the industrial food system. Local food systems with people raising food and establishing rural communities and building local (agri)cultures will need to be renewed and re-created in every part of the country.

4. While the industrialized food system is highly mechanized and dependent on cheap energy, not everything can be done by machines. The industrialized food system also creates an underclass of agricultural workers, often illegal aliens, whose traditional culture is systematically destroyed and who are exploited and treated unjustly for the sake of their labor. These workers are unable to achieve a stake in the system, because they have no legal standing. The stereotypes of agricultural workers feeds the perception of the dominant culture that working with food in its production and processing and preparation is drudge labor, work unfit for normal people. It never seems to occur to the unemployed former blue and white collar workers of our dominant culture that they might engage in raising, preserving, and preparing their own food, so deeply is it ingrained in the dominant culture that the food industry represents drudge labor.

5. The industrial food system transforms agricultural land itself from a community-sustaining resource to a lucrative investment for speculation by corporations and urban elites. In the process, local farmers are dispossessed and local communities lose

control of the land—the most basic and necessary resource for their communal life on the land. During the winter of 2011/12 there were several public auctions of previously farmer/family-owned land in our community. Several sales went for exorbitantly high prices for this area, which ordinary farmers in our community could not afford even if they needed a bit more land to sustain their medium-size operations. With investors paying so much for land, they also demand rents beyond what local farmers can pay, with the result that large corporate farming operations with no stake in the local community come in and rent the land. Meanwhile, local farmers are pressured by these circumstances to pay higher rent for the land they rent.

The analysis of the global food system above is my own, based often on my own observations of the realities I see in the dominant culture and the rural communities where I have lived. This analysis also owes much to a large bibliography of authors and books offering a critique of the industrial food system. I would note the works of Wendell Berry, and particularly the essays collected in *What Are People For?* Also noteworthy is *From Land to Mouth* by Canadian food expert Brewster Kneen, *The Omnivore's Dilemma* by journalist Michael Pollan, and *Folks, This Ain't Normal* by Viriginia farmer Joel Salatin.

In all these ways, and many others that could be discussed, the industrial food system reveals itself to be an agent of the imperial interests of urban civilization—interests that today, as in Jesus' day, translate into the dismantling of rural communities and local cultures throughout the land and around the world. The destruction of these communities and cultures is bad enough, but the fact that this food system is highly unstable and unsustainable makes the re-formation of rural communities and local cultures of food critical for the future of life on earth.

There is an intimate connection between land, culture, community, and agriculture. Agriculture (literally, the culture or cultivation of the field) shapes the culture and the community, but also reshapes the land. I think of the patchwork olive groves and vineyards of Crete, the brilliant juxtaposition of blooming blue flax and yellow canola fields in Saskatchewan, and the alternating corn and soybean fields of my home community here in South Dakota. But agriculture and culture are at the same time shaped by the land in both its promise of abundance and its limitations. Rami Zurayk, writing about the Israeli invasion of south Lebanon in 2007 and their destruction of the agricultural infrastructure in that region, describes the connections this way: "Farming connects people to the land. Land is the source of livelihood, but it is also where local habits, customs, and culture are rooted. When land is rendered unusable and valueless, farmers do not only lose physical and financial assets."[36] They also lose their culture!

Obviously, no local community can be completely self-sustaining by itself, nor should it be. However, every local community, by virtue of the uniqueness of its land and environment, has something unique and special it can provide for itself and for

---

36. Zurayk, *Food*, 27.

neighboring rural and urban communities. We live in a world where unrestrained use of fossil fuels is leading to peak oil and higher energy costs, as well as climate change through global warming. As local food systems become a necessity because of rising energy prices and climate change, every local community will need to learn how it can sustain life through communal labor, and thereby (re)shape and (re)vitalize its local agriculture. Food for the tables of all communities, rural and urban, will become once again the primary calling of every local community as each makes its unique contribution to the welfare of all.

In my lifetime, food has become the topic of many studies and books. In the 1970s and '80s, as the coming global crisis of food began to be evident, there were books entitled *Food First: Beyond the Myth of Scarcity* (Frances Moore Lappé), *Food for Tomorrow?* and *Global Dust Bowl* (C. Dean Freudenberger), *Bread for the World* (Arthur Simon), *By Bread Alone* (Lester R. Brown), *The Food and People Dilemma* (Georg Borgstrom), *How the Other Half Dies* (Susan George), and *Empty Breadbasket?* (The Cornucopia Project). This smattering of titles from my personal library over the past three decades confirms the centrality of food and its necessity for the human family, but they tend to view food as a global problem that must be solved and addressed on a global scale.

At the same time, what are to me more hopeful writings (and movements) are beginning to appear. Writers like Wendell Berry and David Kline address the agrarian life and the culture shaped by agriculture.[37] Novelist Barbara Kingsolver has given us a marvelous journal of transitioning to a life of growing food and buying it locally in *Animal, Vegetable, Miracle: A Year of Food Life*. There are these anthologies with the evocative titles, *Meeting the Expectations of the Land* (edited by Wes Jackson, Wendell Berry, and Bruce Colman), *Learning to Listen to the Land* (edited by Bill Willers), and *Hope for the Family Farm: Trust God and Care for the Land* (edited by LaVonne Godwin Platt). I think also of L. Shannon Jung's books *Food for Life: The Spirituality and Ethics of Eating*; *Sharing Food: Christian Practices for Enjoyment*; and *Hunger and Happiness: Feeding the Hungry, Nourishing Our Souls*, which address the spiritual dimensions of food and table in the life of the community.

We may finally be on the verge of understanding the importance of the table and food in the life of community, whether that community is rural or urban. Perhaps food is not after all a global problem to be solved, but a gift to be nurtured and shared in the life of every local community. Will that require us all to get our hands in the dirt and to do some drudge labor? You bet! But in the process we will discover the profound contentment and satisfaction that comes with living together on the land that God has provided for all. I think of Wendell Berry's description of the hard, hot communal labor of putting up hay in the barn on a summer day, and the deep satisfaction that comes when that hay is fed to the animals in the cold winter.[38]

---

37. Berry, *Unsettling*, chapter 4; Kline, *Great Possessions* and *Scratching*.
38. See Berry's chapter "Looking Ahead," in *Gift of Good Land*, 176–82.

Self-Reliant Mennonite Communities of Food Production

In the rural Mennonite community when I was growing up, farm families were just only moving out of what is usually referred to as a subsistence economy. Most farm families, including my own, produced, preserved, and prepared most of their food from the farm itself. That certainly limited the diet and range of foods consumed to the produce of the garden and farmyard and the slaughter of the animals (an extended family enterprise), but it also inspired creativity, enabling folks to do interesting things with the food choices available to them.

My father's farm was small (80 acres plus a neighboring quarter rented) and diversified. My father had a dairy herd of eight to ten cows (which I first helped milk by hand before we got a milking machine), farrowed out perhaps half a dozen sows twice a year and marketed the offspring after butchering one or two for family consumption, and had a flock of perhaps about two hundred chickens. The grain and alfalfa raised served mostly to feed this livestock, although some excess grain was sold for cash for major purchases, along with the several head of cattle and pigs not needed for food or as replacement stock. In addition, the cream separated from the milk of the cows and the eggs of the chickens were sold and used as grocery money to purchase the staples—flour, sugar, coffee, etc.—that were not available or could not be produced on the farm. The vegetable garden and some of the barnyard work was my mother's responsibility, along with virtually all of the food processing and preparation. My father farmed with horses until the post–World War II era, when he purchased small tractors. The work of harvesting and haying was often done communally, most notably with threshing crews in conjunction with the arrival of the threshing machine. But even after combines replaced threshing machines, my father owned a combine and hay baler with one of his brothers, and they often worked together.

While not specifically organized as a food production unit, farms like this produced more food for off-farm human consumption than conventional farms do today. Not only the cream and eggs, but also the surplus animals sold for slaughter, were used for human consumption.

I confess that describing the farm of my childhood makes me nostalgic for "the good old days." The farm I have briefly described was similar in function and scale to many of the farms in our community, and perhaps in most rural communities throughout the Great Plains and even throughout North America. My father might have been slower than some to innovate new agricultural technologies on the farm. Perhaps it was his age and his conservatism, having come through the Great Depression with his small eighty acre farm intact, that made my father more reluctant to join the rush toward the industrialization of agriculture that transpired in rural communities like mine after the Second World War. Mechanization and cheap fossil fuels enabled farmers to work the land much more efficiently, which led inevitably to larger farms and more specialization, with sometimes fierce competition between neighboring farmers.

The result is that today there are few small, diversified farms like my father's left in our community. Quite a few farmers, to their credit, continue with some kind of livestock enterprise, but all the small, single-family dairies are gone within the past ten years or so, with the exception of some recent small organic dairies. Quite a few farmers have cow/calf beef herds to utilize grazing land and consume livestock feeds produced on the farm, and there are also quite a few confinement units, mostly of swine.

Farmers are hardly to be criticized for the choices made over the past three or four generations due to the industrialization of agriculture. There was of course the incredible pressure of the government-policy-, corporate-bureaucratic-, land-grant university-technical-complex to meet the demands of the emerging global markets for agricultural commodities. The productivity of conventional farms, made possible by cheap energy and high tech developments, is truly phenomenal! I have the utmost respect for the most successful and progressive farmers of our community, some of whom I work for occasionally. Today's successful farmers manage multifaceted entrepreneurial operations that require multiple skills and abilities.

However, it is becoming evident that the evolving agricultural technologies have not served the life of the rural community well. I have described the depopulation of the community and the decline of churches and schools and towns. Now we are also beginning to face the prospect of much higher energy costs as the effects of peak oil begin to be felt. Conventional farming, so dependent on cheap fossil fuels, will be facing a crisis in the years ahead.

For this reason, a faith-based movement of local farmers called Rural Revival has emerged in the Freeman, South Dakota, community in recent years. These are for the most part "alternative" farmers in one way or another—organic or rotational grazing or small fruit U-pick operations. They are banding together with two purposes—to develop a local food system and to assist in the transfer of land to a new generation of farmers. They are attracting and being joined by a number of young adults native to the community who have been moving back with a desire to return to the rural setting of their roots and participate in the revitalization of the community from which they have come. While this movement and organization is local and faith-based and largely Mennonite, it is by no means unique. Across North America, there is a resurgence of interest in rural communities and local food systems.

The farms of the future are likely to be quite different from either the farm on which I grew up or the conventional farm on which I occasionally work these days. They are likely to be small-scale food production units specializing in some facet of local food production to serve the immediate area and its surrounding urban centers. They will require significantly less land (ten acres or less) and considerably more human labor than today's conventional farms. They will be able to use all manner of current and still-to-be-developed machines and technological innovations to assist in food production. Some of these may require fossil fuel energy but many will be solar or wind powered. They will benefit from and likely require a whole range of cooperative endeavors, some used by the producers themselves in their production and some managed by local entrepreneurs in the surrounding towns and villages engaged in processing and adding value to the raw produce of the farms. These new farms of the future will maximize the unique ecology and cultural heritage of their community in the production and sale of food products. They will highlight the particular uniqueness and value of the food they produce. In other words, these communities will develop an agriculture (the cultivation of the fields) in which the land and ecology of a particular place will shape the community even as the community shapes the natural environment.[39]

My own interest and hope is that the churches of these new farmers of the future in communities like mine will also develop special relationships with their urban counterparts in nearby cities. Rural and urban congregations are going to increasingly need and depend upon each other as producers and consumers, both for their own membership but also for the larger circle of communities where they live, both in rural and urban settings. The day of food commodities being produced and processed and shipped and prepared anonymously in faraway places is rapidly coming to its end. People in both urban and rural settings need to know who is producing and who is consuming the food being eaten, where it comes from, what its heritage represents, and what its unique value is. Food is the way local communities in both rural and urban settings will work together to tear down the dividing walls that have existed between the imperial urban culture and the exploited rural culture. In a coming age of the collapse of the industrial food system, this is a prime missional calling for both rural and urban congregations, and Mennonite congregations with their rural heritage and roots are uniquely positioned to provide the link in this endeavor.

I live in a context where the vast majority of the food and fiber required for human life can be produced locally, as one of the Rural Revival members keeps reminding us, even in God-forsaken South Dakota! If producer groups like Rural Revival could supply even a fraction of the food consumed in our area, it would provide livelihoods for all the producer families we can imagine willing to move back to our community, thereby repopulating rural communities, relieving the pressures of urbanization, and openly or subversively undermining the exploitative, wasteful, and unsustainable domination of urban civilization. Rural communities/churches don't have to wait for institutional change in the policies of governments, corporations, universities, or denominations. As Jesus empowered rural communities of his day to stand against the tides of domination and exploitation, rural churches and communities of our time can do the same. With their agrarian heritage and tradition, Mennonite congregations in both rural and urban settings are uniquely positioned to participate in this kind of transformation!

39. In this context see Jackson, *Becoming Native*.

Part D

The Christian Experience

CHAPTER 13

The New Community

From Every Tribe and Language and People and Nation (Rev 5:9)

The Church Assumes the Role of Local Community

IN THE BIBLICAL WITNESS, the divine intervention revealed in the life, death, and resurrection of Jesus of Nazareth resulted in the formation of a new community of faith. The Acts of the Apostles relates the birth of this new community on the day of Pentecost. This formative event is presented as a reversal of the dispersal and confusion of the peoples of the earth at the tower of Babel (Genesis 11 and Acts 2).

In succeeding chapters, Acts chronicles the expansion of this new community to include Hellenists (chapter 6), Samaritans and Ethiopians (chapter 8), the household of a Roman centurion (chapters 10 and 11), and ultimately uncircumcised Gentiles (chapter 15). Geographically, the movement spread from Jerusalem to Judea and Samaria to the ends of the earth (Acts 1:8), but this hardly accounts for the post-resurrection communities of faith that undoubtedly formed the first Christian communities in rural Galilee. More significantly, this new community encompassed people from all the known world, as indicated by the roster of nations present on the day of Pentecost in Acts 2, and by the inclusive vision of John the Revelator.

While the Christian Church has had to be dragged, kicking and screaming, into every new crossing of barriers, while the universality of this new community frequently finds only difficult expression in particular local communities of faith, and while the church has often betrayed this inclusive vision by a retreat into an ethnocentric or privatized spiritual expression, the global Christian Church reflects something of the vision expressed by the idealized portrait of this new community of faith described in Acts. The local community of faith (congregation) becomes the primary expression of the alternative to the dominant culture, but each local community is bound by ties of common faith to all the other local communities of faith, and through them to the global church comprised of those from every tribe and language and people and nation.

The Biblical Story

Saints from Every Tribe and Language and People and Nation (Rev 5:9)

Given the parochial and distinctly ethnic origin of the New Testament, rooted as it is in the first-century Jewish experience, it is striking to observe the ecumenical and universal scope of terms used to describe the composition of the church. Take, for example, the four terms used in Revelation 5:9 to describe those for whom the lamb was slain, saints "ransomed for God" by the blood of the lamb who is also the lion of the tribe of Judah and the root of David (Rev 5:5). These four terms are repeated again in different order in Revelation 7:9 when John beholds a great multitude beyond counting, who are, according to the elder accompanying John, those who "have washed their robes and made them white in the blood of the Lamb" (Rev 7:14).

The four terms are *tribe, language, people,* and *nation. Tribe* (φυλή, phule) is an ethnocultural term, often used to describe a group between nation and people, as for instance in the twelve tribes of Israel. *Language* (γλῶσσα, glossa) is of course a linguistic term, usually referring to one's mother tongue, which is given special prominence in the listing of representatives of the nations of the known world present on the day of Pentecost, all of whom heard the disciples proclaiming "God's deeds of power" in their "own languages" (Acts 2:11). *People* (λαός, laos) is in this context a cultural term, specifying the unique and specific cultural heritage to which each person is heir. And *nation* (ἔθνος, ethnos), rather than suggesting nationalistic, political identifications as it does today, refers in this context primarily to the unique ethnic heritage each person has by birth.[1]

In *World Christian Encyclopedia*, David Barrett identifies six distinct characteristics that define each person's place in the human family—race, color, ethnicity, culture, language, and nationality.[2] My own view is that race and color are categories that should be minimized as human identifiers in favor of ethnicity, since ethnicity is a more specific and less racially charged term than either race or color. In recent years, I have refrained from identifying myself by race or color on census data and other official forms. While we can change our nationality with some ease, our ethnic heritage is given to us by our birth, and our mother tongue and culture by the social context of our formative years. While we can learn other languages fluently and learn to live in diverse cultures, our ethnic, cultural, and linguistic heritage expresses both our uniqueness as individuals and the rich diversity of the human family. Every local culture (community), rooted as it is in a specific location, time, and context, with its own unique mix of members, contributes to the beautiful and amazing diversity of the human family.

---

1. See the discussion of "nation" in chapter 4.
2. Barrett, *World*, 107.

David Barrett goes on to develop an extensive ethnolinguistic classification for the human family, identifying 71 ethnolinguisitic families (nations?), 432 peoples (tribes?), and 8,990 cultures (peoples?), speaking 7,010 languages, and living in 223 nation-states or territories.[3] In this typology, I belong to the Germanic ethnolinguistic family (nation), the United States white people group (tribe, dominant culture), and the Swiss Volhynian/Low German cultural heritage (people), speaking English as my mother tongue, as a citizen of the United States.

The point is that the four terms used in Revelation are descriptive of the entire human family, just as David Barrett's classification is an attempt to develop terms that can describe the whole human family. When we consider that the biblical documents were the product of a specific Jewish ethnic heritage and culture, we must ask where this attempt to be ecumenical and universal came from and why it was deemed important to sound this universal note.

The genius of the Christian faith as it was inaugurated by Jesus is that it affirmed both the unity and the diverse particularity of the human family. In *The Ancient Church as Family*, Joseph Hellerman identifies the early church as a "surrogate kin group." In contrast to contemporary family systems that focus on each individual's ancestry and progeny, the Mediterranean family system of the ancient world was a "patrilinear kinship group" related through descent from a specific male progenitor.[4] In this family system, the family is defined by a blood relation to the patriarch and his male progeny. As Hellerman notes, the key relational dynamic in such a family system is neither the husband/wife relationship nor the parent/child relationship, but instead the sibling bond of brothers and sisters.[5]

Jesus, Hellerman asserts, maintained the priority of the sibling bond in his understanding of family, but instead of defining that in terms of consanguinity (blood relationships), Jesus defined the sibling bond as a "surrogate kin group," in which loyalty to him and God's reign forged the bond of sibling relationships. This was then a "patriarchal kin group," but with God as "father," and with all those who share allegiance to God as siblings—thus the "surrogate kin group."[6] This model of kinship becomes evident in sayings of Jesus like that found in Matthew 23:8–11, where the disciples are instructed not to give honorific titles to one another here on earth, not even that of "father," "for you have one Father—the one in heaven" (Matt 23:9).

It is of course a matter of some controversy whether Jesus himself intended to found the church as a social movement, much less give it the specific shape described here. But Hellerman is not alone in his assessment. N. T. Wright, in *Jesus and the Victory of God*, lists some of the most offensive statements of Jesus about the family: Mark 3:31–35, where Jesus claims those who follow him as "my mother and my brothers"

---

3. Ibid., 110.
4. Hellerman, *Ancient Church*, 27–30.
5. Ibid., 35–51, 57.
6. Ibid., 64–68, 79.

rather than his blood family; Luke 11:27–28, where Jesus honors not his mother, but "those who hear the word of God and obey it"; and Matthew 8:21–22, where Jesus calls a potential follower to "let the dead bury their own dead" and to follow him. Wright concludes, "The only explanation for Jesus' astonishing command is that he envisaged loyalty to himself and his kingdom-movement as creating an alternative family."[7] Jesus "regarded loyalty to himself as taking precedence over family loyalty and identity which was both a universally recognized obligation of the ancient world and a major Jewish cultural and religious identity-symbol."[8] Jesus "did not deny the god-givenness of the Jewish symbols, in this case the national and familial identity. . . . He was . . . creating a fictive kinship group—in less technical terms, a new family—around himself."[9]

This constitutes a radical redefinition of family/community. No longer was community or the familial relationship to rest on patrilineal descent (patriarchy) or on national-ethnic origin. As Hellerman points out, Jesus' rejection of Jewish purity laws regarding Sabbath observance (Mark 2:23–28), food laws (Mark 7:1–23), and table fellowship (Mark 2:15–17) led to a redefinition of the people of God as "a transnational surrogate kinship group—one that would welcome not only unclean Judeans into the family, but Gentiles as well."[10]

So it is not inconceivable to imagine unnamed disciples of Jesus returning to Galilee after the crucifixion and resurrection of Jesus and establishing there in the villages of Galilee assemblies of believers that were inclusive of all those who lived in the village—clean or unclean, ill or whole, Jew or Gentile. These communities might have been, as Ched Meyers suggests, the first audience for the reading of Mark's gospel in 69 CE, in the midst of the Jewish Revolt against Rome.[11] This is not to contradict the more common view of Christian expansion given by Luke in the Acts of the Apostles—from Jerusalem to all Judea and Samaria, and to the ends of the earth (Acts 1:8). In Acts, the church expands from a core of Jewish believers in Jesus to include Hellenists (chapter 6), Samaritans (chapter 8), God-fearing Gentiles (the Ethiopian eunuch in Acts 8 and the Roman centurion Cornelius in Acts 10 and 11), and ultimately all manner of uncircumcised Gentiles in the missions of the Apostle Paul to Asia Minor and Greece. But the whole impetus of the Jesus movement was toward decentralized empowerment of local communities, so it is inconceivable to me that the first Christian churches would not have been established by followers of Jesus in rural villages throughout Palestine, and especially in Galilee.

The point is that Jesus and his followers envisioned local assemblies of redeemed believers in every town and village becoming the core of a redeemed humanity in a restored creation. Every local assembly (church, parish, congregation) of believers was

---

7. Wright, *Jesus*, 401.
8. Ibid., 402.
9. Ibid., 403.
10. Hellerman, *Ancient Church*, 89.
11. Myers, *Binding*, 414–23.

to become an alternative community of faith (people of God) that would subversively and nonviolently challenge the hegemony of the dominant powers ruling that place and empower all who lived there as their neighbors and friends to do so as well. In addition, being bonded with neighboring assemblies (churches, congregations) in neighboring villages who shared their faith, they would become harbingers of the universal reign of God for a redeemed humanity in a restored creation. Together, they would be the "holy nation" and "royal priesthood" the Apostle Peter speaks of in 1 Peter 2:9–10 (cf. Exod 19:6), superseding every other national identity.

The interesting thing about these local assemblies is that they stood in solidarity with similar assemblies in towns and villages near and far. None were asked to give up their unique ethnic and cultural heritage. The devout Jews from throughout the known world gathered in Jerusalem on the day of Pentecost were not asked to learn one language, be that Hebrew or Greek. Instead, each heard about "God's deeds of power" in their *native* tongues, the mother language of the lands from which these acculturated Jews had come to Jerusalem (Acts 2:8–11).

This shouldn't be surprising. It is precisely the diverse uniqueness and particularity of the human family that God values, and you can't have unique diversity in the imposition of a common culture, language, and peoplehood. God doesn't expect anyone to give up their unique ethnic and cultural identity when they come under God's reign. Indeed, God wants that unique diversity to be respected and celebrated as the expression of the human experience in each place and time. It is not the unique diversity of each local community/culture that God wants to erase, but rather the intolerance and prejudice and suspicion that has too often governed relations between local communities. For in fact, you can't have unique diversity unless you have local communities giving expression to what it means to be human in that particular place and time.

This is not to argue against the formation of truly multicultural congregations, which are often held out as the ideal in our current North American context. Of course, every local congregation should always welcome and respect everyone who comes to their doors for their unique ethnic and cultural heritage and identity. However, this is to challenge the notion that it is somehow a sign of unfaithfulness when a particular congregation expresses its ethnic/cultural heritage, even a WASP (white/Anglo-Saxon/Protestant) congregation! Every congregation of believers is required to embody the cultural/ethnic heritage that makes it unique in its particular place and time. There will be no assembly of saints from every tribe and nation and language and people if all evidence of the particular and unique cultural/ethnic heritage of each particular assembly (congregation, church) is not respected and preserved.

Healing God's Earth

There Is One Body (Eph 4:4)

Notwithstanding my defense of the uniqueness and particularity and diversity of the church and the human family, I also affirm the unity of all Christians and all humanity. It has always been easier for the church and for believers to affirm the universality of the human family in theory than to do so in practice. In other words, it is always easy for local assemblies to allow their ethnic/cultural differences to divide them into competing or hostile camps, as usually happens in the world around them.

The book of Acts chronicles the painful steps through which the first Christian church in Jerusalem began to realize the Pentecost vision of people from the whole world celebrating "God's deeds of power" revealed in Jesus Christ (Acts 2:11). The first chasm to be crossed was that between "the Hebrews" (Aramaic-speaking Jewish Christians) and "the Hellenists" (Greek-speaking Jewish Christians) in Acts 6. Marginal members of "the Hellenists" (widows) were being discriminated against by the dominant Hebraic Jewish/Christian community. The community appointed seven "deacons" to ensure that this discrimination ended. This may seem like a minor chasm, but it is in the nature of human community that many of the most intractable divisions between people have the character of these apparently minor differences.

Another major chasm was bridged in Acts 8. With the church in Jerusalem undergoing persecution, members of the church sought refuge in the countryside of Judea and Samaria. Philip, one of the "deacons" in Acts 6, began the transformation of community in Samaria through the proclamation of the gospel. The church in Samaria, representing the bitter foes of true Jewish people, entered the fellowship of the universal church when Peter and John arrived from Jerusalem to examine the local Samaritan church and to pray the Holy Spirit upon them through the laying on of hands (Acts 8:17).

The next chasm crossed in the book of Acts came in Acts 10–11, as Peter was prepared by a divine vision to accept and receive a God-fearing (but still enemy Gentile) Roman centurion as a Christian brother. Jewish purity laws, so blatantly broken by the unclean food Peter was called to eat in the vision of Acts 10:9–16, were revealed as no longer binding upon the Jewish Christian Peter in his relationship to Cornelius. Now it may be that Peter reneged on his fellowship with Gentiles under pressure from the home church in Jerusalem, as Paul accused him of doing in Galatians 2:11–14, but still the precedent had been established by Peter's acceptance of Cornelius and his household as a fellow Christian assembly.

The final and decisive chasm was crossed in the Jerusalem Conference of Acts 15, in which the Gentile assemblies established by the Apostle Paul in Asia Minor were received as assemblies in fellowship with the mother church of Jewish Christians in Jerusalem. With this action, it became clear that the Christian Church would be open to people of all ethno-linguistic and national origins without regard for Jewish purity laws and religious marks of identity.

The New Community

Now it is clear that in most of these instances, there were no intercultural or pluralistic assemblies as such, or at least these were the exceptions rather than the rule. The Jerusalem church likely remained staunchly and conservatively Jewish Christian. The church in Samaria undoubtedly remained primarily Samaritan in its composition. The Gentile churches of Asia Minor and Greece established by Paul, despite Paul's rigorous attempts to recruit fellow Jews as fellow believers in the cities where he brought together assemblies of Christians, were predominantly Gentile—Greek-speaking assemblies of people indigenous to the cities where Paul preached. Yet, despite the extremely varied cultural and ethno-linguistic heritage of these various assemblies, they accepted one another as fellow communities in the faith and acknowledged the members of one another's assemblies as fellow believers, brothers and sisters (siblings) in Christ, under the reign of God their common father, part of God's "holy nation."

While this may not satisfy the proponents of multicultural congregations, it remains a striking feature of Christian faith, then as it is today. For today also, visiting Christians from distant and strange cultural and ethno-linguistic assemblies of Christian faith and diverse denominational heritage routinely visit other assemblies in distant and strange cultural and ethno-linguistic settings and are received as brothers and sisters in Christ. While it is beautiful to see genuinely multiethnic congregations, I find it appropriate that no assembly of Christians anywhere in the world is required to give up its unique cultural and ethno-linguistic heritage, but is accepted into the fellowship of Christian assemblies in all its uniqueness.

We have been looking primarily at the ethno-linguistic and cultural-religious divides in the book of Acts. In the letters of the Apostle Paul, it is also the primary divide Paul addresses, perhaps because it was the largest and most obvious human divide that he could observe. We see this in Romans 1:16, 1 Corinthians 1:22–24, and especially in Ephesians 2:11–22. Here Paul describes how the Gentiles, excluded from God's previous covenants, have now been brought into the "household of God" as "citizens with the saints" through Christ, who on the cross "has broken down the dividing wall" between Jew and Gentile, reconciling "both groups to God in one body through the cross, thus putting to death that hostility through it," and creating "in himself one new humanity in place of the two, thus making peace" (Eph 2:14–19).

Nevertheless, Paul in his letters addresses a whole range of divisions within the human family. In perhaps the most famous passage, Galatians 3:28, in discussing the reality that we have all been adopted into God's family through Christ as children of God (the surrogate family), Paul asserts that there is now no longer either Jew or Greek; there is neither "slave or free" nor "male and female; for all of you are one in Christ Jesus" (Gal 3:28). A similar list of contrasts is made in Colossians 3. You "have clothed yourselves with the new self, which is being renewed in knowledge according to the image of its creator. In that renewal there is no longer Greek and Jew, circumcised and uncircumcised, barbarian, Scythian, slave and free; but Christ is all and in all!" (Col 3:10–11).

In addition to the ethnic/religious divide (*Jew/Gentile, circumcised/uncircumcised*), these passages address the socioeconomic divide (*slave/free*), and the gender divide (*male/female*), as well as the *civilized/barbarian* divide. "Scythian" may simply be Paul's example of an extreme barbarian. Still another divide is highlighted in Romans 1:14 and 1 Corinthians 1:18–25, the *wise/foolish* divide. Later in 1 Corinthians 1, Paul calls attention to another series of divides, *powerful/weak, low/noble birth*, and *strong/weak* (1 Cor 1:26–29). And 1 Corinthians 7:25–31 describes still another divide—the *married/single* divide. While Paul discusses poverty and riches in 2 Corinthians 8–9 and with regard to communion in 1 Corinthians 11:17–22, it is the epistle of James that highlights most clearly the *rich/poor* divide within humanity and in the church (Jas 2:1–7, most directly).

This is quite a list of "divides" that need to be and are overcome within the church and in Christ! A divide we moderns would add is the *hetero/homosexual* divide. I would also note that Paul does not directly mention the *rural/urban* divide, except perhaps as a subset of the *civilized/barbarian* divide. "Barbarian" in the Greek meant "foreigner" or "unintelligible speaker," but in the Latin it also connoted an alien and inferior land, culture, or people. These descriptions and stereotypes surely have and continue to fit with the dominant culture's portrayal of rural people in many respects. So I would respectfully submit that *rural/urban* is still another divide that needs to be bridged through Christ in the church!

There are a number of passages in which Paul addresses the ways in which these divides can be / are bridged within the church. The most familiar are the household codes found in Ephesians 5:21–6:9 and Colossians 3:18–4:1, which discuss the relationships of *husbands/wives, parents/children,* and *master/slaves*. First Peter has similar codes in 2:18–20 (*masters/slaves*), 3:1–7 (*husbands/wives*), and 5:1–5 (*youth/elders*).[12] Romans 13:1–7 and 1 Peter 2:13-17 discuss the relationship of the individual to the ruling authorities of institutions and governments, the *individual/institutional* divide. All of these instructions for domestic divides involved relationships in which there was an imbalance of power, with husbands, masters, and fathers (parents) typically being the dominant figure in relationship to the wives, slaves, and children. Indeed, this imbalance of power is operative in all the divides we have been discussing, if not directly, then in the form of prejudice in relation to the other who is the outsider.

Paul's teachings in this respect are difficult for us as modern people, for Paul does not seem to challenge the institutions of patriarchy and slavery and patronage that foster these divisions within the dominant culture. We should expect Paul to call for the abolishment of these institutions, and for the oppressed parties to be advised to refuse cooperation with the dominant party—the oppressor. Instead, Paul calls for mutual submission on the part of both the stronger and the weaker party, a submission manifested in the form of agape love (Eph 5:21, 33). This approach to these divides within the new community of the church is evident in Paul's counsel regarding our station

---

12. See the essay on "Household Codes" in Waltner and Charles, *1–2 Peter*, 180–83.

in life in 1 Corinthians 7:17–40. In verse 18, Paul advises those who are circumcised/uncircumcised to remain in the condition they were when called. In verse 21, Paul gives the same advice to slaves. Paul's counsel is summed up in verse 20: "Let each of you remain in the condition in which you were called," an admonition repeated again in verse 24. Those married are advised to remain in their marriage, and those single are advised to remain single, in verses 25–31.

The same principles are evident in Paul's counsel to the weak and the strong within the church in Romans 14:1–15:13. Paul is adamant about the freedom of the strong to exercise their strong conscience, but he is equally adamant that they should not exercise that freedom if and when it causes those who are perceived to be weak to stumble (Rom 14:20–21). The general principle is summed up in Romans 15:2: "Each of us must please our neighbor for the good purpose of building up the neighbor," a sentiment repeated often, as in Ephesians 4:1–3, Colossians 3:12–14, and especially Philippians 2:3–4.

Much more can and should be said to describe the way Paul sees the "leveling" and "reconciling" of all human divisions within the church, but that is beyond the scope of this book. Here I am mainly interested in noting that Paul did not function as a reformer of society. Paul exhibits little or no interest in changing the structures of the dominant society, despite their obvious oppressiveness, whether those were the institutions of patriarchy or slavery or patronage. Instead, Paul envisions the church, all these small, local, face-to-face assemblies, as the context for a new communal experience in which the participants on both sides of every human divide find their voice in an egalitarian and caring community. The more powerful yield to the weaker, and the weaker are empowered to own their dignity and make their contribution. In and through these transformed relationships in this new community, Paul and the other writers of the New Testament apparently believed that the oppressive institutions of the dominant culture would be subversively undermined and eventually transformed.

The church, that local, face-to-face assembly of believers established by Christ, becomes the new community of faith planted in every neighborhood and environment of the world as an alternative to the dominant culture. It does not intend to supplant or abrogate any of the existing social forms and institutions of any culture, not even the unjust forms of patriarchy and slavery, or for instance in African societies, polygamy. It is not interested in reforming the existing society structurally. Instead, it creates a new communal experience that transforms the relationships of all the members, empowering them to live freely and subversively within all the relationships of the family, workplace, and institutional roles in the dominant culture.

The dominant culture will lose its hold over those who are a part of this new community. Its ability to oppress and exploit is diminished, whether expressed as patriarchy or slavery or colonization. Every face-to-face community where the assembly of believers resides ("every town", Titus 1:5) is confronted with new possibilities and ways of relating and structuring life. This is the point of the parables of the mustard seed and leaven that Jesus told in Matthew 13:31–33. The church is the seed and the leaven that, however small and seemingly insignificant, is able to change the larger society from within—not from the top down, but from the bottom up!

Do Not Be Conformed To This World, but Be Transformed (Rom 12:2)

In his book *The First Urban Christians*, Wayne Meeks notes that "within a decade of the crucifixion of Jesus, the village culture of Palestine had been left behind, and the Greco-Roman city became the dominant environment of the Christian movement."[13] Meeks goes on to say, "The movement had crossed the most fundamental division in the society of the Roman Empire, that between rural people and city dwellers."[14] Perhaps the divide may have been crossed, but it was hardly bridged! What emerged were two distinctly different modes or expressions of Christian assembly. Thenceforth, the history of the church would be written by the urban communities, which would become the dominant Christian communities, as Meeks correctly notes. The pattern is set in the cosmopolitan center of Antioch in Syria, the base for Paul's mission to the Gentiles and the place where disciples of Jesus were first called "Christians" (Acts 11:19–26). It should be no surprise that in the institutional expression of the church, as in all institutional life, the imperial domination of the urban should overshadow the rural.

Meeks describes rural/urban realities in the Roman Empire in terms very similar to that described for Galilee in the previous chapter. "As cities grew in number and power, their relations with the countryside became more and more ambivalent. Each depended upon the other, but by every measure of physical and social advantage the symbiosis was one sided in favor of the city. Under the principate, agriculture continued to be the base of the whole empire's economy, but the ownership of productive land was increasingly concentrated in the hands of fewer and fewer proprietors—who lived in the city or its extension, their villas. The small, independent landowners living on their own land began to disappear reduced to tenancy or slavery, gone to the city to subsist as laborers, or recruited into the army."[15] Meeks quotes Ramsey MacMullen in *Roman Social Relations* (1975), who says, "The two worlds regard each other as, on the one side, clumsy, brutish, ignorant, uncivilized; on the other side, as baffling, extortionate, arrogant. Peasants who move to a town feel overwhelmed by its manners and dangers and seek out relatives of previous emigrants from the same village to settle among."[16] Meeks concludes, "The cities were where the power was. They were also the places where changes could occur. MacMullen emphasizes the conservatism of the villages, their 'central characteristic.'"[17]

13. Meeks, *First*, 11.
14. Ibid.
15. Ibid., 14.
16. Ibid.
17. Ibid., 15.

These descriptions of the differences between rural and urban in the dominant culture undoubtedly prevailed also in the perspectives of rural and urban congregations, even (especially?) those living in proximity to one another, as rural village congregations adjacent to urban, metropolitan congregations. As Meeks observes, "The conservatism of the villages preserved their diversity; changes in the city were in the direction of a common [dominant] Greco-Roman culture."[18] What an astute and astounding observation, though I suspect I make of it something quite different than Meeks does! The diversity of the Christian church is the contribution of the local village, the rural church, with its unique customs, language, and agrarian culture, shaped by the unique circumstances of the land and ecology of its place. The urban church is a church acculturated, if not accommodated, to the dominant culture. The city is where the peasants from the country lose their distinctive local cultures. The city is where the dominant culture requires the use of a common language and enforces a uniformity of cultural expression.

So I suspect Meeks is quite correct, that the Christian faith spread rapidly from one urban center to the next, as the story of Paul's missionary journeys in the Acts of the Apostles also attests. But given the dependency of urban centers on rural villages, we must also suppose that Christian faith spread quickly to "every town" and village around every metropolitan area, as Paul envisioned happening in Titus 1:5. There Christian faith quickly took expression within the unique context common to every local, agrarian community and gradually brought its influence to bear in the humanization of the relationships governing the life of the community within itself and in relation to neighboring communities and to its dominant urban cultural milieu.

This is the model of Christian faith we observed in the Greek Orthodox Church of Crete during our years living on the island of Crete in the early 1970s. This is the church to which the letter of Titus is addressed, with the local priest and church and weekly liturgy providing the focal point for the life of every village, and with every village expressing Christian faith within its own unique context. This story is, of course, untold in the annals of church history, for the most part, because it is the story of the rural church in the context of urban Christianity.

But ironies abound! While rural assemblies of believers contribute their unique diversity to the universal church, the urban context is much more fertile ground for the emergence of voluntary, alternative communities of faith, which we recognize as the genius of Christian faith. Contemporary scholarship has often noted that urban Christianity mirrors in many ways the "voluntary associations" common to Roman cities.[19] Some of these were pagan religious associations; some were professional associations like the tentmakers with whom Paul seems to have associated; some were domestic associations or philosophical schools. These associations were voluntary in nature, often had religious or cultic significance, and often featured common meals

---

18. Ibid.
19. Ibid., 77–80; see also Stegemann and Stegemann, *Jesus Movement*, 280–84.

and a familial (fictive or surrogate kinship) character. Hellerman has a very helpful chart illustrating both the commonalities and the differences between these various voluntary associations, and highlighting the ways in which the church as an assembly of believers was unique.[20] The church's uniqueness, according to Hellerman, came in being trans-local in nature, socially inclusive, structurally egalitarian, focused on study, being opposed to the dominant culture, and having an exclusive allegiance (in this case to Jesus Christ or God). This last feature also accounts for the church's unique understanding of familial relations, the surrogate kinship model discussed in the first section of this chapter.[21]

According to Hellerman, it was the anomie of urban life that fed the attractiveness of voluntary associations for urban dwellers. "The dislocation and corresponding alienation caused by steady urbanization during the first two centuries of the common era likely encouraged the formation of these alternative models of social organization. This explanation views the voluntary associations as compensatory in nature, offering avenues of relational support and opportunities for acquisition of honor that were unavailable to group members in the society at large. They provided 'fictive families for those uprooted from clan and family and fictive politics for those excluded from political power.'"[22] Christian faith offered an alternative local, face-to-face community in the urban setting more satisfactory to the needs of dislocated and alienated urban residents than either the dominant culture or the other voluntary associations operating in Roman cities could offer.

As indicated in chapter 8, the genius of urban assemblies of believers is that they bring together an assembly of people from diverse backgrounds in the creation of a new, genuinely alternative community to the dominant culture. Recent scholarship emphasizes that the Pauline and post-Pauline urban congregations of the Roman empire had a diverse composition representative of all but the lowest and highest elements of urban society, including slaves, artisans, traders, wealthy and independent women.[23] "A Pauline congregation generally reflected a fair cross-section of urban society," Meeks says, following Abraham Malherbe in *Social Aspects of Early Christianity*.[24] With the membership of these congregations likely being composed of a wide variety of ethnic, class, and religious origins, these urban congregations represented the formation of new, alternative communities of faith, marked not only by their subversive opposition to the oppression and exploitation of the dominant culture but also by their formation of a new cultural expression within the urban setting as a local community of faith. While outwardly conformed to the dominant culture in external

---

20. Hellerman, *Ancient Church*, 6.
21. Ibid., 14–25.
22. Ibid., 4.
23. Meeks, *First*, 72–73; Stegemann and Stegemann, *Jesus Movement*, 314–16.
24. Meeks, 73.

matters, these congregations were indeed transformed communities of faith that empowered their members to live redeemed lives within their urban context.

What I find fascinating and ironic is the reversal of cultural forms within rural and urban congregations. Rural congregations take on or assume the local, (agri)cultural heritage and tradition of their settings, thus exhibiting in their various contexts the diversity of the human cultural heritage. Urban congregations of diverse ethnolinguistic and class origins that exhibit external conformity to the dominant culture create new countercultural expressions in the formation of alternative communities of faith within the dominant culture.

Although Paul in Romans 12:1–2 was writing to Christians in an urban context, his words about not being conformed to this world apply to rural and urban congregations alike. Both rural and urban congregations need to present their corporate bodies as living sacrifices to God, allowing their lives to be transformed by the renewing of their minds in order to discern God's "good, acceptable and perfect will." However, this counsel might mean quite different things in the rural and urban contexts, respectively.

In the rural context, rural congregations would not be asked to give up their unique local and (agri)cultural heritage and traditions, as interpreters from an urban context might advocate, since these local traditions are seen as evidence of a rural community's prejudice, close-mindedness, and traditionalism. Instead transformation and having the mind renewed in a rural context means abandoning the community's ethnocentrism, suspicion, and prejudice toward its neighboring communities both rural and urban, and instead recognizing and learning from the uniqueness and richness present in every local, face-to-face community. The enemy of local communities is the dominant culture characterized by oppression and exploitation, not other local communities. Nonconformity, in the rural context, does not mean withdrawal from the specific, local cultural context that has already shaped human life and creation in that place. Instead, nonconformity means the transformation of communal ethnocentrism that views other communities as rivals, and a healing of the local culture's particular dysfunctions, all of which empowers a subversive response to the oppression and exploitation of the dominant culture.

In the urban context, urban congregations would not be asked to give up their external conformity to the dominant urban culture in which they reside, as interpreters from a rural context (like myself) might advocate, seeing in such conformity the betrayal of genuine Christian faith. Instead, transformation and having the mind renewed in an urban context might require the urban assembly to respect and celebrate the unique heritage of each member in their diversity while also creating a new local cultural identity that enables its members to engage the oppression and exploitation of the dominant culture in creatively subversive ways. In an urban context, nonconformity has more to do with the values by which the community lives than with its cultural forms, the values Paul outlines in passages like Romans 12:1–21.

Ultimately, both rural and urban congregations need to have a renewal of their minds regarding each other, as well. For although the context, character, and roles of rural and urban congregations differ, both are shaped as alternatives to the oppressive and exploitative values of the dominant culture. Rural and urban congregations need to see one another not as enemies or as rivals, but as allies, both no longer "conformed to this world," each in their respective ways, but both now "transformed" by the renewing of their minds (Rom 12:1–2).

What Is the Church: A Brief Analysis of Church History

Pick up any standard history of the Christian Church, and you will read about the history of the institutional (urban) church through the past two thousand years. There may be passing references to the stories of particular, local congregations or assemblies of believers here or there, but the storyline follows the institutional fortunes of the church, whether that be the episcopacy in Catholic and Orthodox churches, or the denominational structures of Protestant or free churches. Just as in the secular world, the history of the church tends to be dominated by the structures of power and influence.

The Christian Church typically takes expression within each faith tradition in four manifestations—local congregations, regional conferences, national assemblies, and global communions. Except for only a few extremely congregational traditions, the pattern in nearly all Christian traditions is that local congregations of a similar faith tradition gather in regional conferences, which in turn form national assemblies, which in their turn form global communions of faith. At each level of organization, churches of a particular tradition also interact, sometimes in cooperation and sometimes in competition, with their counterparts in other communions or traditions of Christian faith. So for instance, in the North American setting, there are local ministerial associations or alliances that bring together leaders of the various congregations in a larger community (city or county) to work together for joint purposes, though all too frequently in larger communities there may be at least two such alliances, one for evangelical and one for mainline denominations. Then there are the corresponding councils at state or provincial, national, and global levels, culminating in organizations like the World Council of Churches. Together, all these manifestations of "church" constitute the church universal, if not triumphant.

Whether denominational or ecumenical, organizations of ecclesiastical relationships beyond the local level are almost inevitably located in urban centers. Even within a distinctly agrarian tradition like the Mennonite Church to which I belong, there is a desire to be properly rooted in an urban context. It is the source of no small distress to many within my denomination that our denominational offices have been and apparently will continue to be in small, backwater cities like Newton, Kansas and Elkhart, Indiana. There are many who argue that we should have a proper corporate headquarters in a proper metropolis (mother-city) like Chicago, Los Angeles, or New York City. Is it not, after all, from such urban centers of communications and technology that the power and influence of the church, with its unique message and concerns, may most easily and effectively be disseminated into the institutions of the dominant culture?

In this way, it has been easy for the church in its trans-local manifestations to share the imperial mindset of the dominant, urban culture. Indeed, the history of the church is written from the perspective of the institutional power of the church as a force to be reckoned with by the secular and non-Christian world. The institutional church has often sought to impose its (perceived to be God's) will both on the local congregations/parishes that comprise it and on the society in which it is operating. For evidence of this we need look no further than the manner in which the conservative Christian right seeks to achieve political power and influence in the American political scene in order to advance its conservative Christian agenda. Its methods are no different than that of any secular party seeking to advance its agenda in the political sphere. It uses all the tools of political power and influence developed within the liberal, democratic context of American society, including vicious attacks on opponents.

The results of a nearly two thousand year experiment with political power and institutionalization by the church are not an unmitigated disaster. Despite what we in the free-church tradition might characterize as the loss of its soul, the institutional church has often enabled societies to become more humane, stable, and moral, not only through the passage of laws and legislation and through influence on secular politicians and rulers, but also through the establishment of institutions for education and health. Universities and hospitals are but two significant secular institutions that have their roots in the ministry and concern of the church. Though one can point to extraordinary abuses of power on the part of the church—the Inquisition and the Crusades, to name but two—it should be clear that the church has sincerely sought to bring the spirit of Christ to the social order in which it has operated. After all, as noted in the essay of chapter 8, what separates the official, institutional church from the subversive, face-to-face assembly of believers is not their commitment to Christ so much as their relationship to and understanding of the social order in which they live.

Still, if the thesis of this chapter holds true, the history of the church is ill written, indeed! It was Jesus' intention to form local, face-to-face communities that would enable its members to undermine the exploitative and oppressive structures and institutions (including ecclesiastical) of the dominant cultures in which they found themselves in subversive and nonviolent ways. If that is true, then we should be looking for some "people's history of the church," or better yet, "histories of the assemblies of believers in Christ." Fortunately, such histories do exist in the archives and historical records of each of the four rural congregations I have served, and this is likely true of most local congregations. I have no doubt that such assemblies have not only existed, but have flourished, in every time and place where Christ's name has been proclaimed, sometimes because of and sometimes in spite of the presence of the institutional church, which may have sometimes been the sponsors for such assemblies and sometimes their persecutors.

What this book contends is that even before the "personal salvation" posited by the official church as the central message of Jesus, it was the formation of local, face-to-face assemblies of believers as alternatives to the dominant culture that was the purpose and intention of Jesus' life, death, and resurrection. Indeed, in this view, "personal salvation" can only take on concrete meaning within the context of a local community of faith in which believers find their identity and their relationships. We can only be saved as our identity and our relationships are transformed within the context of a face-to-face community of believers. However, when the dominant church makes "personal salvation" central, then believers need no transformation from the dominant culture. Then the dominant church remains free to bless the ethics and ethos of the dominant culture, permitting only safe, institutionalized expressions of Christian ethics.

Fortunately, the institutional church has had no more success than other manifestations of imperial culture in silencing or uprooting local communities of faith. As in Jesus' ministry, there is something irresistible and irrepressible about the formation of face-to-face communities of faith. However carefully the gospel message of Jesus is sanitized and packaged by the institutional church, people who respond to the Jesus of the gospels find themselves drawn into local assemblies of believers that end up transforming their lives in subversive ways. This is true regardless of whether the message of Jesus is proclaimed in rural or urban settings, even when it is promulgated as the official faith of the dominant culture, even when it is forced upon a pagan culture by an agent of colonial power! The gospel gratefully always takes on a life of its own in the formation of subversive, local, face-to-face communities, which is the primary fruit of Jesus' life, death, and resurrection. According to his reviewer, Stanley Hauerwas, in his recent book *War and the American Difference: Theological Reflections on Violence and National Identity*, makes this point as well: "Our response to the violence of Constantinianism should not be anti-Constantinianism, but rather faithfulness in church communities defined by 'locality and place.' . . . Although the church is called to be everywhere, it does so in a way that is attentive to the particularities of each place in which it gathers."[25]

The truth is that we humans were created to live in community with one another—the families into which we were born, the extended families that are our heritage, and the face-to-face local communities where and with whom our families choose or are forced to live. When we are deprived of this communal life by the dominant culture, and when these communal forms of life are distorted by human sin, we long to be a part of a face-to-face social structure that defines who we are and how we are and should be related to one another, God, and creation.

25. Smith, "Local Church," 43.

Through the creation of the church, Christian faith reconstitutes or redeems our social relationships distorted by sinful structures or destroyed by imperial powers. So, for example, the surrogate family (local assembly of believers) envisioned by Jesus redeemed the family from the bonds of male dominance and patriarchy. It redeemed economic relationships from the constraints of landlords/tenants, masters/slaves, bosses/workers. It redeemed social relationships from the constraints of teachers/pupils, saints/sinners, clean/unclean, pure/impure, healthy/ill. It redeemed relationships between local communities by removing the constraints of prejudice, hatred, jealousy, and suspicion of the other. And when imperial powers uprooted people from their local, ethnic context and brought them to the anonymity of the city, the local assembly of believers gave to these uprooted strangers of diverse background a new identity and community, a place where they could both reclaim their ethnic identity and shape a new communal identity.

None of this works very perfectly, to be sure. Having been the pastor of four of these local assemblies of believers for nearly four decades, I know the foibles and shortcomings of local congregational life all too well. Still, I consider the church—that local assembly of believers expressing the particularity of its local context united with all other local assemblies of believers—to be the first fruit and great genius of faith in Christ. The local congregation as the unique community of a particular place and time joined together with all other local congregations anticipates the full unity, uniqueness, and diversity of the human family, redeemed through Jesus' life, death, and resurrection. This is the social context in which each of us as individuals find our life within community transformed, redeemed from the grip of the dominant culture and empowered to subversively undermine the domination and exploitation that characterizes the dominant culture.

Mennonite Mission Endeavors: Rural and Urban

Since the inception of Mennonite Church USA in the merger of the former Mennonite Church and the General Conference Mennonite Church in 2002, the prime buzzword in the new denomination has been *missional*. The intention is to become a missional church, not just to engage in "missions." In other words, current Mennonite thought is that local congregations, rather than supporting or even doing "missions," are instead called to be missional in the context of the community and place in which they live. This is well expressed, in terms compatible with the assumptions of this book, in the commentary on Article 10, "The Church in Mission," in the 1995 *Confession of Faith in a Mennonite Perspective*. "The church is called to live as an alternative culture within the surrounding society. Thus, the church is involved in cross-cultural mission whether it reaches out to people of the majority culture, to people of minority cultures within the society, or to various cultural groups in other countries. The church lives within the dominant culture, yet is called to challenge that culture's myths and assumptions when they conflict with Christian faith. Those cultural myths include individualism, materialism, militarism, nationalism, racism, sexism, and a worldview which denies the reality of anything beyond the grasp of the five senses and reason."[26]

This marks a significant advance in what has been a longstanding concern within the Mennonite Church for "missions." The General Conference Mennonite Church, whose history I know best, was formed in 1860 with missions as a primary concern. This was the era of the modern missionary movement, generally attributed to the work of William Carey in Great Britain at the turn of the nineteenth century, but with strong roots in the evangelical revivals of the eighteenth century.[27] Mennonites from South Germany immigrating to the United States in the nineteenth century and instrumental in the founding of the General Conference Mennonite Church were strongly influenced by the missionary movement of the time.[28]

Two critiques can be made of this modern missionary movement. One is its oft-noted alignment with the colonial expansion of European powers in Africa and Asia during this time, which compromised the Christian message severely, making it an adjunct to colonial domination. The other critique I would make is that with its roots in the evangelical revivals of the eighteenth century, it was preoccupied, as Protestantism generally has been, with the issue of personal salvation. The work of missions was seen, more often than not, as the task of bringing persons to a saving knowledge of Jesus Christ one by one, quite irrespective of their cultural context. Worthy and laudable as such a task might be, it neglected the more intricate and in my mind important task of forming communities of faith in vastly differing cultural contexts. Indeed, the cross-cultural dimensions of missions highlighted in the quote from the *Confession of Faith in a Mennonite Perspective* above were largely ignored until the middle of the twentieth century.

Within the General Conference Mennonite Church, two fields of mission work were engaged—home and foreign missions. "Home missions" were understood to be ministries to the scattered Mennonite immigrant communities being established in the North American frontiers as well as "city missions."[29] My own native community at Freeman, South Dakota, was the grateful recipient of the first of these mission efforts, with visits from eastern Mennonite missionaries in the 1870s assisting in the formation of churches in the Freeman community. As for "city missions," this was an effort to do evangelistic work within the urban context, but of course, it rapidly became evident to those engaged in those enterprises that the needs of urban communities required a more holistic ministry. The ironic contrast of rural, agrarian Mennonites doing urban missions was not lost to contemporary observers. At the mid-twentieth

---

26. *Confession*, 44–45.
27. Walker, *History*, 469–72.
28. Pannabecker, *Open Doors*, 61–62.
29. Ibid., 201–3, 205–10.

century, sociologist J. Winfield Fretz "concluded that Mennonites should direct their missionary efforts to rural areas with which they were familiar."[30]

As for "foreign missions," the first foreign mission field engaged by General Conference Mennonite missionaries was, ironically but truly, the American Indian reservations in Oklahoma in the 1880s. This was followed by missions to India (1900), China (1909), and other countries in the post–World War II era.[31] Through the dynamic of the gospel's power to form and reshape community, however compromised the vehicle in which the gospel is first proclaimed, a number of strong and vital indigenous churches resulted from these missionary efforts. Perhaps the most striking of these occurred in the first "foreign" mission field, among the Cheyenne nation of Oklahoma and Montana. Through the efforts of a Swiss linguist, Rudolphe Petter, Scripture was translated into the Cheyenne language, and a Cheyenne hymnbook was eventually published.[32]

In my years of ministry, I was privileged to learn about the ways in which Anabaptist Mennonite faith has taken root in a variety of indigenous cultural settings from leaders who have engaged this task of community formation. I think of Joseph Walks Along, leader among the Northern Cheyenne nation in Montana, Lawrence Hart, leader among the Southern Cheyenne nation in Oklahoma, and Steve Cheramie Risingsun, leader among the Choctaw nation in Alabama and the Houma nation in Lousiana. Each of these leaders has endeavored to allow the gospel to take shape within the cultural context of their traditional communities. The Hispanic, African American, and Asian congregations comprising Mennonite Church USA give further testimony to the variety of traditional, cultural heritages that are now a part of the church.

I also observe the same process at work among mission personnel working in trans-cultural settings around the world. I think of Loren and Donna Entz, who have lived in a Muslim village in Burkino Faso beginning in 1978, where they raised their family. They learned the language and lived in the culture of the Samogho people. Eventually, through telling Old Testament stories common to both Muslim and Christian traditions, the Entz's began to share gospel stories, as well, working with community leaders and respecting the traditions of the culture in which they were living as resident aliens/guests.[33] Another missionary couple in Argentina, Keith and Gretchen Kingsley, "accompany indigenous church leaders in their efforts to grow in spiritual maturity and understanding."[34] In the *Mennonite Weekly Review*, Kingsley writes about Tito, a pastor of a Toba United church. He says there is nothing exceptional about Tito, but he speaks of him because, "like many of his fellow Toba believers, he is rooted in his culture, its language and its hunting-gathering customs.

30. Ibid., 215.
31. Ibid., 278–81.
32. Ibid., 302.
33. *Mission Mosaic*, 42.
34. Ibid., 35.

He is also grasped by an encounter with God. He delights both in the land, which he cultivates, and solidarity with his people, especially in expressions of *alabanza*, the praise of God."[35]

Mennonite "urban mission" has been more problematic for rural Mennonites, as J. Winfield Fretz noted in 1950.[36] I remember the way in which rural congregations and conferences followed their youth to the city in the post World War II era hoping to establish Mennonite congregations in urban settings. But Mennonites migrating to the city were often not interesting in maintaining their rural, Mennonite identity, and these efforts usually failed, although some genuinely urban congregations did emerge from these efforts. Mennonite urban ministry has taken on new life in recent years as young urban Christians of non-Mennonite background began to discover Anabaptist Mennonite theology and to affiliate with the Mennonite Church in their urban ministry settings. New congregations like Missio Dei in Minneapolis, Minnesota, and Shalom Mennonite Church in Eau Claire, Wisconsin, are examples of these new urban congregations in the Midwest.

It is inspiring to learn these stories and see ways in which local and indigenous cultures around the world are not only responding to the gospel but having their own communities transformed. At the same time, it may be the Mennonite agrarian base that is having the greatest struggle in forming missional congregations appropriate to our cultural context. In part, this is a consequence of a crisis in our identity as traditional, rural Mennonite congregations. We have in the past confused our faith and our ethnic, rural identity. Too often, being Mennonite has meant having an ethnic Mennonite heritage, and we have ended up defensively seeking to preserve our ethnocultural heritage. At the same time, as the Mennonite Church has become multiethnic, we have been rebuked for our ethnic, rural heritage. Having been the dominant element in the institutional Mennonite church, rural congregations have presumed the right to perpetuate their forms of worship and cultural expressions inappropriately within the context of the national church. All of this has led to a crisis of identity and vision for the remaining rural congregations in the Mennonite Church.

In the end, however, it is neither our ethnic nor our rural, agrarian heritage that is contributing to the decline of rural congregations, in my view. It is instead our accommodation to the dominant culture of American society. Rural churches need to allow the gospel message of Jesus to transform their congregations into countercultural communities of faith that stand against the dominant culture. Rural congregations need to relearn how to be authentically rural, having a unique identity shaped not only by our ethnic heritage but also by the specific, local place and community where we live. We do not need to abandon or be ashamed of either our rural context or our ethnic heritage. However, our life together must be devoted to the revitalization of the specific, rural community where we live. Alone, as individual Christians living

---

35. Kingsley, "One", 6.
36. See note 30 above.

in the midst of the dominant culture, we will continue to be helpless victims of the dominant culture, which oppresses and exploits rural communities. Together, as alternative communities of faith, we will find the subversive, nonviolent tools required to revitalize our rural communities as unique expressions of humankind living here on God's earth. But the objective of our missional task must be the revitalization of our rural communities, and not the preservation of our ethnic identity or our institutional structures for their own sakes.

CHAPTER 14

The Christian Vision

To Gather Up All Things in Christ (Eph 1:10)

The Mystery of God's Will (Eph 1:9)

THE CHRISTIAN VISION, EXPRESSED most strongly in the Pauline writings, moves beyond the realm of individual and even communal salvation to an encompassing vision for all history and all creation. It sees God's purpose to be the "gathering up of all things" in Christ. This is not intended as an exclusionary reference, but rather as a visionary inclusive reference. In some mysterious way we can't fully understand, Jesus becomes the one through whom God's ultimate purposes will be worked out. Jesus is seen as the agent of creation (Col 1:16), the one who holds all things together (Col 1:17), the one who redeems creation "from its bondage to decay" (Rom 8:21), the one who reconciles to himself all things through the blood of the cross (Col 1:20).

The instrumentality of this mystery is found in Jesus' humiliation, his willingness to empty himself, to take the form of a slave, to become obedient to death (Phil 2:5–11). In this way, Jesus reveals self-giving love as the divine principle through which all things will one day be gathered up (recapitulated, ἀνακεφαλαιόω, **anakephalaioo**). Those who yield themselves to the mystery of this vision discover themselves to be participants with God in the unfolding of history and creation through their own giving of themselves in obedience to God, love for others, and care for the most vulnerable members of the human and natural community of life.

In this view, every choice we make daily—from the food we eat, to the way we relate to others, to the technologies we use, to the work we do, to the energy sources we rely on—has eternal consequences. Every choice is weighed by whether it contributes to or detracts from the "gathering up of all things in Christ." There is no neutral ground, no place where we can stand apart from this judgment. We either participate with God in the "recapitulation" of all things in Christ by the next choice we make, or we do not. Every act we choose is subject to this judgment, in the Christian vision.

The Biblical Story

In Him All Things Were Created, and In Him All Things Hold Together (Col 1:16–17)

The repeated biblical affirmation, made in John 1:1–3 and Hebrews 1:2, as well as in Colossians, is that Jesus Christ, the Word of God, is the agent of creation. As the preexistent Son of God, Jesus was the one through whom all things were created. "All things came into being through him, and without him not one thing came into being" (John 1:3). "But in these last days he has spoken to us by a Son, whom he appointed heir of all things, through whom he also created the worlds" (Heb 1:2). In Colossians 1:15–20, Jesus is held forth as "the image [icon] of the invisible God, the firstborn of all creation, for in him all things in heaven and on earth were created, things visible and invisible, whether thrones or dominions or rulers or powers—all things have been created through him and for him" (Col 1:15–16). "Firstborn" (πρωτότοκος, prototokos) corresponds here to "only begotten" (μονογενής, monogenes) in John 1:14, 18, signifying the unique character of Jesus as the "god/man" or Son of God. These hymnodic passages owe much to the figure of personified Wisdom found in Proverbs 8, Sirach 24, and Wisdom of Solomon 7:22b—8:1.

Beginning in the seventeenth and eighteenth centuries, through the explorations of Copernicus, Galileo, Newton, and many others, and especially in the past century, our understanding of our place within the universe has undergone profound changes. We do not live in a geocentric or even a heliocentric world. But for me, the most significant insight has been that the world is not a static creation formed once and for all, whole and complete in itself. Instead, creation is the result of a long, unfolding process, a process that seems not to be aimless or accidental but purposeful, moving toward the creation of life on a planet like Earth, and within life, toward the existence of self-conscious humans like ourselves. This is not to deny the uniqueness of each kind (species), including humankind, as God's creation. Indeed, uniqueness, diversity, and interdependence seem to be the driving forces of God's creative work.[1]

In recent years, several summaries accessible for the lay reader recount this unfolding of creation. Two of my favorites are *The Universe Story*, by Briane Swimme and Thomas Berry, and Bill Bryson's *A Short History of Nearly Everything*. With the exception of Brian Swimme, these authors are not natural scientists, but seek to present faithfully the current scientific understandings of the natural world in a way the lay reader can understand. These books, as well as more scientifically oriented texts, frequently note the exquisite and extraordinary circumstances that have occurred in the unfolding of the universe that have made this Milky Way galaxy, this solar system of the sun, this planet Earth, this life as we know it, and ourselves as *Homo sapiens*

---

1. Swimme and Berry, *Universe Story*, 71–79, where these characteristics are called *differentiation*, *autopoiesis*, and *communion*.

possible. Written to reflect the scientific viewpoint, these books refrain from ascribing these exquisite and extraordinary circumstances to divine providence, but as I read these accounts I frequently observe that the narrative screams out for the acknowledgement of God's purposeful direction. In any case, far from shaking my conviction about God's role in the creation of the world, books like these increase my sense of wonder and worship for what God has done in directing and arranging, if you will, the progressive unfolding of creation and life.

So it turns out that we humans occupy a specific and unique niche (like all other forms of life) in the space-time continuum that is the universe we are learning to know and understand, composed of atoms and atomic particles governed by the four physical forces—gravity, electromagnetism, and the strong and weak nuclear forces. Beginning with the Big Bang astronomers posit as the inception of the universe some fourteen billion years ago, the universe developed in such a way that millions of galaxies like our Milky Way were spawned some ten billion years ago. In turn, exploding stars called supernovae made possible the rich array of elements required for a world and life as we know it here on Earth.

So it was that some five billion years ago the solar system of our sun came into being in this distant reach of the Milky Way galaxy. From the material left over from the formation of the sun, the planets, including Earth with its moon, coalesced and began their revolutions around the sun. So for the past 4.5 billion years, give or take several million, Earth has become the habitat for life as we know it today. The first bacterial life emerged on Earth about 3.8 billion years ago.[2] Much later Earth saw an explosion of life forms with the dawn of the Phanerozoic eon about five hundred seventy million years ago.[3]

As for us humans, our genus, *Homo*, began to appear some five million years ago.[4] Modern humans, *Homo sapiens sapiens*, are thought to have appeared in Africa about one hundred fifty thousand years ago, spreading from there across Earth and replacing the earlier subspecies of humankind still existing.[5] This, presumably, would be the population granted the biblical designation of being created "in the image of God." The descendants of these first modern humans were those who about ten thousand years ago began the agricultural revolution leading to urban civilization and the historical period that is the subject of this book.

I include this absurdly brief sketch of "the universe story" not only to emphasize dramatically the particular niche we as humans (and all of life on earth) occupy, but also to reemphasize the reality of our mortal, creaturely existence and the way in which our lives are uniquely bound up with all other forms of life on Earth and with the forces of the universe as a whole. As self-conscious and morally free agents able to

---

2. Bryson, *Short History*, 292.
3. Swimme and Berry, *Universe Story*, 113–15.
4. Leakey, *Origin*, 7.
5. Ibid., chapter 5, esp. 97.

choose our destiny, we might be, as we suppose and affirm, the crown of this creation of God, the end toward which all of earthly life for the past nearly four billion years has been moving. But we still, nonetheless, belong to this world that God has created. And that means that our lives as earthbound, mortal creatures are irrevocably bound up with the fate of Earth.

This, in any case, or something very like it, is the world created, in the affirmation of the writer of Colossians, by "the image [icon] of the invisible God, the firstborn of all creation" (Col 1:15). These are the "all things in heaven and on earth . . . visible [to the third power], and invisible [the world of microscopic life, cells, molecules, atoms and atomic particles, and the world of billions of galaxies and stars invisible to our unaided eyes beyond our own Milky Way] . . . created through him and for him" (Col 1:16). Indeed, the writer of Colossians goes on to affirm that it was not only this physical realm that was created by Jesus, the image of God and the firstborn of creation. It was also the spiritual realm of the "thrones, dominions, rulers and powers," all those forces that we find enslaving and oppressing us, that were created "through him and for him" (Col 1:16). Since it is these spiritual powers that are most oppressive in our lives, it is reassuring to be told that these unseen powers are also a part of the created realm, and that indeed they do not stand outside but rather within the creative realm of God.

"For our struggle," Paul says, "is not against enemies of blood and flesh, but against the rulers, against the authorities, against the cosmic powers of this present darkness, against the spiritual forces of evil in heavenly places" (Eph 6:12). These are the unseen spiritual forces, identified in this book as expressed particularly in the spiritual powers inherent in the institutional structures of imperial urban civilization that oppress and exploit and dominate both the human and natural world of this creation. These are the spiritual forces that have led us into rebellion against God and prevented us from fulfilling our God-given vocation as humans, the vocation of reflecting the image of God. Yet, these spiritual forces, too, are not foreign or extraneous to the creation of God. These forces, too, along with all the visible and invisible physical things of God's creation, were created "through him and for him."

But for that matter, there are plenty of physical things created by Jesus to threaten our lives as well. Bill Bryson's book *A Short History of Nearly Everything* might be understood as an exercise in marveling at all the ways we just barely came to be as humans, and at all the ways in which we might just as easily cease to be. Chapter 13 examines the history of asteroids striking the earth and their role in the extinction of the dinosaurs at the end of the Cretaceous Period sixty-five million years ago. There are literally millions of asteroids orbiting the sun in a belt between Jupiter and Mars, and every now and then one of them crosses Earth's path.[6] Contrary to science fiction movies that envision us deploying a nuclear weapon into space to blow up an incoming asteroid, there is no possibility of us protecting ourselves from an asteroid strike; indeed, it is unlikely we would even detect such a threat before it struck the earth.[7]

6. Bryson, *Short History*, 192–94.
7. Ibid., 205.

The next two chapters of Bryson's book, 14 and 15, describe the volcanic threat under which we live (and on which, ironically, life on Earth also depends as part of the rock cycle by which the continental land masses of the earth are renewed). About one hundred miles southwest of where I live, near Orchard, Nebraska, is Ashfall Fossil Beds State Historical Park, where about twelve million years ago "scores of animals—rhinoceroses, zebra-like horses, saber-toothed deer, camels, turtles," met their death beside a dried-up water hole.[8] They were buried in and died from volcanic ash that came from an eruption in southern Idaho, the same volcanic hot spot that now underlies Yellowstone National Park. The volcano beneath Yellowstone Park has had three major eruptions in the last two million years, one about every six hundred thirty thousand years. The last one, about six hundred thousand years ago, ejected about a thousand times more volcanic material than the Mount St. Helens eruption in 1980.[9] Any time now, in not too many thousands of years, Yellowstone will be due for another major eruption, and if Yellowstone erupts, we won't have to worry about global warming anymore.[10]

In view of the physical and spiritual forces that threaten life on Earth, including our own lives, I find special consolation in the affirmation of Colossians 1:17, that in Jesus Christ "all things hold together." The Greek word is συνίστημι (sunistimi), which literally means "to stand together." What the affirmation means for me, and of course it is nothing more than a faith affirmation, is that Jesus not only is the creator of all things, but also the one who manages to hold everything together, to keep everything from falling apart. The spiritual powers that keep seeking to undo creation in rebellion against God ultimately come up against this Jesus who "holds everything together." And who knows, perhaps it is Jesus who also "holds at bay" the natural catastrophes that threaten life on Earth (and ourselves) with destruction. Recognizing these cataclysmic forces capable of destroying life on Earth make it all the more wonderful to me that life has taken the shape that it has, through God's divine providence and Jesus' word, and that we humans have had this last ten thousand year history of living here on planet Earth in an environment so favorable to human life.

Writing in the tumult of the Bolshevik Revolution in Russia and the aftermath of the conflagration of the first Great War of the twentieth century, William Butler Yeats, the Irish poet, felt the cycles of history and civilization coming undone, widening to the point where "Things fall apart; the center cannot hold; / Mere anarchy is loosed upon the world." But in the poem with these lines, "The Second Coming," Yeats also perceives that "some new revelation is at hand." He anticipates a second coming, though perhaps not *the* second coming of Christian hope.[11] The Christian affirmation is that the center will hold, despite all fears and evidence to the contrary, at least so

---

8. Ibid., 207; see also Voorhies, "Ancient Ashfall."
9. Bryson, *Short History*, 226.
10. Ibid., 227–28.
11. Yeats, "Second Coming."

long as it matters to mortal creatures and a finite world, because at the center is Jesus Christ, who holds all things together.

Creation Itself Will Be Set Free from Its Bondage to Decay (Rom 8:21)

To be honest, however, if Jesus is supposed to be holding everything together, we might be pardoned for thinking that he isn't doing a very good job of it! If we look around with any kind of honest appraisal, we must agree with Paul's assessment. "We know that the whole creation has been groaning in labor pains until now" (Rom 8:22). Well, we might even doubt that creation is in labor, giving birth to something new. It seems rather that creation is groaning in its final death pangs! Already in Jeremiah 4:23–28, we read of a de-creation, echoing the creation story in Genesis 1, and culminating in earth's grief. "Because of this the earth shall mourn, and the heavens above grow black" (Jer 4:28).

Consider this short list of environmental disasters:

- The equatorial forests are being cut down and countless species of life snuffed out.
- Land around the world is eroded and mined, both literally and in agriculture, for profit in the production of commodities for the global market place.
- Groundwater is polluted by "fracking" in our frantic effort to find enough fossil fuels to sustain our lavish lifestyle for a few more years.
- The oceans are depleted from overfishing, with huge islands of plastic waste floating in their midst.
- The air and water are fouled by our industrial and energy plants.
- Everywhere the race is on to find the last mineral stores of the earth needed to run all our gadgets, with both natural and social mayhem and warfare accompanying this search.
- An entire coast is polluted by the flow of crude oil from an undersea drilling rig uncontained for three months.
- Another coast is first devastated by an earthquake and tsunami, and then made uninhabitable by radiation from a nuclear plant damaged by the tsunami.
- Extreme weather and storms portend climate changes caused by human use of fossil fuels, leading to flooding and loss of homes and land for millions, especially for those living in low-lying coastal areas in the Third World.

The list could go on, and it is depressing to note that these disasters are mostly the result of human greed and exploitation, not the cataclysmic natural disasters of asteroids, volcanoes, and earthquakes noted in the previous section. Of course, the earth is a big place, and the earth contains within itself immense reservoirs of self-healing and adjustments (though not, it should be noted, without involving immense human suffering and perhaps the loss of humanity itself). These healing powers of earth are indeed a part of God's created order, a part of Jesus' function as the one who "holds everything together," making life on earth possible. Perhaps it is possible to be too pessimistic about the future of life on earth. Perhaps, like the people who built the Tower of Babel in Genesis 11, we overestimate our own power to conquer nature, in either positive or negative ways. Still, it should be clear that we humans have irrevocably changed the natural systems of life on earth in dramatic ways, especially since the Industrial Revolution of the eighteenth century and the onset of our use of fossil fuels to power our way of life.

At the same time, it may be important to note that while the scale of human impact on natural systems has increased exponentially in recent centuries, the exploitative impulse is as old as civilization itself. The roots of human exploitation of God's creation are to be found, if the thesis of this book has any merit, not only in human sin and rebellion itself, but particularly in the rise of urban civilization, in the drive to use earth's resources to make a humanly constructed environment where we humans can live apart from God. The agricultural revolution that began ten thousand or so years ago, resulting in agrarian cultures, also tinkered with natural systems creating the agricultural landscapes of the earth. But traditional agrarian cultures have sought to understand and respect and build upon the natural systems in the environments where they lived. There were in traditional agrarian cultures some built-in restraints preventing the rampant exploitation of the earth characteristic of urban civilization. There were the limitations of the specific environment of each community, and the face-to-face relationships of communal life that curb human greed.

My point, in any case, is that the biblical writers were just as aware as we are today about the exploitative characteristics of urban civilization. Biblical writers felt the same angst about the future of the earth and its life as we do, if the apocalyptic writings of the New Testament age are any indication. It seemed as clear to thoughtful people in the first-century Mediterranean world of the Roman Empire as it does to us today that the way of life which everyone had come to accept as the norm was unsustainable, exploitative, oppressive, and certain to be undone. Revelation 17 and 18, with its description of the fall of Babylon, code word for Rome, makes that very clear. This is why the Apostle Paul is also so clear about the role of the principalities and powers, embodied in the institutional structures of urban civilization, as the primary forces threatening human life and God's creation.

It isn't really surprising, then, that Paul's vision for God's redemptive work in Jesus Christ in Romans 5–8 should culminate in the redemption of creation itself, as it does in Romans 8:18–25. "Creation itself," Paul asserts in Romans 8:21, "will be set free from its bondage to decay!" In my mind, "decay" here is an unfortunate translation for the Greek φθορά (phthora), for it seems to suggest that Paul had in mind a reversal of natural processes of life and death. Elsewhere, most notably in 1

The Christian Vision

Corinthians 15, the term is translated as "corruption," and this is its meaning here as well.[12] When something is corrupted it is made impure or untrue to its original nature, and this is what happened to creation (the natural world we know here on earth) because of human sin, as we saw in Genesis 3.[13]

This is why in the previous verse Paul speaks of creation being "subjected to futility, not of its own will but by the will of the one who subjected it" (Rom 8:20). Most commentators assume that the agent of creation's subjection to futility alluded to here is God, though the agent is not indicated in the Greek text.[14] My own view is that the agent of creation's subjection is none other than ourselves as fallen, sinful humans. It is we who subjected creation to its futility and its corruption, through no fault of its own, by our sin and rebellion against God.

This would explain what is also most striking in this passage, though not often noted—the role of a redeemed humanity in the redemption of the earth (creation)! Though it is in fact Jesus who through his life, death, and resurrection redeemed creation from its "futility" and "corruption," that is never made explicit by Paul in this text. Instead, verse 19 speaks of creation waiting "with eager longing for the revealing of the children of God [a redeemed humanity]." And in verse 21, Paul sets creation's freedom from its bondage to corruption in parallel with our own obtaining "the freedom of the glory of the children of God." That leads finally to verses 22–23, where both "the whole creation" and also "we ourselves, who have the first fruits of the Spirit" groan in unison (and in labor pains), waiting together for "adoption, the redemption of our bodies." Creation's redemption in Romans 8:18–25 is dependent on a redeemed humanity, just as creation's subjection to futility and corruption was caused by the sin of humanity. Creation's groaning as an exploited and corrupted natural world is indeed a form of labor pains, for that groaning anticipates the new birth of creation through a redeemed humanity.

This passage opens with a consideration of "the sufferings of this present time" (Rom 8:18). These sufferings are noted in the first verses of this section (Rom 5:1–5) as the source of Christian hope in Christ.[15] These sufferings cannot be compared with "the glory about to be revealed to us" (Rom 8:18), "the freedom of the glory of the children of God" (Rom 8:21). That glory is our adoption as God's children through "the redemption of our bodies" (Rom 8:23), our freedom from slavery to sin and entry into God's eternal life as followers of Christ. This is something for which we groan (Rom 8:22–23) in hope (Rom 8:24–25) even though we have already seen the first fruits of that bodily redemption in the resurrection of Jesus.

Paul's argument for cosmic (in this case planetary) redemption thus runs something like this. Just as humanity's sin and rebellion led to creation's subjection to futility

---

12. Harder, "φθείρω," 9:104.
13. See chapter 2.
14. See, e.g., Wright, "Romans," 10:596, in an otherwise marvelous exegesis of this passage.
15. Ibid., 595.

and corruption through no fault of its own, so creation's redemption is bound up with the redemption of humanity accomplished through Jesus' death and resurrection. The implication is, of course, as follows: If we have been redeemed from the powers of evil and sin, we will then become participants with Christ in the redemption of God's creation. We will no longer participate in the exploitation (corruption) of creation. Instead we will seek actively to bring to creation the healing and redemption that Christ has already brought to our mortal bodies.

The Christian vision (as articulated in this case by the Apostle Paul) is of a cosmic (planetary) redemption of God's original good creation. This assumes that the tragic exploitation and corruption of creation by human sin is limited to the natural systems of life here on Earth and do not affect the sun and Milky Way galaxy and universe to which Earth belongs. Of course that involves the redemption of humans, individually and as a human family. But just as it was never enough for God to limit salvation to one people (Isa 49:6), so it is never enough for God to limit salvation to humanity alone. It is the whole creation, along with humanity, that needs to be redeemed, and that is what God is doing through Jesus' life, death, and resurrection.

The image we should have is of a Jesus who wanders every nook and cranny of the earth, from the depths of the oceans to the heights of the mountains to the extremes of the polar caps and the equatorial regions, but especially to the wasted and polluted and corrupted and exploited places, pondering how the broken pieces of this creation can be put back together, healed, or redeemed from futility. What is the guiding principle in this redemption? Is it not that love which values the uniqueness, the diversity, and the interconnectedness of all that is, and every form of life? Is it not that love which gives itself for the sake of the weakest and most vulnerable member of each community of life here on earth? This is, after all, the love Jesus had for us in giving his life for us on the cross. This is, after all, the love God has repeatedly enjoined on the human communities God has sought to shape, where the weakest and most vulnerable members of the community are to be shown not just deference, but particular care. Must not this same care then be extended to all the non-human members of the community of life on earth, who are also created and valued by God, the God who sees every sparrow fall?

While the first step in the redemption of creation is to imagine what Jesus would do to redeem the broken and wounded creation of life, the second step for those redeemed in Christ is to enact those redeeming practices in our own lives. This is a very particular and daily exercise for us as humans. It involves learning to know most intimately the specific natural and human community of life in which we share. It means caring for that particular space we occupy each day, whether it be urban apartment, rural town, or agrarian field. Having been redeemed by God in Christ, we are responsible to bring redemption to creation, to redeem that place where we live. This is the task that confronts us in all our daily decisions, our choices about what we will eat, what we will wear, where and how we will live, how much energy we will use, which technologies we will employ, how we will relate to others and to the creatures and forms of life that sustain our lives, and how we trust and worship God in all these choices. After all, the redemption of the earth is not a global problem to be solved, but rather a local mission of caring for the specific place where we live. If we can redeem the place where we live, if we can redeem the lives we live, if we can participate in redeemed local communities in every place around the earth, then the earth is being redeemed.

A discipline that can be helpful for us in accomplishing this redemptive work is that of walking. It is when we put our feet on the ground that we always begin to see and respect the complexity and enormity and specificity of creation and life in all its mystery and wonder. Walking, no matter where we are, on city street, field, or country lane, always reminds us of our relatedness to the other humans who are a part of our neighborhood and to all the other creatures and systems that sustain us. Walking reminds us of our dependence upon God, our inability to manage and control every aspect of our lives. Walking shows us the specific real estate that needs our healing presence—this gully, that ill-advised planting, those creatures whose space we share. If we as local redeemed communities, rural or urban, might begin to heal our yards, our neighborhoods, our farms—whatever piece of real estate we are responsible for by our presence if not our ownership, then we are beginning to set creation free from its bondage to corruption.

God's Plan for the Fullness of Time: The Recapitulation of All Things in Christ (Eph 1:10)

The mature Pauline writings of the New Testament are replete with hymnic passages that celebrate the cosmic work of Jesus Christ in creation and redemption. We have already looked at the first stanza of the hymn in Colossians 1:15–20, which describes Jesus as the cosmic creator, the one who holds all things together. The second stanza of that hymn speaks in parallel cosmic form of Jesus' work as the redeemer: "He is the head of the body, the church; he is the beginning, the firstborn from the dead, so that he might come to have first place in everything. For in him all the fullness of God was pleased to dwell, and through him God was pleased to reconcile to himself all things, whether on earth or in heaven, by making peace through the blood of his cross" (Col 1:18–20).

Here the redeeming work of Christ is highlighted first with Christ's role in the formation of the church as God's vehicle for the redemption of the world, in verse 18. Both Christ's resurrection, "the firstborn from the dead" (Col 1:18), and his atoning death, "making peace through the blood of his cross" (Col 1:20), are mentioned as the instruments of God's redeeming work. Jesus' unique identity as the God/man is affirmed, "For in him all the fullness of God was pleased to dwell" (Col 1:19). All of this leads to the central affirmation of this stanza: "And through him God was pleased to reconcile to himself all things, whether on earth or in heaven" (Col 1:20). Note again the universal and cosmic scope of the affirmation being made about the redeeming/reconciling work of Jesus/God in the cross and resurrection.

The same cosmic view of God's work in Jesus Christ can be seen in the Christ hymn of Philippians 2:6–11. The first stanza (Phil 2:6–8), describes the instrumentality of Christ's redeeming work in terms of his emptying himself of his divine prerogatives in order to become fully human, and indeed, not only human but the least of humans, "taking the form of a slave" (Phil 2:7). This of course meant not only taking on human mortality, but voluntarily and willingly accepting death: "He humbled himself, and became obedient to the point of death—even death on a cross" (Phil 2:8). In this way, the hymn stresses the character of ἀγάπη (agape), self-giving love, as the means by which God redeems the world.

The second stanza of the Christ hymn (Phil 2:9–11) places Jesus at the center of God's redeeming work, this time by declaring that it will be "at the name of Jesus" that "every knee should bend, in heaven and on earth and under the earth, and every tongue should confess that Jesus Christ is Lord, to the glory of God the Father" (Phil 2:10–11). As Christians, we have sometimes read this as an exclusionary reference to Christ and a forced submission. My own view is that Paul had in mind rather his conviction regarding the centrality of Jesus in accomplishing God's redemption of the world, and its universal scope. Here there is nothing left outside the redeeming work of Christ. Every knee will bow and every tongue, in heaven, on earth, and under the earth, will confess the name of Jesus, which presumably includes all the spiritual cosmic powers that oppress and exploit humanity and creation, including those rebellious spiritual powers that first led humans into sin. Christ, the name of Jesus, is the one who accomplishes this cosmic and universal redemption of the world through his humiliation and self-giving love. There is nothing coercive or exclusionary about Jesus' sacrifice of himself upon the cross.

There is still one final Pauline passage that I find particularly intriguing in its description of God's redeeming work in Christ. It is the blessing of the God who is "Father of our Lord Jesus Christ, who has blessed us in Christ with every spiritual blessing in the heavenly places" (Eph 1:3), the opening blessing of Paul's letter to the Ephesians (Eph 1:3–14). This passage is one long, complex sentence in the original Greek. Here our interest is primarily in the first ten verses of this passage, and particularly verses 9 and 10. God is clearly the subject of this long sentence. First, blessing is invoked upon God as the Father of our Lord Jesus Christ. But then it is God who has blessed us "with every spiritual blessing" (Eph 1:3), who "chose us in Christ before the foundation of the world" (Eph 1:4), who "destined us for adoption as his children through Jesus Christ" (Eph 1:5), and finally, who "has made known to us the mystery of his will, according to his good pleasure that he set forth in Christ, as a plan for the fullness of time, to gather up all things in him, things in heaven and things on earth" (Eph 1:9–10). Each action of God is further described in subsidiary clauses, most notably in verse 7, which highlights our redemption in Christ. "In him we have redemption through his blood, the forgiveness of our trespasses, according to the riches of his grace that he lavished on us" (Eph 1:7–8).

Here I am most interested in that mystery of God's will made known to us by God in Christ. God's plan is that in the fullness of time all things in heaven and on earth will be "gathered up" in and through Christ. The Greek term translated as "gathered up" here is ἀνακεφαλαιόω (anakephalaioo), which literally translated means "to recapitulate." The Greek word is derived from the noun κεφάλαιον (kephalaion), which means "the main thing" or "the main point," and is in turn related to the Greek noun for "head," κεφαλή (kephale), which plays such an important role in Pauline theology describing Jesus as the head of the church. To recapitulate, in any case, is to repeat the main points.

"Capitulation" in English has two meanings. The more familiar one refers to the act of surrendering, but it also refers to "a set of terms or articles constituting an agreement between governments."[16] To "recapitulate" is "to repeat the principle points or stages" of something.[17] "Recapitulation" is used in biology to describe the development of an individual organism through "successive stages resembling the series of ancestral types from which it has descended, so that the ontogeny of the individual is a recapitulation of the phylogeny of its group."[18] In music, "recapitulation" refers to the third section of the sonata form, in which the three principle themes of the first exposition section are repeated in their original order and in the home key.[19]

I have found it highly provocative theologically to think of God "recapitulating" everything in heaven and on earth through the life, death, and resurrection of Jesus Christ. Think of the layers of meaning this might involve. God is "replaying" all the movements of creation and history through Jesus Christ, and this time everything is being playing in the "right" key, without the disturbing and disrupting influence of our sin and rebellion against God. In his life, death, and resurrection, Jesus is "recapitulating" the whole history of our lives and our human race, at once playing out the "phylogeny" of our kind in his life, while at the same time by his choices fulfilling the destiny that was to have been ours, and now in Christ can be. In Jesus, God is "summing up" all the principle stages and movements of history and creation, and bringing them all to fruition. In Jesus, God is "gathering up" all the loose ends of creation and history caused by the disruption of human sin and the entry of evil powers into creation, and putting everything in order to reflect the divine purpose for both creation and for humanity.

This recapitulation of all things in Christ has the character of both a "once and for all" event and something that is repeated over and over again, in many lives and places

16. *Merriam-Webster's Collegiate Dictionary*, 10th ed., s.v. "capitulate."
17. Ibid., s.v. "recapitulate."
18. Ibid., s.v. "recapitulation."
19. Machlis, *Enjoyment*, 227.

and times, and indeed in every hour of every day everywhere. Its "once and for all" character is to be seen in the historical life, death, and resurrection of Jesus. We have already noted in chapter 11 how Jesus perfectly fulfilled God's intentions for humanity through his life choices for how he would live, and indeed how he would die. This we confess as Christians is what makes Jesus our Savior, for by his life, death, and resurrection we are redeemed from the powers of evil, shaped into a new community of faith, and empowered to live together against the grain of the dominant culture that until now had enslaved us in rebellion and sin against God. As the writer of Hebrews affirms, "But as it is, he has appeared once for all at the end of the age to remove sin by the sacrifice of himself" (Heb 9:26). "But when Christ had offered for all time a single sacrifice for sins, 'he sat down at the right hand of God.' . . . For by a single offering he has perfected for all time those who are sanctified" (Heb 10:12, 14).

While affirming the "once and for all" character of Jesus' life, death, and resurrection, these verses in Hebrews already point toward the repetitive character of Jesus' recapitulation of all things—the way in which Jesus continues to "recapitulate" everything in our own lives and space and time, both in the choices we make (being perfected as those Jesus sanctified), and in the way that life on earth continues to unfold. As N. T. Wright says: "When Paul declares [in Colossians 1:15–20 and Ephesians 1] that it is now God's intention both to reconcile all things to, through and for him and to sum up all things in the Messiah, he is standing firmly against all kinds of dualism which would envision a final state in which the present created order was abandoned as worthless. Just as at the end of Revelation the new heavens and the new earth are joined together, so in Paul's thought the triumphant goal of eschatology is that there should be one future for the one world made and loved by the one God."[20]

This vision of Christian faith as the "recapitulation" of all things in heaven and on earth through the life, death, and resurrection of Jesus is rooted in the work and the choices made by Jesus himself. But it is worked out also in the choices we make daily as those whose lives have been redeemed from the powers of evil and shaped into the alternative community of faith living against the grain of the dominant culture. As lone individuals, we of course find it difficult even as humans redeemed by Christ to stand against the powers of the dominant culture. But when we find ourselves in a redeemed community, an alternative community of faith, we are empowered to make choices that reflect Jesus' recapitulation of all things in heaven and on earth.

Obviously, the claims made by Christian faith for Jesus Christ in this Christian vision of life and creation are extreme and astounding! They are rooted in the conviction of God's providential role as the Creator of the universe and of life. They are rooted in the conviction of the goodness of God's creation, and of God's purposeful plan for the unfolding of creation and the trajectory of history. They are rooted in the conviction that humankind represents in some way the culmination of God's plan for this particular world we know as planet Earth, with all its abundant life. They are

---

20. Wright, *Paul*, 144.

rooted in the conviction that God's intention for the human family is that we were to reflect the divine image for one another and for God's creation. They are rooted in the realization that as individuals and as a human family, we have distorted this image of God through our rebellion and sin against God, born out of our realization of our mortality and our mistrust and impatience with God's promise. They are rooted in the realization that our sin unleashed into the created world powers of evil that have also bound us and keep us from fulfilling God's intention for our lives. And finally, they are rooted in the conviction that God "loved the world so much" that God acted to redeem it by coming to dwell within it as a mortal human who would give his life in self-giving love.

Sometimes, these faith affirmations about Jesus that comprise the Christian vision are presented as though it has all been accomplished already and done for us. Of course, there is an aspect of truth in this understanding. It is valid for Christians to say that we already know the outcome of both the historical process and the unfolding of creation because of Jesus' life, death, and resurrection. That is in keeping with the Christian vision. But what Christians have often forgotten or neglected is that by our redemption from the powers we are called to become active participants in the redemption of creation. This is particularly the function of the church, that alternative community of faith formed and redeemed by God in Christ. The Christian vision not only affirms the central role of Jesus Christ in the redemption of creation and history through his life, death, and resurrection, but also the role of the church, Christ's body of redeemed people, as the vehicle through which that redemption is being realized.

The Crises of the Dominant Culture: Economic, Energy, Ecological

Throughout this book, I have been writing about rural and local face-to-face communities as alternatives to the dominant cultures of urban civilization. In the New Testament era, there is a sense in which rural and local communities are subsumed by the church as the new community of faith. The church, as a redeemed community, is to model what all local communities, rural or urban, ought to look like. Nevertheless, I believe that all rural, traditional cultures of whatever ethnicity or religious heritage and all face-to-face neighborhoods in urban areas, are the primary places where the values of the dominant culture are subversively undermined, making a humane and sustainable future possible both for the human family and for creation. Indeed, I believe that the risen Christ (God) is present in all these local communities and cultures, empowering their resistance to the dominant cultures in which they live. We in the church need to see every traditional rural culture, every local community, rural or urban, as our ally in resisting the depredations of the dominant culture.

Perhaps I need to be a bit more explicit about what I mean when I speak about *dominant cultures*. I see that local communities and cultures, rural and urban, are required to confront the dominant culture in their society. This dominant culture takes shape in every society or nation in terms of the political, economic, technical, and religious institutional structures of that society. As we saw in chapter 3, the more complex organizational structure of urban (or national) life provides a space for the powers of evil to operate through the institutional structures of society. Within the urban (or national) structures that now exercise dominion over every geographical region of the earth, the institutions of society create a dominant culture, a system of values and a way of living that holds sway over all who are subject to this particular jurisdiction. These values are marked by oppression, injustice, domination, exploitation, and idolatry—all the characteristics of urban civilization noted in the introduction.

In our own time, and perhaps for the past century or so, we also have seen the emergence of a global dominant culture. Despite competing and rival nation-states, the global culture is marked by a global market economy and integrated financial system, in which multinational corporations often wield considerably more power than all but the most powerful of nation-states. The scientific worldview, and in particular the technological revolution of the past century, also informs and shapes the global culture. The information/computer age has hastened and facilitated the dominance of the global dominant culture. To some degree, the Islamic resistance to this global dominant culture represents an alternative representing traditional cultures, though the Arab Spring that began in 2011 may signify the end of even Islamic resistance to the global culture.

It may seem that in this computer age humanity is now closer than ever to realizing the ancient dream of Genesis 11:4: "Come, let us build ourselves a city, and a tower with its top in the heavens, and let us make a name for ourselves; otherwise we shall be scattered abroad upon the face of the whole earth." But while the current global culture seems to be so nearly dominant over the whole world, it is important to recognize that the current global culture varies only in degree from previous attempts to establish global dominance. The Hellenistic world established by Alexander the Great and the Pax Romana of the Roman Empire are both previous efforts to build globally dominant cultures, and indeed in both cases it might be argued that the whole then-known world was brought within the sphere of these imperial projects.

What is less obvious to most of our contemporaries are the crumbling foundations of the global dominant culture, and that is particularly true of the most powerful people who govern and benefit from the oppression and exploitation of the dominant culture. The largest crack in the global dominant culture derives from the fact that it is fueled (literally) by fossil fuels. The Industrial Revolution of the eighteenth and nineteenth centuries that kicked off the current global culture began with the invention of the coal-powered steam engine, since by then most of the forests in Europe had already been exploited for timber for fuel and shipbuilding. With the beginning of the petroleum age in the 1860s, the use of fossil fuels has powered the affluent, consumerist, and gadget-driven global culture.[21]

21. Northcott, *Moral Climate*, 90–93.

It is truly amazing to ponder the amount of energy the human family has taken from the organic material stored in the earth's crust in the form of coal, crude oil, and natural gas. I always am in awe of this driving into a city in steady traffic with all those cars and trucks around me, and with the passenger jets approaching and departing from the nearby airport, and realizing that this energy usage goes on day after day, year after year, not just in this city, but in countless cities around the world. To be fair, I have the same realization when I help with the harvest on a local farm and watch as one diesel engine after another is fueled up daily for all the trucks, tractors, and combines used in the harvest.

Still, we do live on a finite planet. Eventually the last drop of oil might be pumped from the earth's crust. Most analysts believe we have already reached "peak oil," the point at which half the petroleum reserves of the earth will have been used up. It may seem reassuring to note that only half of the petroleum reserves have been used, but in fact, the remaining reserves will be much more difficult and costly to extract, both economically and environmentally. Currently, the dominant culture is reassuring itself that heretofore inaccessible sources of crude oil are available, but the costs of extracting this oil will be immense.[22] This means that the price of gasoline will continue to rise, creating dislocations throughout societies around the world.[23]

Of course, if we continue to burn fossil fuels at current rates, we will in all likelihood have destroyed the possibility of human life on earth by global warming long before the supplies of crude oil are exhausted. At the least, the continued use of fossil fuels as the primary source of energy for human use will create a huge environmental crisis for the poorest residents of the world, who will see their lands lost to droughts and flooding.[24] Since reducing the use of oil has profound implications for economic growth, which has continued to be the primary idolatry of the dominant global culture, politicians and corporations continue to be in grave denial about global warming and its implications for the future, and technical experts continue to trust human ingenuity to fix things. It does not seem likely that the current use of petroleum will be curtailed significantly enough to prevent some level of catastrophic global warming. We should expect massive human dislocations due to climate change, the breakdown of the current global food system, and more wars designed to maintain access to oil and other vital resources, with all the attendant human suffering and ecological devastation these phenomena involve.

Add to all this the intricately integrated global financial systems of the world, and we have a recipe for the dissolution of the current global dominant culture. The United States continues to recover from the 2008 recession caused by the greed of the

---

22. Walsh, "Oil's Messy Frontier," 29–35.

23. See Maynard Kaufman, *Adapting*, chapter 1, for a summary of peak oil and its implications, as well as an excellent overview of pertinent bibliography.

24. See the first two chapters in Northcott, *Moral Climate*, for a brief but thorough scientific analysis of global warming from a Christian biblical-ethical perspective.

financial institutions of our land, but it is doubtful that the American economy can continue to expect strong economic growth in the face of the energy and environmental constraints it is facing. The stresses the Eurozone has had with the indebtedness of countries like Greece and Italy are indicative of the fact that the global financial system is teetering on the brink of collapse. One does not have to resort to apocalyptic language and imagery to imagine what will happen as these global systems continue to unravel and disintegrate. We are witnessing in our time one of those major disintegrations of imperial power that has marked the annals of history.

This makes it all the more urgent that alternative and traditional cultures and communities be revitalized and strengthened, both in the church and in society as a whole. While some institutional reforms may occur that will slow and perhaps cushion the disintegration of the global dominant culture, it will be important for there to be viable local cultures and communities to provide both food and social stability as the structures of the global economic, technical, political, and religious systems unravel. The Jubilee Movement is an example of a biblically-inspired reform movement that has had significant success.[25] The recent Occupy Wall Street movement may indicate the direction of further reforms.[26]

Meanwhile, though the global dominant culture is weakening and disintegrating, we should have no illusions about its continued power. The subversive and revolutionary nature of the efforts of local cultures and communities in standing against the depredations of the global dominant culture involve significant risk for such actions. An example of this subversive action might be seen in the German church's movement toward developing local alternative energy systems.[27] We must assume that both those who hold the reins of governmental, corporate, and technical power, as well as the general public that has benefitted from the status quo of the dominant culture, will continue to resist the growth of local cultures and communities. A primary challenge for local cultures and communities will be to diffuse the current polarization seen in both national and global societies. That might be accomplished by working "beneath the radar" of the powers that be while at the same time luring the public by example into a consideration of sustainable and humane local ways of structuring life without judging the current values by which people are living.

Learning to Know the Uniqueness of Our Land (Place)

Since beginning the writing of this book, I've retired as an active congregational pastor. While I think I had the heart of a pastor, I confess to often being frustrated in congregational ministry. Serving in rural congregations throughout the American Midwest in both Canada and the United States, I was blessed (cursed?) fairly early in

25. Storkey, "Jubilee."
26. Hirschfield, "American Spring?"
27. Eberlein, "Heavenly Energy," 28–31.

being able to understand some of the dynamics that were affecting rural congregations and causing their decline. However, I have always struggled with how to communicate these dynamics in ways that would be helpful and not offensive to the people in the congregations I was serving.

I confess that I often did not succeed in doing this. Since the early1970s, I have understood fairly clearly that the farmers in these communities were caught up in the industrialization of agriculture, with its reliance on fossil fuels, mechanization, technology, and the production of commodity crops for a global market. While many of these farmers understood and did not like what they were feeling pressured to do in their farming operations, they felt their choices were limited if they wanted to stay in agriculture at all. So they were understandably hurt and resentful at my criticisms of commodity, industrialized agriculture, and my sometimes ill-advised attempts to call for a different agricultural paradigm.

Perhaps one of the most effective though impractical practices I sought to employ through the years to help a congregation understand its place as an alternative community of faith in the midst of a dominant culture were the prayer walks I initiated and led at the Salem Mennonite Church, Freeman, South Dakota, in the summer of 2009. The inspiration for these walks was born during my 2008 sabbatical, in which I spent one day weekly, from sunrise to sundown if possible, walking and reading and meditating in an outdoor setting. Given the fact that my sabbatical fell during the winter months and also involved international travel, this was a challenge, but still a very effective spiritual discipline for me. I used the monthly retreat models in *A Guide to Prayer* to guide my meditations.[28] Some of the most memorable days on these retreats occurred in Galilee and on the island of Crete.

After I returned from the sabbatical, I resolved to continue intentional walks as a spiritual discipline. As a part of this resolve, I conceived of doing four eight-mile prayer walks, one per month, around each of the four section quadrants surrounding the rural Salem Mennonite Church. While I did these walks as a personal spiritual discipline, I also invited congregational members to join me, and a total of nine members did so on one or more of the walks. I also involved the congregation by preparing and distributing guides for each of the four walks, as well as some introductory handouts. These handouts explored the natural history and community of life, the history of the land in relation to the various people who have lived upon it or claimed it, the history of the particular Swiss Volhynian community that had settled in this area, a demographic analysis of current and past residents, an analysis of landownership patterns and land utilization, and a study of the residential location of the church members in each quadrant. While the main focus of the walks was on the sixteen square miles around the church—the church's neighborhood—attention was paid to the ministry area of the congregation (thirteen townships in Turner and Hutchinson Counties), as well as the region beyond this ministry area in each quadrant.

28. Job and Shawchuck, *Guide*, 347–415.

Walking the country lanes as we did in the early mornings as the sun began to rise while the full moon was setting in the west, we were made aware of the natural rhythms that govern the world, the rigors of the weather (two of our walks began in light rain), and the variety and diversity of natural life in the neighborhood of the church. We observed the local watersheds over which we walked and witnessed the profusion of life as the growing season progressed from early summer to early fall. We could also witness firsthand the effects of invasive species, including ourselves and our crops and livestock, on this natural environment in the form of eroded land, polluted streams, natural imbalances, and ill health. While agriculture had improved the land and community of natural life in some respects, current agricultural practices were also detrimental to the health of the land in other respects.

Having identified the homesteads of charter Salem members, as well as the current members and other residents within these sixteen square miles, the prayer walks put us in touch with the history and current status of the human population of our church's neighborhood. While there was evidence of at least fifty-five homesteads in these sixteen square miles (3.5 per square mile, or nearly one for every quarter section of 160 acres), only forty of these homesteads (73 percent) were currently occupied, and a quarter of these (eleven) were non-farm, rural residents. We estimated the population of these sixteen square miles to be about 115 (7.2 per square mile), less than half what it had been a century earlier. We also discovered that only about 10 percent of current church members (37 of 369 members) lived within the sixteen square miles of the church's neighborhood—a marked change from the situation when the church was established in the perceived center of the congregation's new membership in 1908.

As for land tenure and land use, we found that the land of these sixteen square miles was owned by at least eighty-four separate parties. About half of these land holdings were farmed by the owners, local farmers living on the land or nearby these sixteen square miles. However, thirty-four parcels of land were rental properties rented out to local farmers, and half of these rental properties were owned by non-residents, individuals who had inherited the land in most cases, but who no longer lived in the community. These statistics indicated an agricultural community losing control of its most basic resource—the land!

However, it was encouraging to see an increased diversity in the usage of the land. No longer was the production of agricultural commodities for a global market the only perceived use of the land. There were organic farms for food production, and within the church's ministry area an even more diverse use of land. The image of a monolithic agricultural paradigm for the use of land, while never entirely true for this community, was clearly no longer valid now.

On the prayer walks themselves, walkers paused for prayer at designated places along the walk. Some of these prayers were related to the physical or natural features present at the site; some were related to the social or historical significance of the site or the residents living at the site. Some prayer stops were also for the villages, towns, and cities, and other institutional powers, present in that quadrant of the church's ministry area and region. However, the main subject for the prayers offered at these prayer stops were the 546 persons (369 members) then a part of the Salem Mennonite Church family. Each of these persons was prayed for by name at the site closest to their home.[29]

My intention for these prayer walks was that just as prayer walks and vigils on city streets aim to reclaim that space for God and to bring God's presence to bear on that space, these prayer walks might do the same for this rural space which was the home for this congregation. It was of course a highly impractical action, doing nothing concrete to change the rural community where we lived. But it was nonetheless highly effective in helping those who participated, and myself first and foremost, to understand the specific, concrete, local situation of our congregation's neighborhood, ministry area, and region. I believe that it is these kinds of intentional, prayerful actions of learning to know and bring before God all the dimensions and features unique to the places we call home that are necessary for local communities to be revitalized.

Exercises such as this would be particularly helpful for Mennonite congregations in rural areas with a long history in their place. Such congregations do not often consider their farming practices to be an integral aspect of their mission as a church. We are often unaware of the extent of changes that have occurred in our neighborhoods. Changes keep occurring, but since we live in these settings we rarely stop to see and understand what has been happening to those familiar places in which we live. We realized on the walks how little we knew about the demographic changes of our neighborhood or about the new rural residents living next to us.

It is even more helpful to deliberately *walk* through the landscape of these changes. Now that automobiles or farm machinery are the primary modes of movement in rural communities, it is surprising how differently things look from the ground itself, moving at the speed of a walk. Even those who work the land rarely actually walk the land they till; they only see it from the insulated cabs of the tractors and trucks they use to work the land, and then only perhaps for several days a year in spring and fall when the crops are planted and harvested. When you cover the land meter by meter, walking, you see things from a different perspective. You see what's actually happening on this particular square meter, square dekameter, hectare, or square kilometer of land.

Mennonites of rural congregations are "peasants," which means inhabitants of a particularly district.[30] While the term "peasant" has come to have a negative connotation as an uneducated person of low social status, in its root meaning it refers to persons who till the soil of a particular area. We have seen how throughout history, agriculture or the agrarian life always reflects the particular possibilities and limitations

---

29. For a more complete description of these prayer walks, see the author's compilation of the papers describing these walks collected in a folder at the Salem Mennonite Church library, as well as Kaufman, "Anatomy of a Rural Church."

30. *Miriam Webster's Collegiate Dictionary*, 10th ed., s.v. "peasant."

of the specific environment in which the human community working the land finds itself. Both "agrarian" and "agriculture" have "field" as their linguistic root, deriving from ἀγρός (agros), the New Testament word for "field."

A genuine agrarian life, a true agriculture (culture of the field), can only emerge from this kind of spiritual and physical intimacy with the land. For rural congregations, it is the formation of an agrarian life, a genuine "culture of the field," which is their primary mission and reason for being in their place. The word agriculture describes the unique blending of human activity (culture) with the natural processes of the field (agros), and this defines the agricultural landscape, as opposed to either the natural landscape or the urban landscape. If rural congregations fail to develop a healthy agriculture, a symbiosis of human activity with natural processes unique to their specific place, they will have failed in their reason for being. In the terms of the biblical portion of this chapter, this symbiosis is how rural congregations participate in the recapitulation of all things that Jesus is accomplishing in his life, death, and resurrection.

CHAPTER 15

An Urban Future or the Garden Renewed?

I Saw the Holy City (Rev 21:2)

The New Creation and the Resurrection of the Body

THE QUESTION IS MOST often posed as an irreconcilable dichotomy, by rural and urban advocates alike. The reality is that the biblical vision for the future involves both the city and the garden, both human achievement (even that compromised by its origins in the domination systems of the world) and the natural systems of God's creation. John the Revelator envisions a time when all the human achievements of the city, all the great architecture and art and music and writing and technology of civilization, all of those achievements purchased at so great a cost in human oppression and suffering, will be adopted and purified by God in the new creation, in order to reflect their true worth in God's presence.

But the new Jerusalem, that holy city that comes down from heaven as God's gift of God's eternal presence with humanity, takes its place upon a newly fashioned heaven and earth, a new creation, brought into being through the life, death, and resurrection of Jesus Christ! The people of God, already under the Old Covenant (Isaiah 65) envisioned new heavens and a new earth, a new reality of social, natural, and divine peace.

The New Testament witness goes on to express the hope for a bodily resurrection in the context of this new creation, not a disembodied gathering of souls in some celestial mansion or city, (nor in the current secular counterpart to this—a spaceflight to another galaxy)! While such language must clearly be understood symbolically rather than literally, as Paul makes clear in 1 Corinthians 15, it is nonetheless the Christian hope that mortal humanity will find its fullest expression in the world to come.

This is a world in some kind of continuity with this earth and these bodies in which we now live, however much this earth and these bodies are only the seeds from which the new creation will emerge, appropriately embodied. Embodied, earthbound creatures we are; embodied, earthbound creatures we shall remain in God's new creation, dependent in both instances on God's life-giving Spirit revealed most clearly in the person of Jesus Christ. And God's persistent call remains—that we reflect God's character clearly and by our choices participate with God in the unfolding of the divine purpose for creation and history.

The Biblical Story

For I Am About to Create New Heavens and a New Earth (Isa 65:17)

Throughout the years, as I have advocated for rural community and excoriated urban civilization for its depredations among rural communities at church conferences and ecclesiastical settings, I have almost invariably been met with the objection: *But the Bible ends in the city, doesn't it?* I suppose the objection might not be made did I not root my argument on biblical premises, the assumption that the biblical message has a bias toward rural community. But since I argue that the biblical materials do in fact reveal a God with a preferential bias toward rural life and creation care, advocates of urban life and ministry are quick to seize upon the penultimate chapter of the Bible as proof that God does indeed love the city after all!

Of course, the critics are right! Revelation 21 does envision the future in urban terms, with the holy city, the new Jerusalem coming down out of heaven to rest upon the earth as the dwelling place of God among humans (Rev 21:2). "See, the home of God is among mortals. He will dwell with them; they will be his peoples, and God himself will be with them" (Rev 21:3). The holy city, it turns out, is *God's* dwelling place among humankind within God's new creation. Coming down out of heaven, however, this is clearly not a humanly created city, any city of history. Nor is it clear that it is *our* human dwelling place within this new creation of God.

But before engaging what will be both the polemic and hopefully also the amicable resolution of the rural/urban debate with regard to the new Jerusalem, perhaps it is important to step back and consider the broader biblical perspective with regard to the future of both humankind and Earth itself as God's creation in this corner of the Milky Way galaxy. As humans so keenly aware of our fleeting, earthly, mortal existence, we have always had a deep interest, to say the least, in what if anything lies beyond this life and this creation. Such interest only grows in eras of societal upheaval and cultural trauma. Such was the case for the people of Israel during the time of the exile and again in the first century CE with the destruction of the Second Temple by the Romans in 70 CE. It is also a characteristic of our own age, as the fractures of the dominant global culture grow more and more evident. So this chapter is about "eschatology," doctrines or beliefs about "end times," the "last things."

In our own age, things are complicated by the fact that it is no longer just the fate of our own lives or our own community that is at stake, but the fate of Earth itself and

An Urban Future or the Garden Renewed?

the whole universe. In other words, it isn't just that our lives are in jeopardy. Now we can contemplate the end of human life on earth, and indeed the end of Earth itself. Now we know that not only are we mortal and finite beings, but so also is Earth itself. Earth is a planet of the sun, a star that now, after some five billion years of existence and in middle age, will eventually begin to use up its fuel reserves and swell into a red giant that will consume the inner planets, likely including Earth itself, before dying out in cold space.[1] In this scenario, the warning of 2 Peter 3:7–10 is prescient: "the present heavens and earth have been reserved for fire" (2 Pet 3:7).

But of course, the universe itself confronts on a cosmic scale the same fate of finitude described for the earth and the solar system in which we live. In the words of John Polkinghorne, either the universe will continue to expand until it "ends in a whimper," or eventually gravity will prevail and the expansion of the galaxies will be reversed until the universe ends in "the big crunch, as the universe collapses back into a singular cosmic melting pot."[2] If the universe has a beginning as current scientific theory holds, it must also have an end. Physicists and cosmologists are busy theorizing about the possible ways in which this fate can be avoided at some cosmic if not personal or planetary level through still-to-be-described and analyzed physical phenomena.[3] Still, currently, fire or ice seem to the only viable options for the fate of the universe, as so succinctly stated in Robert Frost's poem "Fire and Ice."[4]

John Polkinghorne, a British physicist and "bottom up" thinker, who is also a Christian believer and Anglican priest, rejects the desperate and "fantastic" theories of his scientific colleagues[5] regarding the future in favor of the Christian hope expressed in the Nicene Creed. "We look forward to the resurrection of the dead and the life of the world to come."[6] "Cosmic death and human death pose equivalent questions of what is God's intention for his creation."[7] So, Polkinghorne goes on to say, "I believe it is a perfectly coherent hope that the pattern that is me will be remembered by God and its instantiation will be re-created by him when he reconstitutes me in a new environment of his choosing."[8] The same can be said for Earth and the sun and the Milky Way and the universe itself. "We are driven back, as we might have expected, to God alone as the basis of final hope, so that our own and the universe's destiny awaits a transforming act of divine redemption. In Christian thought this is expressed in terms of a new creation (2 Cor. 5:17), a new heaven and a new earth (Rev. 21:1–4)."[9]

1. Davies, *God*, 200–201.
2. Polkinghorne, *Faith*, 162.
3. Davies, *Last Three Minutes*, 127–55.
4. Frost, "Fire and Ice," 242.
5. Polkinghorne, *Faith*, 166.
6. Leith, *Creeds*, 33.
7. Polkinghorne, *Faith*, 163.
8. Ibid.
9. Ibid., 166.

This "new creation" of Christian belief is not a second creation "out of nothing," *ex nihilo*, to replace this first and presumably failed creation of God. It will instead, Polkinghorne says, be a creation *ex vetere* (out of the old), a transformation of this present creation that has the character "appropriate to an evolutionary universe, endowed with the ability through the shuffling explorations of its happenstance to 'make itself.'"[10] This means that the present creation in which we live is highly significant, because as it unfolds both through natural laws and human choices, it is "the raw material from which the new will come."[11] This is why, in the previous chapter, I made a point of highlighting the importance of all the daily decisions we all make about how we live our lives. These decisions and choices become part of the "stuff" from which God in Christ is creating the new heavens and the new earth. In choosing humane, just, and sustainable ways of living, we are not simply concerned with preserving the earth as our home. We are participating with Christ in God's new creation!

I believe it is in the light of this kind of thinking that we are to read the prophetic pronouncements, present already in the Old Testament, of a new creation. As humans, we can only project onto the new creation the hopes and dreams and aspirations we already have for this creation and this life. But if Polkinghorne's point of view has any validity, then this is not mere wishful thinking. By living toward the vision of what we hope for in this life, we participate with God in the new creation that is coming into being through Christ's life, death and resurrection.

So it is that in Isaiah 65, in what was most likely the post-exilic age, the prophet envisions a new creation of God. "For I am about to create new heavens and a new earth; the former things shall not be remembered or come to mind" (Isa 65:17). These "former things" would surely include a devastated Jerusalem and a ruined land, a people ravaged by war and destruction and displaced by exile, and a countryside and natural life that had lost its fruitful balance. So, yes, there will be here already a new "Jerusalem," a city created "as a joy, and its people as a delight" (Isa 65:18). No longer will the city be the place or occasion of weeping and cries of distress (Isa 65:19). Indeed, the full potential of mortal human life shall be within reach. Infant mortality will end and everyone will live to ripe old age (Isa 65:20). Not only will the city be at peace, but the countryside will also flourish. Rural villages will not be uprooted, along with the vineyards and crops. Villagers will live in the houses they build and reap the crops they plant, and people will "enjoy the work of their hands" (Isa 65:21–22). Generation will follow generation in unending succession (Isa 65:23). Finally, this scene of bucolic peace will extend to the world of nature itself, so that, echoing the historical prophet Isaiah in Isaiah 11:6–9, predator and prey will lie down together in a peaceable kingdom (Isa 65:25).

There is always both a discontinuity and a continuity between this world and the next, in the biblical vision. The discontinuity derives from the realization that we are

---

10. Ibid., 167.
11. Ibid., 168.

An Urban Future or the Garden Renewed?

mortal humans living in a finite world. The continuity derives from the affirmation that the future world is created out of this world. In this vision of Isaiah 65, it is interesting to observe that while humans themselves are not granted immortality (people die in full old age, Isa 65:20), humankind is granted the promise of a generational immortality, continuing from generation to generation (Isa 65:23). We also see that all creatures in this new creation conform to the injunction of Genesis 1:29–30, finding nourishment from the plants of the earth and no longer shedding blood (Gen 9:1–5). Finally, the urban center will no longer be experienced as oppressive (Isa 65:18–19), and human labor in caring for the earth will no longer be felt to be a curse (Isa 65:22–23; Gen 3:17).

Our best hopes for the future are descriptions of the world as we would like it to be, with all that we experience as oppressive and domineering and exploitative removed. After we have experienced the trauma of dislocation and destruction that comes from living within and under the domination cultures of the world, and when we open ourselves to the image of God in which we were created, we begin to imagine the world as God intended it and as God is re-creating it in and through Jesus Christ. This is also what John the Revelator did at the end of his visionary perspective on both our current predicament and our future hope.

I Saw the Holy City (Rev 21:2)

After an introduction of the writer and his task in the first chapter, the book of Revelation begins by addressing seven presumably historical churches in seven cities of Asia Minor all facing the difficulty of living with varying degrees of success as alternative communities of faith within the dominant culture of these cities of the Roman Empire in the first century CE (Revelation 2–3). Next come the throne room scenes of Revelation 4–5, which announce the sovereignty of God and proclaim proleptically the outcome of history and creation—the triumph of the Lamb who was slain over all the powers of evil, and the redemption of all the multitudes from every "tribe and language and people and nation," through the blood of the Lamb (Rev 5:9–10).

The bulk of the book of Revelation then consists of several sketches of the End Times crisis in which the seven churches of Asia Minor were living, and in which we still live. End Times, in the view of Revelation I am working with here, is the period of time from Jesus' resurrection until his second coming. The sketches are repetitions, often intensified, of plagues and calamities revealed or announced by (you guessed it) seven seals (Revelation 6–7), seven trumpets (Revelation 8–11), and seven bowls (Revelation 15–16), with a "freehand sketch" of the conflict between Jesus and his church and the powers of evil inserted (Revelation 12–14). This in turn is followed by the writer's vision of events at the end of time (Revelation 17–20), followed by his vision of the new creation (Revelation 21–22), which will be our primary interest here.[12]

Before turning to John's final vision of the new creation in the last two chapters, it is important to note the role of the city in John's development of his vision of these End Times in which we are living as a church. In Revelation 12–13, we have the narrative of the conflict between Jesus and his church and the powers of evil symbolized by the unholy trinity of the dragon, the beast from the sea, and the beast from the earth, representing Satan and the powers that rule the earth. That vision concludes in Revelation 14 with the Lamb and those he has redeemed appearing on Mount Zion (Jerusalem) to witness the fall of Babylon. "Fallen, fallen is Babylon the great! She has made all nations drink the wine of the wrath of her fornication" (Rev 14:8). Again in Revelation 15–16, the bowls of God's wrath are given from the heavenly temple of the tent of witness, corresponding to the temple that had been in Jerusalem (Rev 15:5–8). With the pouring out of the seventh bowl of the wrath of God, the "great city was split into three parts, and the cities of the nations fell. God remembered great Babylon, and gave her the wine-cup of the fury of his wrath" (Rev 16:19). All this leads to the elaborate description of the great whore, Babylon (Revelation 17), and her ultimate destruction to the great grief and consternation of the kings and merchants and traders of the earth (Revelation 18). While Babylon certainly is a code word for Rome in the book of Revelation, it also certainly represents the spiritual power and domination of the city throughout human history, exercised in the kingdoms and nation-states and empires of the world (Rev 18:21–24).

Clearly, there is in Revelation a juxtaposition between Jerusalem (Zion), representing the holy city, and Babylon, representing the spiritual reality of all earthly cities (including the historical Jerusalem) which dominate and oppress humankind and exploit God's creation. Jerusalem began its checkered history as an on-again, off-again holy city within Israelite history when the Jebusite city was conquered by King David and made into the capital of the united kingdom of Israel and Judah (2 Samuel 5). Not content with Jerusalem only as a neutral, political capital, David also sought the sanction of religion for his reign by bringing the ark of the covenant to Jerusalem (2 Samuel 6) and desiring to build a temple in which to house it since he had already built a fine palace for himself (2 Samuel 7). While the Lord through the prophet Nathan prevented David from building the temple, the first temple of Jerusalem was built by his son Solomon as the crowning glory of the Israelite empire (1 Kings 5–6).

Built on Mount Zion within Jerusalem's walls, the temple and the city in which it stood became invested within certain prophetic traditions with a more universal and ecumenical significance, as we have seen.[13] The most classic expression of this significance can be found in Isaiah 2:2–4 (see also Mic 4:1–4) in the sixth century BCE

---

12. I am indebted to Eller, *Most Revealing Book*, inside back cover, for this eminently simple outline of Revelation.

13. See "The end of a national identity" in chapter 10.

An Urban Future or the Garden Renewed?

in the kingdom of Judah, where Zion becomes the destination for all the nations of the earth who will come to be taught the ways of the Lord and where God will establish a reign of global peace. This understanding of Jerusalem (Zion) is also reflected in the Psalms of Zion, of which Psalm 87 is typical, with its adulation of the "city of God" (Ps 87:3), and its enumeration of all the peoples and nations born in Zion (Ps 87:4–6).[14] Also in the post-exilic era of the Persian Empire, Zion is celebrated as the destination not just of those who have been exiled, but of all the nations of the earth (Isaiah 60–62). Indeed, the Jerusalem described in Isaiah 60:3, 5, and 11 has characteristics repeated in Revelation 21, with the wealth of nations brought to Zion, and the gates of the city being always open. Being himself a priest, the exilic prophet Ezekiel also invested Jerusalem with his hopes for the future in his elaborate description of the temple destroyed by the Babylonians being restored (Ezekiel 40–48).

That the historical Jerusalem was never able to fulfill these prophetic hopes and dreams is evident from Jesus' own words regarding the city on the eve of his passion (Matt 23:37–39; Luke 19:41–44; 23:26–31). Jerusalem, with its Herodian temple, would have been a familiar and beloved place for Jesus, as the scene of the annual pilgrimages so pleasantly described in Luke 2:41–52. Virtually all of John's gospel is set in the city of Jerusalem, in contrast to the Synoptic Gospels, which portray Jesus coming to Jerusalem only for the final Passover feast that culminated in his death.[15] So it should not be surprising to see the deep emotion that Jesus expressed as the city of Jerusalem with its Herodian temple came into view from the Mount of Olives on Palm Sunday (Luke 19:41–44). "As he came near and saw the city, he wept over it, saying, 'If you, even you, had only recognized on this day the things that make for peace! But now they are hidden from your eyes'" (Luke 19:41–42). Jesus goes on to announce the total destruction of Jerusalem, "because you did not recognize the time of your visitation from God" (Luke 19:44). This destruction occurred some forty years later after the Roman siege of Jerusalem, when the city and temple were razed to the ground in 70 CE.

These verses describe how profoundly Jesus wished and hoped for the historical Jerusalem to fulfill its prophetic vocation as the place from which God's peace and reign would extend to all the earth. But for that, the historical city of Jerusalem was required to forsake its preoccupation with power and domination and exploitation, recognize "the things that make for peace," and accept Jesus, who represented in his coming "the time of God's visitation." And so the historical Jerusalem, then, and unfortunately still today, faces the same judgment shared by all the cities of the world.[16]

That judgment, in the Bible, is most often expressed in the words of judgment about Babylon, the power responsible for the first destruction of Jerusalem and its

---

14. Waltner, *Psalms*, 424–25.

15. John 2:13—4:3; 5:1–46; 7:1—10:39; 11:7–53; and 12:1—20:31 are all set within Jerusalem or its environs.

16. See the discussion of Jesus and Jerusalem in Ellul, *Meaning*, 135–46.

Solomonic temple in 587 BCE. But its roots, spiritually, go back even further to Genesis 11, and the human resolve to "build ourselves a city, and a tower with its top in the heavens, and let us make a name for ourselves" (Gen 11:4). Perhaps the reference is to the Marduk temple or ziggurat in Babylon.[17]

The character of the city spiritually as a place of idolatry, domination, and exploitation, and its parasitic function, is graphically described in Revelation 18.[18] It is interesting that the agency of the destruction of the city is not identified. The most that is said is that God "gave her the wine-cup of the fury of his wrath" (Rev 16:19), presumably the same cup of abominations she holds with the "impurities of her fornication" (Rev 17:4), and the cup with "the wine of the wrath of her fornication" Babylon herself gives to the nations and kings and merchants of the earth who fornicate with her (Rev 18:3). The city, in other words, dies a natural death, however violent it may well be—a death that comes as a natural consequence of her idolatry and immorality, oppression, and exploitation. However, the lament of the kings and merchants and traders over the fall of Babylon expresses vividly the genuine loss of so much human creativity and achievement represented in the city and its life, despite the oppression and exploitation by which it might have been produced (Rev 18:11–14, 16, 21–23).

So this brings us at last to John's vision of the new Jerusalem in Revelation 21–22. We note first that the new Jerusalem, the holy city, appears in the context of the creation of a "new heaven and a new earth" (Rev 21:1), one in which the sea as the source of the evil beast in Revelation 13 "was no more," but which otherwise might seem to stand in some continuity with the earth as we know it (however unscientific it is to think of the earth without its seas). This new creation stands then also in continuity with the vision of the new creation in Isaiah 65:17–25. So within this new creation, John sees "the holy city, the new Jerusalem, coming down out of heaven from God, prepared as a bride adorned for her husband" (Rev 21:2). The first obvious thing to note is that this city descends down from heaven and rests upon this newly created earth, as resplendent as a bride on her wedding day. In other words, this is no humanly created city, but God's creation. Next, we see that the city seems to represent "the home of God" among mortals, the place in which God comes to dwell with humans on earth in an everlasting relationship in which death and pain and crying and tears will all have passed away (Rev 21:3–4).

When we move on to the description of the heavenly city in Revelation 21:9–27, there are a number of striking features. This city is an immense cube (Rev 21:16), as high as it is long and wide, all perfectly laid out with three gates on each side, presumably opening onto streets that run in a regular grid throughout the city. How big is the city? Commentators pass by this feature, for it is absurd—twelve thousand stadia, which according to most conversions comes to around fifteen hundred miles (Rev 21:16)! I imagine this cube resting like some gigantic pimple on the face of the earth!

---

17. Jacobsen, "Babel," 1:334.
18. See Ellul, *Meaning*, 148–63, on the history of the city.

An Urban Future or the Garden Renewed?

Here is a skyscraper of a city to put all earthly cities to shame, a tower that does not aspire to heaven (Gen 11:4) but belongs squarely upon the earth! The walls themselves are 144 cubits thick, about seventy-five yards (Rev. 21:17). The holy city has the appearance of a jewel (Rev 21:11). Each of its twelve gates (which are never closed, Rev 21:25) is presided over by an angel and each one is inscribed with one of the names of the twelve tribes of Israel (Rev 21:12), and the walls of the city rest on twelve foundation stones named for the "twelve apostles of the Lamb" (Rev 21:14). Each of the foundation stones are adorned with jewels (Rev 21:19–20), and the twelve gates are each made of a single pearl (Rev 21:21). The street of the city is pure gold (Rev 21:21).

The measures of this holy city, foursquare and twelves or multiples thereof, are like numbers throughout Revelation, highly symbolic. Four is the number of creation—the four corners of the earth. Three is the number for God—the trinity. And twelve is the multiple of these—of God and the world. The shape of the city, as a cube, recalls the Holy of Holies in the earthly Jerusalem temple, which had the shape of a cube at the heart of the temple. Perhaps this is why there is no temple in the city (Rev 21:22), for the city itself becomes the Holy of Holies, the place of the presence of "the Lord God Almighty and the Lamb" on earth (Rev 21:22).

This is where John's vision digresses from Ezekiel's vision of the city in Ezekiel 40-48. Though Ezekiel's description begins with the city in Ezekiel 40:2, the whole of chapters 40–46 are preoccupied with a lengthy description of the temple. Ezekiel 47–48, describing the new holy land watered by the river of life flowing from the temple, and the redistribution of the land, only incidentally refer to the city. Only in the last verse, Ezekiel 48:35, is the significance of the city revealed in its new name: "Yahweh-Shammah," (The Lord is There). But as Ellul reminds us, the locus of God's presence shifts from the temple in Ezekiel to the city itself in Revelation.[19] "I saw no temple in the city, for its temple is the Lord God the Almighty and the Lamb" (Rev 21:22).

As noted, a striking feature of John's city is that the gates of the city are never closed by day and, there being no night there since the city is illumined by the presence of God and the Lamb, the gates are never shut (Rev 21:25). But what is perhaps even more striking is what enters the city: "and the kings of the earth will bring their glory into it" (Rev 21:24). "People will bring into it the glory and the honor of the nations" (Rev 21:26). We might justifiably ask where these kings and people come from, presumably having perished in the plagues of the End Time, the destruction of Babylon the Great, and the final judgment of Revelation 19! But this is the New Creation, after all. There are now nations who "will walk by its light" (Rev 21:24; Isa 2:3), and kings and peoples who bring into the city the wealth and glory and honor of their human cities! Of course, we are reminded that nothing nor anyone unclean can enter this city, but only "those who are written in the Lamb's book of life" (Rev 21:27).

The final features of the city in Revelation 22:1–5 seem to bring us full round to Genesis 2. Here we see "the river of the water of life, bright as crystal, flowing from

19. Ibid., 185.

the throne of God and of the Lamb through the middle of the street of the city" (Rev 22:1–2), reminiscent of the river that flowed out of the Garden of Eden in Genesis 2:10. And there, on either side of the river is that old "tree of life" we first met in Genesis 2:9 in the garden God had planted for the first humans. Denied to us by human sin, that tree is now made available to all by the Lamb, offering its fruit for every month of the year with twelve kinds of fruit and with its leaves "for the healing of the nations" (Rev 22:2; Ezek 47:12).

What are we to make of all these images and visions? Do they indeed describe an urban future for humanity? It is in any case a moot question, but it seems to me that the holy city, the new Jerusalem described in Revelation 21, is the place of *God's* dwelling among humanity in the new creation, not the place where we live. Our habitation is out on the earth among the peoples and nations that comprise God's new creation, for we are earthborn, earthbound creatures. We only come to the new Jerusalem to bring our tribute in the form of the glory of the nations into the presence of God and the Lamb, and perhaps also to drink from the river of the water of life and to feast on the fruit of the tree of life.

So why this elaborate symbolism of the city? And in particular, why does John envision God coming to dwell among humans in a city in the new creation? Jacques Ellul is most eloquent on this point. "If God chooses this new form it is simply because man has chosen it. Man wanted this setting, this environment, and scorned the one prepared for him by God. From the beginning man worked desperately to have his own little world, independent of all that God desired. And God will give him the perfect work which he himself could not bring about. God will realize man's setting. . . . Man wanted to build a city from which God would be absent, but he never managed. God will make for him the perfect city, where he will be all in all."[20] "It is in Jesus Christ that God adopts man's work. For Ephesians 1:10, translated literally, tells us that Jesus is the great recapitulator. God formed the plan of uniting 'all things in him,' . . . God's plan also includes things invented by man, what he laboriously put together piece by piece learning from experience and failure. Both his technical failures and the marvels of his cleverness. All this is 'recapitulated' in Christ, summed up by him, taken over by him. In a brilliant transfiguration all of man's work is gathered together in Christ."[21] While the masculine gender Ellul uses dates his work, it is also appropriate in this case, for it is evident in history that the city is the work of men in particular, with the city supplanting the earth-based feminine perspectives that likely preceded the development of urban civilization.[22]

In *Apocalypse: The Book of Revelation*, Ellul further comments: "What does this signify? Very simply that God does not annul history and the work of man, but, on

---

20. Ibid., 174.
21. Ibid., 176.
22. See for example Eisler, *Chalice and the Blade,* and Merchant, *Death of Nature,* among many other works.

the contrary, assumes it. The city is the great work of man. We have seen that. It is well described as the sum of his culture and his inventions; it is his creation. It is the very sign of his history, since it is in the city that the various layers of history and culture are preserved. Well, God takes up the whole history of men and synthesizes it in the absolute city. The symbol of Jerusalem is the strongest sign we can have that the biblical God is a God who accompanies man in his history."[23]

What an astounding vision this is that John gives us of the new creation, in which this broken, oppressive world of our striving becomes a part of the raw material God uses to create the new Jerusalem, the ultimate symbol of God's dwelling with humans through Jesus Christ! As Ellul says, "The city was a place of the dissolution of specificities, of the meeting and mixture of all ideas, values, races, social categories: it receives its complete fulfillment. For in this New Jerusalem all races, peoples, nations, tribes meet. But while the tendency was always toward unity by the disappearance of diversities, now unity appears (in God) in the communion of existing diversities, and human plurality is maintained."[24] Rural communities and local cultures will after all be preserved, in all the races and peoples and nations and tribes of humankind! All the social and technological achievements of human creativity reflected in the reality of the city, purchased often at so great a human travail and cost in suffering and oppression, are not excluded by God from the new creation. They are instead purified and transformed by Christ to form that holy city in which God and the Lamb dwell with us in the new creation.

The Resurrection of the Body

As we began these reflections, it was noted in the second chapter that it may have been our anxiety about our mortality as persons created in God's image that made us susceptible and vulnerable to the temptations of the evil powers. These temptations falsely promised shortcuts to that goal of immortality for which humanity has often striven. If you only do this or that, you will be like God, immortal (Genesis 3)! We have also seen now how the tree of life, that symbol of immortality given to mortal humans in the Garden of Eden and then denied to them because of their sin and rebellion against God (Genesis 2–3), was finally restored to human access in God's new creation, in the form of the tree that bears fruit for each season of the year (Rev 22:1–5).

Still, it is fair to say that John's visions of God's new creation that we have just explored are more cosmic than personal. In addition, this book has focused more on the re-formation of redeemed communities that the redemption of individual persons. I have even argued in chapters 12 and 13 that God's first intention in sending Jesus to earth was not the personal salvation of individuals but the formation of redeemed

---

23. Ellul, *Apocalypse*, 222.
24. Ibid., 224; see also the author's treatment of the church in chapter 13.

communities. Nevertheless, since our mortality had always been such a thorn in our flesh, it may be important to close this book with some reflections on our personal destinies within God's creation. For, however much God's intention is the formation of redeemed human communities on a redeemed earth, we also matter to God as individual persons, and indeed, as noted in chapter 11, Jesus also died for us!

Students of the New Testament have often noted that next to the movement of the church from a Jewish to a multiethnic context, the largest crisis of the early church in the first thirty years of its existence was the natural death of saints, those who had come to faith in Christ. The crisis is most clearly expressed in 1 Thessalonians, where Paul, writing in about 52 CE, seeks to counsel and comfort those experiencing the crisis. It is evident that the first generation of Christian believers anticipated an early return of the risen Lord and the consequent consummation of history. When believers began to die a natural death, their loved ones wondered if they would somehow miss out on Christ's return. Or more directly, they began to question their own faith and hope in Christ. Was what they had hoped for in Christ to be trusted?

So in 1 Thessalonians 4:13–18, the planter of the Thessalonian church provides this reassurance and explanation: "We who are alive, who are left until the coming of the Lord, will by no means precede those who have died. For the Lord himself, with a cry of command, with the archangel's call and with the sound of God's trumpet, will descend from heaven, and the dead in Christ will rise first. Then we who are alive, who are left, will be caught up in the clouds together with them to meet the Lord in the air; and so we will be with the Lord forever" (1 Thess 4:15–17). We do not have to subscribe to the specific details of Paul's cosmology to understand the gist of what Paul intends to communicate. There are indeed grounds to hope for an everlasting life with God in the new creation rooted in Jesus' own resurrection from the dead (1 Thess 4:14). But there is neither an advantage nor a disadvantage to being either alive or dead at the anticipated second coming of Christ. Either way, whether dead or living, we will participate together in our entry into God's new creation, through the resurrection (transformation) of our earthly, mortal bodies.

Writing to the Corinthian church a few years later (perhaps 55 CE), the Apostle Paul provides perhaps his most mature reflections on the resurrection of the body in 1 Corinthians 15. Paul begins (1 Cor 15:3–11) by providing a list of post-resurrection appearances of the risen Lord to his followers, concluding with Christ's appearance to Paul himself, "as to one untimely born," on the road to Damascus (1 Cor 15:8). The core of the significance of Jesus' resurrection for Paul is to be found in 1 Corinthians 15:20–29. Here Paul sees Christ's resurrection as "the first fruits of those who have died" (1 Cor 15:20). The resurrection is the confirmation of the defeat of all the rulers, authorities, and powers (1 Cor 15:24), under which humanity has been enslaved since the sin of Adam. "For since death came through a human being, the resurrection of the dead has also come through a human being; for as all die in Adam, so all will be made alive in Christ. But each in his own order: Christ the first fruits, then at his coming those who belong to Christ" (1 Cor 15:21–23). Our resurrection is closely linked to Christ's resurrection, and particularly to the triumph over sin and death represented by Christ's resurrection. As John Polkinghorne writes, "The resurrection of Jesus is the beginning within history of a process whose fulfillment lies beyond history, in which the destiny of humanity and the destiny of the universe are together to find their fulfillment in a liberation from decay and futility (cf. Rom. 8:18–25)."[25]

As for the character of the resurrection itself, Paul resorts to the natural analogy of the seed to describe "what kind of body" we will have in the resurrection (1 Cor 15:35). We don't sow plants, "the body that is to be," but seeds, which sprout and take the shape determined by the kind of seed that is planted (1 Cor 15:37). "But God gives it a body as he has chosen, and to each kind of seed its own body" (1 Cor 15:38). Here the relationship between our present earthly bodies and our hope for the resurrection of the body is most clearly stated and envisioned. There is a continuity between our present earthly life and the life that is to come. The life we have lived here becomes the seed, the raw material, from which our resurrection bodies are formed.

While not too much should be concluded from the post-resurrection appearances of the risen Lord, it does seem evident that Jesus' resurrection itself involved both a continuity and a discontinuity with his earthly life. The risen Jesus was not immediately recognizable to Mary Magdalene in John 20 or to the disciples on the road to Emmaus in Luke 24. Even when Jesus appeared to the frightened band of disciples on Easter Sunday evening through locked doors, he showed them the wounds on his hands and side to convince them that it was he (Luke 24:36–40; John 20:19–23). He invited the doubting Thomas to touch those wounds (John 20:24–29). Jesus even ate broiled fish in their presence (Luke 24:41–43) to convince them he was no mere ghost. Indeed, it was in his function as host that Jesus was most often recognized, as by the Emmaus disciples in Luke 24:30–35, and by the disciples at the Sea of Galilee in John 21:9–14. Is it saying too much to say that Jesus' resurrection body had a form beyond that of his earthly life and with capabilities no mortal body has, and yet stood in continuity with his earthly body?

It should be clear by now that the Christian hope for the resurrection of the body is quite different from the immortality of the soul, the kind of hope offered by other religions and particularly by gnostic thought. The immortality of the soul is rooted in a rejection of the physical body and physical world in favor of a spiritual union with the divine. The resurrection of the body is of a piece with the restoration of God's creation in God's new creation in Christ. Our future, in Christian faith, is inextricably linked with the future of the earth as God's creation. There is a correspondence, as John Polkinghorne has already noted, between the cosmic and the personal. Being made from the earth, our future is also bound up with the fate of the earth. Whatever else that may involve, both for the earth and for ourselves, ours will always be an embodied existence bound to the earth from which we were made.

25. Polkinghorne, *Faith*, 164.

Christian visions of the future have sometimes been so sterile and removed from the earthly human experience that skeptics have expressed no interest in living on streets of gold for an eternity with nothing to do. The biblical vision of the future envisioned here, on the contrary, is rooted in the dynamic of an emerging, unfolding universe—God's work in the new creation being brought into being through Jesus Christ. As Polkinghorne remarks, "What does seem clear is that if it is intrinsic to humanity to be embodied, then it must be intrinsic to humanity to be temporal. The life of the world to come will doubtless be everlasting, but it will not be eternal in that special and mysterious timeless sense in which the word is applied to God himself. The patient process of this world will find its reflection in the redemptive process of the world to come. Our notion of heaven is delivered from any static, and potentially boring, conception. The life of heaven will involve the endless, dynamic exploration of the inexhaustible riches of the divine nature."[26]

So the truth of John's gospel is borne out. Our everlasting life begins as we begin our journey with the risen Lord, with our physical death being only a gateway into a fuller and more concrete participation in God's new creation. From the moment we come to faith, we become inextricably and blessedly involved in the re-creation of the world in Jesus Christ. That's what makes the Christian story and the Christian journey so powerful as a motivation for doing what we can to redeem the earth and to live in ways that anticipate the future God is bringing into being through Jesus' life, death, and resurrection.

The Collapse of Urban Civilization

We are living in an era of the nearly complete triumph of urban civilization. A global, homogenous culture has emerged to which all nations, peoples, languages, and tribes are subjected. While as noted in the previous chapter this is not a completely unique phenomenon, being anticipated also by the triumph of Hellenism in the ancient world and by the Pax Romana of the first century CE, its global reach is truly evident. There are virtually no people groups (local cultures) anywhere on the globe who are not subjected to the influence, domination, and exploitation of the global culture of urban civilization. By now, fully half the world's population lives within urban centers, and that percentage continues to grow by leaps and bounds.

What makes the current global culture unique, however, is that not only is it global in reach, but it also extends to a domination of the natural world. In previous eras, urban civilizations always had to rely on the agrarian cultures around them to sustain the urban lifestyle with its excesses. (Double entendre intended—the excess production of agrarian cultures sustains the excesses of urban life!) With the industrialization of agriculture, the exploitation of petroleum resources, and the subsequent

---

26. Ibid., 170.

technological control of nature through pesticides, herbicides, and genetically modified organisms, urban civilization no longer needs agrarian cultures. Machines and oil replace human and animal traction and energy. Nature is manipulated to maximize production through technological innovation. Technicians replace agrarian cultures and farmers. One only has to view advertising for agricultural products to see the extent to which agriculture has become a war on nature, and by extension on agrarian culture.

All this feeds the perception, common in the dominant culture, that we really don't need to care for the earth. The earth becomes only an inert and lifeless medium for the inputs we place into the sterile soil before taking the commodities we need from it. We no longer really believe in the possibility of droughts and floods or crop failures. Whatever nature throws at us, we will respond with a technological fix that will allow us to continue our exploitation of the earth. Television may show sentimental images of the family farm, but in reality we don't need the family farm any longer. Indeed, less and less do we need any form of real human labor. The city has now achieved its ultimate goal—the complete subjugation of people and nature to the technological imperative. Now the city no longer has to rely on dominating the people who previously worked the land. Now everyone is free, indeed, obliged, to move to the city, which becomes the only realistic place of human habitation, the earth itself having been made uninhabitable by the technological controls in place to manage the environment. The extreme measures taken to maintain the facade of technological control over every aspect of life is evident in documentaries like *Farmageddon*, which documents the attempts by federal agents to prevent raw milk from being sold and consumed in its natural form.[27] What a hideous proposition!

The same triumph of technological control can be seen in every area of life. Learning, education, and communication are all dominated by ever more sophisticated technological devices (including this laptop on which I am writing). Technology makes ever more sophisticated exploitation of potential energy sources possible, like "fracking" for natural gas, offshore drilling for oil, and the immense tar sand operations in Alberta, Canada. Why, now we no longer even need to send soldiers into combat to protect ourselves from enemies. We simply deploy our drone aircraft and bomb our enemies into oblivion from the comfort of our bases here at home! Truly, we have at last made a name for ourselves!

As noted in the essay of the previous chapter, it is of course a facade, this illusion that we control the earth and every facet of our lives. As the dominant culture of urban civilization confronts the energy, environmental, and economic crises of our time, the foundations of urban civilization are beginning to crumble. It is not so hard to imagine another grand dissolution, another scattering of humankind upon the earth, another confusion of languages (Gen 11:1–9), that will keep humankind from

---

27. Canty, *Farmageddon*.

completely destroying itself and the earth with it. Indeed, there are plenty of dystopian novels and movies that imagine exactly these kinds of scenarios.[28]

What is difficult to imagine is that this "fall of Babylon" will occur either peacefully or without the dissolution of the great cultural achievements of the past few centuries. We can and should anticipate that we are entering a time of "great tribulation" (Rev 7:14), a time that will likely involve immense human suffering in every land and every sector of the globe. We can and should anticipate that the structural organizational and institutional safeguards so carefully constructed in recent centuries to govern humankind and the vast technological controls over nature that we all currently enjoy will disappear. We are likely to be entering once again in human history a time of wilderness. In such an era, those who know and exercise the skills of self-reliant communal living will be best positioned to cope with the extreme dislocations that are likely to occur. This is what lends urgency to the central argument and thesis of this book—that the formation of local, rural communities is of the utmost importance for the future we are entering.

Like Jesus weeping over Jerusalem, and like the kings and merchants and traders grieving Babylon's fall, there is no joy for me in anticipating the collapse of urban civilization, despite its idolatrous, oppressive, and exploitative ways. Much as I am an advocate for rural communities and the agrarian life, I am amazed and astounded at all that humankind has been able to achieve in recent centuries. Though for most of my life I have been something of a Luddite, I yielded to the technological imperative and adopted the use of the computer about a decade ago, and after raising three daughters without television our living room is now graced (cursed?) with a television. (But I still have an almost complete set of the journal *Plain* published in the 1990s that was hand set and extolled an anti-technological stance.) What I most like about the achievements of urban civilization are products of its literature and music, and the exploration of the natural world that technology has made possible. The latter has opened the natural world to human understanding in a way unknown in previous eras, and for that, I am grateful.

So like John in the book of Revelation, I cling to the hope that in the new creation God has begun to create in the life, death, and resurrection of Jesus Christ, the best works of urban civilization will be redeemed and purified and indeed made into a part of the environment of God's future intimate dwelling with us. At the same time, I have no illusions about the future of urban civilization itself. It is well on its way to self-destruction. It is insatiable, idolatrous, oppressive, and exploitative, and nothing with these characteristics can long survive. I nevertheless cling to the hope that enough institutional reforms will be implemented to cushion the inevitable collapse of urban civilization, minimizing the damage to the fragile environment of the earth and the suffering of the human family.

---

28. I think of the movie, *The Postman*, or the more recent novels and movie, *The Hunger Games*.

But in the meantime, it is urgent that the human family seek as best it can to live toward the vision of God's new creation, forming face-to-face communities able to live self-reliant lives upon the earth. The sooner, and the more, people devote themselves to the viability of local, self-reliant communities described in the introduction, in both rural and urban settings, the less traumatic will be the imminent disintegration of the current global culture and the urban civilization it supports, both for the human family and for creation.

The Legacy of the Mennonite Church

Rural Revival, the local rural revitalization nonprofit I relate to here in Freeman, South Dakota, recently sponsored a reading of *Look Who's Knockin'*, a two-person drama written by Doug Nopar for the Land Stewardship Project of Minnesota.[29] The drama features an older farm couple facing the dilemma of retirement. The husband's health is failing, and the children are off on careers of their own in the city. The obvious choice, and the husband's preference, is to sell to a local big farmer for top dollar in order to provide a financial legacy for his wife and children in return for his years of hard labor. But the farm was the wife's family's farm, and her family was very conservation minded. Recently a young couple came knockin', expressing an interest in renting the farm for a small dairy and local food operation. Renting the farm to the young couple would be messy and risky, but it would possibly provide the legacy preferred by the wife in the drama—the continuation of her family inheritance as an operating family farm producing food for the local community and making space for a new young family entering the life of the community. The question of this drama is essentially one of the legacy this couple will choose for their lives and their farm.

As denominations, Mennonite Church USA and Canada also confront the question of the legacy they intend to bequeath to future generations. From my perspective as a lifelong congregational pastor who has participated in conference and denominational activities all my life, I see the Mennonite Church being pulled in two somewhat different and even contrasting directions, both of which represent a viable legacy for the future. On the one hand, there is the push for the denomination to emphasize its evangelical roots and to continue the push to plant new churches, primarily in urban areas, and primarily among non-European ethnic groups, many of whom are new to the North American scene.

On the other hand, there is the pull for the denomination toward establishment Protestantism, which historically saw its role as the conscience of the mainstream culture. With the emergence and dominance of the Religious Right politically, the influence of mainline denominations in the public square has diminished, but it is interesting to observe the fortress-like sanctuaries that still dominate the centers of so

---

29. "Opportunity Knocks," unsigned review of *Look Who's Knockin'*, by Doug Nopar. *Land Stewardship Newsletter* 29, no. 1 (2011) 8–9.

many towns and cities throughout America, reminding us of the time when Lutheran, Presbyterian, Disciples of Christ, Episcopalian, Reformed, and Congregational denominations had a dominant voice in the social and political sphere. Today, there are elements of the Mennonite Church who aspire to claim such a voice for the Mennonite Church, particularly in the realms of peace and justice witness.

Neither of these options takes account of the agrarian heritage so prominent in the earlier history of the Mennonite Church. Indeed, it seems we are quite ready as a denomination to turn our backs on this heritage and plunge ahead into either an evangelical program of evangelism and church growth or a politically active direction of attempting to influence the dominant culture. Perhaps it seems to us that our rural heritage is already lost. After all, few Mennonite congregations in many conferences are any longer rural in any true sense, and even fewer have a substantial membership of active farmers.

Yet even in a more rural conference like the one to which I belong, Central Plains Mennonite Conference, the extent of our rural reality is usually overlooked or downplayed in our attempt to address urban church plants. The fifty-one member congregations of Central Plains in 2009 were quite clearly divided into thirds—a third were rural by location, a third were in villages and towns of less than ten thousand (making them rural by virtue of the typology I developed in chapter 3), and a third were in cities and metropolitan areas of ten thousand or more. There were seventeen congregations in each category. So two-thirds of Central Plains Mennonite Conference congregations were rural. In terms of membership, likely more than 90 percent were rural by the above definition since all of the largest congregations in the conference were rural.[30]

Of course, being rural by location does not mean that all of these congregations were predominantly agrarian culturally. Likely, active farmers are a minority in nearly all of these congregations. However, virtually all of these thirty-four congregations have a rural, agrarian heritage, and even members who no longer farm are only one or two generations removed from a truly agrarian community. Many of these congregations have a good number of retired and aged members who own farms, or urban members who have inherited farm land but now have vocations other than farming. Issues of land tenure and generational land transfer are pressing and often lead to conflict both within families and within congregations. In short, these rural congregations have the agricultural wisdom and experience, as well as the resources of land and equity that can enable the formation of sustainable agrarian communities where now there are merely dying, fractured rural communities.

So like the farm couple in *Look Who's Knockin'*, the Mennonite Church is confronted by the question of the legacy it wishes to have at this juncture in history. Given all the real estate assets to which it is heir in its membership, the Mennonite Church can quite easily cash in and opt for a legacy of either evangelical success or political/

---

30. *Handbook*, 10–19.

cultural witness. It can continue to spurn and turn its back on its agrarian roots. Or, it can choose to make rural revitalization and community formation the primary focus of its missional task. It can support the current wider cultural interest in developing local food systems for urban centers and engage its membership in the economic transitions that such a missional task would represent. It can foster connections between rural and nearby urban congregations in the development of this missional task, both as producers and as consumers and in both urban and rural settings.

This is a much more dicey and risky missional strategy, this effort to reclaim our agrarian roots. It will require us to learn and relearn the skills and practices and disciplines required for local food production. It will require us to reinvest in the rural communities where our rural churches are located rather than seeing rural congregations as primary sources for the funding of denominational programs and institutions in urban areas or overseas. In particular, it will require rural congregations like those I served to gradually abandon commodity-oriented, industrial agriculture in favor of the production of food. It will require these rural congregations to pay attention to land tenure patterns, making sure that as the land is brought into food rather than global commodity production, it is made available to as many people as are willing and able to utilize the land for such purposes, whether or not they share traditional ethnic Mennonite roots.

As for Mennonite Church institutional leadership and bureaucracy, the development of a rural missional strategy will require our leaders to reclaim their rural, agrarian roots (regardless of their ethnic/racial origin), and stop pretending that the future of the church lies in the city. Cities, certainly as metropolitan and mega-metropolitan urbanized centers, are clearly non-sustainable in terms of the future of human life on earth. The sooner the church develops strategies for the decentralization of urban centers, the redistribution of land to many people for food production, and the development of (rural and urban) local food systems, the sooner the church will be able to claim a relevant function in helping to formulate a sustainable future for the human family here on earth, which I think would best reflect God's hopes and intentions for the future.

I began this book by asserting the theological claim that we humans are created in the image of God, and that God's primary intention for the human family is that we represent for one another and for God's creation the character of God. I believe this is best done through the formation of agrarian communities committed to the welfare of the human family and the natural environment in both rural and urban settings. As a Mennonite Church, we are close enough to our historic rural roots that we can model for the church at large what this might look like in the context of our current urban civilization facing severe economic, ecological, and energy crises. What will be our legacy?

Conclusion and Prospect

Summary

CONGRATULATIONS, DEAR READER! IF you have followed me through these fifteen chapters and not cheated too much, you have completed a survey of the entire biblical story, viewed from the perspective of local, rural communities living within the dominant urban civilizations of the ancient world. It is particular and parochial, this biblical story. Historically, it tells the story of particular people—the Israelites, referred to as Jewish people in the New Testament, during some two thousand years of their history, from the time of Abraham and the patriarchs about 2000 BCE until the end of the first century CE, with the formation of the church. Geographically, the biblical story is centered almost exclusively on the land of Palestine, and the various peoples and empires that impacted that land through those two thousand years, though there are forays into Egypt and Mesopotamia (the Fertile Crescent), as well as Asia Minor, Persia, North Africa, and eventually the Mediterranean lands of Europe, most notably Greece and Italy.

Of course, the biblical story itself purports to be something more, as well, as it was presented in this book. It claims to be relevant to creation and history as a whole—from the Big Bang to the last twinkling out of the last star, from the first stirrings of the human species to the full-flowering of urban industrial, computer- and gadget-driven twenty-first-century men and women. The biblical story encompasses both the creation of the earth and human life and all the possible cataclysmic scenarios that mark the possible end of this finite world as we know it. The historical aspect of the biblical story is set in the context of the particular understanding of both the creation and eschatological narratives attempted in chapters 1 and 2, and 14 and 15—the beginning and the end of human life and history, as well as the earth itself as the context for the immense adventure of life in which we humans participate.

Conclusions

It is, to be sure, the weakness of a preacher's life and habits, one who has sought repeatedly and weekly to interpret and exegete some aspect of the biblical story. So I cannot help myself! Now, lest anyone doubt or feel confused by what I have been trying to say in fifteen chapters, I feel compelled to draw some of the conclusions I have made on this extended journey through the biblical story. So, here are a few!

1. The Bible presents a consistent and coherent story of rural community struggling to live in the context of urban civilization. While my reading of Scripture is by no means the only one, nor should it even be the dominant one, what I set out to do in this book is to demonstrate that the biblical story is also about rural community as an alternative living within the context of an already existent dominant, urban civilization and culture. I hope that the readings of Scripture and the historical perspectives presented here have not been stretched too far to be credible, on the one hand, and have, on the other hand, been sufficiently cogent to warrant this conclusion.

2. A corollary of this first conclusion is that the current dynamic between rural community and urban civilization is no new or unique phenomenon. The biblical story presupposes the agrarian revolution of ten thousand and more years ago, as well as the development of cities, urban civilization, and empires during the past six thousand or so years. The relationship between rural community and urban civilization originated with the rise of cities and is the backdrop for the whole biblical story as it unfolds in Scripture, from Abraham on. This conclusion is not meant to provide us with a false security, as though to say our current crisis is nothing new, nor is it to minimize the gravity of the crisis local and rural cultures face the world over in our time. However it is intended to remind us that our situation is not without precedent, and that we might learn from the efforts, however faltering and yet inspiring, of rural communities during the past four millennia who confronted the depredations of urban civilization. Indeed, it is naive for us to imagine that the history of rural communities during these millennia have nothing to teach us about how to confront the current crisis of a disintegrating and yet powerful imperial reality of urban civilization. This history has important lessons to teach us, particularly as Mennonite Christians, as we observe how our own pilgrimage as a people intimately related to the land parallels the experiences of ancient Israel. I hope the final sections of each chapter made these linkages between the biblical story and our own pilgrimage as contemporary Christians clear.

3. As I have already noted above, the biblical story is parochial, originating like so many of the truly humane and life-giving stories of humanity in a particular culture and human tradition at particular times and places and in the experiences of a particular people facing particular challenges. It is, in other words, an Israelite story, a story about this particular people and how they experienced their sojourn with God over two millennia. As though that wasn't particular enough, it is the story of a particular man who lived some two thousand years ago in the land of Palestine. This is, in other words, a story rooted in the responses and experiences of a particular people, and in the case of Jesus Christ, a particular human, to the unique challenges they and he confronted. Of course, it is a story that has come to have universal significance as a global religion and faith in Christianity, a significance that transcends the time and circumstances that gave this story birth. This universalization of the Christian story was not without its ambiguities and deceptions. Indeed, it is a story that the dominant culture of urban civilization has always tried to co-opt to sanction its domination

and exploitation, as it does with every local, rural culture. So it is a story that is most useful to us when we allow it to give voice to the particular experiences of the cultures and people it describes. That is why so much of this book has been an attempt to understand and explain the particular historical dynamics and experiences of both the people of Israel and the person of Jesus Christ in their relationship to the dominant urban cultures in which they lived.

4. Notwithstanding the particularity and historicity of the biblical story, the Christian message of human enslavement to the powers of evil and God's work of redemption in God's covenants with humanity is relevant to the general human predicament occasioned by the rise of urban civilization. Indeed, there is evidence throughout the biblical story that the actors in this story understood that what they were experiencing with God was paradigmatic for humanity generally. This is in the end a claim of faith that cannot be substantiated by historical evidence in significant ways. It has to do finally with whether the story itself is perceived to be convincing and authoritative, something credible enough to "stake one's life on." But for those who do find the Christian story convincing, it lends encouragement, direction, and empowerment to those who struggle with the domination, oppression, and exploitation of urban civilization. Those who like myself believe that everything in heaven and on earth is being recapitulated in Jesus Christ—his life, death, and resurrection, have a framework for working with persistence, hope, and courage toward the redemption and renewal of the earth and the human family.

5. In the biblical story, God's consistent strategy for redeeming humanity from the powers of evil unleashed by human sin is the formation of local, countercultural communities of subversive and nonviolent resistance to the dominant cultures of idolatry, oppression, and exploitation. This is already clearly seen in the formation of ancient Israel as a collection of agrarian communities establishing themselves in the midst of the dominant Canaanite city-states and the larger empires of the ancient world. It is seen again in the formation of the church as the primary fruit of Jesus' ministry as God's Messiah in the context of first-century Roman political and Jewish temple imperialism. Only local, face-to-face, intentional communities like those that characterize Israelite agrarian society or congregational communities of the church are able to function as effective countercultural communities of subversion and resistance to imperial power.

In this book, I have tried to present the formation of Israel and the church, alternative communities of faith, as the primary locus of divine activity within what we usually refer to as the Old and New Covenants or Testaments. This stands in contrast to traditional hermeneutical stances that see Israel's existence as a national/ethnic entity and the church as an adjunct to God's main mission of saving individuals. I view both of these hermeneutical stances as betrayals of what God intended in the formation of both Israel and the church. Our best hope, and God's chosen instrument, for the redemption of creation and humanity is the re-formation of small, local communities and cultures, both rural and urban. Indeed, it is such communities that are required for the restoration of creation and the sustenance of urban civilization if it is to survive its current economic, energy, and ecological crises at all.

6. I have perhaps been less clear than I had hoped at the outset of this book in describing the particular character of these local, countercultural communities. I began with the thesis that such communities would be primarily rural and agrarian in character. But, particularly with the emergence of the church in its local congregational manifestation as the heir of the mantle of local community, I was forced to acknowledge that local community is as much an urban as it is a rural or agrarian reality and need. My discussion of the unique character of both rural and urban congregations in chapter 13 is instructive in this respect. Nevertheless, I remain fairly confident in affirming the character of local communities, rural or urban, as described in the introduction, as indicative of the kind of communities required to cope with the exploitation, idolatry, and oppression of urban civilization. Urban communities will be more clearly multicultural, celebrating the unique heritage of all their members, by virtue of their external conformity to the dominant culture. But rural communities must also learn to respect and value and learn from diverse cultures even while preserving the distinctive agrarian culture unique to their heritage, circumstances, and locations.

It should be evident that while the local communities described in this book are assumed to be Christian in faith, the characteristics of local community required for resistance to and subversion of imperial power are not uniquely Christian. Indeed, it should be the mission of every local, Christian congregation to actively pursue and support the (re-)formation of local communities of all kinds and faith orientations within the larger rural and urban settings where they live. We should strive, as Jesus did, for communities in which humans can live in a relation of trust and humility and obedience before the divine, a relation of justice and peace and love with one another, and a relation of harmony and care and respect for creation.

7. Where local, countercultural communities already exist in the form of local Christian congregations of whatever denomination, the primary vocation/mission of these communities is to be the church—to live out their being as countercultural communities. This is not to argue against saving souls or sending missionaries abroad. But to do either of those things authentically requires the church to be the church where it is located, in the first place. Unless, or until, the congregation is an intentionally countercultural presence in its particular setting, whatever it attempts to do will be a perversion or distraction or worse. But once a congregation is truly a countercultural presence, I believe its primary mission is to invest itself in the formation of community within the specific rural or urban setting in which it finds itself. It is a matter of bringing the gospel to bear on "every town" (Titus 1:5), every place on earth in which humans dwell. This may involve the formation of new congregations within the larger community when there is no Christian presence in a particular place. Perhaps, in the

North American setting, it will more likely involve forging alliances with other Christian congregations of all denominations in both rural and urban settings to make sustainable, local communities a reality.

Prospect

This book was inspired by the trauma of seeing for a lifetime the dismantling of rural communities at the hands of urban civilization, which has often felt not only depressing, but also hopeless. The power of the dominant culture of urban civilization seems overwhelming. Rural and local cultures like those among whom I have worked seem to be doomed. It is tempting to feel that I have thrown my life away by devoting so much energy to the revitalization of rural communities when there is so little prospect of such communities surviving and thriving. Each of the congregations I served as pastor declined in membership during the years of my ministry.

Yet, even while all this was happening in rural communities, it was becoming increasingly clear that urban civilization as we know it—the global economy (corpocracy, to coin a word for the rule of corporations), the US empire (bureaucracy, nationalism, and militarism), and technological sophistication (technocracy)—is in crisis and in decline. While I am glad to see the power of urban civilization, which occasions so much oppression and idolatry and exploitation, waning, I grieve the loss of human achievements this will involve. As well, I grieve the immense human suffering occasioned not only by the oppression of urban civilization but also by the natural and social catastrophes that already are and undoubtedly will fall upon the already poor and struggling masses of people the world over. While I have tried to avoid too apocalyptic a tone in this book, I have no doubt that the events of the next decades will appear increasingly apocalyptic to the people who are suffering and whose world will be increasingly broken and fragmented, and that may very well include myself and my family, my church, and my community.

As though all this wasn't traumatic enough, I also deplore what I experience and perceive to be the intransigence and resistance to change in so much of the institutional church and among so many ordinary members of the church to the issues I have been discussing in this book. The institutional church in America, including Mennonite Church USA and Canada, busies itself with questions of self-preservation as membership declines, and distracts itself with theological controversies regarding sexual ethics imposed upon it by the dominant culture. The institutional church increasingly patterns itself after the polarizations evident in the dominant culture and is thus unable to creatively address the crises of the dominant culture.

Despite all this bad news and all my impatience and frustration with the way things are in our society and in the church, I confess that I remain strangely optimistic and hopeful about the future. This is first of all a function of my faith—my conviction that in Christ, God is recapitulating all things on earth and in heaven. I don't know how this is going to work itself out, but I have this stubborn belief, contrary to all the evidence, that in Christ everything is going to come out alright.

My optimism also rests on my conviction that it is indeed through the travail of nature and the suffering of humanity, as it was in the passion of Christ, that God is at work overcoming the powers of evil and redeeming both creation and history. So, like John in Revelation, the worse things get, the more hopeful we can be! Of course, that sounds far too facile and crass, too resigned to suffering, too disrespectful of all those creatures and humans who innocently bear in their passion the sins of the world. Still, the heart of Christian faith is the assertion that it is through nonviolent, suffering, sacrificial love that the vicious cycle of violence and oppression and exploitation and domination is broken. So it is in the groaning of creation and the groaning of an oppressed humanity that the fate of urban civilization is sealed. For as always, God hears those groans (Exod 2:24; Rom 8:22–23; Rev 6:10), and acts to bring new life out of the shards and splinters of a shattered civilization.

As though in answer to this hope, I have begun to see the resurgence of local and traditional cultures and communities in all sorts of surprising ways and places. Through family and church connections, I have been blessed to witness personally the resurgence of Lakota culture in South Dakota, the persistence of Palestinian communities in the West Bank, the creativity of young adults in urban centers seeking local food, and the revitalization of traditional rural congregations and communities.

My hope is that this book, which articulates a particular biblical theology of rural community in the context of urban civilization, will provide the biblical and theological rationale for a reorientation of the church's understanding of its mission. This book is rooted in the particular places and communities where the struggle of rural communities with urban civilization is being played out. Here is a biblically sound, pastorally concerned, missionally based rationale for the re-formation of local communities in both rural and urban settings.

Bibliography

Ardrey, Robert. *African Genesis: A Personal Investigation into the Animal Origins and Nature of Man.* New York: Dell, 1961.

Barraclough, Geoffrey, ed. *Harper Collins Atlas of World History.* Ann Arbor, MI: Borders, 1999

Barrett, David B., ed. *World Christian Encyclopedia: A Comparative Study of Churches and Religions in the Modern World, AD 1900–2000.* Nairobi: Oxford University Press, 1982.

Bender, Harold S. "The Anabaptist Vision." *Church History* 13 (March 1944) 3–24. Reprinted in *Mennonite Quarterly Review* 18 (April 1944) 67–88 and in pamphlet form as *The Anabaptist Vision.* Scottdale, PA: Herald, 1944.

Berkhof, Hendrik. *Christ and the Powers.* Translated by John Howard Yoder. Scottdale, PA: Herald, 1962.

Berry, Wendell. *The Gift of Good Land: Further Essays Cultural and Agricultural.* San Francisco: North Point, 1981.

———. *The Unsettling of America: Culture and Agriculture.* San Francisco: Sierra Club, 1977.

———. *What Are People For?* San Francisco: North Point, 1990.

Boers, Arthur Paul. *The Way Is Made by Walking: A Pilgrimage along the Camino de Santiago.* Downers Grove, IL: InterVarsity, 2007.

Borgmann, Albert. *Technology and the Character of Contemporary Life: A Philosophical Inquiry.* Chicago: University of Chicago Press, 1984.

Borgstrom, Georg. *The Food and People Dilemma.* North Scituate, MA: Duxbury, 1973.

Boulding, Kenneth. *There Is a Spirit: The Nayler Sonnets.* Nyack, NY: Fellowship, 1964.

Braght, Thieleman J. van. *The Bloody Theatre; or, Martyr's Mirror of the Defenseless Christians.* Scottdale, PA: Herald, 1950.

Bright, John. *A History of Israel.* Philadelphia: Westminster, 1959.

Brown, Lester R. *By Bread Alone.* New York: Praeger, 1974.

Brueggemann, Walter. "Exodus." In *New Interpreter's Bible,* edited by Leander D. Keck, 1:677–981. Nashville: Abingdon, 1994.

———. *The Land: Place as Gift, Promise, and Challenge in Biblical Faith.* Philadelphia: Fortress, 1977.

———. "Theses on Land in the Bible." *Catholic Rural Life* 34, no. 5 (November 1984) 5–9.

Bryson, Bill. *A Short History of Nearly Everything.* New York: Broadway, 2003.

Byler, J. Ron, ed. *Mennonite Church USA 2009 Directory.* Scottdale, PA: Mennonite Publishing Network, 2008.

Canty, Kristin, dir. *Farmageddon: The Unseen War on American Family Farms.* Canty Productions, 2012.

Capra, Fritjof. *The Web of Life: A New Scientific Understanding of Living Systems.* New York: Anchor, 1996.

Confession of Faith in a Mennonite Perspective. Mennonite Church and General Conference Mennonite Church. Scottdale, PA: Herald, 1995.

Coogan, Michael D., ed. *The New Oxford Annotated Bible: With the Apocryphal/Deuterocanonical Books.* 3rd ed. Oxford: Oxford University Press, 2001.

Crossan, John Dominic. *God and Empire: Jesus against Rome, Then and Now.* New York: HarperOne, 2007.

———. *The Historical Jesus: The Life of a Mediterranean Jewish Peasant.* San Francisco: HarperSanFrancisco, 1991.

Dale, Tom, and Vernon Gill Carter. *Topsoil and Civilization.* Toronto: McClelland and Stewart, 1961. First published in 1955 by University of Oklahoma Press.

D'Arcy, Martin C. *The Mind and Heart of Love: Lion and Unicorn; A Study in Eros and Agape.* Rev. ed. Cleveland: World, 1956.

Bibliography

Davies, Paul. *God and the New Physics*. New York: Touchstone, 1983.

———. *The Last Three Minutes: Conjectures about the Ultimate Fate of the Universe*. New York: BasicBooks, 1994.

Dyck, Cornelius J., ed. *An Introduction to Mennonite History: A Popular History of the Anabaptists and the Mennonites*. Scottdale, PA: Herald, 1967.

Eberlein, Sven. "Heavenly Energy." *Sojourners* 41, no. 3 (March 2012) 28–31.

Eisler, Riane. *The Chalice and the Blade: Our History, Our Future*. San Francisco: HarperSanFrancisco, 1995.

Eller, Vernard. *The Most Revealing Book of the Bible: Making Sense out of Revelation*. Grand Rapids: Eerdman's, 1974.

Ellul, Jacques. *Apocalypse: The Book of Revelation*. Translated by George W. Schreiner. New York: Seabury, 1977.

———. *The Meaning of the City*. Translated by Dennis Pardee. Grand Rapids: Eerdman's, 1970.

Empty Breadbasket? The Coming Challenge to America's Food Supply and What We Can Do About It. Study of the US Food System by the Cornucopia Project. Emmaus, PA: Rodale, 1981.

Flora, Cornelia Butler, and Jan L. Flora. *Rural Community: Legacy and Change*. 2nd ed. Boulder, CO: Westview, 2004.

Freudenberger, C. Dean. *Food for Tomorrow? A Christian Agronomist Calls for Renewal of the Biblical Covenant to Meet the World Crisis in Agriculture*. Minneapolis: Augsburg, 1984.

———. *Global Dust Bowl: Can We Stop the Destruction of the Land Before It's Too Late?* Minneapolis: Augsburg, 1990.

Freyne, Sean. *Galilee and Gospel: Collected Essays*. Boston: Brill Academic, 2000.

Frost, Robert. "Fire and Ice." In *A Pocket Book of Robert Frost's Poems*, 242. Edited by Louis Untermeyer. New York: Washington Square, 1962.

George, Susan. *How the Other Half Dies: The Real Reasons for World Hunger*. Montclair, NJ: Allanheld, Osmun, 1977.

Gottwald, Norman K. *The Tribes of Yahweh: A Sociology of the Religion of Liberated Israel, 1250–1050 B.C.E.* Maryknoll, NY: Orbis, 1979.

Granberg-Michaelson, Wesley. *A Worldly Spirituality: The Call to Redeem Life on Earth*. San Francisco: Harper & Row, 1984.

Greenfield, J. C. "Philistines." In *Interpreter's Dictionary of the Bible*, edited by George Arthur Buttrick, 3:791–95. New York: Abingdon, 1962.

Groff, Anna. "Church Harvests Help End 'Food Desert.'" *Mennonite* 14, no. 12 (December 2011) 44.

Habel, Norman C. *The Land Is Mine: Six Biblical Land Ideologies*. Minneapolis: Fortress, 1995.

Hamlin, E. J. "Nations." In *Interpreter's Dictionary of the Bible*, edited by George Arthur Buttrick, 3:515–23. New York: Abingdon, 1962.

Handbook of Information. Freeman, SD: Central Plains Mennonite Conference, 2009/2010.

Harder, Günther. "φθείρω." In *Theological Dictionary of the New Testament*, edited by Gerhard Friedrich, translated by Goeffrey W. Bromiley, 9:93–106. Grand Rapids: Eerdman's, 1974.

Hart, John. *The Spirit of the Earth: A Theology of the Land*. Ramsey, NJ: Paulist, 1984.

Hellerman, Joseph H. *The Ancient Church as Family*. Minneapolis: Fortress, 2001.

Hirschfield, Robert. "American Spring?" *Sojourners* 40, no.11 (December 2011) 44–49.

Hoebel, E. Adamson. *Anthropology: The Study of Man*. 3rd ed. New York: McGraw-Hill, 1966.

Horsley, Richard A. *Sociology and the Jesus Movement*. 2nd ed. New York: Continuum, 1994.

Huber, Tim. "World Membership Rises." *Mennonite World Review* 91, no. 5 (March 2013) 1–2.

Jackson, Wes. *Becoming Native to this Place*. Washington, DC: Counterpoint, 1996.

Jackson, Wes, et al., eds. *Meeting the Expectations of the Land: Essays in Sustainable Agriculture and Stewardship*. San Francisco: North Point, 1984.

Jacobsen, T. "Babel." In *Interpreter's Dictionary of the Bible*, edited by George Arthur Buttrick, 1:334. New York: Abingdon, 1962.

Jeschke, Marlin. *Rethinking Holy Land: A Study in Salvation Geography*. Scottdale, PA: Herald, 2005.

Job, Rueben P., and Norman Shawchuck. *A Guide to Prayer*. Nashville: Upper Room, 1983.

Jung, L. Shannon. *Food for Life: The Spirituality and Ethics of Eating*. Minneapolis: Fortress, 2004.

———. *Hunger and Happiness: Feeding the Hungry, Nourishing Our Souls*. Minneapolis: Augsburg, 2009.

———. *Sharing Food: Christian Practices for Enjoyment*. Minneapolis: Fortress, 2006.

Bibliography

Kanagy, Conrad L. *Road Signs for the Journey: A Profile of Mennonite Church USA*. Scottdale, PA: Herald, 2007.

Kauffman, J. Howard, and Leo Driedger. *The Mennonite Mosaic: Identity and Modernization*. Scottdale, PA: Herald, 1991.

Kaufman, Maynard. *Adapting to the End of Oil: Toward an Earth-Centered Spirituality*. Xlibris, 2008.

Kaufman, S. Roy. "The Anatomy of a Rural Church." *Mennonite* 14, no. 9 (September 2011) 16-19.

———. *Roots that Nourish Our Congregational Life*. Fifteen sermons marking the centennial of the Salem Mennonite Church in 2008. In *Centennial Sermons and Talks*. Unpublished booklet located at Salem Mennonite Church Library and Heritage Hall Museum and Archives, Freeman, SD.

Kingsley, Keith. "One Who Will Inherit the Kingdom." *Mennonite Weekly Review* 90, no. 2 (January 2012) 6.

Kingsolver, Barbara, et al. *Animal, Vegetable, Miracle: A Year of Food Life*. New York: HarperCollins, 2007.

Kline, David. *Great Possessions: An Amish Farmer's Journal*. San Francisco: North Point, 1990.

———. *Scratching the Woodchuck: Nature on an Amish Farm*. Athens: University of Georgia Press, 1997.

Kneen, Brewster. *From Land to Mouth: Understanding the Food System*. 2nd ed. Toronto: NC Press, 1993.

Kraybill, Donald B., and C. Nelson Hostetter. *Anabaptist World USA*. Scottdale, PA: Herald, 2001.

Kraybill, Donald B., Steven M. Nolt, and David L. Weaver-Zercher. *Amish Grace: How Forgiveness Transcended Tragedy*. San Francisco: Jossey-Bass, 2007.

LaCugna, Catherine Mowry. *God for Us: The Trinity and Christian Life*. San Francisco: Harper Collins, 1991.

Lambdin, T. O. "Hyksos." In *Interpreter's Dictionary of the Bible*, edited by George Arthur Buttrick, 2:667. New York: Abingdon, 1962.

Landes, G. M. "Midian." In *Interpreter's Dictionary of the Bible*, edited by George Arthur Buttrick, 3:375–376. New York: Abingdon, 1962.

Lappé, Frances Moore, and Joseph Collins. *Food First: Beyond the Myth of Scarcity*. Boston: Houghton Mifflin, 1977.

Leakey, Richard. *The Origin of Humankind*. New York: BasicBooks, 1994.

Leith, John H., ed. *Creeds of the Churches: A Reader in Christian Doctrine from the Bible to the Present*. Garden City, NY: Doubleday, 1963.

Lorenz, Konrad. *On Aggression*. Translated by Marjorie Kerr Wilson. New York: Bantam, 1966.

Machlis, Joseph. *The Enjoyment of Music: An Introduction to Perceptive Listening*. 3rd ed. New York: Norton, 1970.

Meadows, Donella H., et al. *The Limits to Growth: A Report for the Club of Rome's Project on the Predicament of Mankind*. New York: Signet, 1972.

Meeks, Wayne A. *The First Urban Christians: The Social World of the Apostle Paul*. New Haven, CT: Yale University Press, 1983.

Mendenhall, George E. *The Tenth Generation: The Origins of the Biblical Tradition*. Baltimore: Johns Hopkins University Press, 1973.

Merchant, Carolyn. *The Death of Nature: Women, Ecology, and the Scientific Revolution*. San Francisco: Harper Collins, 1980.

Mesarovic, Mihajlo, and Eduard Pestel. *Mankind at the Turning Point: The Second Report to the Club of Rome*. New York: Signet, 1974.

Mission Mosaic, 2008–2010: The Mennonite Mission Network Prayer Directory. Elkhart, IN: Mennonite Mission Network, 2010.

Morgenstern, J. "Week." In *Interpreter's Dictionary of the Bible*, edited by George Arthur Buttrick. 4:826–27. New York: Abingdon, 1962.

Morris, Desmond. *The Naked Ape*. New York: Dell, 1967.

Morrison, Philip, and Phylis Morrison. *Powers of Ten: About the Relative Size of Things in the Universe*. New York: Scientific American Library, 1994.

Myers, Ched. *Binding the Strong Man: A Political Reading of Mark's Story of Jesus*. Maryknoll, NY: Orbis, 1988.

Nolt, Steven M. *A History of the Amish*. Intercourse, PA: Good Books, 1992.

Northcott, Michael S. *A Moral Climate: The Ethics of Global Warming*. Maryknoll, NY: Orbis, 2007.

Owen, David. *Green Metropolis: Why Living Smaller, Living Closer, and Driving Less Are the Keys to Sustainability*. New York: Riverhead, 2009.

Bibliography

Pagels, Elaine. *The Gnostic Gospels*. New York: Vintage, 1979.

Pannabecker, Samuel Floyd. *Open Doors: A History of the General Conference Mennonite Church*. Newton, KS: Faith and Life, 1975.

Petry, Ray C., ed. *A History of Christianity: Readings in the History of the Early and Medieval Church*. Englewood Cliffs, NJ: Prentice-Hall, 1962.

Platt, LaVonne Godwin, ed. *Hope for the Family Farm: Trust God and Care for the Land*. Newton, KS: Faith and Life, 1987.

Polkinghorne, John. *The Faith of a Physicist: Reflections of a Bottom-Up Thinker*. Princeton, NJ: Princeton University Press, 1994.

Pollan, Michael. *The Omnivore's Dilemma: A Natural History of Four Meals*. New York: Penguin, 2006.

Salatin, Joel. *Folks, This Ain't Normal: A Farmer's Advice for Happier Hens, Healthier People and a Better World*. New York: Center Street, 2011.

Sansom-Flood, Renee, and Shirley A. Bernie. *Remember Your Relatives: Yankton Sioux Images, 1851–1904*. 2nd ed. Marty, SD: Marty Indian School, 1985.

Schrag, Martin H. *The European History (1525-1874) of the Swiss Mennonites from Volhynia*. 2nd ed. North Newton, KS: Harley J. Schrag / Graphic Images, 1999.

Schrock, Jennifer Halteman. "Featured 100 Shades Congregation: Berea Mennonite Church." *Mennonite Creation Care Network* 2, no. 3 (November 2011) 1–2.

Simon, Arthur. *Bread for the World*. New York: Paulist, 1975.

Smith, C. Christopher. "Local Church as Radical Witness." Review of *War and the American Difference: Theological Reflections on Violence and National Identity*, by Stanley Hauerwas. *Sojourners* 41, no. 1 (January 2012) 42–43.

Snyder, C. Arnold. *Anabaptist History and Theology: An Introduction*. Kitchener, ON: Pandora, 1995.

Sonne, I. "Synagogue." In *Interpreter's Dictionary of the Bible*, edited by George Arthur Buttrick, 4:476–91. New York: Abingdon, 1962.

Stegemann, Ekkehard W., and Wolfgang Stegemann. *The Jesus Movement: A Social History of Its First Century*. Translated by O. C. Dean Jr. Minneapolis: Fortress, 1999.

Stoddard, W. H., comp. *Turner County Pioneer History*. Freeman, SD: Pine Hill, 1991. Reprint of the 2nd ed., published by the Turner County Historical Society, 1975.

Storkey, Elaine. "Jubilee and Beyond." *Sojourners* 41, no. 3 (March 2012) 24–26, 45.

Swimme, Brian, and Thomas Berry. *The Universe Story: From the Primordial Flaring Forth to the Ecozoic Era—A Celebration of the Unfolding of the Cosmos*. San Francisco: Harper Collins, 1992.

Tennyson, Alfred Lord. "In Memoriam." In *The Poems of Alfred Lord Tennyson*. Roslyn, NY: Black's Readers Service, 1932.

"Turner County, South Dakota." State & County QuickFacts. United States Census Bureau. Online: http://quickfacts.census.gov/qfd/states/46/46125.html.

Unruh, John D. *A Century of Mennonites in Dakota: A Segment of the German Russians*. [Freeman, SD?]. Reprinted from volume 36 of the South Dakota Historical Collections, 1972.

Unruh, John D., and Gary J. Waltner. *An Andreas Schrag Document with Some Implications*. Freeman, SD: Unruh and Waltner, 1982.

Urban Agglomerations 2007. Department of Economic and Social Affairs, Population Division. New York: United Nations, 2008. Online: http://esa.un.org/unup/pdf/WUP2011_Highlights.pdf.

Voorhies, Michael R. "Ancient Ashfall Creates a Pompeii of Prehistoric Animals." *National Geographic* 159, no. 1 (January 1981) 66–75.

Waldner, Marie J., and Marnette D. Ortman Hofer. *Many Hands, Minds, and Hearts: A History of Freeman Junior College and Freeman Academy, 1900-2000*. Sioux Falls, SD: Pine Hill, 2000.

Walker, Williston. *A History of the Christian Church*. 3rd ed. Revised by Robert T. Handy. New York: Scribner's Sons, 1970.

Walsh, Bryan. "Oil's Messy Frontier." *Time*. April 9, 2012.

Waltner, Emil J. *Banished for Faith*. Freeman, SD: Pine Hill, 1968.

Waltner, Erland, and J. Daryl Charles. *1-2 Peter, Jude*. Believers Church Bible Commentary. Scottdale, PA: Herald, 1999.

Waltner, James H. *Psalms*. Believers Church Bible Commentary. Scottdale, PA: Herald, 2006.

Weaver, J. Denny. *The Nonviolent Atonement*. Grand Rapids: Eerdman's, 2001.

Willers, Bill, ed. *Learning to Listen to the Land*. Washington, DC: Island, 1991.

Williams, William Appleman. *Empire as a Way of Life: An Essay on the Causes and Character of America's Present Predicament along with a Few Thoughts about an Alternative.* New York: Oxford University Press, 1980.

Wilson, J. A. "Egypt." In *Interpreter's Dictionary of the Bible*, edited by George Arthur Buttrick, 2:39–66. New York: Abingdon, 1962.

———. "Ramses." In *Interpreter's Dictionary of the Bible*, edited by George Arthur Buttrick, 4:10–12. New York: Abingdon, 1962.

Wink, Walter. *Engaging the Powers: Discernment and Resistance in a World of Domination.* Minneapolis: Fortress, 1992.

———. *Naming the Powers: The Language of Power in the New Testament.* Philadelphia: Fortress, 1984.

———. *Unmasking the Powers: The Invisible Forces That Determine Human Existence.* Philadelphia: Fortress, 1986.

World Almanac and Book of Facts, 1990. New York: World Almanac, 1989.

World Almanac and Book of Facts, 2000. Mahwah, NJ: World Almanac, 1999.

Wright, Christopher J. H. *God's People in God's Land: Family, Land, and Property in the Old Testament.* Grand Rapids: Eerdman's, 1990.

Wright, N. T. *Jesus and the Victory of God.* Minneapolis: Fortress, 1996.

———. *Paul in Fresh Perspective.* Minneapolis: Fortress, 2005.

———. "Romans." In *New Interpreter's Bible*, edited by Leander E. Keck. 10:395–770. Nashville: Abingdon, 2002.

Yeats, William Butler. "The Second Coming." In *An Approach to Poetry*, edited by Wayne Shumaker, 372–73. Englewood Cliffs, NJ: Prentice-Hall, 1965.

Yoder, John Howard. *The Politics of Jesus: Vicit Agnus Noster.* 2nd ed. Grand Rapids: Eerdman's 1994.

Zinn, Howard. *A People's History of the United States.* New York: Harper Colophon, 1980.

Zurayk, Rami. *Food, Farming, and Freedom: Sowing the Arab Spring.* Charlottesville, VA: Just World, 2011.

Subject Index

Abraham / Sarah, 23, 49, 51–56
    as surrogate parents / broken family, 55
agrarian culture and the agricultural revolution, 33, 34–35, 222, 236, 254
    Israel as, 90, 93–96
agriculture, 186, 187
    "culture of the field", 188, 236
    industrialization of, 102, 233
    landscapes of, 188
Ahab and Jezebel, 119, 122–125
alternative community of faith, 1, 5, 49, 60, 88, 132, 133, 135, 178, 179, 199, 259, 260
    challenge of being, 105, 106–108
    summary of Old Testament paradigms/models for, 135–136
Amish, 31, 32, 170
Anabaptist movement, 18, 131–133
    missional implications of, 133
Assyrian Empire, 137, 138
atonement, 169–170
    Christus Victor theory of, 169
Babylonian empire, 138, 143
Babylonian exile, 79, 134, 136, 138, 139, 143
Bender, Harold, 131
Berry, Thomas, 11, 217, 218
Berry, Wendell, 188, 189
biblical story, 257, 258
    parochial nature of, 17, 258
Boers, Arthur Paul, 60
Borgmann, Albert, 71
Boulding, Kenneth, 164
boundaries / limitations / constraints, 22–23, 30
Brueggemann, Walter, 67, 84, 122, 123, 125
Bryson, Bill, 217, 218, 219, 220
Cain and Abel, 34, 36

Canaan, 52, 53, 89, 91, 92, 105, 137
Capra, Fritjhof, 166
Catherine the Great, 72, 73
church, 3, 168, 259
    as counter-cultural community of faith, 116–118
    as God's new community, 195, 203
    as local assembly of believers, 198, 199, 203, 206
    as transnational surrogate kinship group, 199
    as voluntary association, 205, 206
    characteristics of urban New Testament church, 207
    chasms and divides bridged or crossed by, 200–203
    composition of New Testament church, 206
    from rural to urban in New Testament in first century, 204–208
    history of, 208–211
    institutional character of, 208
    multicultural and ethno-cultural congregations, 199
    subversive or imperial, 114
    unique character of rural and urban assemblies, 207
city, 37, 39, 42, 134, 139, 204, 246, 247
    emergence of, 35
    origin of, 33
    pluralism of, 58
    spiritual power of, 178, 244
    welfare of, 134, 139, 141
commodification of goods and services, 80, 82, 186
common table / open commensality / communion, 183–185

Subject Index

community, 111, 210
   and neighborhood, 43
   ideal character of, 3–5
   redemption of, 168
   shaped by food/table, 184, 185, 186
Confession of Faith in a Mennonite Perspective, 1, 20, 211, 212
Constantine / Constantinian synthesis of church and state, 112–113, 210
cosmology, 11, 217–218, 238, 239
covenant code / holiness code / deuteronomic code, 93, 94
creation, 3, 9, 16, 153, 217
   and evolution, 11, 13
   Genesis accounts of, 11–12, 19
   redemption of, 221–224
Crete, church of, 116, 205
Crossan, John Dominic, 172, 177, 184–185
culture as marker of identity, 115, 116
D'Arcy, M. C., 155, 156
David, 5, 110, 119, 125, 242
demon possession as symptom of socio-economic oppression, 159, 176, 177
disease, 175, 176
disenfranchisement of rural communities, 62
dominant culture, 49, 60, 88, 106, 119, 156, 185, 203, 205, 206, 209
   crises of, economic / ecological / energy, 16, 46, 229–232
   defined, 2, 229
   redemption from, 170
domination systems, 153, 167, 171
earth, 9, 11, 14, 16, 218, 220
ecological concerns, 2, 16, 17, 19, 154, 221, 231
economic crisis, 231, 232
economic functions of production and consumption, 4, 38
economic sharing in community, 182
eonomy of abundance, divine, 80
economy of scarcity, human, 80
Egypt / Egyptian empire, 76, 81, 106, 138
Elijah / Elisha, 79, 124–125
Ellul, Jacques, 35, 39, 244, 245, 246, 247
empire / imperialism, 62, 100, 101, 120, 134
   as subjugation of one ethnicity by another, 69
   association with emperors, 70
   character of, 67–69
   defined, 63, 69
   relationship to colonialism and nationalism, 70
   role in environmental exploitation, 68
   sponsorship of arts, works of civilization, 71

end times in Revelation / eschatology, 238
energy, 230, 231
   solar, 12
Enoch, 33
environmental disasters, 221
Epistle to Diognetus, 61
ethnic identity, 97, 109, 141
   ethnocentrism, 136, 137
evil, 28–31
exploitation, 141, 156
exiles / aliens, 134, 135, 138–141
Ezekiel, 126, 141–142
Ezra / Nehemiah, 135, 136
fall, 27, 28, 223
farms, 190, 191
"father's house" in Israel, 92, 95, 111
Fertile Crescent, 49, 54, 105, 137
focal practices, 72
food system, industrial, 186–188, 191
   local, 187, 191, 192, 255
forgiveness, 36, 160, 170, 179
Freeman, South Dakota community, 44–46, 59, 102, 148, 186, 191, 212
Freyne, Sean, 172, 173, 174, 177, 178, 179, 181, 182, 183
Frost, Robert, 239
Galilee, as scene of Jesus' ministry, 171
   as setting for early Christian church, 198
   cities in, 172, 173, 178
   socio-economic condition of, 172–174
garden of Eden, 15, 28, 246, 247
Gates, Bill, 128, 130, 160
Gentiles, 158, 198, 200, 201
Gideon, 108
global warming / climate change, 231
gnosticism, 5, 154–157
God, 9, 11, 14, 25, 27, 33, 40, 50, 79, 153
   breath of, 12
   covenant promises of, 51
   intention of for humanity/creation, 3, 13, 216, 224, 225–229
   promise of eternal life, 24
   realm of, 172, 174
   trinitarian character of, 12
   trust in, 179
Gottwald, Norman, 65, 90, 91, 92
Habel, Norman, 52–53
Hellerman, Joseph, 197, 198, 206
Herod Antipas, 158, 172
Herodians, 158, 163, 178
history, who and what makes, 127–128
   historical process, 77
Hmong Mennonite churches, 149

Homestead Act of 1862, 74, 87, 101
Hosea, 126, 127
household, earth as God's, 15
human life, 153
    calling / vocation of, 13–16
    dominion over creation, 14
    earthly mortal character of, 11–12
    identifying characteristics of, 196
    in cosmic setting, 9–11, 218
    made in God's image, 12
    origin of, 11–13
human migrations, 52, 56–58
    nomadic and modern migrations contrasted, 57
Hyksos, 65–67, 76
    shared ethno-linguistic heritage with patriarchs, 65–66
hymns to Christ (Col 1:15-20; Phil 2:1-11; John 1:1-18; Heb 1:1-3), 216, 225, 226
icon, 14
idolatry, 141
illness, 175
image of God, 12–14, 27, 217
incarnation, 153, 157–158
Isaiah, 126–127, 142–143, 162, 237, 240, 242
Israel, as kingdom/empire, 105, 110, 120, 135
    constitutional foundations of, 93–96
    northern kingdom of, 121, 122, 134, 137
    origins, 91–93
    social organization, 91–93
Jackson, Wes, 189, 192
Jacob and his family, 63–66
    as local community, 64
Jeremiah, 126, 134, 138–139, 221
Jerusalem conference, 200
Jerusalem / Zion, 243
    juxtaposed with Babylon, 242
Jeschke, Marlin, 56
Jesus, 23, 26, 36, 79, 153, 171, 216
    agent and sustainer of creation, 217–220, 221
    and community formation, 159, 171, 178, 192
    and Jerusalem, 249
    and riches, 183
    and spiritual empowerment, 159
    and women, 182
    announcements of his passion, 163, 180
    as a healer, 175–177, 179
    as cosmic lord, 157–160
    as divine savior, 154–157
    as image of God, 14, 217, 219
    as proclaimer of God's realm, 172–175
    as revealer of God's nature / purpose, 159
    as Son of God, 160, 217
    as suffering servant, 160–164
    as the host, 183–185
    as the strong man, plundering Satan's house, 159, 177
    as the Word, 157, 217
    authority of, 157, 159
    divinity of, 158
    his community of resistance, 179–185
    his life, death and resurrection, 164, 170, 224, 225, 229
    his trust in God, 163
    rurally based ministry of, 177–179
    temptations of, 161
    the resurrected, 249
John the Baptist, 171, 174
John the Revelator, 195, 196, 237, 242
Joseph, 65
    his role in disenfranchising Egyptians, 66–67
Judah, kingdom of, 134, 136, 138
Jubilee, Year of, 89, 95, 162, 174
Jung, L. Shannon, vii–viii, 189
Kaufman, Maynard, ix, 231
kinship groups in Israel, 89
Kingsolver, Barbara, 189
Kline, David, 189
LaCugna, Catherine, 12
land tenure, 234
    among the Amish, 102
    as speculative investment, 187
    in ancient Israel, 96
    in Hutterite colonies, 103
    in Mennonite communities, 101–104
    land trust, 101, 103
landedness / landlessness, 75, 135
    among Mennonites, 85–88
    character of landlessness, 78–81
    dependence and security in, 83
    in Israel, 90–93
    lure of landedness, 81–83
    movement back and forth from, 84, 141
    oppressive landedness, 76–78
language, 39, 195, 196, 199
"light to the nations", 134, 141–144
love (agape), as God's instrument for overcoming powers of evil, 153, 162–164, 224, 226, 262
Martyr's Mirror, 18
Maccabeans, 136
Meeks, Wayne, 204, 205, 206
Mendenhall, George, 84
Mennonite acculturation, 32, 87
    influenced by Fundamentalism, 156

Subject Index

Mennonite Church USA & Canada, 5, 32, 261
    communal / agrarian heritage of, 116–117, 190–192, 254
    global, 18
    legacy of, 253–255
Mennonite migrations, 59
    in imperial contexts, 72–74
    parallel to Israel's descent to Egypt, 73
    to America, 73, 74
Mennonite mission, rural and urban, 117, 149, 211–215, 262
Mennonite urbanization, 147–149
Mesopotamia, 52, 54
metric system, 10
metropolis / megalopolis, 42
Micah, 126, 127
missional calling of church, 1–2, 5–6
    changing focus of, in rural setting, 45–46, 214
    implications in rural Mennonite history, 19–20, 255
    of Israel, 96–97, 143
missionary movement, 212
models / paradigms for living as God's people, 135–136
mortality, 21, 28
    fear of as cause of sin, 23
Moses, 77, 82
Myers, Ched, 159, 176, 184, 198
"myth of redemptive violence", 165–168
Naboth of Jezreel, 119, 122–125
nation / nationhood / nationality, 109, 137, 139, 195, 196
    ethnolinguistic vs. political, 57
Nazareth, 157, 158, 171
new creation / new heavens, earth, 237, 238–241, 244
New Jerusalem in Revelation, 237, 238, 244–246
Noah / flood, 106
    Noachic covenant, 30
Northcott, Michael, 16, 230, 231
Owen, David, 145, 146, 147
Palestinian communities, 124, 188
Palestine/Canaan, geopolitical reality of, 49, 53–54, 137
Paul, 219, 221, 222, 223, 224, 237, 248, 249
    as witness to the Christian vision, 216, 225–228
    on divisions within the church, 201–203
    on mutual submission within one's station in life, 202, 203
peak oil, 231
Peasant Revolt / Wars, 131–132
peasants, 204, 235
    of first century Galilee, 158

Pentecost, 195, 200
people, as ethno-cultural term, 195, 196
Persian Empire, 143
Peter, 200, 239
Pharisees, 158, 163
Philistines, 105, 106, 107
pilgrimage of faith, 50–51
    Christian life as, 60–61
    elements of, 60
pioneer life in South Dakota, 87
Polkinghorne, John, 239, 240, 249, 250
Pollan, Michael, 188
population, rural/urban, 40–44
power, 63, 136, 202, 209
    centralization of, 111, 112
    egalitarian sharing of, 180
    exercising power for security, 63–64
powers, 26, 29–30, 38, 158, 167, 219, 226
"priestly kingdom / holy nation", 90, 96, 162, 199
property, private, 96, 97, 98, 100
    and national sovereignty, 98–99
    communal, 98
    "fictive" nature of private property, 99–101
    in capitalism and socialism, 99–100
    in traditional cultures, 98
promised land, 75, 135, 139
    America as Mennonite, 86
    Israel's entry into, 91, 94
prophetic movement in Israel, 119, 124–127
"quiet in the land", 2, 20
"recapitulation" (Ephesians 1:9-10), 6, 216, 227–228, 246
relationships with God, others, creation, 2, 9, 153, 216
religious faith, used to sanction imperial power, 67, 111, 113
    disparate visions of, 113
resident aliens, 49, 51–54, 60, 61, 135
    marginality of, 54–55
    Mennonites as, 59
    missional aspects of being, 54
resurrection of the body, 153, 237, 247–250
Revelation, 241, 242
Roman Empire, 113, 158, 176, 179, 204, 222, 250
rural community, 171, 177, 178, 247, 258
    defined as sphere of spiritual power, 2
rural development as missional task, 44, 46, 117
Rural Revival, 148, 191, 253
Sabbath / sabbatical year/pentcontad calendar, 4, 80, 89, 94, 99, 174
Salem / Salem-Zion Mennonite churches, 44, 61, 87, 102, 233
Samaria / Samaritans, 195

Subject Index

Samuel, 105, 107
Satan, 167, 176
    as tempter, 25, 161
Saul, 110
Schmeckfest, 71, 186
servant songs, 143
signs and wonders, 158, 175
sin, consequences of, 21, 26–28
Solomon, 110, 120, 121
speech, confusion of and understanding of, 40
Stegemann, Ekkehard and Wolfgang, 173–174, 205, 206
stewards / stewardship, 15
surrogate familial relationships, 181, 197
Swimme, Brian, 11, 217, 218
Swiss Volhynian community at Freeman, 32, 44, 72, 87, 102, 233
Table of Nations, 39, 54
technology, 33, 39, 81, 252
    triumph of, 251
temptation, 161, 163
    as shortcut to desired end, 23–26, 160
theocentric worldview, 16–18
tower of Babel, 39, 195, 222, 230
traditional cultures, constraints of, 31–32
    also fallen / sinful, 31, 38
    parochial (local) stories of, 17–18
tree of life, 21, 22–23, 28, 246, 247
tree of the knowledge of good and evil, 21, 22–23
tribe, 195
Turner County, South Dakota, 45, 233
universe, 10–11, 217, 218
urban civilization, 33, 39, 54, 90, 111, 112. 144–147, 167, 222, 258, 259
    collapse of, 250–253
    defined as sphere of spiritual power, 2
    redemption of, 246, 252
urban gardening, 140
urbanization, 45, 145, 172
vengeance, 36, 165
violence, 166
walking, 10, 146
    as spiritual discipline, 60, 225, 233–235
war, 37, 165, 166
Weaver, J. Denny, 169, 170
wilderness, 75, 78–81, 135, 140
    as context for character shaping, 80, 161
    Mennonite experiences of, 86
    wandering of Israel, 81
Williams, William Appleman, 42, 69, 70
Wink, Walter, 30, 165–169
women, 27, 166, 182, 246
work, 128–130
    creative / fulfilling, 128, 129, 130
    routine / drudge, 30, 129
Wright, Christopher J. H., 92, 95
Wright, N. T., 197, 198, 228
Yankton Sioux Treaty of 1858, 44, 74
    destruction of Lakota culture, 74
Yeats, William Butler, 220
Yoder, John Howard, 168, 169
Zinn, Howard, 128

www.ingramcontent.com/pod-product-compliance
Lightning Source LLC
Chambersburg PA
CBHW080546230426
43663CB00015B/2724